Big Game Hunter's Guide to
Montana™

Big Game Hunter's Guide to
Montana™

Ron Spomer

Wilderness
Adventures
Press

Gallatin Gateway, Montana

Published by Wilderness Adventures Press
P.O. Box 627
Gallatin Gateway, MT 59730
800-925-3339
Website: www.wildadv.com
email: books@wildadv.com

10 9 8 7 6 5 4 3 2 1

Printed in the United States of America

Library of Congress Cataloging-in-Publication Data
Spomer, Ron
    Big game hunter's guide to Montana / Ron Spomer.
        p.   cm.
    Includes index.
    ISBN 1–885106–31–9
    1. Big game hunting—Montana—Guidebooks.   2. Montana—Guidebooks.
I. Title.
SK99.S67   1999
799.2′6′09786—dc21   98–50090
                                                                              CIP

Table of Contents

Acknowledgments

The author and publisher would like to thank the Montana Department of Fish, Wildlife & Parks for providing us with information regarding regulations and animal behavior, and the Information Services Unit of Kalispell in particular for providing statewide species distribution maps. We also thank the Boone and Crockett Club for kindly granting us permission to reprint scoring charts for the trophy species listed in this book.

Tips on Using this Book

The area code for the entire state of Montana is 406; when no area code precedes a phone number, you can assume this is the area code. All in-state long distance calls must be dialed with that prefix.

This guide is divided into the seven regional administrative divisions of Montana Fish, Wildlife & Parks (FWP). Each section includes: distribution maps for each big game species present in the region; maps of federal lands, climax vegetation, land use, and mountain ranges; descriptions of physical terrain, land use, and local weather patterns; descriptions detailing regional hunting opportunities; listings of guides and outfitters; and information on regional hub cities, including accommodations, camping, restaurants, veterinarians, sporting goods, gun sales and gunsmiths, taxidermists, meat processors, auto repair and rental, air service, and medical services. While this information is current at the time of printing, we cannot guarantee it will be accurate in subsequent years. Always check in advance.

Animal distributions are subject to change over the course of years based on migrations, weather patterns, predation, and disease; thus, the maps contained herein are approximations only. In addition, hunting regulations, prices, and seasons change on a yearly basis; those within are current only for the 1998–1999 season. Call the regional FWP offices for current information.

It is illegal to hunt big game on private land without permission of the landowner; always ask before hunting or fishing on private land.

Getting Around in Montana

Montana is the fourth largest state in the U.S. and has a good system of federal and state highways and county roads. Nevertheless, vast sections of mountain and plains counties have few roads, and many of these are gravel, dirt, or clay, often in poor condition at best.

Major access from the south is via Interstates 15 and 90, from the west via I-90, and from the east via I-94. Secondary roads are generally paved and well maintained, but those that pass over mountains may be temporarily blocked by heavy snows. Highways passing through Yellowstone National Park are often closed as early as mid-September. You might want to call a Montana road report (phone numbers are on the next page) before starting your trip.

There are no major airports in the state, but several national and regional airlines serve the largest cities and towns. As Spokane, Washington, is only 2 hours from the western Montana border, hunters might want to consider flying there and driving a rental to their hunting grounds.

Amtrak and several bus companies serve Montana; however, buses do not permit transport of firearms. Amtrak service is fun but often slow and unpredictable. Proceed with care.

To save precious hunting time, fly to the airport nearest your hunting area and rent a car or 4-wheel-drive rig to reach your camp. Though many Forest Service roads and most county roads through BLM lands are suitable for standard 2-wheel-drive cars, most require high clearance, 4-wheel-drive rigs, particularly by the time hunting season sets in. They are absolutely necessary for backcountry trails and rocky or muddy lanes. With careful planning and extra hiking, one can reach and effectively hunt all but the wildest, most isolated lands.

Road Conditions

For up-to-date road conditions across Montana, phone 800-226-ROAD (7623) or 406-444-6339. For local road reports:

Billings 406-252-2806
Bozeman 406-586-1313
Butte 406-494-3666
Glendive 406-365-2314
Great Falls 406-453-1605
Havre 406-265-1416
Kalispell 406-755-4949
Lewistown 406-538-7445
Miles City 406-232-2099
Missoula 406-728-8553
Wolf Point 406-653-1692

Because winter weather can arrive early and delay travel, consider giving yourself an extra day or two at the end of your trip in order to reach your flight out. Carry chains for your car or truck and a good snow shovel.

Major Roads and Rivers of Montana

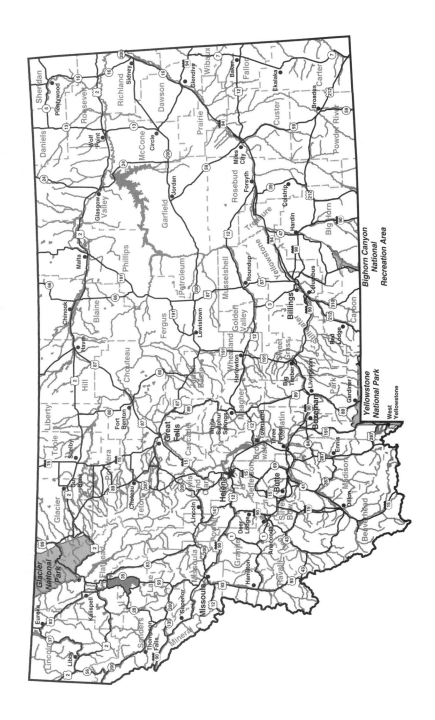

Montana Facts

Fourth largest state in the union
147,138 square miles
93,157,953 acres
550 miles east to west
275 miles north to south

Elevations: 1,820 feet to 12,798 feet
Counties: 56
Towns and Cities: 126
Population (as of 1996): 879,372
   7 Indian Reservations
   2 National Parks
  11 National Forests
  68 State Recreation Areas
  12 Wilderness Areas
  11 State Parks

Nicknames: Treasure State, Big Sky Country, Land of the Shining Mountains
Primary Industries: Agriculture, timber, mining, tourism
Capital: Helena
Bird: Western Meadowlark
Animal: Grizzly Bear
Flower: Bitterroot
Tree: Ponderosa Pine
Gemstone: Montana Agate
Grass: Bluebunch Wheatgrass
Fossil: Maiasaur

MOUNTAIN RANGES OF MONTANA

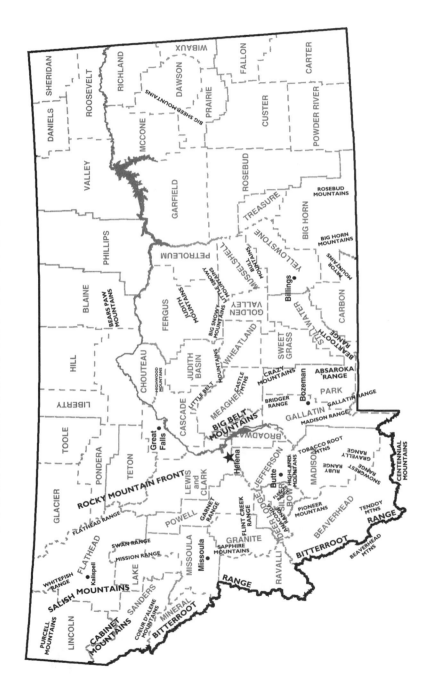

Land Use of Montana

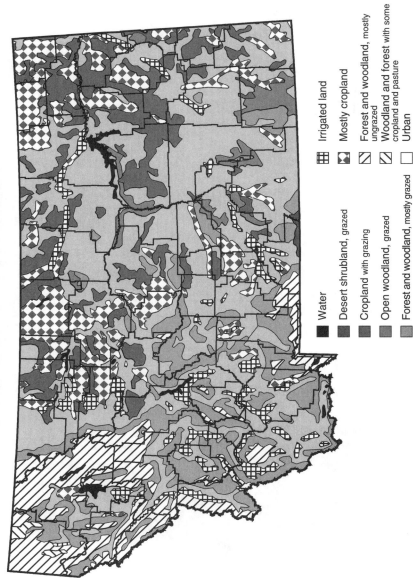

Water

Desert shrubland, grazed

Cropland with grazing

Open woodland, grazed

Forest and woodland, mostly grazed

Subhumid grassland and semiarid grazing land

Irrigated land

Mostly cropland

Forest and woodland, mostly ungrazed

Woodland and forest with some cropland and pasture

Urban

Climax Vegetation of Montana

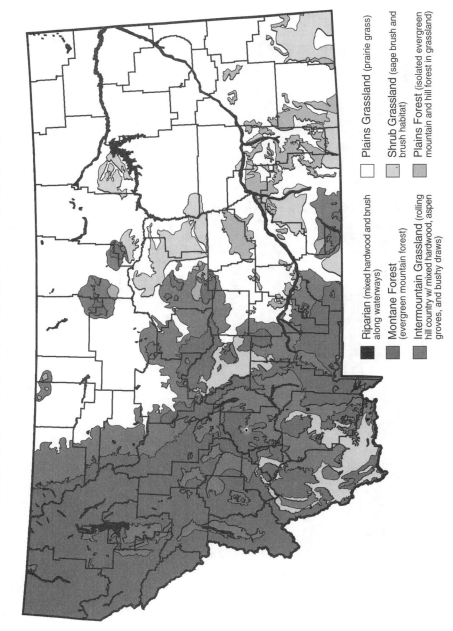

Riparian (mixed hardwood and brush along waterways)

Montane Forest (evergreen mountain forest)

Intermountain Grassland (rolling hill country w/ mixed hardwood, aspen groves, and bushy draws)

Plains Grassland (prairie grass)

Shrub Grassland (sage brush and brush habitat)

Plains Forest (isolated evergreen mountain and hill forest in grassland)

Federal Lands of Montana

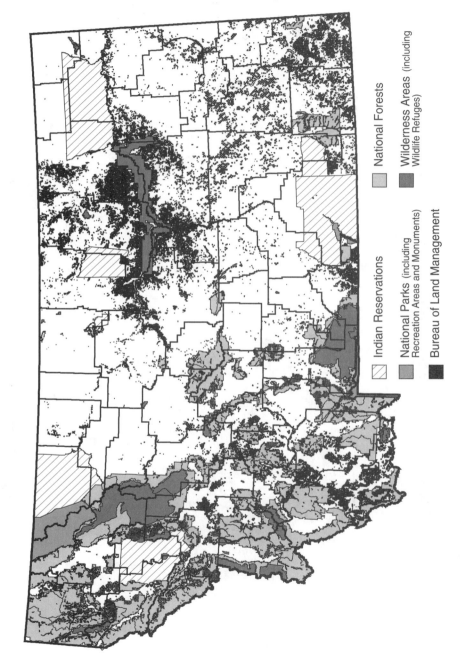

Indian Reservations

National Parks (including Recreation Areas and Monuments)

Bureau of Land Management

National Forests

Wilderness Areas (including Wildlife Refuges)

MONTANA FISH, WILDLIFE & PARKS REGIONS

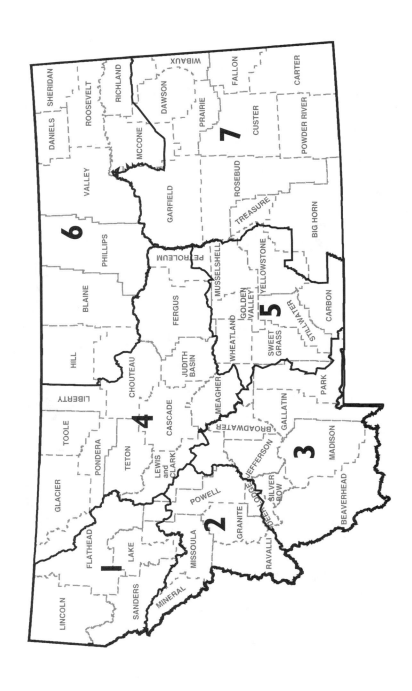

MONTANA FISH, WILDLIFE & PARKS OFFICES

State Headquarters
Montana Fish, Wildlife & Parks
1420 East 6th Avenue, P.O. Box 200701
Helena, MT 59620-0701
406-444-2535
fwp.state.mt.us

Region 1
490 North Meridian Road
Kalispell, MT 59901
406-752-5501
fwprg1@mt.gov

Region 2
3201 Spurgin Road
Missoula, MT 59804
406-542-5500
fwprg2@mt.gov

Region 3
1400 South 19th
Bozeman, MT 59718
406-994-4042
fwpgen@mt.gov

Helena Area Resource Office
930 Custer Avenue West
Helena, MT 59620-0701
406-444-4720

Butte Area Resource Office
1820 Meadowlark Lane
Butte, MT 59701
406-494-1953

Region 4
4600 Giant Springs Road
P.O. Box 6610
Great Falls, MT 59406-6610
406-454-5840
fwprg4@mt.gov

Region 5
2300 Lake Elmo Drive
Billings, MT 59105
406-247-2940
fwprg5@mt.gov

Region 6
Rural Route 1-4210
Glasgow, MT 59230
406-228-3700
fwprg6@mt.gov

Havre Area Resource Office
2165 Hwy 2 East
Havre, MT 59501
406-265-6177
fwphao@mt.gov

Region 7
P.O. Box 1630
Miles City, MT 59301
406-232-0900
fwprg7@mt.gov

Montana Hunting Regulations, Seasons, and Licensing

GENERAL REGULATIONS AS OF 1998

Firearms Regulations

Caliber

There is no caliber limitation during the general big game hunting season (except as specified for shotguns) for the taking of big game animals in Montana. However, the use of poisonous, explosive, or deleterious substances on or in any bullet or projectile is prohibited.

Shotgun

Hunters are prohibited from shooting deer or elk with shotguns, except with lead loads of 0 buck or larger, or rifled slugs.

Restrictions for Traditional Muzzleloader/Handgun Areas Only

- Muzzleloader and firearm must meet the following criteria:
  1. Cannot be loaded from the breech of the barrel.
  2. Must not be loaded with any prepared paper or metallic cartridge.
  3. Must be charged with black powder, pyrodex, or an equivalent.
  4. Must be ignited by a percussion, flintlock, matchlock, or wheellock mechanism.
  5. Must be a minimum .45 caliber.
  6. Cannot have more than two barrels.
  7. Must fire only lead projectiles, no sabots.

- Handguns: "Traditional" handguns must meet the following criteria:
  1. Not capable of being shoulder mounted.
  2. Has a barrel of less than 10½ inches.
  3. Chambers a straight wall cartridge, not originally developed for rifles.

Archery Regulations

The following archery equipment is *legal* to use during the archery only season:

- A long, recurve, or compound bow.
- Broadhead arrows with at least 2 cutting edges when hunting big game animals.

The following archery equipment is *prohibited* from being used *during the archery only season*:

- A crossbow or any device attached to any bow that holds an arrow at partial or full draw. Crossbows may be used during the general rifle season.
- A bow sight, bow, or arrow using artificial light, luminous chemicals such as tritium, or electronics.

The following archery equipment is prohibited at all times:

- Any chemical or explosive device attached to an arrow to aid in the taking of wildlife.

Hunters may hunt with a bow and arrow during the rifle season. However, they must conform to the rifle season regulations. This includes wearing a minimum of 400 square inches of hunter orange (fluorescent) material above the waist. Crossbows may be used during the general rifle season.

Basic Hunting Laws

Hunters or persons in possession of a game animal or game animal parts are prohibited from wasting or rendering unfit for human consumption any part of a game animal that is "defined as suitable for food." For big game animals excluding mountain lions, all of the four quarters above the hock, including loin and backstrap, are considered suitable for food. A person harvesting a black bear or mountain lion is prohibited from abandoning the head or hide in the field.

Hunters are prohibited from shooting on, from, or across the right-of-way of a publicly maintained road open to vehicular traffic. The right-of-way includes the road, shoulders, berms, and borrow pits and generally extends from fenceline to fenceline along fenced roadways.

Hunters are prohibited from shooting or attempting to shoot any game animal from any motorized vehicle (car, truck, boat, snowmobile, motorcycle, all terrain vehicle, airplane, etc.) Even if the vehicle is not moving, hunters must be off or out of the vehicle.

Hunters may in some instances drive off established roads and trails to retrieve game. In all cases, when on private lands, hunters must first obtain permission from the landowner. In the case of public lands, the policy or law varies. BLM public lands are open to motorized travel unless designated as closed. On National Forest lands, restrictions to motorized travel are described on Travel Plan maps available at local U.S. Forest Service offices. On National Wildlife Refuges, all off-road travel is prohibited. For further information, contact the appropriate land management agencies.

Hunters may not use a motorized vehicle or aircraft to concentrate, drive, rally, stir-up, corral, or harass any wildlife except predators.

Hunters are prohibited from hunting or taking any game animals by the aid or with the use of any set gun, jacklight or other artificial light, trap, snare, scent station, or salt lick, nor may any such aforementioned device to entrap or entice game animals be used, made, or set.

Youths under 14 years of age must be in the company of a parent, legal guardian or other responsible adult when carrying or using firearms for any reason.

Hunters may possess, transport, sell or purchase naturally shed antlers or the antlers with a skull or portion of a skull attached from a game animal that has died from natural causes and that has not been unlawfully or accidentally killed. Roadkilled animals have not died from natural causes, and the carcass or parts may not be salvaged or possessed. It is illegal to possess a sheep head picked up in the wild.

Party hunting is not legal in Montana; each hunter must shoot his or her own animal.

Hunters are prohibited from loaning or transferring their licenses to others or using a license issued to another person.

Montana is a member of the Wildlife Violator Compact. Violation of Montana laws or regulations leading to loss of privileges in Montana may also result in the loss of privileges in the other member states: Arizona, Colorado, Idaho, Nevada, Oregon, Utah, Washington, and Wyoming.

Airplane Spotting

Aircraft may not be used to locate big game animals for the purpose of:

1. Hunting those animals within the same hunting day after a person has been airborne.
2. Providing information to another person for the purpose of hunting those animals within the same hunting day after being airborne.

A hunting day is defined as between the earliest and latest legal shooting hours.

Two-Way Communication

Two-way communication may not be used to:

1. Hunt big game animals as defined in MCA 87-2-101(8). ("Hunt" means to "pursue, shoot, wound, kill, chase, lure, possess or capture.")
2. Avoid game checking stations, department enforcement personnel, or to facilitate unlawful activity. When hunting mountain lions or bobcats with dogs, this rule applies when hounds are placed on tracks in a district open to lion or bobcat harvest. The rule shall not be interpreted to prohibit the possession or use of two-way radios for safety or other legitimate purposes, nor does it prohibit the use of radio tracking equipment to locate hounds when hunting mountain lions or bobcats.

Night Vision Equipment

Use of night vision equipment or electronically enhanced light gathering optics for locating or hunting game is prohibited.

Checking Stations

All hunters and anglers are required by law to stop as directed at all designated check stations on their way to and from hunting and fishing areas, even if they have no game or fish to be checked.

Clothing Color

Any person hunting or accompanying hunters as an outfitter or guide must wear a minimum of 400 square inches of hunter orange (fluorescent) material above the waist, visible at all times.

The hunter orange requirement is not in effect for bowhunting during the special archery seasons. Bowhunters pursuing big game animals with bow and arrow must wear a minimum of 400 square inches of hunter orange (fluorescent) above the waist if firearm season is open in the hunting district and for the species being hunted or pursued.

Glandular Scents

Natural or artificial glandular scents may be used by licensed hunters to attract game animals by spraying or pouring scent on the ground or other objects. Hunters may not create a scent station where the scent continues to be dispensed without the hunter's direct action, such as an automatic device that drips or otherwise continues to dispense scent. Scents may not be used to attract bears. No scents other than glandular may be used for attracting animals, but other scents may be used to mask human odor.

Hunting Hours

Authorized hunting hours for the taking of big game animals begins one-half hour before sunrise and ends one-half hour after sunset each day of the hunting season.

Marked Animals

It is legal to shoot big game animals that have radio collars, neck bands, or markers, but markers and radio collars must be returned to the nearest Montana Fish, Wildlife & Parks office.

When a Mistake is Made in Wrongly Killing an Animal

Field dress the animal to keep it from spoiling. Leave it where it was killed, preferably with a person watching it. As soon as possible, contact the nearest regional FWP office, the local sheriff's office, game warden's home office, or 1-800-TIPMONT. Report what happened and wait for instructions from a game warden. Do not transport the animal unless you are told to do so by a game warden.

Procedures To Follow Upon Harvesting an Animal

License Validation and Tagging

IMMEDIATELY after harvesting a game animal, hunters must cut out the proper month and the day of the harvest from the appropriate license and attach it to the animal in a secure and visible manner. To properly validate a license, locate the appropriate month and day the animal was killed and completely cut away (notch out) the month and day designations. Be careful! The correct and appropriate month and day designations must be removed completely from the license. Removing more than one month or one day designation invalidates the license. It is recommended that black electrician's tape be used to secure the license to the animal's leg or antlers. The properly validated license/tag shall remain with the meat until consumed (including cold storage). If quartered, the license/tag should remain with the carcass or largest portion of the carcass.

For mountain lions, hunters must present the hide and skull for inspection to FWP officers for the purpose of tagging. A hide tag must remain attached to the hide until tanned; the skull tag must remain attached to the skull for one year.

Black bear licenses must be attached to the carcass of the bear immediately upon kill, where it shall remain until the hide, carcass, and skull are presented for inspection to an FWP officer. At that time, a tag will be attached to the hide and the license will be placed with the meat.

Evidence of Sex Requirements

It is illegal to possess or transport the carcass of any big game animal unless evidence of the animal's sex and species remains naturally attached to its carcass or a portion of the carcass.

In most cases, the easiest way to meet this requirement is to leave the animal's head attached to the carcass. However, if the animal's head is removed, including quartered or skinned animals, some other evidence of sex must remain naturally attached to the carcass or a portion of it.

The following are considered lawful evidence of sex:
- Horned or antlered game animals:
  Male: Head with the horns or antlers naturally attached, penis, testicles, or scrotum.
  Female: Head or udder (mammaries).
- Bears and Mountain Lions:
  Male: Testicles or baculum.
  Female: Vulva.

Evidence of an animal's sex and species must be retained until the animal's meat is processed (cut and wrapped) or until a bear or mountain lion is checked by a FWP employee or delivered to a taxidermist.

As a condition of hunting in Montana, persons may be required to return to the kill site if requested to do so by a department employee.

Transporting Big Game

Transporting properly tagged animals that comply with the "Evidence of Sex Requirements" and that were lawfully taken by the license holder may be transported by an individual other than the license holder. It is a violation of the Federal Lacy Act to transport an illegally taken game animal across state boundaries; Federal Lacy Act violations could result in a criminal penalty of $20,000 and 5 years in prison. All shippers of fish, game, or nongame birds, game animals, furbearing animals, the skins of furbearing animals or predator animals, or parts thereof are required to label all packages offered for shipment by parcel post, common carrier (airlines or UPS, etc.), or otherwise. The label should be securely attached to the address of the package and shall plainly indicate the names and addresses of the consignor and consignee and the complete contents of the package.

Hunter Education for Firearm and Archery

Youth applying for the 1998 special drawings must be at least 12 years of age before September 15, 1998, and provide required proof of successfully completing a Hunter Education Program at the time of applying for the special drawings.

Resident hunters 12–17 years of age are required by law to have a Montana Hunter Education Certificate of Competency in the safe handling of firearms before they may purchase a hunting license. The Certificate of Competency is awarded to resident youths who have successfully completed Montana's Hunter Education Program. Duplicate Montana Hunter Education certificates may be obtained by contacting any FWP regional office or the Hunter Education Office in Helena (406-444-3188).

New residents of Montana 12–17 years of age need to check with their local Fish, Wildlife & Parks Office to determine if their out-of-state hunter education certificate can be transferred to a Montana Hunter Education Certificate. Regardless, new residents are encouraged to complete the Montana Hunter Education Course to increase their knowledge of Montana's hunting laws and practices.

Nonresident youths 12–17 years of age are required by law to submit a copy of their home state hunter education certificate verifying successful completion of the course when applying for any hunting license in Montana.

Both resident and nonresident youths 12–17 years of age are required to purchase the bow and arrow stamp to archery hunt during the archery only season, and must provide a Certificate of Competency in the safe handling of bow hunting tackle from the National Bowhunter Education Foundation NBEF, in addition to the Certificate of Competency in the safe handling of firearms. Duplicate Montana Bowhunter Education certificates may be obtained by contacting any FWP regional office or the Hunter Education Office in Helena (406-444-3188). Bowhunters seeking information where to find a NBEF course in their state may call the National Archery Hotline at 1-800-461-2728.

Adult (18 years of age or older) bowhunters must show proof of NBEF Bowhunter Education Certificate or present any prior year's bowhunting/archery stamp, tag, permit, or license from any state or province to purchase a Montana bow and arrow license.

Montana law requires members of the armed forces and their dependents stationed in Montana to present a Montana Hunter Education Certificate or similar certificate from any state or province when purchasing any Montana license.

Property Laws

Permission to Hunt Big Game

Montana law requires that big game hunters must have permission of the landowner, lessee, or their agent before hunting big game animals on private property, regardless of whether the land is posted or not. Hunters should secure landowner permission well before applying for a special license/permit to hunt on these lands. It is recommended that hunters receive written permission from the landowner or landowner's agent.

Trespass

Montana law states that lands can be closed to the public either by posting the land or through verbal communication by the landowner or his/her agent. If permission is granted, the landowner may revoke permission by personal communication at any time.

Posting Requirements

Notice denying entry to private land must consist of written notice on a post, structure or natural object or by painting a post, structure or natural object with at least 50 square inches of fluorescent orange paint. In the case of a metal fencepost, the entire post must be painted. This notice must be placed at each outer gate and at all normal points of access to the property, as well as on both sides of a stream, where it crosses an outer property boundary line.

Closed Areas

State Game Preserves and National Parks are closed to hunting of big game animals. For hunting privileges on Federal Wildlife Refuges, inquire at the local refuge office. Big game hunting privileges on Indian Reservations are limited to tribal members only. For questions, contact the tribal headquarters.

Wildlife Management Areas with big game winter range, unless otherwise posted, are closed to public entry from the day following the end of the general deer-elk season or December 1, whichever is later, to May 15 each year, as posted. EXCEPTION: Blackfoot-Clearwater WMA closes November 10.

Recreational Use of State Land

A State Lands Recreational Use License, which is available from FWP license agents, is required to conduct all recreational activities (including hunting and fishing) on state school trust land. Pamphlets which provide information regarding the rules, regulations and restrictions governing these activities on state school trust land are available from FWP license agents, FWP offices and the Department of Natural Resources and Conservation, 1625 11th Avenue, Helena MT 59620, 406-444-2074.

Access to Hunting on Private Land

Block Management Program: The block management program is a cooperative effort between private landowners, Montana Fish, Wildlife & Parks and hunters to provide public hunting on private lands. Over 7.5 million acres of land throughout the state are enrolled in the program, offering a variety of hunting opportunities. The dollars to administer the block management program come from nonresident variable priced outfitter sponsored licenses.

Each region administers the block management area (BMA) for that portion of the state. Hunters wishing to learn more about BMA opportunities should contact the regional office in the area where they wish to hunt. Regional tabloids listing lands enrolled in the program will not be available until August 15, which is also the earliest date for making BMA reservations.

For general information about the block management program, contact the Field Services Division at 406-444-2602.

Miscellaneous Laws and Information

Protected—Gray Wolf

Gray wolves are present in Montana and are protected by state and federal laws. To assist in wolf management, please report any wolf sightings or sign to the U.S. Fish and Wildlife Service at 406-449-5225, the Flathead National Forest at 406-755-5401, or Fish, Wildlife & Parks State Headquarters at 406-444-2612.

Operation of an Off Highway Vehicle (OHV) on Public Lands

OHVs (which includes motorcycles) operating on public land must be registered and display current decals. Residents must register their OHV at their County Treasurer's office. Nonresidents must register their OHV in their home state or purchase a temporary Off Highway Vehicle use permit from any Fish, Wildlife & Parks office. The permit is $5 and expires on December 31, 1998.

Transporting Horses and Mules in Montana

- The Montana Department of Livestock requires a veterinary inspection certificate and an import permit prior to entry into Montana.
- A brand inspection certificate is required for movement within Montana. For information, call the Montana Department of Livestock at 406-444-2976.

- Weed Free Hay Programs: All federal land in Montana requires visitors and per-mittees to use certified weed free hay, grain, straw, mulch, cubes, and pelletized feed on their lands. Please contact offices of Montana Fish, Wildlife & Parks, U.S. Forest Service, Bureau of Land Management, US Fish and Wildlife Service, and Montana Department of Agriculture for information about the area where you will be hunting.

GENERAL LICENSING INFORMATION

One of the world's greatest unsolved mysteries would appear to be the Montana FWP licensing morass. Anyone setting out to discourage participation in hunting would be wise to copy this system. Nevertheless, if you want to hunt big game in Montana, you must wade through its licensing swamp.

Actually, the system does an excellent job of managing game herds and of appor-tioning licenses fairly (more or less) to residents, nonresidents (restricted to no more than 10 percent of available licenses even though 35% of the state is public land), landowners, and outfitters. That's why it's so complicated. The following information should help cut through some of the fog.

As a starting point, think of Montana licenses as carcass tags. They license you to bag an animal. Think of permits as adjuncts to the license. Permits don't let you take an additional carcass but do grant you special privileges to help fill your license. For instance, an elk license entitles you to kill one elk. A special elk permit might make it legal for you to kill a cow elk in a hunting district where non-permit holders may take only bulls. Generally, you buy your licenses first, then apply for special permits to enhance those licenses.

Resident Licensing

Resident licensing is fairly straightforward. The Conservation License is a pre-requisite to all others. You can buy it alone for $4 or get it in a package like the Sportsman's License. This $64 combination license includes the conservation license plus deer "A", elk, and black bear licenses. It's also good for fishing and upland bird hunting. You can get the Sportsman's License without the bear tag for $54. Residents may also buy just a deer "A" license for $13, an elk license for $16, an antelope license for $14, a black bear license for $15, or a mountain lion license for $15. Moose, sheep, and mountain goat licenses are available via limited quota drawing only at $78 each. An $8 bow and arrow license is needed in conjunction with specific species licenses to hunt them during extended archery only seasons.

Nonresident Licensing

As of July, 1998, there were several ways a nonresident could obtain a license to hunt deer and/or elk in Montana. Most required applying for a limited quota of licenses by March 16, 1998. This date may change in subsequent years. To make certain you don't miss the application period, write to Fish, Wildlife & Parks, Attn: License Section, P.O. Box 200701, Helena, MT 59620-0701, or phone 406-444-2950 in December of the year before you hope to hunt and request all information and application forms for the upcoming seasons. This will put you on the FWP mailing list. You'll receive information and notices on all special drawings and emergency regulations for the year. Do not trust friends or outfitters to provide you with this information. They may miss something. You may also glean much of this information off the FWP web site at **fwp.state.mt.us.** You can download some application forms as well as check drawing results. Annual permit drawing results are also available at 1-900-225-5397 for a charge of $1.50 per minute.

When your paperwork arrives, set aside several evenings to begin deciphering them. Be prepared to telephone FWP for clarification.

SEASONS AND LICENSES BY SPECIES
Deer and Elk

Seasons

Generally, the regular Deer/Elk season runs from the last Sunday of October through the last Sunday of November; in 1998, this was October 25–November 29. The archery only season runs from the first Saturday of September to the third Sunday of October; in 1998, this was September 5 through October 18.

Special seasons occur in most districts and are available by special permit only. As the seasons change from year to year and from district to district, consult your regulations thoroughly each year.

Licenses

The following is a rundown of the various nonresident deer and elk licensing options:

1. Nonresident General Deer/Elk Combination $478
   11,500 licenses available in 1998
   This license includes tags for deer, elk, upland birds, and fishing. About 40 percent of the people who applied received one. Half of them had preference points from an unsuccessful try for this license the previous year. The more often you apply for and do not receive this license, the better your chance of getting it in the following year.

2. Nonresident General Elk Combination $428
   11,500 licenses available in 1998 (counted within General Deer/Elk Combination Licenses)
   Good for elk, upland birds, and fishing. This license is included within the 11,500 quota for the Nonresident General Deer/Elk Combination

licenses above and is subject to the same preference system. Again, about 40 percent of those applying in 1998 received this license.

3. Nonresident Elk/Deer Combination (Outfitter Sponsored) $835
   Unlimited license numbers
   Good for elk, deer, upland birds, and fishing. Applicants must be sponsored by a certified Montana outfitter and must hunt under his guidance at all times. If you've got the money, this is the ticket for guaranteed elk and deer tags. There is no drawing to worry about. Plunk down your money, pay your outfitter his fees, and go hunting.

4. Nonresident Elk Combination (Outfitter Sponsored) $735
   Unlimited license numbers
   Good for elk, upland birds, and fishing. Applicant must be sponsored by a certified Montana outfitter and must hunt under his guidance at all times. This is the route to go if you just want to hunt elk, not deer, and want to be absolutely certain of getting a license.

5. Nonresident General Deer Combination $248
   2,300 licenses available in 1998
   Good for deer, upland birds, and fishing. The price is reasonable, but your odds of drawing are slim. In 1998, only 20 percent of applicants drew this license. There is no preference system for this one, so each year you essentially enter a lottery with one chance in five for hitting the jackpot.

6. Nonresident Deer Combination (Outfitter Sponsored) $720
   Unlimited license numbers
   Good for deer, upland birds, and fishing. Applicant must be sponsored by a certified Montana outfitter and must hunt under his guidance at all times. Again, this is the best and most expensive way to get a guaranteed license for deer only.

7. Nonresident Deer Combination (Landowner Sponsored) $253
   2,000 licenses available in 1998
   Good for deer, upland birds and fishing. Applicant must be sponsored by a Montana landowner and must hunt on the landowner's property only. Only 60 percent of 1998 applicants won this tag.

All of the above licenses provide you with something called a deer "A" license. In 1998, this "A" license was valid for hunting statewide in accordance to season dates and sex/species restrictions in individual hunting districts, except for several hunting districts in the special Southwest Montana Antlered Buck Mule Deer Areas. In order to hunt mule deer bucks in this area, you had to have your "A" license validated for one of 8 special units within the area as described on pages 20 and 21 of the 1998 Big Game Hunting Regulations. Study each annual Big Game Regulations pamphlet for this and similar special regulations which change as game populations, hunting pressure, and management goals change from year to year.

Both nonresident and resident hunters are allowed to purchase just one "A" deer tag each year, but they can also often buy one or more "B" licenses, depending on the year. Usually "B" licenses are for doe/fawn harvest and are used as a management tool to reduce overpopulation of whitetails or mule deer, though species available for these tags vary between the regions and are usually valid only in restricted areas. Some "B" licenses are available over the counter from FWP offices and license agents; others must be applied for through special drawings. Consult current regulations for details.

Special deer permits are also issued through special drawings for the harvest of trophy mule deer bucks within specific hunting districts closed to general buck harvest on the "A" license. Once you have your "A" tag, you may enter one of these special permit drawings. The application deadline in 1998 was June 1. If you win, you will be restricted to hunting only mule deer and only in the district specified on your special permit. You may not hunt antlered buck mule deer anywhere else in the state, but you may use your "A" tag to hunt whitetail bucks or does or mule deer does in other hunting districts where they are legal game.

Antelope

Seasons

Generally, the antelope season runs from the second Sunday of October through the second Sunday of November; most districts in 1998 had seasons from October 11 through November 8. However, some districts open earlier—as early as September 15; check the regulations for the district(s) you plan to hunt.

Archery only season runs from the first Saturday in September through the second Saturday of October (in 1998, September 5–October 10). The Multi-Region archery season runs from the second Saturday in September through the second Sunday in November (in 1998, September 5–November 8). See the bowhunting regulations section below for more details on these hunts.

Licensing

Resident $14
Nonresident $153

Nonresident antelope licenses are not included in any of the deer-elk combination licenses above, for whatever reason. To get a license for hunting pronghorns with a firearm, a nonresident must apply for a limited number of licenses in specific hunting districts. Non-residents are limited to, but not guaranteed, 10 percent of the available licenses in each region. In 1998, the application deadline was June 1. Each hunter gets one application; each hunter gets one license. Up to 5 people can apply as a party. If successful, they all get licenses.

Trophy Species

Applying for mountain goat, moose, and sheep tags is not complicated. Request licensing application forms from the FWP state headquarters in Helena in January of the year you wish to hunt. Be sure to specify which species you want to apply for. You must select a specific hunting district for each species. Licenses are extremely limited and highly contested. In 1997, for instance, 272 people tried to draw 8 mountain goat tags in hunting district 100-00. Would you believe 1,261 competed for 15 bighorn licenses in unit 680-01? Fully 702 would-be moose hunters vied for 10 licenses in unit 270-00. All this was despite nonresident license fees of $478 per species and resident fees of $78. Deadline for applications was May 1 in 1998. Successful applicants in limited areas cannot apply for that species license again for 7 years, regardless of whether or not they fill their tags; unsuccessful hunters in unlimited areas can reapply in subsequent years, but successful hunters cannot.

Mountain Goat

Resident $78
Nonresident $478
Seasons generally run from September 1 or 15 through the end of November. Any person taking a mountain goat must present either the intact head or skull with horns attached to an FWP office within 10 days of the kill.

Moose

Resident $78
Nonresident $478
The moose season generally runs from September 15 through the end of November, though some districts have a November 15–December 15 season. Red Rock Lakes NWR in Region 3 delays the beginning of its season until October 15.

Bighorn Sheep

Resident (limited or unlimited hunt) $78
Nonresident (limited or unlimited hunt) $478
Several bighorn sheep hunting units in Region 3 and Region 5 north and northwest of Yellowstone National Park are open for unlimited hunting—to an extent. Residents or nonresidents may apply for and receive a license to hunt districts 300, 301, 303, 500, and 501, but they must apply through the standard special drawing process and select one of these districts as their first and only choice.

Seasons run from the 1st or 15th of September through October 31, November 15, or November 29, depending on the district. Legal rams must have a minimum ¾ curl. Kills must be presented to any FWP office within 10 days of harvest.

The catch to this seemingly ideal opportunity is that in all but one of the units hunting ceases within 48 hours after a predetermined quota of rams has been harvested—usually 1 to 3 animals. District 301 in the Spanish Peaks district of the

Madison Range has no quota, but the season is just 6 days long. In 1997, 169 hunters were licensed to hunt rams in this district, and they harvested six rams.

Each of these districts is wild, rugged, and relatively inaccessible—miles from the nearest road. Rams are scarce and widely scattered, often disappearing into heavy timber for days on end. Finding them is extremely difficult. Serious hunters roam and comb their chosen districts (year after year) for days, sometimes weeks, before the season to locate rams. They move and camp as near the sheep as possible and try to take them at the crack of dawn on opening morning. Many hunts end within minutes.

So don't rush out and drop $478 on "the most accessible bighorn hunting in the world" until you've studied the maps and hiked the districts. Then make your decision. This isn't the best way to harvest a ram, but it is the best way to enjoy, practice, and learn sheep hunting. Go for those reasons, and you'll have a great hunt.

Mountain Lions

1. General License
   Resident $15
   Nonresident $320
2. Trophy License (to be purchased upon reporting a harvest)
   Resident and nonresident $50

All Montana mountain lion hunting is conducted under the quota system. Each region sets a quota of lions that may be killed within its boundaries in a given year. The winter season runs December 1 through February 15 of the following year, and some regions also allow hunting during the general fall season. When the annual harvest quota is reached in any region, the season is closed on 24-hours notice regardless of the previously set closing date.

An unlimited number of licenses are sold to residents and nonresidents. Hunters must submit application forms to FWP headquarters by November 15 each year. In addition, should you bag one, you will be required to purchase a $50 trophy license upon presenting the animal for inspection. You must report any kill within 24 hours and present the head and hide for inspection within 5 days to an FWP office. FWP will retain the skull for processing and examination before returning it.

Hounds may be used to hunt mountain lions during the winter season. To do so, you must first obtain a free hound handler permit from FWP no later than August 31 of the year you plan to hunt. Females with kittens and spotted juveniles may not be taken. Wildlife Managment Areas are closed to mountain lion hunting during the winter season, and all National Wildlife Refuges are closed to mountain lion hunting at all times.

Black Bears

Resident $15

Nonresident $120

Considering all the regulations, limited licenses, and special permits swirling around elk and deer, Montana's black bear regulations are surprisingly simple. Any resident or nonresident can simply buy an annual black bear license by August 31 and go hunting in any black bear hunting district as described in the annual Black Bear Big Game Hunting Regulations. Note, however, that two districts, 510 and 520 in the Beartooth and Pryor Mountains areas, are under a quota system.

There is a spring season from mid-April to mid- to late May, depending on the hunting district, and a fall season from mid-September until late November or early December. If you wish to hunt the spring season, you must purchase your license before the season starts (in 1998, this was April 14); after that date, it is only valid for the fall season. This regulation was instigated because some unethical hunters were purchasing their tags after opportunistically killing bears during other spring hunts; this will prevent such future poaching. In addition, you may take only one bear per year, so if you get one in the spring, you can't hunt in the fall.

Since Montana regulations prevent you from wasting or rendering unfit for human consumption any part of an animal suitable for food, you'll need to keep the meat from any bear you shoot. However, you should be aware that black bears in Montana commonly carry trichinella, the parasite that causes trichinosis; trichinosis can cause intestinal disorders, fever, nausea, and muscular pain. FWP has a free program to test for this disease, and you need but send a portion of the tongue or muscle tissue to their laboratories: FWP Wildlife Research Lab, Box 173220, Bozeman, MT 59717-3220.

Any black bear of either sex is legal except females with cubs. All harvested bears must be presented to a FWP official for inspection within 5 days of the kill. All National Wildlife Refuges are closed to black bear hunting. Neither dogs nor scents may be used hunt bears.

BOWHUNTING MONTANA

Understanding Licensing

If you bowhunt for deer, elk, or antelope during archery only seasons, you must buy an $8 Bow and Arrow License. These seasons usually run for about 6 weeks before the rifle seasons open. Some archery only seasons run into January and are a good way to extend your season.

Early archery only seasons (and some wider choices in several hunting districts as outlined below) are the only "special favors" bowhunters get in Montana; no extra tags, no extra animals. All resident and nonresident bowhunters buy and use the same licenses firearm hunters buy (with one exception, the Multi-Region Archery Only License, also outlined below). If hunters arrow an animal and notch their tag, they are finished hunting that species for that year, regardless of what equipment they used. If they do not take an animal during the archery only season, they may use their license to hunt during the rifle season and extend their repertoire of equipment to include a crossbow. There are no special archery only seasons for bighorn sheep, mountain goat, black bear, moose, or mountain lion, though you still have the option of using a bow and arrow instead of a firearm to hunt those animals—and save yourself the cost of purchasing a bow and arrow license.

Montana archers in recent years have been able to hunt deer and elk beginning in early September and press on into mid-October. In addition they have been allowed—with a few exceptions—to hunt in nearly any hunting district in the state for mule deer or whitetails. In many districts where rifle hunters are limited to branch-antlered bull elk only, bowhunters are allowed to take cows and spikes.

Regulations change from year to year to accommodate fluctuations in big game populations, so carefully check current Montana Big Game Hunting Regulations. There has been some talk about limiting hunters to either bow or firearm hunting, the so-called "choose your weapon" option.

Unlimited Archery Antelope Licenses

Archery antelope hunting regulations as spelled out in the 1998 Montana Big Game Hunting Regulations are confusing, but this is what they boil down to: Hunters may possess only one antelope tag per year (unless over-the-counter doe/fawn licenses are sold that year) and may kill just one antelope whether with rifle or bow. However, depending on which license you apply for, you can hunt with bow and rifle or with bow only. Confused? I should think so.

Here's how it works: If you apply for a limited quota license valid for a specific hunting district as listed in the Big Game Regulations, and if you are drawn for that license, you may then use that license to hunt in that district and take one antelope of the sex specified on that license. You can hunt with a bow during the archery only season (September 5–October 10 in 1998); you can wait and hunt with a rifle during the firearm season (October 11–November 8 in 1998); or you can hunt with a bow, and if you don't fill your tag, you can still hunt the rifle season with rifle or bow, your choice. Get it? Good, because here comes a curve.

If you don't want to risk failing in the limited quota license drawing, you can instead apply (by June 1 again) for a Multi-Region Archery Only License which is valid for most antelope hunting districts in the state beginning with the numbers 3, 4, 5, 6, and 7. These licenses are unlimited, so you will get one, but you must hunt with bow and arrow only. You may use this license to hunt during the antelope firearm season but you may not use a rifle. The archery only season runs September 5—November 8 in 1998.

The difference, then, boils down to how serious a bowhunter you are. If you wish to hunt strictly with a bow, go for the Multi-Region Archery Only License. If you want to try bowhunting but would like the option of a rifle-hunt back-up just in case, try for one of the limited quota licenses, realizing that you risk not drawing a license. After June 1, it's too late to buy a Multi-Region Archery Only tag.

Bowhunter Certified

In an effort to raise the standards of bowhunters, Montana now requires for the purchase of a Bow and Arrow License (required for archery only seasons) that all hunters show proof of:

- an NBEF National Bowhunters Education certificate, or

- any prior year's bowhunting stamp, tag or permit from any state or province.

Hunters under age 18 must have a standard hunter education certificate and a NBEF National Bowhunters Education certificate. Contact FWP for details.

Bows Legal in Special Restricted Areas

In a few heavily populated areas such as those around Kalispell, Missoula, and Bozeman, centerfire rifles are not legal for hunting big game, but bows are. In some of these "restricted weapons" zones, muzzleloaders, shotguns, and traditional handguns may also be used. Always consult current regulations for complete information before hunting in any hunting district.

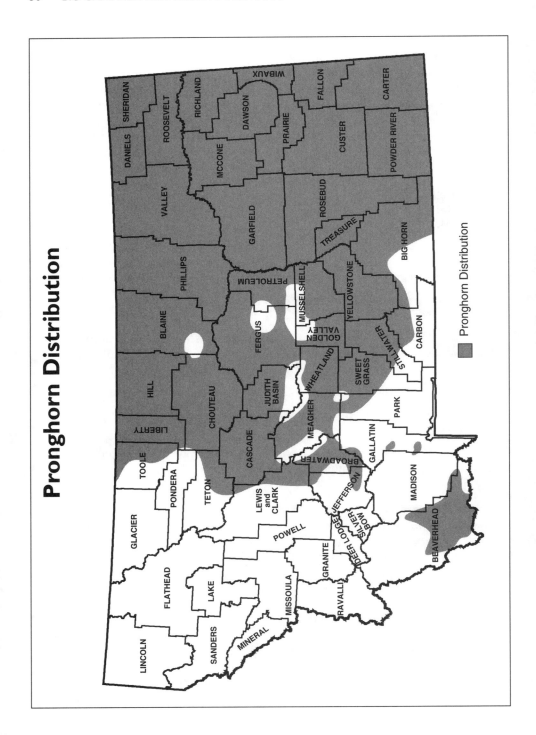

Pronghorn Distribution

Pronghorn Distribution

Pronghorn

Antilocapra americana

The North American pronghorn is the High Plains distilled into flesh and bone. Fast as the wind, pale as seared buffalo grass, tough as cactus, this sharp-eyed ungulate is the ultimate rifleman's game.

Fascinating Facts

- Pronghorns are not antelopes, as they are commonly called, but a unique family —*Antilocapridae*—native to North America.
- Pronghorns are the only horned animals that shed their horns each year.
- The pronghorn, with the exception of the short-burst speed of a cheetah, is the world's fastest land mammal, reaching 50, 60, and even 70 miles per hour depending on which eyewitness accounts you believe.
- Pronghorns are physically capable of jumping fences; they just don't know how. When pushed or badly frightened, they've cleared six-foot fences. The proliferation of fences in the West is slowly forcing pronghorns to learn to jump.
- Fossil pronghorns with four horns have been dated back 20 million years.
- A five-day-old fawn can outrun a human.
- Bucks herd and protect doe groups, but the does ultimately decide with which buck they'll mate.
- Pronghorns, although mostly diurnal, can and do move and feed at night.

Local Names
Antelope, prairie goat, speed goat, scape goat, goats, 'lopes

Size
Bucks stand 35 to 40 inches at shoulder and weigh 110 to 135 pounds. Does stand 33 to 36 inches and weigh 90 to 110 pounds.

Coat & Color
Hairs are short, stiff, dense, and spongy feeling. Each hair is filled with tiny air pockets for insulation. Pelage is reddish-tan over the top of the head, neck, and back, running down the outsides of the legs and the top of the tail. Rump, sides, belly, chest, inside legs, inner ears, muzzle, lower face, and the crown between the horns are bright white. Three white chevrons or bands run from under the neck halfway up the sides, giving pronghorns an elegant, exotic look. Mature males sport black upper noses and "cheek patches" that cover an oil-producing scent gland used to mark territories. These black patches can be the best way to distinguish bucks from does.

*Note the black horns, nose, and oily scent gland below the eye
of this mature pronghorn buck.*

Horns

Both sexes have horns. Doe horns vary from bumps to 4-inch black spikes that usually curve back at their tips. Male horns are black, flattened laterally, and commonly reach 14 inches, sometimes 16 inches, and very rarely 18 to 20 inches. They usually hook back or inward several inches at their tops, and the tips are often white. Halfway up this main horn is the forward projecting paddle or prong which gives the animal its name. The area from the back of the main horn to the tip of the prong measures 3 to (rarely) 8 inches. Not uncommonly, some horns spread widely to each side, project forward until they nearly touch the nose, or otherwise diverge from the standard conformation.

From the tip of a bony core, a new black horn sheath begins to grow in early fall each year. By late October, this new growth pushes off the old sheath. This is why pronghorn hunting seasons are held before November. By June, the new horn is finished growing; thus, winter conditions determine horn quality. Mild, open winters mean adequate food and good horn growth. Cold, snowy winters limit food, and horn growth takes a back seat to survival. If you want a big, long horn, don't look for one following a hard winter.

Voice & Communications

Does and fawns communicate with soft bleats, blatts, and whines. Bucks whine and smack their lips while courting does. Of most significance to hunters, bucks blow a snort-wheeze, a rapid series of five to twelve loud snorts that carry up to a mile on a calm morning and from a distance sound like high-pitched barks. This is a territorial call meant to warn away competing males during the rut, and imitating it can often lure bucks within bow shooting range. Alarmed pronghorns flare their rump hairs to visually alert others. A variety of scent glands on the face, feet, and back convey messages poorly understood by humans.

Senses

While pronghorns probably detect odors and hear as well as mule deer or whitetails, they don't appear to use those senses fully. Instead, they trust their eyes to spot danger. A noisy hunter crawling through grass or casting his body odor downwind to a herd may put them on alert, but they usually won't flee until they see him. Pronghorns have been recorded spotting small moving animals up to 4 miles away. Normally, however, even hunted herds don't spook until humans approach within a mile or less.

Tracks and Sign

Like most deer-sized ungulates, the pronghorn leaves a heart-shaped hoof print. These vary from 2 to 3¼ inches in length and are easily confused with

Pronghorn tracks. Above, front, 3¼" long; below, rear, 2¾" long.

mule deer and whitetail prints. Droppings are dry pellets, sometimes segmented masses when the animals have been feeding on fresh grass. Territorial bucks routinely SPUD mark: they *sniff* the ground, *paw* it bare with a front hoof, *urinate* in it, then *defecate* in it. Find a few of these markers, and you'll know there's a buck about.

If your nose is sensitive, you may discover a buck's olfactory signposts. Watch for stiff, protruding vegetation such as yucca stems, isolated sagebrush, or thick weeds. Sniff their tips for a pungent, pronghorn odor. These are the places bucks rub their oily, odoriferous cheek-patch glands.

Last, watch for beaten and broken brush. Like deer, pronghorn bucks thrash vegetation with their horns during the rut.

Reproduction and Young

Antelope breed in September and usually produce twin fawns in May or June. Each weighs about 4 pounds. They can walk on their first day, follow their dam on the second, and run with the herd in little more than a week. Until they are mobile and strong enough to evade predators, they hide in the grass until summoned to nurse several times each day.

A pronghorn buck in open grasslands scans the horizon for danger during September.

Habitat

Pronghorns live on flat-to-rolling, short-grass to mixed-grass plains and prairies, including sagebrush flats and grassy mountain foothills. Pronghorns adapt readily to wheat and alfalfa fields and feed in them, but too many fences hamper their movements.

Home Range

Despite living in the wide open, pronghorns are strongly territorial over most of their range. Doe groups and their fawns select a summer range of one to five square miles based on quality forage and convenient watering holes. Mature bucks adopt these same territories and attempt to control them by marking and patrolling. Rather than flee the country when spooked, territorial pronghorns run from danger within their familiar territories, so if you see a big buck one day, you should be able to find him nearby the next. Hard winters can drive pronghorns from their summer territo-

During the September rut, a pronghorn buck trots around does to herd them back into his harem.

ries, forcing them to migrate dozens of miles to find forage, but such movements rarely occur during hunting seasons.

Forage Plants

Surprisingly, pronghorns eat little grass. Instead, they pick broad-leafed forbs like prairie clover, dandelions, and wild lilies from between the grasses. They also feed heavily on sagebrush, bitterbrush, and other native shrubs, as well as succulent commercial crops like clover and alfalfa. Irrigated crop fields often lure hungry herds of late-summer pronghorn, and ranchers are often eager to have hunters collect a few while harassing the others back to the prairies.

Daily Patterns

Unlike many members of the deer family, pronghorns eat, sleep, and make love right out in the open, often in the same place. There is rarely a daily movement pattern between feeding and bedding areas. In hot, dry areas they go to water at least once per day, but more often in the morning and evening, and they move in and out of green farm fields when natural forage is at a premium.

Rutting Behavior

Pronghorns rut from late August to mid-October with most activity occurring in mid-September. Bucks try to control territories, groups of does, or both. Early in the rut they scent mark brush with their cheek glands, SPUD mark ground throughout their territories, patrol territory boundaries, snort-wheeze, and chase off rivals.

Watching for danger from atop a grassy ridge, this buck pronghorn displays massive, 15-inch horns.

Bucks often spar like whitetails, locking horns and trying to push one another down. During the peak of rut, bucks are usually so busy attempting to keep does collected in one herd and running off challengers that they give up territorial defenses, though they still scent mark, SPUD, and snort-wheeze. Where bucks are numerous, a herd buck may spend up to 90 percent of his time each day running off rivals and herding does. Expect erratic behavior and movements, but expect bucks to remain within their territories. Bucks with the largest horns usually, but not always, run with the doe herds while hopeful satellite bucks revolve around them. Sometimes two or three big bucks are mixed with a big bunch of does.

Trophy Dimensions

The longest antelope horn ever officially recorded was 20⅛ inches from base to tip. It came out of Arizona in 1899. The longest Montana horn ever entered in the Boone & Crockett record book measured 17⅘ inches and came out of Rosebud

OFFICIAL SCORING SYSTEM FOR NORTH AMERICAN BIG GAME TROPHIES

Records of North American
Big Game

BOONE AND CROCKETT CLUB®

250 Station Drive
Missoula, MT 59801
(406)542-1888

Minimum Score: Awards All-time
80   82

PRONGHORN

SEE OTHER SIDE FOR INSTRUCTIONS		Column 1	Column 2	Column 3
A. Tip to Tip Spread		Right Horn	Left Horn	Difference
B. Inside Spread of Main Beams				
C. Length of Horn				
D-1. Circumference of Base				
D-2. Circumference at First Quarter				
D-3. Circumference at Second Quarter				
D-4. Circumference at Third Quarter				
E. Length of Prong				
TOTALS				

	Column 1		Exact Locality Where Killed:
ADD	Column 2		Date Killed: Hunter:
	Subtotal		Owner: Telephone #:
	SUBTRACT Column 3		Owner's Address:
			Guide's Name and Address:
	FINAL SCORE		Remarks: (Mention Any Abnormalities or Unique Qualities)

I certify that I have measured this trophy on _____ 19 _____

at (address) _____ City _____ State _____
and that these measurements and data are, to the best of my knowledge and belief, made in
accordance with the instructions given.

Witness: _____ Signature: _____

B&C Official Measurer

I.D. Number

Reprinted courtesy of the Boone and Crockett Club, 250 Station Dr., Missoula, MT 59801, 406-542-1888

INSTRUCTIONS FOR MEASURING PRONGHORN

All measurements must be made with a 1/4-inch wide flexible steel tape to the nearest one-eighth of an inch. Enter fractional figures in eighths, without reduction. Official measurements cannot be taken until horns have air dried for at least 60 days after the animal was killed.

A.   Tip to Tip Spread is measured between tips of horns.

B.   Inside Spread of Main Beams is measured at a right angle to the center line of the skull, at widest point between main beams.

C.   Length of Horn is measured on the outside curve on the general line illustrated. The line taken will vary with different heads, depending on the direction of their curvature. Measure along the center of the outer curve from tip of horn to a point in line with the lowest edge of the base, using a straight edge to establish the line end.

D-1. Circumference of Base is measured at a right angle to axis of horn. **Do not** follow irregular edge of horn; the line of measurement must be entirely on horn material.

D-2-3-4. Divide measurement C of longer horn by four. Starting at base, mark **both** horns at these quarters (even though the other horn is shorter) and measure circumferences at these marks. If the prong interferes with D-2, move the measurement down to just below the swelling of the prong. If D-3 falls in the swelling of the prong, move the measurement up to just above the prong.

E.   Length of Prong: Measure from the tip of the prong **along the upper edge** of the outer side to the horn; then continue around the horn to a point at the rear of the horn where a straight edge across the back of both horns touches the horn, with the latter part being at a right angle to the long axis of horn.

FAIR CHASE STATEMENT FOR ALL HUNTER-TAKEN TROPHIES

FAIR CHASE, as defined by the Boone and Crockett Club®, is the ethical, sportsmanlike and lawful pursuit and taking of any free-ranging wild game animal in a manner that does not give the hunter an improper or unfair advantage over such game animals.
Use of any of the following methods in the taking of game shall be deemed **UNFAIR CHASE** and unsportsmanlike:

   I.   Spotting or herding game from the air, followed by landing in its vicinity for the purpose of pursuit and shooting;

  II.   Herding, pursuing, or shooting game from any motorboat or motor vehicle;

 III.   Use of electronic devices for attracting, locating, or observing game, or for guiding the hunter to such game;

  IV.   Hunting game confined by artificial barriers, including escape-proof fenced enclosures, or hunting game transplanted for the purpose of commercial shooting;

   V.   Taking of game in a manner not in full compliance with the game laws or regulations of the federal government or of any state, province, territory, or tribal council on reservations or tribal lands;

  VI.   Or as may otherwise be deemed unfair or unsportsmanlike by the Executive Committee of the Boone and Crockett Club.

I certify that the trophy scored on this chart was taken in **FAIR CHASE** as defined above by the Boone and Crockett Club. In signing this statement, I understand that if the information provided on this entry is found to be misrepresented or fraudulent in any respect, it will not be accepted into the Awards Program and all of my prior entries are subject to deletion from future editions of *Records of North American Big Game* and future entries may not be accepted.

Date: _____   Signature of Hunter:_____
                                        (Signature must be witnessed by an Official Measurer or
                                        a Notary Public.)

Date: _____   Signature of Notary or Official Measurer:_____

Reprinted courtesy of the Boone and Crockett Club, 250 Station Dr., Missoula, MT 59801, 406-542-1888

*Outfitter and guide
Keith Atcheson with the
author's Boone & Crockett
82-point pronghorn taken
on snowy grassland.*

County. Keep this in mind when hunters tell you about the 18-inch heads they routinely shoot in Big Sky Country.

Length, important as it is to trophy quality, isn't the sole requirement. The "prong" in pronghorn refers to a forward jutting piece of the horn that some old-timers call a paddle. During jostling matches, it serves to stop an opponent's horns from sliding down to a defendant's eyes. In trophy measuring, its length taken from the back of the main horn to the tip of the prong is added to the total score. A 5-inch prong is good, a 6-inch is bragging rights, and anything over 7 inches is outstanding. The world's record is 8⅝ inches, again from an Arizona head.

The only other requirement for trophy horns is mass. The fatter the horns throughout their length, the higher the score. Circumference measurements are made at four quarters. Inside and tip-to-tip spreads are not counted in the score.

Trophy status, like beauty, is in the eyes of the beholder. Some hunters seek only bucks with wide, flaring horns. Others want to find tips that curve in and almost

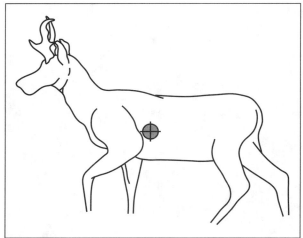

Shot Placement:
Top: Broadside shot.
Aim for the center of the chest just behind the bend of the front leg or shoulder; this should penetrate the lungs.

Below: Quartering shot.
Aim for the off-side shoulder by drawing an imaginary line from your rifle or bow to the far-side shoulder; aim slightly behind the shoulder if you don't wish to damage any meat.

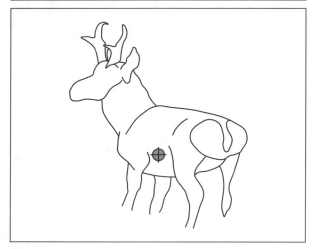

touch. Others like oddball, deformed horns that droop or curve at strange angles. Some hunters even seek out old does with big horns. Any pronghorn that is hunted hard and fairly and taken cleanly is a trophy and should be honored as such. Conversely, a 17-inch horn shot from the side of a road after a vehicular chase is a shame and a black-eye on the fine tradition of sport hunting.

Hunting Tactics

The hunter's challenge is to slip within rifle range unseen and place one true shot, often at extreme distances. Stalking, patience, and accurate range estimation are essential skills. Resisting the urge to chance overly long shots is another.

The most common hunting technique is to scan with binoculars to locate your quarry, then stalk it. Magnifications of 8× to 10× are about right for this work. Particular hunters often use spotting scopes of 15× to 45× power to scour the plains for miles in search of a trophy head. This saves considerable walking. When you do spot a suitable animal, study the lay of the land, looking for hills, ditches, folds, and brush to cover your stalk. Also note what your game is doing and is likely to do while you're stalking. A whirling, unsettled rutting herd is liable to bolt. A bedded herd is likely to stay.

A second tactic is to wait beside a popular feeding field. A sharpshooter can cover several hundred yards of an alfalfa field from one position. This is popular with hunters unable to walk and stalk.

In heavily hunted areas, especially on opening day, another trick is to take up a position along a fence, near a fence crossing (look for tracks going under a high bottom wire and hair on the barbs), or in a natural saddle. Wait there for animals to move past as they run and shift positions to avoid other hunters. Study a herd's movements and you'll often detect a pattern. Move to intercept.

Muzzleloader and bow hunters often build blinds beside water holes. Isolated ponds far from other water supplies are best for this.

One of the most exciting hunting tactics is calling and decoying, recommended only for bow hunters, for obvious reasons. The idea is to crawl within the territory of a herd-master buck, then erect a smaller buck decoy in his sight. Sometimes it is necessary to imitate the snort-wheeze call of a buck to attract attention to the decoy. The archer hides behind the decoy, watching for his opportunity to shoot. Often angry bucks run within 10 or 20 yards of a decoy before stopping. WARNING: do not use a decoy during firearm seasons or where rifle shooters (poachers) are likely to spot it!

Recommendations for Loads and Rifle Cartridges

This light-framed, thin-skinned animal can be handled quite well with the 6mm Rem. and .243 Win., but for a bit better long-range performance, the .25–06 and .270 Win. are perfect.

Too Many Pronghorns

Perhaps the best part of pronghorn hunting is the open country. Forget head-down searching for tracks and droppings. Just sweep your gaze across miles and miles of prairie and see your game. A half-dozen does and fawns there, three small bucks over there, a big band with a boss buck crossing that butte. Let's go!

After more than a dozen pronghorn hunts to my credit, I was used to spotting lots of the animals, but not the numbers Keith Atcheson guided me to one bright October day.

"See that little band on the horizon?" Keith asked as the two of us sat on a hillside glassing. "Looks like a pretty good buck with them. If they drop over the other side we'll get closer for a better look."

Fifteen minutes later we bellied over that ridge. A wide basin—almost a four-square-mile bowl surrounded by low hills and grassy ridges—was swarming with pronghorns. "Look at the buck in that bunch of 13," I said. "He's gotta be at least 15 inches."

"How about these two," Keith countered. "They're both 15s if they're an inch." The longer we looked, the more we saw until we'd counted at least a dozen bucks most hunters would have traded their rifles for. But stalking them in that short-grass bowl was nigh impossible. That's when my guide really earned his keep. "I'll hike out and circle behind them," he said. "They usually make for these hills. You just stay on this ridge and keep track of them, then use the cover to sneak in for a shot."

By noon I was scrambling from hill to hill, trying to intercept a big band that had drifted away from Keith. At least two bucks in the bunch of 18 animals looked good. Real good. But when I crawled over a crest to look down on the band, it had grown to more than 30. Apparently two groups had merged in the jumbled little hillocks, and both were close enough to hit with a rock.

I faced a problem all hunters should have to endure—too many choices. I quickly tallied 11 bucks in the herd, nearly half worth studying. Four in particular, walking abreast, looked like 15-inch contenders, maybe 16-inch. I would have to judge them on more than just length, so I traded my 8X binocular for a 15–35× spotting scope and started studying. I quickly ruled out one. Good length, but weak prongs. A second became an also-ran because of spindly tops. That left two, and they'd already ambled more than 200 yards away. Both looked the same length and showed good curl at the tips, always worth an extra inch or more. Both had wide, long prongs and good bases. Peas in a pod except one sported a series of bumps and protrusions on his horn bases, not uncommon to the species. The other was smooth. It came down to aesthetics. I chose the buck with the clean bases and leveled my Ruger .22–250.

Author with guide Keith Atcheson, admiring a pronghorn buck with 15-inch horns taken in sagebrush and grass hills.

White-tailed Deer Distribution

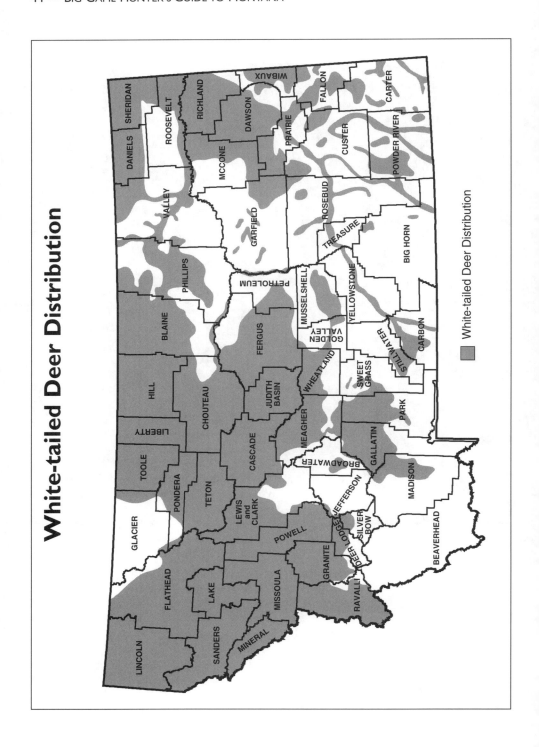

White-tailed Deer Distribution

White-tailed Deer

Odocoileus virginianus

Overshadowed by mule deer and elk, whitetails are nevertheless native to Montana and increasingly popular quarry, given their trophy size and wary natures. A small buck by Montana standards is considered a trophy by hunters from many eastern states.

Fascinating Facts

- Unlike elk, moose, and caribou, which migrated to North America over the Bering Land Bridge, whitetails developed natively 10 to 20 million years ago.
- Because whitetails have red coats in summer and gray pelage in winter, they were once thought to be two species.
- Whitetails may be homebodies in the East, but in Montana bucks may walk 10 straight-line miles in a night looking for does. Mountain whitetails may migrate across several major valleys to reach winter habitat.
- Spooked mule deer bounce uphill and run toward broken country. Whitetails dash full speed toward dense cover, usually downhill.
- A whitetail can high-jump 8 feet and broad-jump 28 feet, but run only 35 mph.
- Scientists have surgically repositioned buck antler bases, called pedicles, to nose, rumps, and even ears. In each case, antlers grew in the new position. Thus, if pedicles are damaged or knocked out of position during fights, antlers may grow in new positions. This explains three-antlered bucks, forehead antlers, and "unicorn" bucks.
- Bucks run heedlessly through woods and fields during the rut because does intentionally lead them on courting chases to stir up competition. She picks the most fit.

Local Names
Whitetail, fantail, flagtail

Size
Highly variable by age. Does and young bucks weigh around 150 pounds and stand 2½ to 3 feet at the shoulder. Mature bucks can reach 3½ feet and top 350 pounds. Most good bucks will field dress about 200 pounds.

Coat & Color
Because they sport red coats in summer and gray in winter, whitetails were once thought to be two species. Hunters will see the winter coat: gray-brown above with snowy-white belly, white inner ears, white throat patch, white ring around the nose

just behind its black muzzle, and that long, wide white undertail and rump waving bye-bye.

Antlers

For symmetry, you can't beat a whitetail rack. Main beams rise to each side on an angle with the alert ears, then curve forward and inward to varying degrees. Some almost touch at the tips, others flare wide with little or no curve at the tips. Jutting up from these beams are typically 3 to 6 tines per side, including a sizable brow tine. Each tine typically leans or curves in slightly, creating a "basket" shape designed for grasping opponents' antlers for secure holds during wrestling matches.

Number of points says nothing about a buck's age, but antler mass does. Since the bases widen every year of a buck's life, its antlers get more massive each year. Spread and length usually peak between ages five and eight.

Voice and Communication

Like so many deer, whitetails probably say more with scent than vocalization. Fawns and does bleat, of course, and bucks blatt or grunt. When following does in heat, they grunt often and repeatedly (the tending grunt), much like pigs. Both sexes snort by exhaling loudly through the nose. This is an alarm call, as is stomping with the front foot. The bright rump and wagging white tail are visual signals, probably so the herd can stay in touch while running in woods.

As for scent, whitetails are virtual walking olfactory factories. Glands on the forehead, in front of the eyes, and in the mouth are used to mark twigs over scrapes and at licking branches. Bucks also rub their foreheads against trunks as they work them with their antlers, making these tree rubs both scent and visual markers. When a buck paws a scrape on the ground, he urinates into it over his hock or tarsal glands to deposit scent. Females that walk through or near scrapes leave a trail of scent from interdigital glands between their hooves. Metatarsal glands low on the outside of the rear legs produce an odor—for what purpose, only the deer know.

Senses

Whitetails see, hear, and smell evil, but they trust their noses most. Any animal that lives in dense cover can't flee from every sound or motion it detects; it could be birds, squirrels, or the wind. But odor is singular. Cat, wolf, man. A deer trusts its nose and uses it well. Beware.

Tracks and Sign

The cloven hoof of a whitetail looks just like that of a mule deer. Figure on any hoof print longer than 3 inches being left by a really old, big doe or a buck. Overall, mature buck tracks are slightly rounder and blunted at the tips, and in soft ground or snow they more readily leave dew claw prints than do lighter-weight females. Hoof drag marks are usually buck tracks, too. Figure about 18 inches between the left and right prints of a walking adult deer, 6 feet between clusters of galloping deer, and 10 to 25 feet between clusters when they're really motivated.

Whitetail droppings are variable, depending on diet, and virtually identical to mule deer scat. Expect pellets of ½-inch to 1 inch in fall and winter, more clustered to cow-like droppings in spring and summer when they feed on grass and lush forbs. Honestly, you don't need to spend a lot of time examining scat to find whitetails. If you're in suitable habitat, the droppings will be there and so will the deer.

Sign that should excite you include rubs and scrapes. The bigger the rub, the bigger the "rubber." Rubbed trees indicate a buck's territory, nothing more. Scrapes are not as indicative of size, but they do point out a buck's home court. Isolated scrapes in a line suggest a travel route to or from food or doe groups. Clusters suggest proximity of a core or bedding area.

Reproduction and Young

A doe usually produces a single fawn her first time, then twins thereafter. The bulk of breeding occurs during one or two weeks in mid-November, but some whitetail does cycle as early as late October or as late as December or January if they haven't bred during their first and second heats (about 28 days apart). Fawns lie low their first couple of weeks in the world, rising only when mom visits to suckle and clean them. By two months they are browsing heavily, and by fall they can make it on their own, but they usually try to reconnect with their dam as soon as she's done entertaining the bucks. She'll drive them off before her next twins drop.

Habitat

In a word, lush. The more brush and the more variety of brush, the better whitetails like it. Thus, in Montana they are primarily river bottom and wet forest creatures. They'll slip deep into the plains along watercourses, especially if alfalfa, corn, beans, or other crops are available. In the Long Pines country of extreme southeast Montana, whitetails live in dry

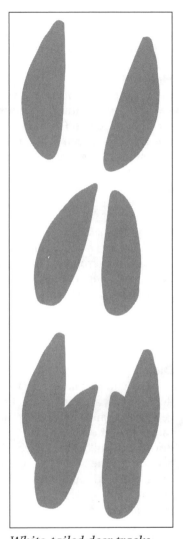

White-tailed deer tracks.
Top: *Front foot, average length of 2¾"; notice the spread of the hooves.*
Middle: *Rear foot; notice the traditional heart shape.*
Bottom: *Often the tracks double-register, overlapping by an inch or more.*

ponderosa pine forests that look better suited to mule deer. Indeed, both species occur side-by-side here. Logging and fire in the northwest encourages brush which improves whitetail habitat there.

Home Range

As mentioned above, Montana whitetails are not such homebodies as many eastern deer, primarily because of changing habitat. When suitable cover is a quarter-mile wide and 60 miles long in a river valley, deer naturally travel long distances up- and downriver. In the northwest mountains, deep snow often forces migrations over several ridges and across several valleys. Nevertheless, one can consider whitetails fairly faithful to their home ranges, such as they are. If you see a buck in one alfalfa field in October, you can be pretty sure he's still around in November. Still, don't be afraid to go looking for him eight miles downriver if you have to.

Forage Plants

What will a whitetail eat? Anything from poison ivy to sagebrush will do, but they are partial to crops. In the northwest, brush such as chokecherry, serviceberry, snowberry, and Oregon grape are favored. The "beard" lichens hanging from fir trees is relished in winter. In a study back in the 1960s, the most consistent food source in all seasons was snowberry in the Missouri River bottoms. Cottonwood ranked second. They didn't much care for willow. Corn and alfalfa, of course, are heavily used where available.

Daily Patterns

Early to bed and early to rise makes a whitetail buck aged and wise. You'll catch does, fawns, and young bucks stepping into the open before the sun has set and lingering long after it's up, but don't expect to find the big bucks with them—unless it's the peak of the rut. As a rule, whitetails trek to dense brush to chew their cud and rest during the bulk of the day, perhaps catching a drink along the way or at midday when it's hot. As the sun lowers, they drift out again, nibbling here and there until they reach the feed field or a favored brushy area for dining. Mature bucks, by nature lazy and by training wary, wait longer before rising. It's often nearly dark before they step into the clear, and the stars are still shining when they head back to the brush. But for a few short days in mid-November, they reluctantly abandon caution to trail hot does thither and yon, and that is the hunter's best chance.

Rutting Behavior

The whitetail deer may be the only animal whose sex life has been analyzed more than that of humans. What 40 years ago was mystery is now understood by every serious hunter in the country. In late August, antlers have finished growing. Bucks rub off their velvet and begin sparring to see who's on top. In October, bachelor bands begin to break up, and younger bucks begin sniffing after does. The big guys wait until the time is riper, but even they can't contain themselves. By mid-

Note the scars on the neck of this 5×5 point whitetail standing in brush and breathing hard after a fight.

October, they're rubbing trees and fighting brush vigorously. They lay a few preliminary scrapes. By early November, they're scraping, staying out of one another's way, and fighting when they don't. For the week before the first doe comes into estrus, they're about to explode with pent-up energy, criss-crossing their territories and sniffing for tracks. Then there's a flurry of doe chasing and battling at all hours of the day, peaking about mid-month and tapering off by December. Antlers are broken, eyes poked out, ears torn, hides ripped. Old, hard-driving bucks retire from the fray to recuperate in heavy cover, leaving the also-rans to finish the last of the procreating.

Trophy Dimensions

A respectable Montana whitetail rack will have 4 to 5 points per side, spread 16 to 18 inches, and tape 130 to 145 B&C points. A darned good one will go 150 to 160 B&C points, and anything bigger is a monster. The state record typical taken from

This hunter took a 4×5 whitetail buck along a trail at the edge of a fir forest.

Missoula County in 1974 had 27⅛-inch beams, 22⅜-inch inside spread, and had 6 points on the right, 7 on the left, for a total score of 199⅜. It ranks 10th in the world.

The Montana record nontypical scored 252⅛ and came out of Hill County in 1968. Its longest beam was 28⅜, inside spread 19⅝, and it had a total of 18 points. Flathead and Missoula Counties figure heavily in the trophy count.

Hunting Tactics

There are as many ways to hunt a whitetail as to skin a cat. Because eastern Montana is relatively open, glassing and stalking or shooting at long range are popular. In the thick river bottoms, it's best to learn a buck's stomping grounds and set up an ambush along a trail to his bed or feeding field. Do not let him see or smell you in his core area, or he may vacate it for days, even weeks. Bowhunters like to sit in tree stands over good trails—which aren't always the heavily traveled ones. It's essential to play the wind and remain scent-free by washing your body, clothes, and

OFFICIAL SCORING SYSTEM FOR NORTH AMERICAN BIG GAME TROPHIES

Records of North American
Big Game

BOONE AND CROCKETT CLUB®

250 Station Drive
Missoula, MT 59801
(406) 542-1888

TYPICAL
WHITETAIL AND COUES' DEER

Kind of Deer: _____

Minimum Score:	Awards	All-time
Whitetail	160	170
Coues'	100	110

Abnormal Points	
Right Antler	Left Antler
Subtotals	
Total to E	

SEE OTHER SIDE FOR INSTRUCTIONS				Column 1	Column 2	Column 3	Column 4
				Spread Credit	Right Antler	Left Antler	Difference
A. No. Points on Right Antler		No. Points on Left Antler					
B. Tip to Tip Spread		C. Greatest Spread					
D. Inside Spread of Main Beams		(Credit May Equal But Not Exceed Longer Antler)					
E. Total of Lengths of Abnormal Points							
F. Length of Main Beam							
G-1. Length of First Point							
G-2. Length of Second Point							
G-3. Length of Third Point							
G-4. Length of Fourth Point, If Present							
G-5. Length of Fifth Point, If Present							
G-6. Length of Sixth Point, If Present							
G-7. Length of Seventh Point, If Present							
H-1. Circumference at Smallest Place Between Burr and First Point							
H-2. Circumference at Smallest Place Between First and Second Points							
H-3. Circumference at Smallest Place Between Second and Third Points							
H-4. Circumference at Smallest Place Between Third and Fourth Points							
TOTALS							

ADD	Column 1	
	Column 2	
	Column 3	
	Subtotal	
SUBTRACT Column 4		
	FINAL SCORE	

Exact Locality Where Killed: _____

Date Killed: _____ Hunter: _____

Owner: _____ Telephone #: _____

Owner's Address: _____

Guide's Name and Address: _____

Remarks: (Mention Any Abnormalities or Unique Qualities) _____

Reprinted courtesy of the Boone and Crockett Club, 250 Station Dr., Missoula, MT 59801, 406-542-1888

I certify that I have measured this trophy on _____ 19 _____

at (address) _____ City _____ State _____

and that these measurements and data are, to the best of my knowledge and belief, made in
accordance with the instructions given.

Witness: _____ Signature: _____

B&C Official Measurer

I.D. Number

INSTRUCTIONS FOR MEASURING TYPICAL WHITETAIL AND COUES' DEER

All measurements must be made with a 1/4-inch wide flexible steel tape to the nearest one-eighth of an inch. (Note: A flexible steel cable can be used to measure points and main beams only.) Enter fractional figures in eighths, without reduction. Official measurements cannot be taken until the antlers have air dried for at least 60 days after the animal was killed.

A. Number of Points on Each Antler: To be counted a point, the projection must be at least one inch long, with the length exceeding width at one inch or more of length. All points are measured from tip of point to nearest edge of beam as illustrated. Beam tip is counted as a point but not measured as a point.

B. Tip to Tip Spread is measured between tips of main beams.

C. Greatest Spread is measured between perpendiculars at a right angle to the center line of the skull at widest part, whether across main beams or points.

D. Inside Spread of Main Beams is measured at a right angle to the center line of the skull at widest point between main beams. Enter this measurement again as the Spread Credit if it is less than or equal to the length of the longer antler; if greater, enter longer antler length for Spread Credit.

E. Total of Lengths of all Abnormal Points: Abnormal Points are those non-typical in location (such as points originating from a point or from bottom or sides of main beam) or extra points beyond the normal pattern of points. Measure in usual manner and enter in appropriate blanks.

F. Length of Main Beam is measured from the center of the lowest outside edge of burr over outer side to the most distant point of the main beam. The point of beginning is that point on the burr where the center line along the outer side of the beam intersects the burr, then following generally the line of the illustration.

G-1-2-3-4-5-6-7. Length of Normal Points: Normal points project from the top of the main beam. They are measured from nearest edge of main beam over outer curve to tip. Lay the tape along the outer curve of the beam so that the top edge of the tape coincides with the top edge of the beam on both sides of the point to determine the baseline for point measurements. Record point lengths in appropriate blanks.

H-1-2-3-4. Circumferences are taken as detailed for each measurement. If brow point is missing, take H-1 and H-2 at smallest place between burr and G-2. If G-4 is missing, take H-4 halfway between G-3 and tip of main beam.

FAIR CHASE STATEMENT FOR ALL HUNTER-TAKEN TROPHIES

FAIR CHASE, as defined by the Boone and Crockett Club®, is the ethical, sportsmanlike and lawful pursuit and taking of any free-ranging wild game animal in a manner that does not give the hunter an improper or unfair advantage over such game animals.

Use of any of the following methods in the taking of game shall be deemed **UNFAIR CHASE** and unsportsmanlike:

I. Spotting or herding game from the air, followed by landing in its vicinity for the purpose of pursuit and shooting;

II. Herding, pursuing, or shooting game from any motorboat or motor vehicle;

III. Use of electronic devices for attracting, locating, or observing game, or for guiding the hunter to such game;

IV. Hunting game confined by artificial barriers, including escape-proof fenced enclosures, or hunting game transplanted for the purpose of commercial shooting;

V. Taking of game in a manner not in full compliance with the game laws or regulations of the federal government or of any state, province, territory, or tribal council on reservations or tribal lands;

VI. Or as may otherwise be deemed unfair or unsportsmanlike by the Executive Committee of the Boone and Crockett Club.

I certify that the trophy scored on this chart was taken in **FAIR CHASE** as defined above by the Boone and Crockett Club. In signing this statement, I understand that if the information provided on this entry is found to be misrepresented or fraudulent in any respect, it will not be accepted into the Awards Program and all of my prior entries are subject to deletion from future editions of *Records of North American Big Game* and future entries may not be accepted.

Date: _____ Signature of Hunter:_____

(Signature must be witnessed by an Official Measurer or a Notary Public.)

Date: _____ Signature of Notary or Official Measurer:_____

Reprinted courtesy of the Boone and Crockett Club, 250 Station Dr., Missoula, MT 59801, 406-542-1888

OFFICIAL SCORING SYSTEM FOR NORTH AMERICAN BIG GAME TROPHIES

Records of North American
Big Game

BOONE AND CROCKETT CLUB®

250 Station Drive
Missoula, MT 59801
(406) 542-1888

Minimum Score:	Awards	All-time
whitetail	185	195
Coues'	105	120

NON-TYPICAL
WHITETAIL AND COUES' DEER

Kind of Deer: _____

Abnormal Points	
Right Antler	Left Antler
Subtotals	
E. Total	

Detail of Point
Measurement

SEE OTHER SIDE FOR INSTRUCTIONS				Column 1	Column 2	Column 3	Column 4
A. No. Points on Right Antler		No. Points on Left Antler		Spread Credit	Right Antler	Left Antler	Difference
B. Tip to Tip Spread		C. Greatest Spread					
D. Inside Spread of Main Beams		(Credit May Equal But Not Exceed Longer Antler)					
F. Length of Main Beam							
G-1. Length of First Point							
G-2. Length of Second Point							
G-3. Length of Third Point							
G-4. Length of Fourth Point, If Present							
G-5. Length of Fifth Point, If Present							
G-6. Length of Sixth Point, If Present							
G-7. Length of Seventh Point, If Present							
H-1. Circumference at Smallest Place Between Burr and First Point							
H-2. Circumference at Smallest Place Between First and Second Points							
H-3. Circumference at Smallest Place Between Second and Third Point							
H-4. Circumference at Smallest Place Between Third and Fourth Point							
			TOTALS				

ADD	Column 1	
	Column 2	
	Column 3	
	Subtotal	
SUBTRACT Column 4		
	Subtotal	
ADD Line E Total		
	FINAL SCORE	

Exact Locality Where Killed:

Date Killed: Hunter:

Owner: Telephone #:

Owner's Address:

Guide's Name and Address:

Remarks: (Mention Any Abnormalities or Unique Qualities)

Copyright © 1997 by Boone and Crockett Club®

Reprinted courtesy of the Boone and Crockett Club, 250 Station Dr., Missoula, MT 59801, 406-542-1888

I certify that I have measured this trophy on _____ 19 _____

at (address) _____ City _____ State _____

and that these measurements and data are, to the best of my knowledge and belief, made in accordance with the instructions given.

Witness: _____ Signature: _____

B&C Official Measurer

I.D. Number

INSTRUCTIONS FOR MEASURING NON-TYPICAL WHITETAIL AND COUES' DEER

All measurements must be made with a 1/4-inch wide flexible steel tape to the nearest one-eighth of an inch. (Note: A flexible steel cable can be used to measure points and main beams only.) Enter fractional figures in eighths, without reduction. Official measurements cannot be taken until the antlers have air dried for at least 60 days after the animal was killed.

A. Number of Points on Each Antler: To be counted a point, the projection must be at least one inch long, with the length exceeding width at one inch or more of length. All points are measured from tip of point to nearest edge of beam as illustrated. Beam tip is counted as a point but not measured as a point.

B. Tip to Tip Spread is measured between tips of main beams.

C. Greatest Spread is measured between perpendiculars at a right angle to the center line of the skull at widest part, whether across main beams or points.

D. Inside Spread of Main Beams is measured at a right angle to the center line of the skull at widest point between main beams. Enter this measurement again as the Spread Credit if it is less than or equal to the length of the longer antler; if greater, enter longer antler length for Spread Credit.

E. Total of Lengths of all Abnormal Points: Abnormal Points are those non-typical in location (such as points originating from a point or from bottom or sides of main beam) or extra points beyond the normal pattern of points. Measure in usual manner and enter in appropriate blanks.

F. Length of Main Beam is measured from the center of the lowest outside edge of burr over the outer side to the most distant point of the main beam. The point of beginning is that point on the burr where the center line along the outer side of the beam intersects the burr, then following generally the line of the illustration.

G-1-2-3-4-5-6-7. Length of Normal Points: Normal points project from the top of the main beam. They are measured from nearest edge of main beam over outer curve to tip. Lay the tape along the outer curve of the beam so that the top edge of the tape coincides with the top edge of the beam on both sides of the point to determine the baseline for point measurement. Record point lengths in appropriate blanks.

H-1-2-3-4. Circumferences are taken as detailed for each measurement. If brow point is missing, take H-1 and H-2 at smallest place between burr and G-2. If G-4 is missing, take H-4 halfway between G-3 and tip of main beam.

FAIR CHASE STATEMENT FOR ALL HUNTER-TAKEN TROPHIES

FAIR CHASE, as defined by the Boone and Crockett Club®, is the ethical, sportsmanlike and lawful pursuit and taking of any free-ranging wild game animal in a manner that does not give the hunter an improper or unfair advantage over such game animals.

Use of any of the following methods in the taking of game shall be deemed UNFAIR CHASE and unsportsmanlike:

I. Spotting or herding game from the air, followed by landing in its vicinity for the purpose of pursuit and shooting;

II. Herding, pursuing, or shooting game from any motorboat or motor vehicle;

III. Use of electronic devices for attracting, locating, or observing game, or for guiding the hunter to such game;

IV. Hunting game confined by artificial barriers, including escape-proof fenced enclosures, or hunting game transplanted for the purpose of commercial shooting;

V. Taking of game in a manner not in full compliance with the game laws or regulations of the federal government or of any state, province, territory, or tribal council on reservations or tribal lands;

VI. Or as may otherwise be deemed unfair or unsportsmanlike by the Executive Committee of the Boone and Crockett Club.

I certify that the trophy scored on this chart was taken in FAIR CHASE as defined above by the Boone and Crockett Club. In signing this statement, I understand that if the information provided on this entry is found to be misrepresented or fraudulent in any respect, it will not be accepted into the Awards Program and all of my prior entries are subject to deletion from future editions of Records of North American Big Game and future entries may not be accepted.

Date: _____ Signature of Hunter: _____
(Signature must be witnessed by an Official Measurer or a Notary Public.)

Date: _____ Signature of Notary or Official Measurer: _____

Reprinted courtesy of the Boone and Crockett Club, 250 Station Dr., Missoula, MT 59801, 406-542-1888

Shot Placement:

Top: Broadside shot.
Aim for the center of the chest just behind the bend of the front leg or shoulder; this should penetrate the lungs.

Below: Tail/Rump shot.
Take this shot only if using a powerful cartridge and a heavy, premium bullet. Aim for the base of the tail. The shot should break several vertebrae and paralyze the animal; rush in for a finishing shot. If it hits to the left or right, it should break the pelvis or one of the legs. Be aware that these types of shots will destroy a lot of meat.

gear religiously in scent-free soap, applying scent-killer sprays, or wearing carbon-filtered, scent-absorbing clothing or saturating odor-free clothes with natural scents. As the rut nears, try rattling antlers and grunting to imitate bucks fighting. This works best before the first doe comes into heat and on smaller bucks. Decoys also help lure some bucks within range for a bow shot. For obvious reasons, don't use them during rifle seasons.

Rifle hunters often team up to drive brushy islands or manageable strips of cover along rivers or near crop fields.

Still-hunting remains popular in the western mountains where visibility is limited. Walking quietly along old logging roads during the rut often does the trick.

Checking the trail behind, this big whitetail buck, complete with 5×5 antlers, stands in a pasture that is still green in October.

Recommendations for Loads and Rifle Cartridges

So many cartridges have been used to hunt whitetails over the years that virtually any legal centerfire will work, but most open country hunters like a minimum of .243 Win. up through the .300 magnums. You don't really need the power of the mags, but their higher velocities perform a bit better in big winds and add a few extra yards to their range, making them ideal for open country where shots are often long. The best compromise for adequate power and flat trajectory with minimum recoil might be the .25–06 Rem., .270 Win., .284 Win., and .280 Rem. The venerable .30–06 will shoot within an inch of any of them out to 300 yards. The .240 and .257 Weatherby Mags. make awesome long range rifles for the eastern plains.

In the northwest where cover is thick and shooting ranges often short, any of the above cartridges will work fine, but you won't be handicapped with older short-range calibers like the .30–30 Winchester. Carbines, and other short barrel rifles, are handy in heavy cover.

Mule Deer Distribution

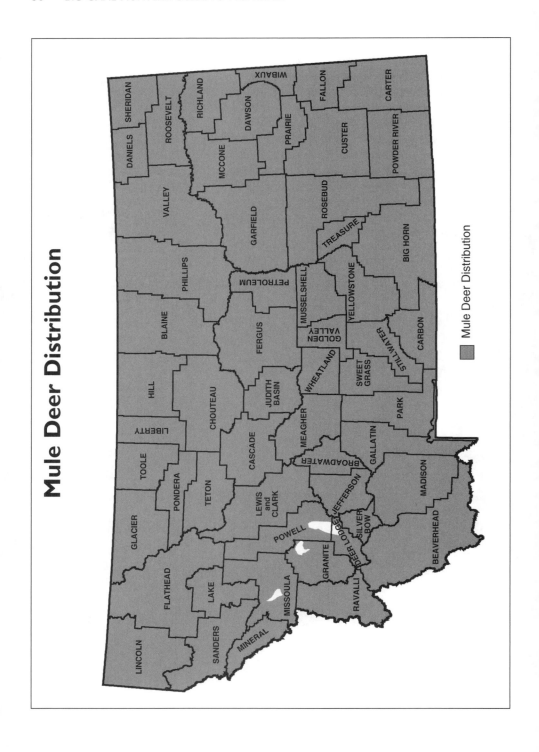

■ Mule Deer Distribution

Mule Deer

Odocoileus hemionus

Quiet, cautious, reserved, the common western mule deer is an antlered Houdini. Giant bucks can live undiscovered for years in creases and folds of the prairie hills, until one day they appear on the horizon for an instant like a glorious apparition, never to be seen again. The species itself, once common across Montana, was thought to be virtually extinct by many residents in the 1920s. Now it is again the most widespread big game animal in the state.

Fascinating Facts

- DNA testing suggests that mule deer are the product of matings between whitetails and Pacific Coast blacktails tens of thousands of years ago.
- A muley buck will manufacture his largest antlers when about 7 years old.
- The "pogo-stick" bounce of a mule deer is designed to enable it to change direction on a dime and scan the area until it clearly identifies the point of danger and a suitable escape route. Only then does it break into a direct-line run.
- Courting bucks mimic the behavior of fawns to entice does into letting them get close.
- Mule deer do indeed cross breed with whitetails. Whitetail and mule deer bucks have even been seen sparring.

Local Names
Muleys, blacktails

Size
Bucks stand 3 to 3½ feet at the shoulder and weigh 110 to a maximum of 475 pounds; average weight is around 200 pounds. Females are about 3 feet tall and weigh 70 to 160 pounds. Nose to tail, a big buck will stretch 6½ feet.

Coat and Color
Short, smooth, but relatively stiff guard hairs that are reddish-brown in summer, gray in winter. Fine, wooly underfur provides insulation. Belly, inside back legs, inside ears, rump, and the top half of the tail are white; the tail tip is black. Bucks and does sport a white throat patch. Mature bucks develop a white rutting face mask accented by black nostrils and a black "shield" on the forehead.

Antlers
Unlike whitetails and elk, muleys have bifurcated (forked) antlers. Instead of many tines sprouting from the main beam, the beam itself forks into roughly equal branch tines. Each of these tines may fork again, and so on. Bucks in their second

A nice mule deer buck with tall, 5×5 point antlers standing in sagebrush.

summer grow spikes or small fork-horns. When 2½-years-old, they generally manufacture bigger fork-horns or spindly 4-point racks. Each year thereafter, antlers increase in diameter, height, and width. Brow tines are sometimes missing and rarely longer than a few inches. Non-typical points protruding at odd angles are fairly common, especially on older bucks.

Between 5 and 8 years of age, bucks can grow some truly awesome racks atop their heads. Inside spread and main beam length may reach 30 inches, circumference just above the burr over 10 inches. A mature mule deer rack is one of the most impressive sights in nature. Like all deer except caribou, mule deer does do not develop antlers.

Voice and Communications
Body language and scent are the muley's preferred methods of communicating. Bucks do grunt softly and hiss/growl at competitors. Both sexes sound alarms by

snorting and stamping their front hooves to warn of danger or to flush out a preda-tor. They can also blatt much like a sheep, but seldom do. Fawns bleat. Bucks show aggression by pulling back their ears and erecting their tails and body hairs. Crouching low is an appeasement posture.

Numerous glands on the face, feet, and legs emit a variety of odors for identifi-cation, tracking, and probably displaying fear, threats, or dominance. Master bucks urinate on the tarsal glands inside their legs, becoming walking olfactory advertise-ments of their virility. Horning a sapling or shrub is a buck's version of bugling. The sound doesn't carry far, but it telegraphs aggression and dominance. The more a buck horns, the more confident it is.

Senses

Despite their large ears, mule deer probably depend more on their noses to detect danger. They might guess a strange sound is a rolling rock, falling pine cone, or wandering porcupine. Movement can be mistaken for a bird, small mammal, cow, or another deer. But the scent of a human is distinctive. One whiff and bye-bye. Nevertheless, old, experienced bucks often slink away from an area if they hear a sus-picious sound or glimpse a suspicious form at considerable distance. A stalking hunter, out of sight, usually never sees his quarry depart. If surprised by a human at close range, crafty bucks often flatten themselves and stick to cover like cottontails until nearly stepped on.

Tracks and Sign

Muley tracks look identical to whitetail tracks—a heart-shaped, cloven hoof, pointed at the tips, rounded at the back, 2½ to 3¼ inches long. Older deer usually show blunter tips due to wearing against rocks. Dew claws may show in snow or mud. When a mule deer is running, however, its spoor is distinctive. All four feet are closely bunched beneath the animal as it bounds. As a result, tracks show in tight clusters of four hoof prints with 9 to 21 feet of space between the clusters, depending on how motivated the runner was.

When feeding on grass and lush forbs, usually in summer, scats are soft and clumped. Browse and dry vegetation produce the classic pellet shape ½- to ¾-inch long.

During the November rut, observant hunters may notice on dry ground or snow the spot where a muley buck urinated on its tarsal glands. The buck stands with its feet close together, then urinates onto its hocks while rubbing its long tarsal gland hairs together. This shows on the ground as a concentra-tion of tracks in a small oval with urine mixed in. It carries a strong, musky odor.

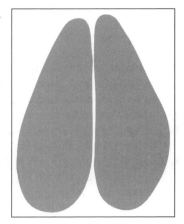

Mule deer track, running to 3¼" in length.

A mature 4×4 mule deer buck with a wide antler spread stands in sagebrush during a snowstorm.

Watch also for shrubs and small trees stripped raw from horning. Branches may also be twisted and broken. If you find a bed—usually depressed snow, flattened grass, or dirt scraped clear of small stones—look for urination signs. Bucks usually urinate in the bed, while does urinate outside it.

Reproduction and Young

Most Montana muley does breed in mid-November and drop twin spotted fawns (a single fawn if it's their first time) in June. The fawns weigh about 6 pounds, but grow quickly on their rich milk diet. Like all deer, muley's hide their new, scent-free fawns and return several times a day only to nurse them quickly and clean them. Within one week, the little ones are following their dam short distances. They'll stay with her through winter, but she'll run them off before bearing her next fawns.

Habitat

Mule deer range from alpine mountain tops to sagebrush plains and cotton-wood river bottoms. They thrive on prairies far from mountains if there are a few brushy draws or rimrock hills in which to bed. Crop fields are favored feeding sites.

The author poses with a mule deer buck on a steep, grassy slope at the edge of a Douglas fir forest.

Home Range

While mule deer often do have home ranges, they do not stick to them as faithfully as do whitetails or pronghorns. Ranges also tend to be large and divided into distinct summer and winter territories. When living is easy in late summer, bands of bachelor bucks may move less than a quarter-mile each day, but as the rut nears, they break up and often move many miles a night. When hard-pressed by man or coyotes, bucks and does will readily abandon their home range for long periods, sometimes for years. More than one hunter has watched a big buck all summer, only to return for the hunting season to find no sign of him. Mountain muleys generally move to bordering lowlands for the winter.

Forage Plants

Mule deer are rather catholic in their tastes. Dozens of native and introduced plants suit their palates, things like huckleberry, sagebrush, mountain mahogany, bitterbrush, Douglas fir, serviceberry, aspen, clover, wheat, and alfalfa, to name a few. During drought years on the plains, muleys flock to irrigated crop fields for obvious reasons.

Daily Patterns

Mule deer are crepuscular and nocturnal—active at sunrise and sundown and during the night. Left undisturbed, they will feed and move fairly early in the evening and late in the morning. When hunted hard, they can become almost completely nocturnal. Where forage and escape cover are far apart, muleys will walk miles daily to access them. They'll also go to water regularly when it is hot and dry. Generally, does move earlier than bucks. Bucks like to bed on high, open, rocky ridges where they can see for miles and catch scents on rising thermals. In forested mountains, they often bed just under a ridgetop in open woods.

Rutting Behavior

Bucks will rub off their summer velvet in early September and begin sparring, but they remain in bachelor parties of 2 to 20 well into October. They then begin roaming widely in search of receptive does, the young bucks sniffing around the maternal herds first before they are ready. Master bucks usually move in and take over in early November. While it appears they have rounded up and are controlling a harem, they are really only waiting for the first doe to ripen. If she were to break from her maternal herd, he'd abandon it to accompany her, but muley does generally remain in their familiar family groups of aunts, grandmas, and cousins. Thus, a big buck can remain with one group for two weeks or more, servicing each female in turn.

In order to prevent frightening any of the does and driving them off, a wise buck courts slowly and cautiously, scent-checking their urine, keeping his head low, sticking out his tongue and calling softly like a fawn until the females allow him to touch them. While waiting for his chance to breed, he'll frequently horn shrubs, rubbing his oily forehead scent glands against them, and urinate on his tarsals. If smaller bucks approach, he'll bristle and walk stiff-legged toward them to push them back. Nearly equal bucks will walk parallel, hissing, bristling, laying their ears back, and snort-wheezing. If neither backs down, they clash antlers and attempt to throw one another over or gain an opening to impale their opponent. The victor chases the vanquished a short distance before turning to his spoils.

Hunters who locate a buck attending one or more does should try not to alarm the females. Where they go, the buck will follow, unless he is severely spooked.

Trophy Dimensions

The B&C world record typical mule deer rack—from a deer killed in southwest Colorado in 1972—totaled 226⅛ inches, spread 30⅞ inches inside, and had 11 points, a base circumference of 5⅜ inches, and a main beam length of 30⅛ inches. The top-ranked nontypical totaled 355⅔ inches. It spread only 22⅛ inches inside, but had 43 points!

OFFICIAL SCORING SYSTEM FOR NORTH AMERICAN BIG GAME TROPHIES

Records of North American
Big Game

BOONE AND CROCKETT CLUB®

250 Station Drive
Missoula, MT 59801
(406) 542-1888

Minimum Score:	Awards	All-time
mule	180	190
Columbia	125	135
Sitka	100	108

**TYPICAL
MULE DEER AND BLACKTAIL DEER**

Kind of Deer: _____

Detail of Point Measurement

Abnormal Points	
Right Antler	Left Antler
Subtotals	
Total to E	

SEE OTHER SIDE FOR INSTRUCTIONS				Column 1	Column 2	Column 3	Column 4
				Spread Credit	Right Antler	Left Antler	Difference
A. No. Points on Right Antler		No. Points on Left Antler					
B. Tip to Tip Spread		C. Greatest Spread					
D. Inside Spread of Main Beams		(Credit May Equal But Not Exceed Longer Antler)					
E. Total of Lengths of Abnormal Points							
F. Length of Main Beam							
G-1. Length of First Point, If Present							
G-2. Length of Second Point							
G-3. Length of Third Point, If Present							
G-4. Length of Fourth Point, If Present							
H-1. Circumference at Smallest Place Between Burr and First Point							
H-2. Circumference at Smallest Place Between First and Second Points							
H-3. Circumference at Smallest Place Between Main Beam and Third Point							
H-4. Circumference at Smallest Place Between Second and Fourth Points							
			TOTALS				

	Column 1		Exact Locality Where Killed:
ADD	Column 2		Date Killed: Hunter:
	Column 3		Owner: Telephone #:
	Subtotal		Owner's Address:
SUBTRACT Column 4			Guide's Name and Address:
	FINAL SCORE		Remarks: (Mention Any Abnormalities or Unique Qualities)

Reprinted courtesy of the Boone and Crockett Club, 250 Station Dr., Missoula, MT 59801, 406-542-1888

I certify that I have measured this trophy on _____ 19 _____

at (address) _____ City _____ State _____

and that these measurements and data are, to the best of my knowledge and belief, made in accordance with the instructions given.

Witness: _____ Signature: _____

B&C Official Measurer [ ][ ][ ]

I.D. Number

INSTRUCTIONS FOR MEASURING TYPICAL MULE AND BLACKTAIL DEER

All measurements must be made with a 1/4-inch wide flexible steel tape to the nearest one-eighth of an inch. (Note: A flexible steel cable can be used to measure points and main beams only.) Enter fractional figures in eighths, without reduction. Official measurements cannot be taken until the antlers have air dried for at least 60 days after the animal was killed.

A.   Number of Points on Each Antler: To be counted a point, the projection must be at least one inch long, with length exceeding width at one inch or more of length. All points are measured from tip of point to nearest edge of beam. Beam tip is counted as a point but not measured as a point.

B.   Tip to Tip Spread is measured between tips of main beams.

C.   Greatest Spread is measured between perpendiculars at a right angle to the center line of the skull at widest part, whether across main beams or points.

D.   Inside Spread of Main Beams is measured at a right angle to the center line of the skull at widest point between main beams. Enter this measurement again as the Spread Credit if it is less than or equal to the length of the longer antler; if greater, enter longer antler length for Spread Credit.

E.   Total of Lengths of all Abnormal Points: Abnormal Points are those non-typical in location such as points originating from a point (exception: G-3 originates from G-2 in perfectly normal fashion) or from bottom or sides of main beam, or any points beyond the normal pattern of five (including beam tip) per antler. Measure each abnormal point in usual manner and enter in appropriate blanks.

F.   Length of Main Beam is measured from the center of the lowest outside edge of burr over the outer side to the most distant point of the Main Beam. The point of beginning is that point on the burr where the center line along the outer side of the beam intersects the burr, then following generally the line of the illustration.

G-1-2-3-4.   Length of Normal Points: Normal points are the brow tines and the upper and lower forks as shown in the illustration. They are measured from nearest edge of main beam over outer curve to tip. Lay the tape along the outer curve of the beam so that the top edge of the tape coincides with the top edge of the beam on both sides of point to determine the baseline for point measurement. Record point lengths in appropriate blanks.

H-1-2-3-4.   Circumferences are taken as detailed for each measurement. If brow point is missing, take H-1 and H-2 at smallest place between burr and G-2. If G-3 is missing, take H-3 halfway between the base and tip of G-2. If G-4 is missing, take H-4 halfway between G-2 and tip of main beam.

FAIR CHASE STATEMENT FOR ALL HUNTER-TAKEN TROPHIES

FAIR CHASE, as defined by the Boone and Crockett Club®, is the ethical, sportsmanlike and lawful pursuit and taking of any free-ranging wild game animal in a manner that does not give the hunter an improper or unfair advantage over such game animals.

Use of any of the following methods in the taking of game shall be deemed **UNFAIR CHASE** and unsportsmanlike:

   I.   Spotting or herding game from the air, followed by landing in its vicinity for the purpose of pursuit and shooting;

  II.   Herding, pursuing, or shooting game from any motorboat or motor vehicle;

 III.   Use of electronic devices for attracting, locating, or observing game, or for guiding the hunter to such game;

  IV.   Hunting game confined by artificial barriers, including escape-proof fenced enclosures, or hunting game transplanted for the purpose of commercial shooting;

   V.   Taking of game in a manner not in full compliance with the game laws or regulations of the federal government or of any state, province, territory, or tribal council on reservations or tribal lands;

  VI.   Or as may otherwise be deemed unfair or unsportsmanlike by the Executive Committee of the Boone and Crockett Club.

I certify that the trophy scored on this chart was taken in **FAIR CHASE** as defined above by the Boone and Crockett Club. In signing this statement, I understand that if the information provided on this entry is found to be misrepresented or fraudulent in any respect, it will not be accepted into the Awards Program and all of my prior entries are subject to deletion from future editions of *Records of North American Big Game* and future entries may not be accepted.

Date: _____   Signature of Hunter:_____

(Signature must be witnessed by an Official Measurer or a Notary Public.)

Date: _____   Signature of Notary or Official Measurer:_____

Reprinted courtesy of the Boone and Crockett Club, 250 Station Dr., Missoula, MT 59801, 406-542-1888

OFFICIAL SCORING SYSTEM FOR NORTH AMERICAN BIG GAME TROPHIES

Records of North American
Big Game

BOONE AND CROCKETT CLUB®

250 Station Drive
Missoula, MT 59801
(406) 542-1888

Minimum Score: Awards 215 All-time 230

NON-TYPICAL
MULE DEER

	Abnormal Points	
	Right Antler	Left Antler
Subtotals		
E. Total		

SEE OTHER SIDE FOR INSTRUCTIONS			Column 1	Column 2	Column 3	Column 4
A. No. Points on Right Antler	No. Points on Left Antler		Spread Credit	Right Antler	Left Antler	Difference
B. Tip to Tip Spread	C. Greatest Spread					
D. Inside Spread of Main Beams	(Credit May Equal But Not Exceed Longer Antler)					
F. Length of Main Beam						
G-1. Length of First Point, If Present						
G-2. Length of Second Point						
G-3. Length of Third Point, If Present						
G-4. Length of Fourth Point, If Present						
H-1. Circumference at Smallest Place Between Burr and First Point						
H-2. Circumference at Smallest Place Between First and Second Points						
H-3. Circumference at Smallest Place Between Main Beam and Third Point						
H-4. Circumference at Smallest Place Between Second and Fourth Points						
TOTALS						

ADD	Column 1		Exact Locality Where Killed:	
	Column 2		Date Killed: Hunter:	
	Column 3		Owner:	Telephone #:
	Subtotal		Owner's Address:	
SUBTRACT Column 4			Guide's Name and Address:	
	Subtotal		Remarks: (Mention Any Abnormalities or Unique Qualities)	
ADD Line E Total				
FINAL SCORE				

Reprinted courtesy of the Boone and Crockett Club, 250 Station Dr., Missoula, MT 59801, 406-542-1888

I certify that I have measured this trophy on _____ 19 _____

at (address) _____ City _____ State _____

and that these measurements and data are, to the best of my knowledge and belief, made in accordance with the instructions given.

Witness: _____   Signature: _____

B&C Official Measurer ☐☐☐☐

I.D. Number

INSTRUCTIONS FOR MEASURING NON-TYPICAL MULE DEER

All measurements must be made with a 1/4-inch wide flexible steel tape to the nearest one-eighth of an inch. (Note: A flexible steel cable can be used to measure points and main beams only.) Enter fractional figures in eighths, without reduction. Official measurements cannot be taken until the antlers have air dried for at least 60 days after the animal was killed.

A. Number of Points on Each Antler: To be counted a point, the projection must be at least one inch long, with length exceeding width at one inch or more of length. All points are measured from tip of point to nearest edge of beam as illustrated. Beam tip is counted as a point but not measured as a point.

B. Tip to Tip Spread is measured between tips of main beams.

C. Greatest Spread is measured between perpendiculars at a right angle to the center line of the skull at widest part, whether across main beams or points.

D. Inside Spread of Main Beams is measured at a right angle to the center line of the skull at widest point between main beams. Enter this measurement again as the Spread Credit if it is less than or equal to the length of the longer antler; if greater, enter longer antler length for Spread Credit.

E. Total of Lengths of all Abnormal Points: Abnormal Points are those non-typical in location such as points originating from a point (exception: G-3 originates from G-2 in perfectly normal fashion) or from bottom or sides of main beam, or any points beyond the normal pattern of five (including beam tip) per antler. Measure each abnormal point in usual manner and enter in appropriate blanks.

F. Length of Main Beam is measured from the center of the lowest outside edge of burr over the outer side to the most distant point of the main beam. The point of beginning is that point on the burr where the center line along the outer side of the beam intersects the burr, then following generally the line of the illustration.

G-1-2-3-4. Length of Normal Points: Normal points are the brow tines and the upper and lower forks as shown in the illustration. They are measured from nearest edge of main beam over outer curve to tip. Lay the tape along the outer curve of the beam so that the top edge of the tape coincides with the top edge of the beam on both sides of point to determine the baseline for point measurement. Record point lengths in appropriate blanks.

H-1-2-3-4. Circumferences are taken as detailed for each measurement. If brow point is missing, take H-1 and H-2 at smallest place between burr and G-2. If G-3 is missing, take H-3 halfway between the base and tip of G-2. If G-4 is missing, take H-4 halfway between G-2 and tip of main beam.

FAIR CHASE STATEMENT FOR ALL HUNTER-TAKEN TROPHIES

FAIR CHASE, as defined by the Boone and Crockett Club®, is the ethical, sportsmanlike and lawful pursuit and taking of any free-ranging wild game animal in a manner that does not give the hunter an improper or unfair advantage over such game animals.

Use of any of the following methods in the taking of game shall be deemed **UNFAIR CHASE** and unsportsmanlike:

I. Spotting or herding game from the air, followed by landing in its vicinity for the purpose of pursuit and shooting;

II. Herding, pursuing, or shooting game from any motorboat or motor vehicle;

III. Use of electronic devices for attracting, locating, or observing game, or for guiding the hunter to such game;

IV. Hunting game confined by artificial barriers, including escape-proof fenced enclosures, or hunting game transplanted for the purpose of commercial shooting;

V. Taking of game in a manner not in full compliance with the game laws or regulations of the federal government or of any state, province, territory, or tribal council on reservations or tribal lands;

VI. Or as may otherwise be deemed unfair or unsportsmanlike by the Executive Committee of the Boone and Crockett Club.

I certify that the trophy scored on this chart was taken in **FAIR CHASE** as defined above by the Boone and Crockett Club. In signing this statement, I understand that if the information provided on this entry is found to be misrepresented or fraudulent in any respect, it will not be accepted into the Awards Program and all of my prior entries are subject to deletion from future editions of **Records of North American Big Game** and future entries may not be accepted.

Date: _____   Signature of Hunter: _____
                  (Signature must be witnessed by an Official Measurer or a Notary Public.)

Date: _____   Signature of Notary or Official Measurer: _____

Reprinted courtesy of the Boone and Crockett Club, 250 Station Dr., Missoula, MT 59801, 406-542-1888

This mule deer showed up during a winter hunt displaying a tall, 5×5 rack with one tine broken off.

The Montana B&C record typical, shot in Lincoln County in 1963, ranks 107 and scored 202 points. Its 6×6 rack spread just 27⅝ inches; consider that when searching for the hallowed 30-inch buck. In fact, none of the 16 biggest B&C muleys, and just two of the nontypicals, taken in Montana exceed a 30-inch inside spread.

The best Big Sky state nontypical scored 275⅞ inches, spread an incredible 34⅜ inches, and had 29 points. It was taken from the Highland Mountains in 1962.

The bulk of record heads have come from the western and northwestern mountain counties. These days, all but fanatical trophy hunters should be tickled with a heavy 4×4 wider than its bearer's ears and as high as it is wide. Prairie bucks are appreciably smaller, although fine heads are taken in central and eastern Montana each year.

Hunting Tactics

Terrain and habitat dictate one's approach to mule deer. In the heavily forested mountains, rely on sign to locate likely areas. Then watch meadows early and late, or still-hunt timber. Tracking snow helps. If you find buck sign but are unable to see bucks in heavy timber, try horning brush with a castoff antler, rattling antlers

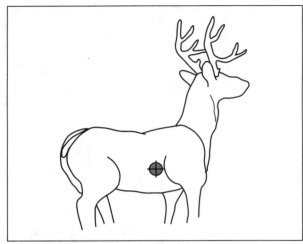

Shot Placement:
Top: Broadside shot.
Aim for the center of the chest just behind the bend of the front leg or shoulder; this should penetrate the lungs.

Below: Quartering shot.
Aim for the off-side shoulder by drawing an imaginary line from your rifle or bow to the far-side shoulder; aim slightly behind the shoulder if you don't wish to damage any meat.

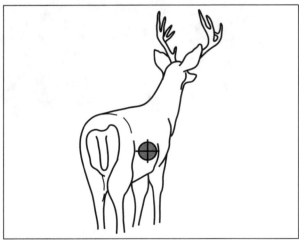

together to mimic a fight, or grunt calling. These whitetail tactics have been working for a few innovative muley hunters.

Above timberline, glass brushy basins and the bases of rimrock ridges. Big bucks especially like this habitat before the snow falls. Watch traditional migration corridors when the migration begins from high country to low. Saddles between high peaks are usually a good bet.

Two or more hunters can work a wooded draw or basin. Place one at its head overlooking likely escape routes, as many others as are available to cover the sides, and one still-hunting up the bottom. There is no need to make a lot of racket to move out old bucks.

On the high plains, watch feeding fields early and late in the day, particularly lush, green croplands. Expect the biggest bucks to move near dark. They usually head for distant broken country at the first hint of dawn and don't come out of it until nearly dark. Take a stand near this escape cover to intercept them. Does and young bucks linger in open fields much longer. High, rocky buttes are popular bedding sights for old bucks. Glass them from afar with a spotting scope, then stalk in. Badlands and isolated draws beyond reach of motor vehicles are also good bets. Glassing is the key in open country. The trick is to see them before they see you.

Bowhunters do best watching waterholes in early season, waiting along trails to and from feed, or glassing and stalking bachelor bucks before rutting begins. Don't be afraid to try a decoy to lure a buck into the open.

Recommendations for Loads and Rifle Cartridges

The perfect plains whitetail cartridges are also ideal for plains mule deer: you can't beat the .270 Win. or .280 Rem.; try the 7mm Rem. Mag. if you don't mind a touch more recoil.

Disappearing Mule Deer

More than once, friends and I have spotted mule deer, circled to stalk within range, and never found them again. We'd been out of sight and kept the wind in our favor—what went wrong?

I got an answer one November while hunting the big-eared deer with a camera at the edge of Yellowstone National Park near Gardiner. Two large bucks were working a matriarchal group of does and fawns in the hills above the Gardner River. As the sun rose, more and more tourists began stopping and edging closer to the animals. The bigger and shyer of the two bucks eventually slipped behind a screening ridge, a sharp edge of ground that climbed at a steep angle.

Hoping for a little quiet myself, I decided to break away from the crowd, get out of view, and rejoin the buck in privacy. But I couldn't. When I slipped within view of the shadowy slope on which the buck had sought refuge, he was nowhere to be seen. Yet the slope was big and open enough that he couldn't have walked out of it without my seeing him. Unless he'd doubled back to the crowd.

I walked part-way back and checked the group with my binocular, but the big buck wasn't near them. Puzzled, I returned to the shadowy slope and began glassing it. Nothing. Finally I decided that the buck had somehow crossed the slope and disappeared over its far shoulder. I hiked over. No buck.

Eventually I gave up and walked back toward the truck. En route, I crossed that shadowy hillside again and, as luck would have it, practically stepped on the buck. He was lying quietly behind a few clumps of sagebrush, brush that I'd glassed carefully several times. In the shadowy winter light, his gray coat perfectly matched the sage, the short grass on the slope, and even the patches of bare soil. He had bedded within 100 yards of the sharp rim of ground behind which he'd disappeared initially. I'd walked within 50 yards of him on my way through.

Some of those mule deer that had disappeared on us over the years had probably been within easy rifle range all along.

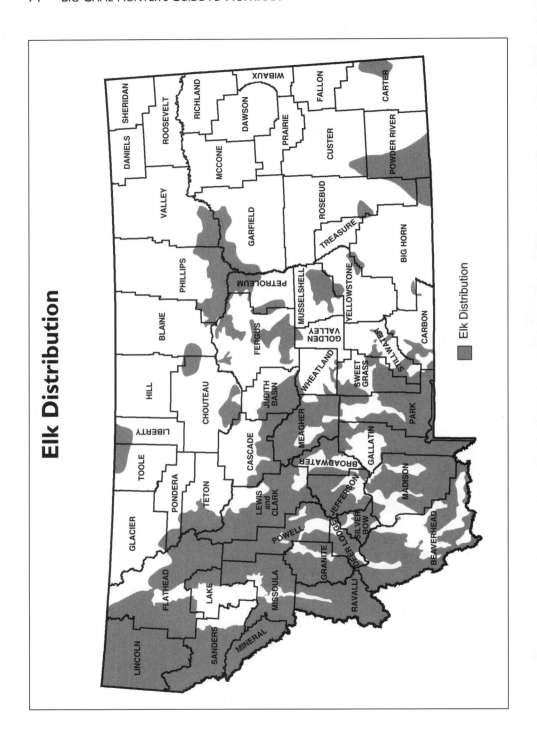

Elk Distribution

Elk Distribution

Elk

Cervus elephus

The North American elk is arguably our most coveted big game trophy, the stuff of dreams for thousands of hunters coast to coast. A regal six-point bull is the essence of the Rocky Mountain wilderness.

Fascinating Facts

- A mature bull elk cannot ingest enough nutrients to grow its huge antlers every year, so it absorbs minerals from its own rib bones to supply the growing tines.
- During the past 20 years, elk populations have increased significantly throughout Montana and the West.
- Elk range from between the grass and sagebrush flats along the Missouri River to above treeline.
- Even the biggest herd bull cannot maintain control of a harem of cows the entire breeding season. After days of endless bugling, chasing, and fighting, it often wears out and retires or is run off by another bull.
- Elk migrated to North America from Siberia and are closely related to the red deer of Europe.
- Because bulls burn their candles at both ends during the rut, they rarely live past 13 years. Cows often last 7 years more.

Local Name
Wapiti

Size
Mature bulls average 5 feet at the shoulder and are 8 to 10 feet from nose to tail. They weigh 600 to 1,000 pounds; a real monster may go 1,200 pounds. A spike bull is roughly the size of an average cow (450–650 pounds), and stands about 4½ feet at the shoulder.

Coat & Color
Most folks overestimate the darkness of an elk's coat. While the face, nose, legs, and long neck hairs are a deep russet-brown, the back and sides are a light tan to nearly white on an old bull (the native Shawnee word wapiti means "pale" or "white"). The rump patch has been variously described as yellow, peach, or tan-orange.

Antlers
Only bulls carry antlers. A long main beam juts up and back from the forehead, usually flaring outward and curving in about halfway to the tips, which often bend down. Off this main beam protrude from 1 to 7 or 8 tines, rarely more even in a

At sunrise, a big, 6×6 bull elk blows some steam in a brushy meadow.

nontypical conformation. Elk hold their noses high when running, so their massive racks seem to flow across their backs. A big rack will seem to touch its bearer's rump.

An 18-month-old bull generally carries spikes up to 2 feet long. Two- and 3-year-olds sport what is called a "rag horn," a rather spindly, 3- to 4-point precursor of a mature bull's splendid rack. At 4 or 5, a bull will grow medium-sized 6-point antlers. Only when in its prime years, 7 to 12, will a bull produce its most massive rack with beams 10 inches in circumference that stretch 4 to 5 feet. Tines will protrude 6 to 24 inches, and the spread between the beams may exceed 4 feet, truly an impressive armament.

Voice and Communications

The bugle or squeal of a bull elk is one of the grandest sounds of the wilderness. It begins as a low growl that quickly rises several octaves to a high-pitched scream. This sounds like a lovely whistle at a distance, but up close it is loud, harsh, and impassioned. A bugle is often concluded with a series of short grunts that sound somewhat like a dog whining. Cows can and do bugle, usually in spring and at reduced volume. Mostly they and their calves mew like kittens and chirp like birds to maintain contact in heavy timber. They bark loud warnings. Bulls bark and chirp less often. Bulls bugle during the rut not so much to challenge other bulls as to attract and hold cows. While sparring, bulls keep up a steady, thin, high-pitched series of squeals that sound more like impatient birds than 800-pound mammals.

In addition to calling, bulls communicate by spraying themselves with urine. They can aim a stream between their forelegs and hit themselves in the neck and face or spray a mist over their belly hairs. The ranker a bull's odor, the higher his status. Even dullnosed humans can smell a bull elk from far downwind.

Senses

Elk see, hear, and smell well, but depend mostly on their noses to detect trouble. A hunter walking through brush unseen might be taken for another elk. Standing still he is often unseen by elk mere feet away. But let one whiff of human odor touch sensitive elk nostrils and that animal is gone. Mix this defense with swirling, unpredictable mountain drafts, and a hunter has his work cut out for him.

Tracks and Sign

Elk tracks are much rounder than deer tracks and, of course, larger. They resemble small cattle tracks more than deer tracks. In snow or mud, hoof prints are usually 4 to 4½ inches long and 3 to 3½ inches wide. Dew claws show in soft mud or snow. The toes of galloping elk splay out at the tips, and tracks range between 8 and 14 feet apart, depending on speed. When walking, an elk strides 5 feet. Because elk are by nature herd animals, single tracks usually indicate a satellite bull or a lost cow or calf. Herds leave obvious trails when walking single file from bedding to feeding areas.

In summer and early fall when they feed on moist, lush vegetation, elk leave loose, cow-like patties or segmented masses. When they feed on dry vegetation, droppings become pellet-like, pointed at one end and usually concave at the other, ¾-inch to 1 inch long. A dry, fibrous browse diet produces pellets that resemble cylinders of sawdust up to 1⅜ inches, very similar to winter moose droppings.

Elk at water often splash and frolic, thoroughly muddying the pool. Bulls during the rut dig shallow pits in moist or muddy ground with hooves and antlers, then urinate and wallow in them.

Like all deer, bull elk strip antler velvet by rubbing brush and trunks. They also "fight" springy saplings and branches, thrash brush, and rub bark from

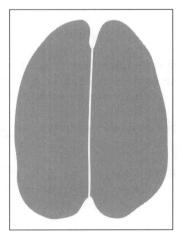

Elk track. Usually, an adult elk print runs around 4" in length.

trunks. Don't confuse these rubs with gnawing marks made when hungry wintering elk scrape bark from aspens with their lower incisors.

Reproduction and Young

Breeding occurs in September or October, and about 8 months later a cow will separate from her herd and drop a single calf, rarely twins, just when new forage is lush. For the first week, the spotted 35-pound newborn hides and suckles. Then the cow rejoins her maternal herd where numerous females provide round-the-clock protection for all the calves. Within a month, calves are sampling vegetation, but they still nurse as often as their dams allow. By August, they are pretty much weaned, though they'll try for milk from time to time well into winter. Their spotted coats are replaced by traditional elk pelage by September when bachelor bands of bulls break up and rejoin the cows for the annual rut.

Habitat

Like whitetails, elk are not particular about their living quarters. So long as they have undisturbed escape cover and plenty to eat, they will thrive on mountain tops, in conifer forests, deciduous river bottoms, prairies dotted with pockets of trees, dry juniper woods, temperate rainforests, and even sagebrush. After the invasion of settlers 150 years ago, only elk living in rugged, isolated mountains survived, but today, thanks to reintroductions and hunter-funded management programs, herds are again growing in more open country. Further expansion is hampered mainly by human development and landowner intolerance. In general, Montana elk like to summer high and winter low. Bulls especially stay high until deep snows push them toward lower slopes and valleys.

Home Range

Unlike whitetails and pronghorns, elk are not slaves to their territory. Herds will remain in small drainages for weeks if undisturbed and while forage lasts, but if spooked they'll often line out and run for miles, crossing two or three ridges before settling down. If food and security are adequate in their new surroundings, they have no uncommon urges to return to their old haunts.

As a general rule, elk migrate from cool, lush, high country summer pastures to warmer valleys when winter hits, then return to the peaks for easy, cool summer living.

Forage Plants

Elk eat an amazing variety of grasses, sedges, forbs (weeds and wildflowers), shrubs, and trees. More important than what they eat is when they eat it. They key on the freshest, most protein-rich foliage in early spring, then switch as necessary to maintain this freshness and nutrition. They will start on early grass and forbs in the valleys, then move to south-facing mountain slopes when they first green. As south slopes dry out, the elk switch to wetter north-facing slopes to feed. By the start of fall

There's no sign of snow, even in Novemeber, in the tall grasslands where this bull elk was found. The partially wooded pine hills make a nice backdrop.

hunting seasons, high mountain meadows and north-facing slopes are usually the prime feeding sites. Grass constitutes 85 percent of their diet in spring and early summer. Where both grass and brush are available, elk usually prefer grass. In winter, they feed heavily on shrubs and twigs because shorter vegetation is often buried. Alfalfa, rape, green wheat, and other crops are eagerly sought.

Daily Patterns

Elk are both nocturnal and crepuscular, meaning active at night and at dawn and dusk. Normally they rest in cool, dark thickets and woods all day, then move to favored grazing meadows at dusk. Here they forage off and on throughout the night before filling up again at dawn and trekking back to secure cover for the day. Rutting activity revolves around foraging, resting, and traveling, the bulls trying to keep the cows together while the latter do pretty much what they please unless corralled by those deadly tines. Where hunting pressure is light, bulls will bugle all day, even while bedded or with a mouth full of grass.

Rutting Behavior

You could write a book on the elk rut. Of primary interest to the hunter is the fact that rutting bulls are more easily found than post-rut bulls. They bugle to announce their location, they respond to other bugles and cow calls, they are active during more hours each day, and they are so preoccupied with sex that they sometimes let down their defenses.

Watch undisturbed elk in Yellowstone, and you quickly see that cow herds pretty much go about their usual business, feeding, bedding, and traveling between these sites on their normal morning/evening schedules. Early in the rut, young bulls gravitate toward these cow bands and delude themselves into thinking they'll later mate with them. There's lots of bugling, thrashing, chasing, and changing of the guard as different bulls come and go. Mature bulls wait in the wings. When the time is right, one of these big boys saunters down and assumes command while the lesser bulls hang about the edges, hoping to steal some action. The herd bull will defend his cows from real challengers, but he won't waste time chasing distant bugling bulls. They have to come to him. To avoid confrontations, he'll often push his cows away from any approaching antagonist. Some herd bulls will tolerate spikes in the herd, but no branch antlered bulls.

Trophy Dimensions

To a novice, any 6-point elk rack looks huge. Truly record-class antlers are phenomenal. According to the 10th Edition Boone & Crockett Club Record Book, the longest main beam ever recorded was 64⅝ inches long. The greatest circumference at the smallest place between the burr (base) and first tine was 12⅖ inches, the greatest inside spread 61⅛ inches, and the most typical points on one antler 9. Added up, the scoreable inches of antler on the current world record Rocky Mountain elk totaled 442⅜ inches. To put that in perspective, an average 6-point rack scores around 300 inches, and a 350-inch rack is considered huge. A bull scoring 419⅘ that came out of Madison County in 1958 is the largest Montana head in the book. It stands in 6th place.

Reasonable trophy hunters on public land know that anything over 300 inches these days is a real find. The average hunter is happy to bag any legal elk. Considering how much work and expense is involved in that undertaking, such an elk is also a trophy. Unless you're extra finicky and willing to go home meatless, don't turn down any branch antlered bull.

Hunting Tactics

Seeing an elk within shooting range is the biggest challenge. Despite their bulk, elk are masters of secrecy, able to slip through dog hair timber silently and disappear from a mountainside like morning mist. If you can hunt during a bugle season, you

OFFICIAL SCORING SYSTEM FOR NORTH AMERICAN BIG GAME TROPHIES

Records of North American
Big Game

BOONE AND CROCKETT CLUB®

250 Station Drive
Missoula, MT 59801
(406) 542-1888

Minimum Score: Awards 360 All-time 375

TYPICAL AMERICAN ELK (WAPITI)

Detail of Point Measurement

Abnormal Points	
Right Antler	Left Antler

Subtotals

Total to E

SEE OTHER SIDE FOR INSTRUCTIONS				Column 1	Column 2	Column 3	Column 4
A. No. Points on Right Antler		No. Points on Left Antler		Spread Credit	Right Antler	Left Antler	Difference
B. Tip to Tip Spread		C. Greatest Spread					
D. Inside Spread of Main Beams		(Credit May Equal But Not Exceed Longer Antler)					
E. Total of Lengths of Abnormal Points							
F. Length of Main Beam							
G-1. Length of First Point							
G-2. Length of Second Point							
G-3. Length of Third Point							
G-4. Length of Fourth Point							
G-5. Length of Fifth Point							
G-6. Length of Sixth Point, If Present							
G-7. Length of Seventh Point, If Present							
H-1. Circumference at Smallest Place Between First and Second Points							
H-2. Circumference at Smallest Place Between Second and Third Points							
H-3. Circumference at Smallest Place Between Third and Fourth Points							
H-4. Circumference at Smallest Place Between Fourth and Fifth Points							
			TOTALS				

ADD	Column 1		Exact Locality Where Killed:
	Column 2		Date Killed: Hunter:
	Column 3		Owner: Telephone #:
	Subtotal		Owner's Address:
SUBTRACT Column 4			Guide's Name and Address:
	FINAL SCORE		Remarks: (Mention Any Abnormalities or Unique Qualities)

Copyright © 1997 by Boone and Crockett Club®

Reprinted courtesy of the Boone and Crockett Club, 250 Station Dr., Missoula, MT 59801, 406-542-1888

I certify that I have measured this trophy on _____ 19 _____

at (address) _____ City _____ State _____
and that these measurements and data are, to the best of my knowledge and belief, made in
accordance with the instructions given.

Witness: _____ Signature: _____

B&C Official Measurer

I.D. Number

INSTRUCTIONS FOR MEASURING TYPICAL AMERICAN ELK (WAPITI)

All measurements must be made with a 1/4-inch wide flexible steel tape to the nearest one-eighth of an inch. (Note: A flexible steel cable can be used to measure points and main beams only.) Enter fractional figures in eighths, without reduction. Official measurements cannot be taken until the antlers have air dried for at least 60 days after the animal was killed.
   A. Number of Points on Each Antler: To be counted a point, the projection must be at least one inch long, with length exceeding width at one inch or more of length. All points are measured from tip of point to nearest edge of beam as illustrated. Beam tip is counted as a point but not measured as a point.
   B. Tip to Tip Spread is measured between tips of main beams.
   C. Greatest Spread is measured between perpendiculars at a right angle to the center line of the skull at widest part, whether across main beams or points.
   D. Inside Spread of Main Beams is measured at a right angle to the center line of the skull at widest point between main beams. Enter this measurement again as the Spread Credit if it is less than or equal to the length of the longer antler; if greater, enter longer antler length for Spread Credit.
   E. Total of Lengths of all Abnormal Points: Abnormal Points are those non-typical in location (such as points originating from a point or from bottom or sides of main beam) or pattern (extra points, not generally paired). Measure in usual manner and record in appropriate blanks.
   F. Length of Main Beam is measured from the center of the lowest outside edge of burr over the outer side to the most distant point of the main beam. The point of beginning is that point on the burr where the center line along the outer side of the beam intersects the burr, then following generally the line of the illustration.
   G-1-2-3-4-5-6-7. Length of Normal Points: Normal points project from the top or front of the main beam in the general pattern illustrated. They are measured from nearest edge of main beam over outer curve to tip. Lay the tape along the outer curve of the beam so that the top edge of the tape coincides with the top edge of the beam on both sides of point to determine the baseline for point measurement. Record point length in appropriate blanks.
   H-1-2-3-4. Circumferences are taken as detailed for each measurement.

FAIR CHASE STATEMENT FOR ALL HUNTER-TAKEN TROPHIES

FAIR CHASE, as defined by the Boone and Crockett Club®, is the ethical, sportsmanlike and lawful pursuit and taking of any free-ranging wild game animal in a manner that does not give the hunter an improper or unfair advantage over such game animals.
   Use of any of the following methods in the taking of game shall be deemed UNFAIR CHASE and unsportsmanlike:

   I. Spotting or herding game from the air, followed by landing in its vicinity for the purpose of pursuit and shooting;

   II. Herding, pursuing, or shooting game from any motorboat or motor vehicle;

   III. Use of electronic devices for attracting, locating, or observing game, or for guiding the hunter to such game;

   IV. Hunting game confined by artificial barriers, including escape-proof fenced enclosures, or hunting game transplanted for the purpose of commercial shooting;

   V. Taking of game in a manner not in full compliance with the game laws or regulations of the federal government or of any state, province, territory, or tribal council on reservations or tribal lands;

   VI. Or as may otherwise be deemed unfair or unsportsmanlike by the Executive Committee of the Boone and Crockett Club.

I certify that the trophy scored on this chart was taken in FAIR CHASE as defined above by the Boone and Crockett Club. In signing this statement, I understand that if the information provided on this entry is found to be misrepresented or fraudulent in any respect, it will not be accepted into the Awards Program and all of my prior entries are subject to deletion from future editions of Records of North American Big Game and future entries may not be accepted.

Date: _____ Signature of Hunter:_____
(Signature must be witnessed by an Official Measurer or a Notary Public.)

Date: _____ Signature of Notary or Official Measurer:_____

Reprinted courtesy of the Boone and Crockett Club, 250 Station Dr., Missoula, MT 59801, 406-542-1888

OFFICIAL SCORING SYSTEM FOR NORTH AMERICAN BIG GAME TROPHIES

Records of North American
Big Game

BOONE AND CROCKETT CLUB®

250 Station Drive
Missoula, MT 59801
(406) 542-1888

Minimum Score: Awards All-time
385   385

NON-TYPICAL
AMERICAN ELK (WAPITI)

Detail of Point
Measurement

Abnormal Points	
Right Antler	Left Antler
Subtotals	
E. Total	

SEE OTHER SIDE FOR INSTRUCTIONS			Column 1	Column 2	Column 3	Column 4
A. No. Points on Right Antler		No. Points on Left Antler	Spread Credit	Right Antler	Left Antler	Difference
B. Tip to Tip Spread		C. Greatest Spread				
D. Inside Spread of Main Beams		(Credit May Equal But Not Exceed Longer Antler)				
F. Length of Main Beam						
G-1. Length of First Point						
G-2. Length of Second Point						
G-3. Length of Third Point						
G-4. Length of Fourth Point						
G-5. Length of Fifth Point						
G-6. Length of Sixth Point, If Present						
G-7. Length of Seventh Point, If Present						
H-1. Circumference at Smallest Place Between First and Second Points						
H-2. Circumference at Smallest Place Between Second and Third Points						
H-3. Circumference at Smallest Place Between Third and Fourth Points						
H-4. Circumference at Smallest Place Between Fourth and Fifth Points						
		TOTALS				

ADD	Column 1		Exact Locality Where Killed:
	Column 2		Date Killed: Hunter:
	Column 3		Owner: Telephone #:
	Subtotal		Owner's Address:
SUBTRACT Column 4			Guide's Name and Address:
	Subtotal		Remarks: (Mention Any Abnormalities or Unique Qualities)
ADD Line E Total			
	FINAL SCORE		

Reprinted courtesy of the Boone and Crockett Club, 250 Station Dr., Missoula, MT 59801, 406-542-1888

I certify that I have measured this trophy on _____ 19 _____

at (address) _____ City _____ State _____

and that these measurements and data are, to the best of my knowledge and belief, made in accordance with the instructions given.

Witness: _____ Signature: _____

B&C Official Measurer ☐☐☐

I.D. Number

INSTRUCTIONS FOR MEASURING NON-TYPICAL AMERICAN ELK (WAPITI)

All measurements must be made with a 1/4-inch wide flexible steel tape to the nearest one-eighth of an inch. (Note: A flexible steel cable can be used to measure points and main beams only.) Enter fractional figures in eighths, without reduction. Official measurements cannot be taken until the antlers have air dried for at least 60 days after the animal was killed.

A. Number of Points on Each Antler: To be counted a point, the projection must be at least one inch long, with length exceeding width at one inch or more of length. All points are measured from tip of point to nearest edge of beam as illustrated. Beam tip is counted as a point but not measured as a point.

B. Tip to Tip Spread is measured between tips of main beams.

C. Greatest Spread is measured between perpendiculars at a right angle to the center line of the skull at widest part, whether across main beams or points.

D. Inside Spread of Main Beams is measured at a right angle to the center line of the skull at widest point between main beams. Enter this measurement again as the Spread Credit **if** it is less than or equal to the length of the longer antler; if greater, enter longer antler length for Spread Credit.

E. Total of Lengths of all Abnormal Points: Abnormal Points are those non-typical in location (such as points originating from a point or from bottom or sides of main beam) or pattern (extra points, not generally paired). Measure in usual manner and record in appropriate blanks.

F. Length of Main Beam is measured from the center of the lowest outside edge of burr over the outer side to the most distant point of the main beam. The point of beginning is that point on the burr where the center line along the outer side of the beam intersects the burr, then following generally the line of the illustration.

G-1-2-3-4-5-6-7. Length of Normal Points: Normal points project from the top or front of the main beam in the general pattern illustrated. They are measured from nearest edge of main beam over outer curve to tip. Lay the tape along the outer curve of the beam so that the top edge of the tape coincides with the top edge of the beam on both sides of point to determine the baseline for point measurement. Record point length in appropriate blanks.

H-1-2-3-4. Circumferences are taken as detailed for each measurement.

FAIR CHASE STATEMENT FOR ALL HUNTER-TAKEN TROPHIES

FAIR CHASE, as defined by the Boone and Crockett Club®, is the ethical, sportsmanlike and lawful pursuit and taking of any free-ranging wild game animal in a manner that does not give the hunter an improper or unfair advantage over such game animals.

Use of any of the following methods in the taking of game shall be deemed **UNFAIR CHASE** and unsportsmanlike:

I.   Spotting or herding game from the air, followed by landing in its vicinity for the purpose of pursuit and shooting;

II. Herding, pursuing, or shooting game from any motorboat or motor vehicle;

III. Use of electronic devices for attracting, locating, or observing game, or for guiding the hunter to such game;

IV. Hunting game confined by artificial barriers, including escape-proof fenced enclosures, or hunting game transplanted for the purpose of commercial shooting;

V.   Taking of game in a manner not in full compliance with the game laws or regulations of the federal government or of any state, province, territory, or tribal council on reservations or tribal lands;

VI. Or as may otherwise be deemed unfair or unsportsmanlike by the Executive Committee of the Boone and Crockett Club.

I certify that the trophy scored on this chart was taken in **FAIR CHASE** as defined above by the Boone and Crockett Club. In signing this statement, I understand that if the information provided on this entry is found to be misrepresented or fraudulent in any respect, it will not be accepted into the Awards Program and all of my prior entries are subject to deletion from future editions of *Records of North American Big Game* and future entries may not be accepted.

Date: _____ Signature of Hunter:_____

(Signature must be witnessed by an Official Measurer or a Notary Public.)

Date: _____ Signature of Notary or Official Measurer:_____

Reprinted courtesy of the Boone and Crockett Club, 250 Station Dr., Missoula, MT 59801, 406-542-1888

Shot Placement:
Top: Broadside shot.
Aim for the center of the chest just behind the bend of the front leg or shoulder; this should penetrate the lungs.

Below: Quartering shot.
Aim for the off-side shoulder by drawing an imaginary line from your rifle or bow to the far-side shoulder; aim slightly behind the shoulder if you don't wish to damage any meat.

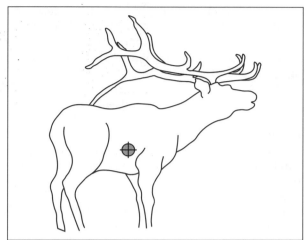

might bugle in a satellite bull. Where calling is overdone, try chirping like a cow, reserving your bugle call only to locate distant elk or when you know you're between a herd bull and his cows. Hike the high ridges, bugling every half-mile or so until you get a response. You might pass by dozens of elk, but you'll find the vocal ones most willing to play ball. The more miles you cover, the better your chances. If bulls won't come to a call but will answer it consistently, send a partner around to stalk while you keep your quarry talking.

When elk are not calling, hunt for tracks, trails, and fresh scat. Then analyze the habitat to deduce where they might bed (cool, thick, isolated cover) and feed (lush meadows). Watch for old wallows and rubbed trees.

Where you see elk or evidence of elk feeding in a meadow, sit and watch that meadow mornings and evenings, hoping to catch them before they slip into dark timber. Or sit along trails leading back to bedding cover. Low crossing points (saddles) between basins are good ambush sites. Elk will remain in an area and reuse foraging sites until spooked out.

Some hunters attempt to drive elk from thick timber. Blockers watch suspected escape routes such as trails and saddles.

During drought, it often pays to watch watering holes, especially where they are few and far between.

When big snows hit, traditional migration corridors are the places to watch or still hunt. Alternatively, find a lone bull track and follow it until you come upon its maker.

Recommendations for Loads and Rifle Cartridges

The wapiti is a major step up from whitetail-sized game. Cows and spike bulls are handled easily enough with the .25–06 and .270, but mature bulls with their extra muscle and heavy bones call for precise shot placement or a stouter cartridge/bullet, of which the latter is most important. Use a long, heavy, premium bullet, and even a 7mm–08 Rem. will punch through to a big bull's vitals. Generally, most westerners concur that the .270 Win. is a good starting point for elk, the .300 Win. Mag. and .300 Weatherby Mag. just about perfect, and the .338 Win. Mag. big medicine. A few big bore fans like the .375 H&H Magnum, but it's really more than necessary.

Wet Elk Hunt

The Bitterroots west of Missoula could have been under a flood watch for all we knew. Drizzle on our first day of elk hunting turned to rain on our second, thundershowers our third and a steady dripping fog our fourth. Then it started snowing, and our dome sleeping tent collapsed, forcing us into the cramped canvas cooking tent. We hadn't seen a single elk.

On day five, the three of us split up to scout more territory. Someone had to find game. The atmosphere was dreary as I hiked a high ridge before dawn, but at sunrise the clouds began to break. Blue sky. By midmorning, I was 5 miles from camp following fresh elk tracks. "Might as well try a call," I mumbled to myself. It was mid-September, and the bulls should have been bugling. They soon were.

Within seconds after my bugle, the real thing wafted back to me, a wild, lonesome whistle as illuminating as sunshine. I still-hunted around the shoulder of the mountain toward it and bugled again. Another reply. And another farther away. A third downslope! I bugled; elk bugled. I bugled; elk bugled. Within five minutes, antlers appeared over the huckleberry brush, five points to a side, ivory tips rocking as the unsuspecting bull strode purposefully to confront his challenger. At 35 yards, he broke into the clear, his neck dark and glistening wet, his shoulders almost white. At 26 yards, I loosed an arrow and watched it slap branches over my quarry's back. The surprised bull turned tail and fled down the mountain.

Hoping to calm the fleeing animal, I bugled again. An immediate response, but from a different quadrant. A second bull was coming in, and several others were screaming. It was as if every bull in the Bitterroots was making up for lost time. I nocked a fresh arrow and listened to approaching hooves.

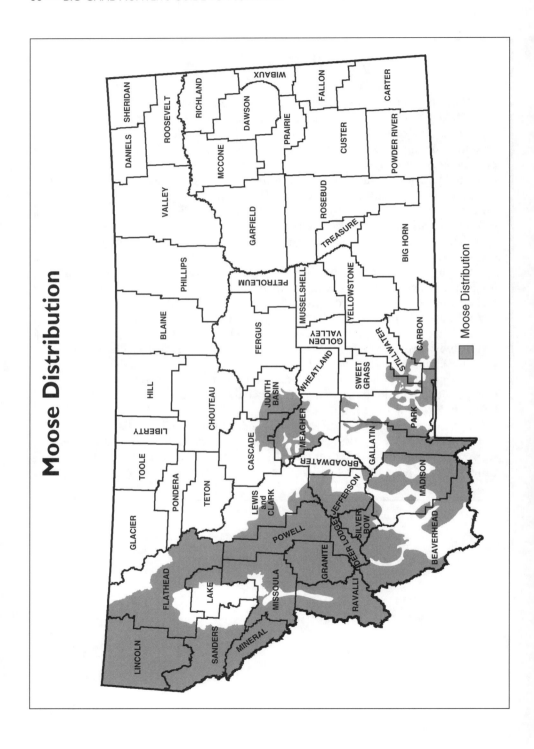

Moose Distribution

Moose

Alces alces

The Shiras moose in Montana is the king of deer, the boss of bosses, and a rare quarry for the hunter. It isn't the wariest animal walking the woods, but the beautiful country it calls home, its sheer size, its impressive antlers, and the difficulty of drawing a permit to hunt it make it a coveted trophy.

Fascinating Facts

- The moose is the largest deer in the world. Even though the Shiras is the smallest subspecies, a mature bull will still weigh over 1,100 pounds.
- Moose antlers are the fastest growing bone known to science. A bull can manufacture ¾-inch of new antler in 24 hours, and up to 90 pounds in 90 days.
- Moose may look clumsy, but they can run 35 mph and swim 6 mph.
- The Montana moose season closed in 1897 due to overharvest and didn't reopen for nearly 50 years. The population is now growing.
- The flap of skin hanging from a moose's neck is called a bell or pendant and has no known function.
- In Europe, moose are called *elch*. Early settlers erroneously applied that to the North American wapiti, now called elk. They adopted the Algonquin word for moose.
- Moose have been seen to completely submerge while feeding on pond weeds.

Local Name
Bullwinkle

Size
Bulls tower 6½ feet at the shoulder and weigh 800 to 1,100 pounds. Cows stand 6 feet and weigh 700 to 1,000 pounds. Stretched on the ground, a moose will tape 7 to 9 feet from nose to tail. Circling one is like walking around a Suburban.

Coat and Color
The moose body is dark brown to nearly black with its shoulder hump sometimes lighter brown. The lower legs of the Shiras moose are light gray to nearly white. Do not confuse moose with elk, which have light bodies and dark legs. A moose's long, overhanging nose is also distinctive.

Antlers
Who could mistake the broad palms of a bull moose for anything else? Those canoe-paddles are as distinctive as a beaver's flat tail. Nevertheless, many young moose antlers have been mistaken for elk racks because they have little or no

An excellent head-on view of a big Shiras bull moose walking toward camera in autumn grassland.

palmation, just a few long tines. Be careful. Look for that long moose nose, dark shoulder hump, and other signs before shooting any odd-looking bull elk.

A mature Shiras moose's antlers will spread 40 to 50 inches between their widest points. Palms may be 2 to 3 feet long and 6 to 15 inches wide with as many as 18 points projecting off the palm's edges. There may be one or more distinct brow tines or a cluster of them joined by palmated bone. This brow cluster may blend almost imperceptibly into the main palm or be separated by a fairly distinct indentation between the two.

Voice and Communication

Though not as vocal as bull elk, moose do a lot of "singing" during their rut. Cows moan long and loudly to attract males, sounding much like sick milk cows. Bulls grunt nasally much like overfed puppies do when you pick them up, only louder. If you hear a long moaning in Montana forests between mid-September and mid-

October, expect to find a cow moose making it. Calves bleat.

Unlike whitetails and mule deer, moose have few obvious scent glands. Mature bulls do dig shallow pits in which they urinate and roll to mark themselves. Young bulls attempt to steal the distinctive, mature odor to make themselves more attractive to cows.

Senses

Much like a whitetail, the moose depends on its nose more than any other sense. One sniff of man-stink and it's bye bye. It also hears well, but may mistake snapping branches and rattling brush for another moose, especially during rut or if you grunt like a moose. Eyesight is poor. Stand still and you often escape detection.

Tracks and Sign

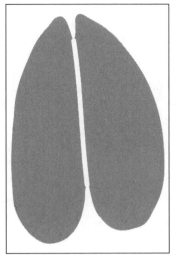

Moose track. Average length is 5".

A moose print is longer and narrower than most hunters imagine. Depending on the age and hoof wear of the individual moose, its track may measure anywhere from 5¼ to 6½ inches long and between 4 and 5 inches wide. In soft mud or snow, dew claws often show, extending the total hoof length to 10 inches. A moose will stride about two feet and trot at four-foot spacings. Dewclaws almost always show when the animal is trotting.

Droppings vary from soft, clumped masses to long, dry pellets and every shape between. They are much larger than deer pellets and slightly larger than elk pellets.

Because moose browse regularly on willows and young cottonwoods, watch for nipped branches and leaves plus large beds pressed into vegetation amid thick stands of willow and cottonwood saplings. Ponds in which moose have been feeding will be muddied and should show tracks in perimeter mud. Look also for floating vegetation that has been ripped from the bottom. Listen for the splashing of water dripping off a foraging moose's head, nose, or antlers.

Like all deer, bull moose thrash brush and rub trunks with their antlers. You may find strands of stripped velvet hanging from broken brush in late August or early September.

Reproduction and Young

Moose mate in late September and early October, each cow accepting a bull's advances for one or two days. Often several cows will attach themselves to a single mature bull, but usually he travels with one after another as they cycle.

Twin calves (after a single calf her first time) are born in late May or June and weigh about 20 pounds each. Unlike other deer, they are not spotted. They lie motionless and hide to escape predators, although they are usually strong enough at one week to outrun a human. Calves may temporarily lose contact with their dam during her estrus, but the family reunites to spend winter together. Before her next calves are born, the cow chases her previous young away and they proceed to live alone.

Habitat

Most people associate moose with ponds, swamps, and willow bottoms, but the animals are surprisingly adaptable to other habitats, including mountainous spruce-fir forests, Douglas fir forests, and mixed deciduous forests, as well as cottonwood and willow river bottoms. They are sometimes spotted foraging in alfalfa fields. Look for them nearly anywhere in the mountains, but especially along streams and lowlands where forage is lush and moist. They generally winter in valleys with abundant willows.

Home Range

Moose are great wanderers when young and in search of a place they can call their own. Once established, they tend to remain in familiar haunts seasonally. Bulls often summer high, returning to valleys for the rut and to winter. Individuals may live for years within a few square miles of territory.

Forage Plants

More than any other deer, moose are browsers, concentrating on twigs and leaves rather than grasses. Favorite vegetation includes willows, red osier dogwood, cottonwood, aspen, currents, mountain ash, snowberry, spiraea, and birch, plus aquatic vegetation like sedges, water lilies, and pondweed. They eagerly munch on garden vegetables, ornamental shrubs, and orchard trees when they discover them.

Daily Patterns

Moose are crepuscular, meaning they're most active at dusk and dawn. But when unharried by humans they'll forage well into the morning and long before sunset if temperatures are not too high. When it's hot and sunny, they lay up in deep shade. Because they often feed in the same cover that hides them, they needn't move much. Late summer bulls often travel less than a mile per day. During the rut, bulls wander all day in search of cows. Deep snows drive mountain moose to sheltered valleys where they can feed on willow shrubs out of the wind. They bed in these same thickets.

Rutting Behavior

In late August, bulls begin thrashing shrubs and mock fighting saplings to clear velvet from their antlers and warm up for the rut. By mid-September, they've abandoned summer lethargy and begun wandering in search of cows, grunting in response to the loud moaning of calling females. Before cows reach estrus, mature bulls dig pits in low, wet ground, then urinate and wallow in them. Their rank odor

In an open, grass meadow, two Shiras bull moose lock horns while sparring.

apparently stimulates ovulation in the cows. Because young bulls cannot produce this strong urine odor, they try to steal the scent from the older bulls' wallows; thus, one often finds aggregates of moose together during the early rut. Normally they are solitary animals. Cows actually guard their chosen bulls to a degree, chasing off rival cows that get too close. Bulls show off their antlers to impress females and warn away other males. Matched bulls clash antlers and try to shove one another over. Sometimes antlers lock, and both bulls perish. The bulk of breeding occurs in the last week of September and first week of October. Some worn out old bulls shed their racks by late November; youngsters may hang on to theirs until March.

Trophy Dimensions

The current B&C world record Shiras moose's antlers spread only 53 inches, but its paddles were 16⅞ and 15⅝ inches wide and over 38 inches long. It was taken in

*In a wet meadow, a Shiras bull moose browses
amid sedges and summer wildflowers.*

Wyoming and scores 205⅘. The widest Shiras antlers ever recorded were 62⅜ inches and came out of Idaho. The biggest registered Montana moose scored 195⅛. It had a 55⅞ inch spread, a palm 43⅛ inches long and 15⅛ inches wide on the right side, slightly smaller on the left, and bases 7⅜ inches in circumference. It had 14 points per side, and was taken near Red Rock Lakes in extreme southeast Beaverhead County in 1952. Minimum score for the all-time book is 155.

Judging moose for the book isn't easy. You must consider spread (measured between the widest outside points), length of palm, width of palm, number of points, and circumference of beam. In addition, symmetry counts, and moose are notorious for sporting one antler considerably smaller than the other. There are no hard and fast rules regarding trophy antler shape or dimensions. Spreads of less than 40 inches have made B&C.

To estimate, you might try the following steps. First, figure a moose stands 7 feet at the shoulder hump. Compare palm height to that; if it seems to be one-third to one-half the bull's shoulder height, the palms are in the 36-inch class and in contention. Next, assess palm width at the narrowest point in comparison to length. If they look half as wide as they are long, they're again trophy class. Finally, try to count

OFFICIAL SCORING SYSTEM FOR NORTH AMERICAN BIG GAME TROPHIES

Records of North American
Big Game

BOONE AND CROCKETT CLUB®

250 Station Drive
Missoula, MT 59801
(406)542-1888

MOOSE   Kind of Moose: _____

Minimum Score: Awards All-time
  Alaska-Yukon   210   224
  Canada   185   195
  Wyoming   140   155

Detail of Point Measurement

	Abnormal Points	
	Right Antler	Left Antler
Number of Points		
Total to B.		

SEE OTHER SIDE FOR INSTRUCTIONS	Column 1	Column 2	Column 3	Column 4
		Right Antler	Left Antler	Difference
A. Greatest Spread				
B. Number of Abnormal Points on Both Antlers				
C. Number of Normal Points				
D. Width of Palm				
E. Length of Palm Including Brow Palm				
F. Circumference of Beam at Smallest Place				
TOTALS				

ADD	Column 1		Exact Locality Where Killed:
	Column 2		Date Killed: Hunter:
	Column 3		Owner: Telephone #:
	Subtotal		Owner's Address:
	SUBTRACT Column 4		Guide's Name and Address:
	FINAL SCORE		Remarks: (Mention Any Abnormalities or Unique Qualities)

I certify that I have measured this trophy on _____ 19_____

at (address) _____ City _____ State _____
and that these measurements and data are, to the best of my knowledge and belief, made in
accordance with the instructions given.

Witness: _____ Signature: _____

B&C Official Measurer

I.D. Number

Copyright © 1997 by Boone and Crockett Club®

Reprinted courtesy of the Boone and Crockett Club, 250 Station Dr., Missoula, MT 59801, 406-542-1888

INSTRUCTIONS FOR MEASURING MOOSE

Measurements must be made with a 1/4-inch wide flexible steel tape to the nearest one-eighth of an inch. Enter fractional figures in eighths, without reduction. Official measurements cannot be taken until antlers have air dried for at least 60 days after animal was killed.

A. Greatest Spread is measured between perpendiculars in a straight line at a right angle to the center line of the skull.

B. Number of Abnormal Points on Both Antlers: Abnormal points are those projections originating from normal points or from the upper or lower palm surface, or from the inner edge of palm (see illustration). Abnormal points must be at least one inch long, with length exceeding width at one inch or more of length.

C. Number of Normal Points: Normal points originate from the outer edge of palm. To be counted a point, a projection must be at least one inch long, with the length exceeding width at one inch or more of length. Be sure to verify whether or not each projection qualifies as a point.

D. Width of Palm is taken in contact with the under surface of palm, at a right angle to the inner edge of palm. The line of measurement should begin and end at the midpoint of the palm edge, which gives credit for the desirable character of palm thickness.

E. Length of Palm including Brow Palm is taken in contact with the surface along the underside of the palm, **parallel** to the inner edge, from dips between points at the top to dips between points (if present) at the bottom. If a bay is present, measure across the open bay if the proper line of measurement, parallel to **inner edge**, follows this path. The line of measurement should begin and end at the midpoint of the palm edge, which gives credit for the desirable character of palm thickness.

F. Circumference of Beam at Smallest Place is taken as illustrated.

FAIR CHASE STATEMENT FOR ALL HUNTER-TAKEN TROPHIES

FAIR CHASE, as defined by the Boone and Crockett Club®, is the ethical, sportsmanlike and lawful pursuit and taking of any free-ranging wild game animal in a manner that does not give the hunter an improper or unfair advantage over such game animals.
Use of any of the following methods in the taking of game shall be deemed **UNFAIR CHASE** and unsportsmanlike:

   I. Spotting or herding game from the air, followed by landing in its vicinity for the purpose of pursuit and shooting;

   II. Herding, pursuing, or shooting game from any motorboat or motor vehicle;

   III. Use of electronic devices for attracting, locating, or observing game, or for guiding the hunter to such game;

   IV. Hunting game confined by artificial barriers, including escape-proof fenced enclosures, or hunting game transplanted for the purpose of commercial shooting;

   V. Taking of game in a manner not in full compliance with the game laws or regulations of the federal government or of any state, province, territory, or tribal council on reservations or tribal lands;

   VI. Or as may otherwise be deemed unfair or unsportsmanlike by the Executive Committee of the Boone and Crockett Club.

I certify that the trophy scored on this chart was taken in **FAIR CHASE** as defined above by the Boone and Crockett Club. In signing this statement, I understand that if the information provided on this entry is found to be misrepresented or fraudulent in any respect, it will not be accepted into the Awards Program and all of my prior entries are subject to deletion from future editions of *Records of North American Big Game* and future entries may not be accepted.

Date: _____ Signature of Hunter:_____
                         (Signature must be witnessed by an Official Measurer or a Notary Public.)

Date: _____ Signature of Notary or Official Measurer:_____

Reprinted courtesy of the Boone and Crockett Club, 250 Station Dr., Missoula, MT 59801, 406-542-1888

Shot Placement:
Top: Broadside shot.
Aim for the center of the chest just behind the bend of the front leg or shoulder; this should penetrate the lungs.

Below: Tail/Rump shot.
Take this shot only if using a powerful cartridge and a heavy, premium bullet. Aim for the base of the tail. The shot should break several vertebrae and paralyze the animal; rush in for a finishing shot. If it hits to the left or right, it should break the pelvis or one of the legs. Be aware that these types of shots will destroy a lot of meat.

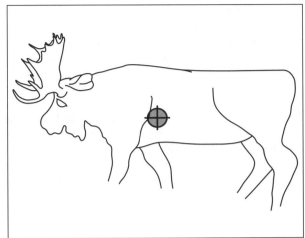

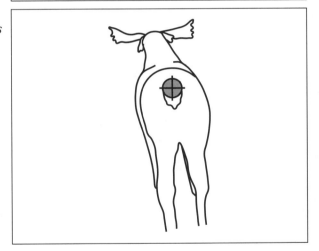

the points. They must be 1 inch long and longer than they are wide to count. Most record book heads have at least 8 tines per side; the best have 12 to 16. Don't worry about beam circumference. That usually takes care of itself on a mature bull.

Hunting Tactics

The generous moose season from mid-September through late November accommodates a variety of hunting tactics. During the first three weeks, still-hunt mountain valleys, cool north slopes, and high lakes and streams, watching for fresh tracks and droppings and listening for grunting and mooing. Call bulls with a typical dairy cow "mooo" modified by pitching it higher, straining as you say it, and pinching the sound through your nose for a nasal quality. Once you hear a real moose, you'll understand. In open areas you may glass suitable habitat to locate game, then stalk in. Hunt early and late if temperatures are high.

After the rut, bulls lay low to recover. This is not the best time to hunt. But once snow begins falling, search valleys, wet meadows, and willow thickets. Deep snows reduce available habitat and force many moose to winter in close proximity.

Recommendations for Loads and Rifle Cartridges

Whatever applies to elk applies to moose. Although they are slightly heftier than elk, they aren't as durable. A well placed, premium 150-grain slug from a .270 Win. will do the job every time, but the .30–06 with a premium 180-grain to 200-grain slug is even better. And if you like carrying heavier guns, by all means go with any of the magnums. The .338 Win. Mag. should be perfect.

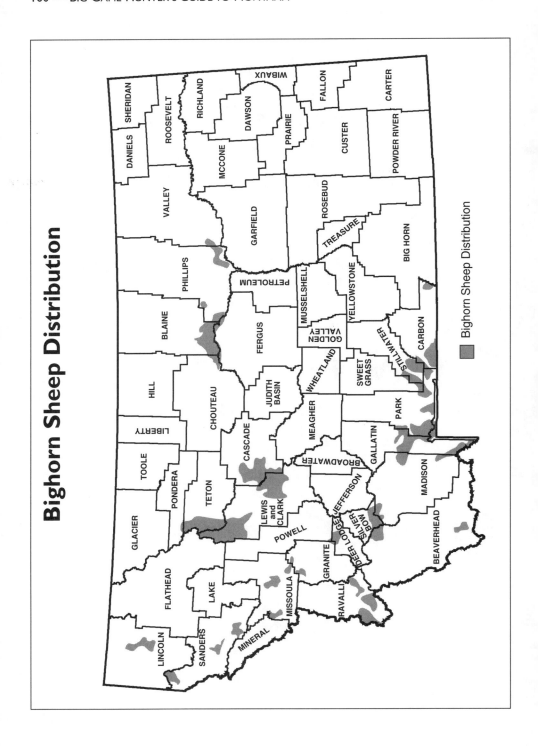

Bighorn Sheep Distribution

Bighorn Sheep

Ovis canadensis

A bighorn ram standing atop a mountain rampart, its magnificent horns curving against a pristine blue sky, is one of the most magnificent sights in nature. Such a beast may be the ultimate trophy of the American West.

Fascinating Facts

- Two battling rams crash together with the energy of a 130-grain bullet leaving the muzzle of a .270 Winchester.
- A ram's horn tips are "broomed" back by splintering and breaking during butting contests, not by rubbing against rocks to clear the tip for better vision.
- Rams butt horns throughout the year to establish and maintain a dominance order.
- Bighorns are the most recent evolutionary rendition of a long line of sheep that originated in North Africa and spread across Asia, down through Alaska, and down to the tip of Baja, Mexico.
- Sheep horns are not weapons of defense but secondary sexual displays that reflect genetic superiority. The larger a ram's horns, the faster it has grown and the more prolifically it breeds.
- Ewes live apart from rams to protect themselves and their lambs from head-butting harassment.
- A large set of ram horns may weigh over 20 pounds.

Local Names

Bighorns, sheep, rams

Size

Bighorns are comparable in size to mule deer but shorter and blockier in build. Rams are about 20 percent larger than ewes and stand 36 to 42 inches at the shoulder, measure 5 to 6 feet nose to tail, and weigh 175 to 280 pounds. Ewes stand 30 to 36 inches, stretch 4 to 5 feet, and weigh 100 to 200 pounds.

Coat and Color

Short, dense hairs of mostly uniform length give a smooth appearance. Pelage is brown-gray, darkening to nearly chocolate in some old rams. White is apparent around the muzzle, inside ear, and to varying degrees around the eyes. The large, white rump extends down the backside of its legs to its black hooves. The belly and backside of the forelegs may be white, too. Its short tail is dark brown to nearly black. This color often extends several inches up the white rump patch above the tail. Horns are tan-brown to amber.

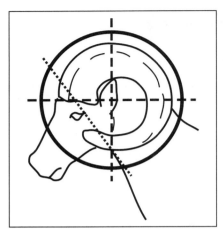

A sheep has a legal curl (¾ curl) if you can draw a straight line from the horn base through any part of the eye to the tip. A full curl would reach past the eye, creating a circle.

Horns

Both sexes bear horns. Ewe horns are short and thin, never forming more than a half-curl. Ram horns grow quickly to a half curl, eventually to a full curl or more; the horns usually stay close to the face, but sometimes flare out to the sides. Horns are made of keratin and grow from a bony core throughout the ram's life. They grow out from their base and increase in diameter as they grow; some reach 17 inches in circumference at the base. Due to limited forage in winter, horns have distinctive growth rings marking these periods of reduced production. They are never shed, though they may exfoliate due to disease. Rarely do horns break off; more often, the tips will splinter, creating a fat, blunted tip that helps distinguish mature rams from sharp-tipped youngsters.

Voice and Communication

Like domestic sheep, bighorns baaa, but not often. Ewes and lambs stay in touch this way. The most common ram sound is the whack of horns, which can be heard as far as a mile in high mountain air. Most sheep communicate via posture and display. Staring is an aggressive challenge; thus, sheep bed facing away from one another, which also provides the flock with optimum predator defense.

A foreleg kick to another sheep's belly or chest is a challenge. The other sheep either backs away or turns to meet the challenger. Approaching another sheep with the head parallel to the ground and the neck outstretched is a threat display. Inferior rams rub their horn tips against a dominant ram's nose to signify appeasement. Head butting can be a casual means to maintain the pecking order. Serious clashes are reserved for two evenly matched rams disputing rights to a female.

Bighorns indulge in no known scent marking, scraping, or sign-post rubbing as do members of the deer tribe; however, they do rub preorbital glands against one anothers' faces and horns, perhaps as a communal scent marking to aid nocturnal recognition.

Senses

Sheep hear and smell well, but they mostly depend on their eyes to avoid danger. That is normal for diurnal, open-country animals. Rocks shift and tumble so often in typical sheep habitat that the animals mostly ignore such sounds. They generally see trouble before it's close enough to smell, but can and do flee when merely scenting danger. Hunters must play the wind, move slowly, and stay out of sight when stalking bighorns.

Tracks and Sign
While most sheep are located visually, many flocks in Montana live much of their lives in open forests. Here one often resorts to tracks and droppings to discover quarry. Hoof prints are less heart-shaped than deer prints, each toe tip being nearly as wide at the heel. A mature ram's print will be about 3½ inches long and rather blocky looking. There are about 18 inches between the prints of walking sheep.

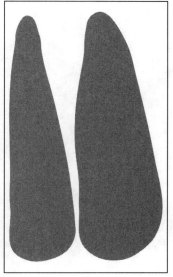

Bighorn sheep track. On average, they run 3½" in length.

Bighorns use their front hooves to scrape beds into rocky slopes, on rocky points, and at the bases of large pines and firs. These beds are used again and again and droppings accumulate around them. Mule deer also scrape out beds in similar areas, but re-use them less often. Rams generally stand and urinate in their beds before walking off; mud in a bed therefore indicates recent occupation. Since deer beds don't usually smell strongly, sniff suspect beds to detect sheep odor.

Sheep also follow trails regularly along steep talus slopes and the very tops of mountain ridges. Backpackers often follow these hard-packed, high country sheep highways.

Sheep scat is as variable as deer scat and similar in appearance. During fall, pellets are generally short with concave ends and sharp, tapering opposite ends. They look like little bells or acorns. Succulent forage in spring and summer makes for clumped masses.

Reproduction and Young
Ewes are bred as early as 15 months on good range. Rams are capable of breeding successfully at 2 years but rarely get the chance. Five- to 10-year-old rams are the prime breeders. Often young, vigorous rams outcompete older rams with larger horns simply because the old timers are too slow to keep up with running ewes.

After a 6-month gestation, one or two lambs are born in late May or early June. They begin to graze soon after birth, are weaned by fall, and remain with the maternal flock for the next two years. Young females remain with the matriarchal band, but the males are ignored and harried until they leave to join bachelor ram groups.

Habitat
Classic sheep range consists of rolling grassland with nearby cliffs, ledges, and rocky mountain slopes for escape cover; contrary to popular conception, this range

A herd of bighorn sheep walks along a steep, barren slope.

does not have to be at high elevation. Lewis and Clark found bighorns on the chalk bluffs along the Missouri River in eastern Montana in 1805. They've been reintroduced to that area and many others across the state, but competition from domestic sheep and cattle keeps numbers depressed. Bighorns are particularly susceptible to diseases carried by domestic sheep, including lungworm and pneumonia. Purchases and management of critical wintering ranges, reduced hunting pressure, and restocking efforts after 1940 helped flocks rebound from historic lows. In many Rocky Mountain ranges, bighorns live in forests with scattered meadow openings where they feed, and rock outcrops where they bed. Montana FWP monitors 42 distinct bighorn sheep herds statewide totaling 4,890 animals as of January, 1997.

Home Range

Bighorns are traditionalists, following older sheep to long-established seasonal ranges. Most movements are from low elevation winter range, usually grassy slopes blown clear of snow, to higher elevation summer ranges where grasses grow fast and rich. But rams may have as many as six seasonal ranges including winter, spring, summer, pre-rut, rut, and post rut. These are traditional and used year after year;

thus, it is possible to pattern both individual sheep as well as flocks. A standard rule is that outside of the rut, rams will not be mixed with ewes and lambs.

Sheep are notorious for refusing to pioneer new territory across brushland or through woods, but if forests gradually grow up around familiar, long-used habitat, they adapt and continue to travel through or live in those forests.

Forage Plants

Sheep are adapted to thrive on coarse, dry grasses and forbs in steep, windswept terrain other ungulates can't easily reach. They feed on a wide variety of grasses, sedges, and forbs year round but include brushy plants such as willow, sage, mountain mahogany, and rabbitbrush in winter.

Daily Patterns

While sheep are slaves to traditional ranges and migration patterns, they live somewhat unpredictable daily patterns, wandering thither and yon over their mountain territories, feeding on this peak three days, then suddenly hiking three miles to a new slope. Sometimes they progress slowly but steadily in the same direction around a peak or down a long mountain valley. Primarily diurnal in habits, they generally graze for two or three hours at dawn and dusk and again at midday, bedding to ruminate and rest between feeding times. Where escape cover—usually steep, often rocky, terrain—lies above grazing pastures, they move up to bed. When cover is below pastures, such as a steep canyon, they move down to rest, usually kicking a flat bed under a rimrock or atop a projection of rock where they can see trouble approaching. Where good grazing and good bedding habitat are intermixed, they lay themselves down at the nearest comfortable spot. When alarmed or badly spooked by wolves, grizzlies, or men, they run uphill when possible and may cross one or more high ridges and valleys to settle in an undisturbed area. They don't hesitate to swim rivers to reach safety, nor do they balk at dropping several thousand feet to reach a drinking stream in dry country where high lakes and snow patches are not available. Mineral licks are also popular, especially in spring. Because bighorns are relatively easy to locate and watch from long distances in most habitats, patterning them isn't usually necessary. Just spot them, plan your stalk, and move in.

Rutting Behavior

The bighorn rut starts in late October when rams move from pre-rut territories to their respective rutting grounds, usually the mountainside where they first followed a lead ram after they were kicked out of the maternal band at 2 or 3 years of age. This rutting site may be miles from the ram's summer and winter grazing territories, or right next door, depending on the migration traditions he learned as a youngster. Peak breeding occurs around Thanksgiving and tapers off through December.

Because bachelor groups often break up as individual males migrate to different rutting areas, rams often meet new rams or associates they haven't seen since the last rut. This requires much chest kicking and head butting to re-establish the pecking order. Brash young rams regularly challenge bigger-horned males. They also harass and chase ewes, often in unruly gangs that fight one another. A ram attempting to mount a ewe may be battered off by another, he by another, and so on. Ewes try to run away, squeeze into rock crevices, or lie down to dissuade their overbearing suitors who kick, butt, and pry them up for more spirited chases.

Ewes prefer to mate with older, bigger rams because these males are smart enough to court slowly and cautiously until ewes are ready to accept them. As a ewe approaches estrus, a big ram follows, stretching his head forward and twisting his horns to show their size. He scent checks her urine and lip curls. A ewe that sticks close to a big male is protected from gangs of smaller rams, but if she breaks and runs, her old protector is often too slow to keep up, putting her at the mercy of the feisty, unmannerly, younger males. Two rams with nearly equal-sized horns may contest supremacy with repeated 20 mph charges and head butts lasting as many as 20 hours. Unfortunately for them, while they battle, smaller rams often run off with their ewes.

After breeding, rams may remain with the ewes they've bred or migrate to a different ewe band per the migratory patterns they learned as youngsters. By spring, males are back in their bachelor bands, isolated from the lambing females.

Trophy Dimensions

Montana rams carry some of the largest sheep horns in North America. Officially, the largest Montana B&C bighorn scores 200⅞ points and ranks #8 in the world, but larger horns have reportedly been picked up in recent years. The world-record head came out of Alberta in 1911. The largest horn is 45 inches long, 16⅝-inches in circumference at it base, and 11⅞ inches around its third quarter. Total score for both horns is 208⅛. Many Montana bighorns score 180 or more. If you draw a permit, you owe it to yourself to hunt hard for such a ram.

To novices, all ram horns look huge, but really big ones drop below their bearer's jaw line, curve up above his nose, and forward halfway between eye and nose. They also look as fat halfway to their tips as they do at their bases, and the tips are usually blunt and fat rather than thin and pointed. Often it is possible to sneak close enough to rams to count horn growth rings through a spotting scope. Rams showing 8 or more rings are fully mature and likely to be trophies, but not every ram carries trophy-sized horns due to genetics. Some slow-growing rams might reach 14 years and never produce B&C class horns.

Hunting Tactics

Sheep hunting is almost exclusively a glass-and-stalk affair. Hunters hike or ride mountain valleys and ridges, glassing long, far, and carefully until they spot rams. Magnifications of 8× to 10× are best. Spotting scopes of 15× to 40× are almost essen-

OFFICIAL SCORING SYSTEM FOR NORTH AMERICAN BIG GAME TROPHIES

Records of North American
Big Game

BOONE AND CROCKETT CLUB®

250 Station Drive
Missoula, MT 59801
(406) 542-1888

SHEEP

Kind of Sheep: _____

Plug Number: _____

Minimum Score:	Awards	All-time
bighorn	175	180
desert	165	168
Dall's	160	170
Stone's	165	170

Measure to a
Point in Line
With Horn Tip

SEE OTHER SIDE FOR INSTRUCTIONS		Column 1	Column 2	Column 3
A. Greatest Spread (Is Often Tip to Tip Spread)		Right Horn	Left Horn	Difference
B. Tip to Tip Spread				
C. Length of Horn				
D-1. Circumference of Base				
D-2. Circumference at First Quarter				
D-3. Circumference at Second Quarter				
D-4. Circumference at Third Quarter				
TOTALS				

ADD	Column 1		Exact Locality Where Killed:
	Column 2		Date Killed: Hunter:
	SUBTOTAL		Owner: Telephone #:
SUBTRACT Column 3			Owner's Address:
			Guide's Name and Address:
FINAL SCORE			Remarks: (Mention Any Abnormalities or Unique Qualities)

I certify that I have measured this trophy on _____ 19 ____
at (address) _____ State ____
and that these measurements and data are, to the best of my knowledge and belief, made in
accordance with the instructions given.

Witness: _____ Signature: _____

B&C Official Measurer

I.D. Number

Copyright © 1997 by Boone and Crockett Club®

Reprinted courtesy of the Boone and Crockett Club, 250 Station Dr., Missoula, MT 59801, 406-542-1888

INSTRUCTIONS FOR MEASURING SHEEP

All measurements must be made with a 1/4-inch wide flexible steel tape to the nearest one-eighth of an inch. Enter fractional figures in eighths, without reduction. Official measurements cannot be taken until horns have air dried for at least 60 days after the animal was killed.

A. Greatest Spread is measured between perpendiculars at a right angle to the center line of the skull.

B. Tip to Tip Spread is measured between tips of horns.

C. Length of Horn is measured from the lowest point in front on outer curve to a point in line with tip. **Do not** press tape into depressions. The low point of the outer curve of the horn is considered to be the low point of the frontal portion of the horn, situated **above** and slightly medial to the eye socket (not the outside edge). Use a straight edge, perpendicular to horn axis, to end measurement on "broomed" horns.

D-1. Circumference of Base is measured at a right angle to axis of horn. **Do not** follow irregular edge of horn; the line of measurement must be entirely on horn material.

D-2-3-4. Divide measurement C of longer horn by four. Starting at base, mark **both** horns at these quarters (even though the other horn is shorter) and measure circumferences at these marks, with measurements taken at right angles to horn axis.

FAIR CHASE STATEMENT FOR ALL HUNTER-TAKEN TROPHIES

FAIR CHASE, as defined by the Boone and Crockett Club®, is the ethical, sportsmanlike and lawful pursuit and taking of any free-ranging wild game animal in a manner that does not give the hunter an improper or unfair advantage over such game animals.

Use of any of the following methods in the taking of game shall be deemed **UNFAIR CHASE** and unsportsmanlike:

I. Spotting or herding game from the air, followed by landing in its vicinity for the purpose of pursuit and shooting;

II. Herding, pursuing, or shooting game from any motorboat or motor vehicle;

III. Use of electronic devices for attracting, locating, or observing game, or for guiding the hunter to such game;

IV. Hunting game confined by artificial barriers, including escape-proof fenced enclosures, or hunting game transplanted for the purpose of commercial shooting;

V. Taking of game in a manner not in full compliance with the game laws or regulations of the federal government or of any state, province, territory, or tribal council on reservations or tribal lands;

VI. Or as may otherwise be deemed unfair or unsportsmanlike by the Executive Committee of the Boone and Crockett Club.

I certify that the trophy scored on this chart was taken in **FAIR CHASE** as defined above by the Boone and Crockett Club. In signing this statement, I understand that if the information provided on this entry is found to be misrepresented or fraudulent in any respect, it will not be accepted into the Awards Program and all of my prior entries are subject to deletion from future editions of *Records of North American Big Game* and future entries may not be accepted.

Date: _____ Signature of Hunter:_____
(Signature must be witnessed by an Official Measurer or a Notary Public.)

Date: _____ Signature of Notary or Official Measurer:_____

Reprinted courtesy of the Boone and Crockett Club, 250 Station Dr., Missoula, MT 59801, 406-542-1888

*The size of the horns on this bighorn ram are an excellent example
of trophy size horns, showing the horn dropping below the jaw line,
curling back above the nose, and forward halfway between eye and nose.*

tial for assessing trophy quality. They save a lot of cross-canyon hiking. When a suitable ram has been selected, you attempt to sneak within range. Since sheep prefer to run uphill when alarmed, it is best to approach from uphill. If you miss but they don't know where you are when the shot is fired, they'll often run up and be quite near for a second shot.

In overgrown ranges where sheep have adapted to living in forests, you can use deer and elk tactics to hunt them. Often they live about two-thirds up mountain slopes. Cruise for sign at this elevation, checking meadows, rocky ledges, and points for droppings and beds. If you come upon fresh but empty beds, mark them on your map and return on subsequent days, glassing them from afar. Still-hunt carefully in areas with fresh sign and you'll eventually come upon your quarry. Watch rams as long as possible so that you can look over the entire band before selecting one. If you shoot the first one you see, you're liable to regret it when a larger one jumps into view at the shot.

Recommendations for Loads and Rifle Cartridges

Remember the cartridges recommended for mule deer? They're perfect for sheep and goats, too. But because serious mountain hunters appreciate minimum weight,

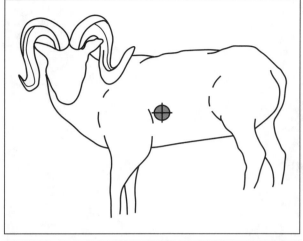

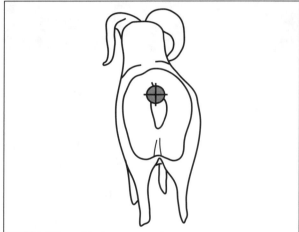

Shot Placement:
Top: Broadside shot.
Aim for the center of the chest just behind the bend of the front leg or shoulder; this should penetrate the lungs.

Below: Tail/Rump shot.
Take this shot only if using a powerful cartridge and a heavy, premium bullet. Aim for the base of the tail. The shot should break several vertebrae and paralyze the animal; rush in for a finishing shot. If it hits to the left or right, it should break the pelvis or one of the legs. Be aware that these types of shots will destroy a lot of meat.

the 7mm and .30 caliber magnums become a bit heavy. Again, you can't beat the .270 Win. and .280 Rem. cartridges. For even more weight savings with no loss in velocity, try the short, fat .284 Win. cartridge and 140-grain bullets. This cartridge cycles through short action lengths, thus saving a few ounces of weight while giving you a shorter, quicker bolt throw. While the .243 cartridges are acceptable, they're a bit on the light side for these stocky trophy animals. You want to anchor them quickly.

Mountain Goat Distribution

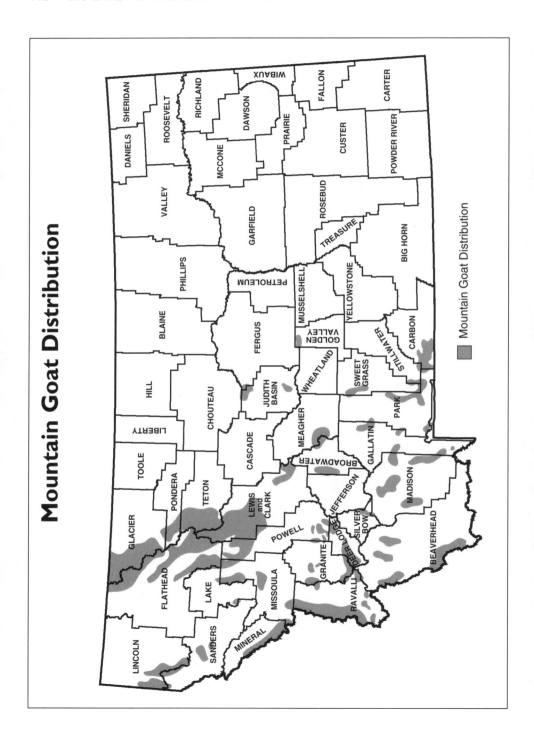

Mountain Goat Distribution

Mountain Goat

Oreamnos americanus

The shaggy white mountain goat is not a true goat, but it is Montana's premiere mountaineer, living in higher, steeper, rockier, snowier, and more barren terrain than any other big game animal. The white goat endures some of the harshest living conditions in North America and thrives on them. Hunting one is a rare treat.

Fascinating Facts

- A mountain goat's short, stiletto horns are not sexual ornamentation like sheep horns, but deadly stabbing weapons for defense and dominance contests. Both billies and nannies grow and use them.
- The guard hairs over the back of a mountain goat commonly exceed 7 inches in length and are underlain with a dense, woolly, insulating layer.
- Gravity is the goat's worst enemy. Falls from rotten ledges, avalanches, and just poor footing kill goats regularly.
- Goats have evolved in their harsh environment to take advantage of isolated vegetation no other ungulates can reach and to utilize escape cover few predators can negotiate.
- Early explorers and mountain men once thought the mountain goat was a form of buffalo or even grizzly bear, based on skins and distant sightings. Goats were the last Western big game animal to be identified by scientists.
- All historic Montana mountain goat range is still inhabited, but since 1941 transplant efforts have established populations in isolated ranges where they didn't naturally occur.
- A slow, cautious nature and unique hooves with convex, leathery inner pads enable mountain goats to climb vertical cliffs via small cracks and ledges
- Goats are by nature ornery and belligerent toward one another because their resources are limited. They can't afford to share small clumps of forage or narrow ledges, so they travel in small groups rather than large herds and stab at other goats that get too close.

Local Names
Goat, billy, nanny

Size
At best, the size difference between males and females is maybe 15 percent. They stand 36 to 42 inches at the shoulder hump, stretch 5 to almost 6 feet from nose to tip of their short tails, and weigh 120 to 300 pounds.

Against a blue sky, a Rocky Mountain Goat stands atop a rocky ridge.

Coat and Color

A goat's coat is easy to describe: long, thick, and white. Summer hair is short, winter hair is nothing short of magnificent. Guard hairs 7 inches long rise over the back and dangle from the forelegs, giving goats that famous pantaloon look. Side and belly hairs are so long that they give the animal a short-legged appearance. Only on the face, small pointy ears, and lower feet are hairs short. One of the most distinguishing characteristics of mountain goats, male and female, is the long beard hanging below the throat (not off the chin.) This gives them an old, slightly amusing persona reminiscent of cartoon versions of "Uncle Sam." Nose, lips, hooves, and horns are black. Old males often take on a yellow patina. During rut, their coats are usually stained and dirty from rolling in dirt or mud.

Horns

Compared to their lush pelage, mountain goat horns are almost an afterthought. They are daggers 7 to 10 inches long (with world class horns going to 12 inches), slightly ribbed by annual growth rings on the base half, nearly smooth and glossy over the terminal half. Billy horns are slightly thicker than nanny horns and tend to curve more uniformly. Nanny horns often rise straight up for several inches before hooking back with a noticeable kink. Horns are rather brittle, as is the underlying skull. Mountain goats are designed for stabbing, not butting.

Voice and Communication

Like most open country ungulates, goats are mostly silent. There's little need to sound off when you can see your associates hundreds, even thousands, of yards away. Nannies and kids bleat to one another, and billies make a buzzing sound when courting. Aggressive goats growl to warn others away. Body language is the more useful communication. Staring is aggressive. The lesser animal should back down. If it doesn't, the aggressor may walk or trot toward it, stomp its front hooves, and toss its horns. Yielding goats turn and walk away or sometimes crouch and slink away. Goats stand broadside to one another, arch their backs, flare body hairs to maximize size, lower their heads and aim horns at opponents as a maximum threat display. If displays don't deliver the message, horn pokes and punctures do. Goats have been seen skewering one another off 15-foot cliffs and into raging rivers. Dead goats have been found with deep puncture wounds.

Senses

Goats are so phlegmatic and slow in their responses that it's sometimes difficult to detect what alerts them. Sound, scent, sight? Vision is probably their first line of defense, with scent and sound tying for distant seconds. Generally, they feel so secure in their steep, rugged habitat that they are not all that alert. A cautious approach from downwind does the trick. A few dislodged rocks are not going to ruin the stalk, dislodged rocks being common in high mountains.

Tracks and Sign

A goat print is quite similar to a sheep print, 3 inches long, blunter at the tip than deer prints and the hooves fairly widely spread, giving the print a blocky look. A walking goat strides about 15 inches. Droppings are typical—pellets when forage is dry, clumped masses when moist. Individual pellets are often smaller than deer and sheep pellets, usually a ½-inch long or less. Goats like to bed atop projecting rimrock, at the base of rock ledges, and in shallow caves. Search these places for droppings. Like sheep, they'll also scratch beds into steep slopes. They rub convenient "scratching" rocks and leave long white hairs behind. They'll sometimes rub their horns on isolated tree trunks within their territories. The wood will be grooved or gouged, not ripped or cut as by sharp bear claws. Finally, look for shallow dusting pits on ridge tops and benches where soil is deep. The pits are actually shallow pans covering 2- to 4-feet square, and roughed up by violent pawing. You should find white hairs in and around pits, and possibly a strong barnyard odor.

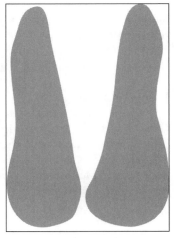

Mountain goat print.
Average length is 3".

Reproduction and Young

Mountain goats have a slower reproduction rate than deer or sheep. Nannies usually don't breed until 2½ years old, and then they'll have one or two kids each year. After a late November mating, gestation lasts until late May or early June. The 7-pound newborn follows mom across broken terrain within a few hours of birth. After several days, the maternal group will join with other nannies and kids to form a small flock, usually no larger than 16 animals, for the summer. Soon the precocious kids are foraging. By late summer they are weaned, but they stay with their dams until the following spring when they are run off so that mom can have her next kid. Young females usually stay with the maternal herd until they, too, become mothers. Young billies may hang around for two years before wandering off for the bachelor life.

Habitat

Mountain goats inhabit barren rocks, ridges, and talus slopes mostly above timberline, as well as steep ledges and cliffs interspersed with small benches and meadows. In Montana, most such habitat lies between 5,000 and 11,000 feet. Winter habitat is usually below summer range, but may be above it in areas where high elevation winds blow grazing meadows near cliffs clear of snow.

Home Range

Maternal bands of 3 to 18 members remain within fairly small territories 3 to 6 miles across, drifting up and down slopes and along ridgetops to access fresh forage. Often they'll remain on a single mountaintop for weeks on end, sometimes whole summers, moving only to reach better winter range. In spring they often travel miles to reach mineral licks. One famous lick is the Walton Goat Lick Overlook above the Flathead River along Highway 2 south of Glacier National Park.

For most of the year, billies live alone or with a few other males apart from females mostly because the ladies are so aggressive that the boys don't want to risk puncture. At the start of the rut in late October, billies cross high passes and deep snows to find isolated nanny groups. Otherwise, they remain in their small territories where they can be located again and again by persistent searching.

Forage Plants

A wide variety of grasses, sedges, forbs, and woody plants fill the goat's stomach. Grasses and forbs are most important in summer. Deep snows force them to browse on firs, aspen, dwarf birch, willows, and junipers, in addition to windblown clumps of cured grasses. Unlike deer or even pronghorns, goats do not make daily hikes to concentrated food sources, but find it scattered throughout their range. Essentially, they live in their kitchens.

Daily Patterns

There is nothing too predictable in daily patterns. With escape cover and forage available pretty much throughout their habitat, diurnal mountain goats are free to

A Rocky Mountain goat stands on a rocky promontory high above a dark canyon.

wander, eating and sleeping nearly anywhere. On some mountains they do walk downhill to reach rich forage, uphill to bed on ledges. In some dry ranges they trek regularly to isolated water holes, but usually snow patches provide all they need. Mineral licks are concentration points, but not on regular schedules. Feeding is most common at the start and end of each day with a brief foraging period at midday. The rest of their time is given to resting and digesting.

Rutting Behavior

Few people ever watch rutting goats because deep snows usually block access to their ranges before the November festivities get under way. It is quite a peculiar show. Because nannies are so belligerent, billies approach cautiously. They wander in after mid-October and stand a respectful distance from the gals, staring longingly, sometimes for hours, letting the nasty nannies get used to them. Over weeks they gradually move closer. At this same time, billies indulge in pit digging with their front hooves. They sit in these and kick dirt up on their chests and bellies. Then they urinate, roll, and rub in the dirt. Some authorities claim they also rub the pit edge plus nearby twigs and other plant stems with a leathery, black scent pad at the back base of their horns.

As hormonal changes within the nannies bring them closer to estrus in late November, they permit the males to approach closer. Fearful of getting skewered, the husky suitors crouch, even crawl toward the females, buzzing softly and flicking their tongues in a submissive posture designed to turn away wrath. Eventually a persistent billy is permitted access.

Contesting billies indulge in pit wallowing contests that sometimes escalate into broadside threat displays and even fights in which combatants circle one another, throwing roundhouse horn jabs at each other's flanks. More than a few such altercations have ended in deep punctures and death. Usually one goat is wise enough to retreat before blood is drawn. Often several males hang around a nanny band through November. Two-year old males seldom breed.

Trophy Dimensions

The official recording groups such as B&C tally horn length plus circumference at base and first, second, and third quarters up the horn. Spread counts for nothing. Minimum score for B&C is 47 inches, 50 inches for the all time record book. More than 20 Montana goats are listed in the 1993 B&C book. The highest scoring one is tied at 67th place. It was taken in Lewis & Clark County in 1981 and totaled 52⅝ inches. Its horns were 10⅞ inches long, and 5⅝ inches around their bases. Because goat horns are so difficult to estimate for trophy quality, most hunters are happy with a 9-inch horn with reasonable mass.

When assessing a goat, compare the horn length to the length of the goat's face from nose to base of horn, a distance of about 8 inches. Horns that look as long as the face are at least 9 inches long due to their backward curve. Horns that seem to touch together at their bases are heavier than thin, widely spaced horns. Horns with heavy bases that don't seem to taper on top should have excellent quarterly circumference scores.

Hunters often appreciate the mountain goat's pelt more than its small horn. Given the extremely limited numbers of goat hunting permits allotted annually, plus the 7-year wait period after a successful draw, many hunters preserve their unique trophies as full- or half-body mounts to show off the pantaloons and rich, lustrous pelage.

Hunting Tactics

Goat hunting is like sheep hunting. You hike high and glass likely habitat. Find a billy, size him up, and start stalking. Due to the broken nature of goat habitat, stalking close enough for a rifle shot is not too difficult. Bow range is tougher to achieve, but still not a major undertaking. Archers usually ease over a rimrock ledge to find their quarry as close as 10 feet. Just go slow and watch the breeze. And remember that

OFFICIAL SCORING SYSTEM FOR NORTH AMERICAN BIG GAME TROPHIES

Records of North American
Big Game

BOONE AND CROCKETT CLUB®

250 Station Drive
Missoula, MT 59801
(406)542-1888

Minimum Score: Awards All-time   ROCKY MOUNTAIN GOAT
                  47   50

SEE OTHER SIDE FOR INSTRUCTIONS		Column 1	Column 2	Column 3
A. Greatest Spread		Right Horn	Left Horn	Difference
B. Tip to Tip Spread				
C. Length of Horn				
D-1. Circumference of Base				
D-2. Circumference at First Quarter				
D-3. Circumference at Second Quarter				
D-4. Circumference at Third Quarter				
TOTALS				

ADD	Column 1		Exact Locality Where Killed:
	Column 2		Date Killed: Hunter:
	Subtotal		Owner: Telephone #:
SUBTRACT Column 3			Owner's Address:
			Guide's Name and Address:
			Remarks: (Mention Any Abnormalities or Unique Qualities)
FINAL SCORE			

I certify that I have measured this trophy on _____ 19 _____

at (address) _____ State _____

and that these measurements and data are, to the best of my knowledge and belief, made in
accordance with the instructions given.

Witness: _____ Signature: _____

B&C Official Measurer

I.D. Number

Reprinted courtesy of the Boone and Crockett Club, 250 Station Dr., Missoula, MT 59801, 406-542-1888

INSTRUCTIONS FOR MEASURING ROCKY MOUNTAIN GOAT

All measurements must be made with a 1/4-inch wide flexible steel tape to the nearest one-eighth of an inch. Wherever it is necessary to change direction of measurement, mark a control point and swing tape at this point. Enter fractional figures in eighths, without reduction. Official measurements cannot be taken until horns have air dried for at least 60 days after the animal was killed.

A.   Greatest Spread is measured between perpendiculars at a right angle to the center line of the skull.

B.   Tip to Tip spread is measured between tips of the horns.

C.   Length of Horn is measured from the lowest point in front over outer curve to a point in line with tip.

D-1.   Circumference of Base is measured at a right angle to axis of horn. **Do not** follow irregular edge of horn; the line of measurement must be entirely on horn material.

D-2-3-4. Divide measurement C of longer horn by four. Starting at base, mark **both** horns at these quarters (even though the other horn is shorter) and measure circumferences at these marks, with measurements taken at right angles to horn axis.

FAIR CHASE STATEMENT FOR ALL HUNTER-TAKEN TROPHIES

FAIR CHASE, as defined by the Boone and Crockett Club®, is the ethical, sportsmanlike and lawful pursuit and taking of any free-ranging wild game animal in a manner that does not give the hunter an improper or unfair advantage over such game animals.
Use of any of the following methods in the taking of game shall be deemed **UNFAIR CHASE** and unsportsmanlike:

I.   Spotting or herding game from the air, followed by landing in its vicinity for the purpose of pursuit and shooting;

II.   Herding, pursuing, or shooting game from any motorboat or motor vehicle;

III.   Use of electronic devices for attracting, locating, or observing game, or for guiding the hunter to such game;

IV.   Hunting game confined by artificial barriers, including escape-proof fenced enclosures, or hunting game transplanted for the purpose of commercial shooting;

V.   Taking of game in a manner not in full compliance with the game laws or regulations of the federal government or of any state, province, territory, or tribal council on reservations or tribal lands;

VI.   Or as may otherwise be deemed unfair or unsportsmanlike by the Executive Committee of the Boone and Crockett Club.

I certify that the trophy scored on this chart was taken in **FAIR CHASE** as defined above by the Boone and Crockett Club. In signing this statement, I understand that if the information provided on this entry is found to be misrepresented or fraudulent in any respect, it will not be accepted into the Awards Program and all of my prior entries are subject to deletion from future editions of *Records of North American Big Game* and future entries may not be accepted.

Date: _____ Signature of Hunter:_____
                                        (Signature must be witnessed by an Official Measurer or
                                        a Notary Public.)

Date: _____ Signature of Notary or Official Measurer:_____

Reprinted courtesy of the Boone and Crockett Club, 250 Station Dr., Missoula, MT 59801, 406-542-1888

Shot Placement:
Top: Quartering to Shooter
Aim for the off-side shoulder. Draw an imaginary line from your rifle or bow to that far-side shoulder, or slightly behind it if you don't want to damage any meat. Aim accordingly, which in this case would be in front of the near-side shoulder.

Below: Tail/Rump shot.
Take this shot only if using a powerful cartridge and a heavy, premium bullet. Aim for the base of the tail. The shot should break several vertebrae and paralyze the animal; rush in for a finishing shot. If it hits to the left or right, it should break the pelvis or one of the legs. Be aware that these types of shots will destroy a lot of meat.

whenever shooting at extreme up and down angles, bullets always strike higher than normal. Generally you needn't worry about this effect until the angle becomes greater than 30 degrees and the distance more than 150 yards. To be safe, never aim off the hair for your first shot. Settle the sight on the lower brisket. Only if the first shot misses should you compensate and hold lower. It helps to have a spotter to call your shots.

You should be in excellent shape for goat hunting and comfortable working on steep slopes, cliffs, and ledges above long drops. Wear lug sole boots with solid ankle support and stiff soles for lateral support. Carry about 20 feet of rope able to hoist 300 pounds, just in case. You might need it to haul up a pack, rifle, or goat.

A happy hunter packs out his mountain goat pelt.

Recommendations for Loads and Rifle Cartridges

Remember the cartridges recommended for mule deer? They're perfect for sheep and goats, too. But because serious mountain hunters appreciate minimum weight, the 7mm and .30 magnums become a bit heavy. Again, you can't beat the .270 Win. and .280 Rem. cartridges. For even more weight savings with no loss in velocity, try the short, fat .284 Win. cartridge and 140-grain bullets. This cartridge cycles through short action lengths, thus saving a few ounces of weight while giving you a shorter, quicker bolt throw. While the .243 cartridges are acceptable, they're a bit on the light side for these stocky trophy animals. You want to anchor them quickly.

Practicing Mountain Goats

I have yet to draw a Montana mountain goat hunting license, but I've already hunted Montana mountain goats. You can, too.

The way I figure, should I ever get a tag, I don't want to waste it on ignorance. One doesn't learn where animals live, how they behave, and how to spot them by sitting home staring at the mailbox. So I hunt them with binocular and camera.

Ideally, one should search for goats, sheep, and moose where one hopes to someday hunt them. This way you learn the terrain, discover the trails, bedding sites, and honey holes. If you want to observe animal behavior or get close-up pictures, however, you're better off visiting the National Parks, and Glacier is the perfect place for watching mountain goats.

Glacier's goats are high on the spine of the Rockies. In a normal year, the only road leading to the top, the Going-to-the-Sun highway, is snowbound by late September. Mountain goats don't rut until November. The options are to visit in early September, ski to the crest (which requires winter camping skills, among others), or await a drought. I took advantage of a drought year in the late 1980s. The highway was open into November. Tim Christie and I drove to the Park on a Friday night, slept in the camper and began hiking north along the Highline Trail at dawn. By midmorning we were miles from the road and surrounded by white goats.

With nannies and billies together, it was easy to see the differences in their appearance and behavior. The nannies were nearly pristine white, the billies yellow. In addition, the males were stained brown from pawing and rolling in rutting pits. We noticed the "kinked" tips of the nannies' horns, and the smooth, even curve of the billies'. While females fed placidly, billies roamed nervously, checking one female after another, lip curling, hiking up and down the rocky slopes. Tim and I were both surprised at how difficult the white goats were to pick out through binoculars from a distance. White boulders and even the glare from dark rocks confused the issue.

"I might still have trouble separating a 10-inch billy from a 9-incher," I said as we hiked back after a successful day of exposing film, "but I won't have any trouble telling which ones are nannies."

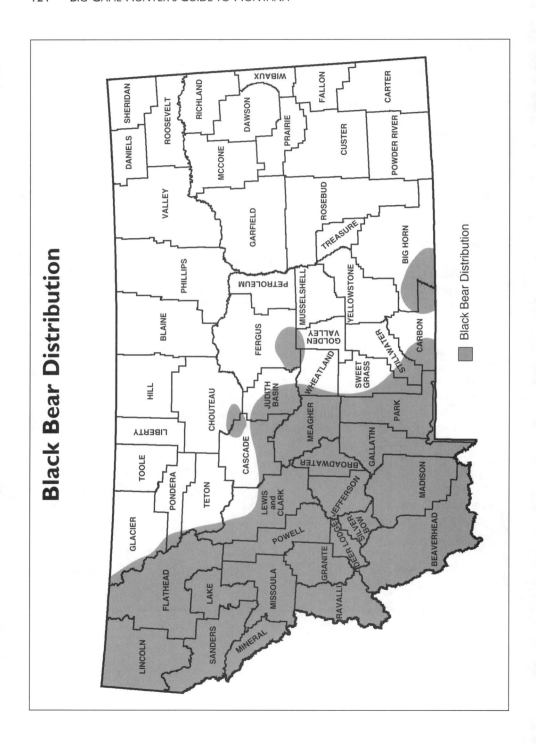

Black Bear Distribution

Black Bear

Ursus americanus

Richly furred, heavily muscled, armed with claw and fang, the elusive black bear is as much man's predator as his prey. Though rarely as aggressive as the grizzly, black bears still inspire us to whistle in the dark and glance over our shoulders—even as we track them.

Fascinating Facts

- Though normally shy and reclusive, black bears have mauled and killed more humans than have grizzly bears simply because there are so many more of them in settled areas of North America.
- Black bears do not truly hibernate, but for as long as six months fall into a deep sleep from which they can be roused. During this period, they do not eat, drink, defecate, or urinate, but they do burn up to 4,000 fat calories per day.
- Cubs normally stay with their mother for 1½ to 2½ years, but cubs as young as six months and as small as 18 pounds can survive on their own.
- Bears do not stand on their hind legs to charge or as prelude to a charge, but to better see or smell something. A charging bear lays its ears back and runs on all fours as fast as 30 mph.
- Mature males kill and eat cubs. In some areas they are their own worst predator. Ecological benefits of this behavior could be to decrease competition for food or to induce estrus in the female so the male who killed the cubs can breed her and pass on his genes. Research has shown that a black bear population can increase in areas where human hunters shoot only old male bears.

Local Names

Blackie, bear, Yogi, Boo Boo (cubs)

Size

Black bears over 700 pounds have been shot in Eastern states. Typically, Montana males stretch to 5½ feet, stand 40 inches at the shoulder, and weigh 170 to 300 pounds. Females average 20 percent smaller than males, measuring 4½ to 5 feet from nose to tail, standing 24 to 34 inches high, and weighing 130 to 180 pounds. First-year cubs are half the size of mature females and second-year cubs nearly adult size.

Coat and Color

Most hunters know that black bears may also be brown, blonde, or a combination of tones. In Montana, 50 percent of hunter-killed black bears have jet black, glossy hair; 30 percent are brown; and 20 percent light brown to blonde. Some have dark brown legs, blonde sides, and dark heads, making them look much like a grizzly bear.

Early spring found this black bear (brown color phase) browsing in a meadow containing dandelions, a favorite of bears.

Grizzlies, however, have distinctive shoulder humps and slightly dished faces compared to the almost Roman-nose profile of a black bear. Since grizzlies are strictly protected, don't shoot any bear you can't positively identify. Most black bears have brown snouts and varying amounts of white on the chest. Hairs vary from coarse to silky and can be several inches long. Pelts are thick and rich in late autumn and early spring.

Voice and Communication

Bears bawl and roar when fighting, "woof" or cough when false-charging, and pop their teeth when agitated, but generally are silent. Cubs bawl and cry when frightened or separated from their dams. And yes, true to legend, dying bears sometimes give a heart-rending death moan.

Most actual communication among individual bears is visual and olfactory. Territorial males reach up and break off small trees along their trails and reach as high as they can to claw and bite large trunks. This has been construed by humans to be a visual marker saying, in effect, "I've been here, and I'm this big, so don't mess with me." Whether that is accurate only the bears know for sure. Males also straddle small trees and walk them down, perhaps depositing scent onto them from their belly hairs or anus. Boars and sows regularly rub their necks, backs, and heads on trees they claw and break off, possibly another form of visual and olfactory marking.

Senses

An old bit of Native American wisdom holds that if a butterfly flits through the forest, the whitetail sees it, the moose hears it, and the bear smells it. Indeed, a black bear's sense of smell is highly acute, enabling it to follow its nose to berries, honey, and of course, garbage from long distances. It depends very little upon its vision, but hears quite well and often slips away unseen after it hears hunters. As long as hunters keep the breeze in their faces, step lightly, and freeze when their quarry looks up, they can stalk within bow range of black bears.

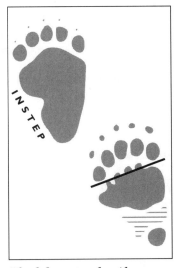

Tracks and Sign

The soft pads of black bears do not leave tracks as regularly as do the hooves of deer. You'll spot the human-like hind footprints and wide, but short, front pads most often in mud, sand, silt and snow, rarely on packed trails. Width of the front heel pad of a big bear is 5 inches, 3½ to 4½ inches on younger animals. Walking black bears stride about one foot and generally put down their rear feet slightly ahead of their front feet, sometimes directly atop them. Five toes show ahead of the pads, but the smallest, innermost toe sometimes doesn't register. Claw marks usually show 1 to 1½ inches in front of the toes of the front feet. Grizzly tracks are similar but slightly bigger. The longer grizzly claws project farther ahead of the toes —usually 1¾ inches or more. You can generally lay a straight edge along the back rim of a grizzly's front toe prints and intersect the back edge of all of them. A black bear's toes are laid out in more of an arc.

A running black bear puts its hind feet well ahead of its front and clears 3 feet between clusters of tracks.

Bear droppings are either cylindrical, like dog scat, or loose masses. The larger the pile and the diameter, the bigger the bear. Seeds, grass stems, hair, and the like indicate what the bruin has been eating.

*Black bear tracks. Above, right **rear** foot, approx. 7" long by 3½" wide; below, **front** foot, approx. 4½" from toes to rear of palm print and 3¾" wide. Note: **the rear foot registers ahead of the front.** The toes of the front foot should arc forward from a line drawn from big toe to little toe (they will form a straight line on grizzlies). The rear foot will have a wedge in the instep (a grizzly's rear foot shows no instep).*

Foraging bears regularly flip over boulders, logs, and even cow chips to uncover insects and grubs. They'll also rip open rotting stumps and logs to extract insect larvae.

Watch for clawed, chewed, and broken trees during the breeding season and the clawed trunks of large "marker" trees that bears supposedly stand up to scratch as if to indicate their size to other bears.

Reproduction and Young

Bears mate from May through July, the females delaying implantation of the fertilized eggs in the uterus until late fall. A sow in poor condition will re-absorb the eggs. One to four embryos grow for only 10 weeks before the nearly naked, blind, 8-ounce cubs are born in the January or February den. They suckle the sleeping female until she emerges from the winter den in May or June. By then, they weigh about 5 pounds and are strong enough to follow her as she roams and forages. Because sows refuse to breed with males while they still have cubs, males attempt to kill and eat every cub they come across. Sows protect their young, but not as ferociously as do grizzly sows, preferring instead to "woof" them up trees when danger threatens. Researchers who have captured hundreds of cubs report that the protective females false charge, but almost never actually touch a human. Yearling cubs weigh about 55 pounds and again hibernate with their mothers, but the maternal unit breaks up the next spring or fall and the 2-year-olds go their own ways, often getting into trouble around farms and towns while establishing home ranges and learning survival techniques.

Black bears in productive, Eastern habitats breed at 3 years of age, but in Montana breeding doesn't usually begin until females are 4½ to 6½ years old. They do not successfully rear cubs until age 6 or 7. Commonly they breed only every third or fourth year. Males, while capable of breeding successfully at 2 or 3, don't usually get the chance until 5 or 6, due to competition from older, stronger boars.

Habitat

About 45 percent of Montana is considered occupied black bear habitat. They live in dry to wet forests on both sides of the continental divide, most abundantly in the wetter northwest counties, with densities declining to the south and east as average annual moisture declines. Because throughout their history they've needed to climb trees to escape grizzlies, they don't venture too far into the eastern prairies, sticking to wooded river bottoms when they do. A combination of dense forests of varying ages, brush, and small meadows up to the alpine zone suits them fine. Grizzlies, because they are bigger, stronger, and more aggressive, do better in open country with less escape cover. There are few blacks in areas with lots of grizzlies. Conversely, dense populations of mature black bears can suppress expansion of grizzlies into their territories by chasing out small, subadult grizzlies trying to move in.

Home Range

Instead of defending specific geographic territories, black bears move in response to food. As seen around garbage dumps, they'll congregate and tolerate one another

A black bear looks out cautiously from the edge of a forest.

to varying degrees. Thus, home ranges overlap and fluctuate seasonally and from year to year. Boars may roam territories from 50 to 225 square miles, females 10 to 137 square miles. Densities in productive, wet northwest forests have been estimated as high as .56 per square mile. They are much lower in dry forests with less forage.

Forage

Like humans and raccoons, black bears are omnivorous. They are also more vegetarian than most folks assume or their teeth suggest. While they use their gripping claws and wolf-like canines to kill ground squirrels, fawns, elk calves, and sometimes even adult elk, mostly they consume vast quantities of grass, sedges, forbs, and berries. Carrion and insects are also on the menu. Apparently bee stings don't bother them, because they've been found with up to 2 quarts of bees in their stomachs. Montana forage plants include dandelion, horsetail, cow parsnip, sweetvetch, huckleberry, gooseberry, serviceberry, mountain ash, and hawthorn. Of course, human garbage, honey, orchard fruits, and some grain crops are relished. Spring bears concentrate on fresh greens and winter-killed carrion. In early summer, in some areas, they prey heavily on elk calves. In fall, they concentrate on berries, insects, and any meat they can find, including the leavings from human hunters' kills.

Daily Patterns

Black bears are most active at night, but where they feel safe they feed and roam at all hours. Old boars are first to leave their dens in late March through early April. Next up are subadult males, then adult females without cubs, then adult females with cubs, and finally subadult females. They spend a week or more near the den, relatively inactive, eating and drinking little as their metabolism changes from fat metabolism back to protein metabolism. Mature males begin prowling their territories below the snow line, marking trees and feeding on new vegetation. Sows with cubs seek safe, often dense forest cover well away from males. Young males seek to establish their own home ranges while keeping out of the way of bigger males.

As snow melts, bears follow tender, new growth up mountainsides, searching avalanche chutes for carcasses, prowling meadows, brushy burns, or logged areas for browse and berries. Roadsides, because they are open to sunlight and extra runoff rainwater, are popular feeding sites as well as easy travel lanes.

Bears generally forage heavily at dawn and dusk, and rest in shade during the heat of the day. They often remain near a patch of vegetation, berries, or a large carcass for several days. When food is scarce they range widely. By late summer, they are often high up mountains and on wet, north-facing slopes or in valleys near human-made food sources. During droughts, they wander into ranches and towns looking for food. In dry areas they return to isolated watering holes daily.

Rutting Behavior

Bears have few of the dramatic rutting behaviors of horned and antlered game. Old boars walk their territories in spring, breaking, biting, clawing, and marking trees while sniffing for ripe females. When they find one, they follow her until she is ready to mate. Then they are off for the next conquest. Two males of equal stature may meet over a receptive female, and the fur will fly until one flees or is killed.

Trophy Dimensions

Bears are officially scored by measuring their bare skulls (minus the lower jaw) front to back and side to side at their widest points and adding the dimensions. The world record B&C black bear scores 23¹⁰⁄₁₆ inches and was found dead in Utah in 1975. Montana blackies are quite a bit smaller than this. The largest ever registered with B&C measures 21³⁄₁₆ inches. It came out of Madison County in 1974 and is tied for 203rd place with 32 others. Only one other Montana bear is in the book!

Some hunters prefer to judge trophy status by weight, but hauling whole bears out of rugged, backcountry terrain is tough. Others prefer to measure hides from one

<u>OFFICIAL SCORING SYSTEM FOR NORTH AMERICAN BIG GAME TROPHIES</u>

Records of North American
Big Game

BOONE AND CROCKETT CLUB®

250 Station Drive
Missoula, MT 59801
(406) 542-1888

Minimum Score:	Awards	All-time
Alaska brown	26	28
black bear	20	21
grizzly	23	24
polar	27	27

BEAR

Kind of Bear: _____

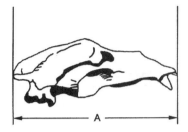
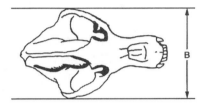

SEE OTHER SIDE FOR INSTRUCTIONS	Measurements
A. Greatest Length Without Lower Jaw	
B. Greatest Width	
FINAL SCORE	

Exact Locality Where Killed:

Date Killed: _____ Hunter: _____

Owner: _____ Telephone #: _____

Owner's Address:

Guide's Name and Address:

Remarks: (Mention Any Abnormalities or Unique Qualities)

I certify that I have measured this trophy on _____ 19_____

at (address) _____ City _____ State _____
and that these measurements and data are, to the best of my knowledge and belief, made in
accordance with the instructions given.

Witness: _____ Signature: _____

B&C Official Measurer

I.D. Number

Reprinted courtesy of the Boone and Crockett Club, 250 Station Dr., Missoula, MT 59801, 406-542-1888

INSTRUCTIONS FOR MEASURING BEAR

Measurements are taken with calipers or by using parallel perpendiculars, to the nearest **one-sixteenth** of an inch, without reduction of fractions. Official measurements cannot be taken until the skull has air dried for at least 60 days after the animal was killed. All adhering flesh, membrane and cartilage must be completely removed **before** official measurements are taken.

A. Greatest Length is measured between perpendiculars parallel to the long axis of the skull, without the lower jaw and excluding malformations.

B. Greatest Width is measured between perpendiculars at right angles to the long axis.

FAIR CHASE STATEMENT FOR ALL HUNTER-TAKEN TROPHIES

FAIR CHASE, as defined by the Boone and Crockett Club®, is the ethical, sportsmanlike and lawful pursuit and taking of any free-ranging wild game animal in a manner that does not give the hunter an improper or unfair advantage over such game animals.
Use of any of the following methods in the taking of game shall be deemed **UNFAIR CHASE** and unsportsmanlike:

   I.   Spotting or herding game from the air, followed by landing in its vicinity for the purpose of pursuit and shooting;

   II. Herding, pursuing, or shooting game from any motorboat or motor vehicle;

   III. Use of electronic devices for attracting, locating, or observing game, or for guiding the hunter to such game;

   IV. Hunting game confined by artificial barriers, including escape-proof fenced enclosures, or hunting game transplanted for the purpose of commercial shooting;

   V.   Taking of game in a manner not in full compliance with the game laws or regulations of the federal government or of any state, province, territory, or tribal council on reservations or tribal lands;

   VI. Or as may otherwise be deemed unfair or unsportsmanlike by the Executive Committee of the Boone and Crockett Club.

Were dogs used in conjunction with the pursuit and harvest of this animal?

Yes _____   No _____

If the answer to the above question is yes, answer the following statements:

1. I was present on the hunt at the times the dogs were released to pursue this animal.
   True _____ **False** _____
2. If electronic collars were attached to any of the dogs, receivers were not used to harvest this animal. **True** _____ **False** _____

I certify that the trophy scored on this chart was taken in **FAIR CHASE** as defined above by the Boone and Crockett Club. In signing this statement, I understand that if the information provided on this entry is found to be misrepresented or fraudulent in any respect, it will not be accepted into the Awards Program and all of my prior entries are subject to deletion from future editions of *Records of North American Big Game* and future entries may not be accepted.

Date: _____   Signature of Hunter:_____
                                  (Signature must be witnessed by an Official Measurer or
                                  a Notary Public.)

Date: _____   Signature of Notary or Official Measurer:_____

Reprinted courtesy of the Boone and Crockett Club, 250 Station Dr., Missoula, MT 59801, 406-542-1888

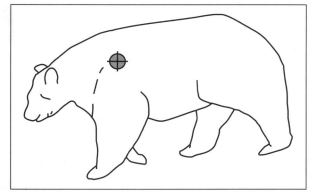

Shot Placement:
Broadside shot.
Unlike ungulates, the heart and lungs are directly between the shoulders. Aim high on the shoulder. This should hit the scapular or spine and drop the bear instantaneously.

Alternatively, a front-on chest shot presents a good target of the heart/lung area.

front paw across to the other or from nose to tail or even from left front paw to right rear paw, but these measurements are inconsistent since hides can be stretched. A more consistent approach might be to tape the unskinned bear from nose to tip of tail plus around its middle at the greatest diameter. For Boone & Crockett, Pope & Young, and SCI books, however, only the skull dimensions count. Montana bear hunters should probably concentrate on finding a large-bodied male with a pretty pelt.

Hunting Tactics

Neither dog pursuit nor baiting is allowed in Montana, so the most popular hunting tactic is glassing meadows for feeding bears, then stalking within range for a clean shot. In open, dry forests this is quite productive. Sit high and carefully glass meadows and forest road edges. Watch young Douglas fir plantations. Spring bears like to feed on the inner bark of these trees. Of course, if you discover sign of a bear feeding on a naturally killed carcass, you may watch it. This is not considered baiting. You may also watch deer and elk gut piles in fall.

Another way to locate spring bears is to walk or drive trails in dense forests, watching edges for tracks, fresh scat, and broken trees. These in abundance indicate the daily stomping grounds of a mature boar. With the wind in your face, slowly and quietly walk these roads early and late each day, watching for the bear. You might also erect a stand overlooking one of these trails, especially a fork or crossing of two trails.

In autumn, glass and still-hunt high in the huckleberry patches and sub-alpine ridges as well as on north-facing slopes. In dry regions, check ponds for fresh tracks.

Recommendations for Loads and Rifle Cartridges

Our smallest native bear isn't as tough as many would like to believe. Punch a hole through his chest with a 6mm Rem., and he'll expire quickly. To anchor the bear on the spot, aim for the scapular, high on the shoulder. But you want to use a premium bullet for the job, not some thin-skinned slug that will tear apart on impact and fail to penetrate. Rather than take chances, stick to the .270 Win. and up. Really, you can't beat the .30–06 with 180-grain slugs. If you anticipate long, cross canyon shots, go with the 7mm and .30 caliber magnums.

Bear Attack

My brother, Bob, and our friend, Tom Lowin, and I were hunting the Gravelly Range one year, camped out in an old miner's shack, committed for the duration. We were still that age when we were dumb enough to get into trouble but strong enough to get out of it. We'd seen a wide, dark, heavily beamed muley buck at the top of the range two days before the season opened and were determined to see him again. We'd seen elk on the opener, including a decent five-point other hunters had stirred up and pushed through a saddle. There were enough fresh bear droppings to keep us alert for anything big and black.

Despite the good portents, by mid-November we were meatless. Snow had fallen on opening day, partially melted, frozen. You couldn't step without crunching. We tried glassing grassy parks at dawn and dusk, following spoor into dark, dog-hair timber, pushing the heads of little canyons. We loaded packs and hunted from spike camps four days running, then returned to our little cabin for a real meal and cook-stove fire.

A mountain stream cascaded past the cabin door, less than ten yards away, convenient for scooping kitchen water. Tom was out filling a bucket after supper one star-shot night when, to our horror, he flew back in with a whoosh, slamming the pine plank door closed almost faster than he'd shoved it open. "Bear!"

Bob pulled his .357 Magnum from its holster hanging beside his bunk. I grabbed my .270 Winchester and bolted home a round. Tom barred the door. We looked at one another. "Are you sure?" we asked.

"Yeah. Maybe. I don't know. It's dark out there."

"Well, what happened? Did you see it?"

"I couldn't see nothin'. But I heard it. In the creek. Something big splashing."

"It was probably just a trout."

"No way. I mean big. Heavy. Splashing and running at me. Right past me."

"Shut up for a minute. Maybe we can hear it." We listened. The steady murmuring of the creek. The pop of the stove. We wouldn't hear the shuffling of a bear unless it decided to come through that flimsy old door.

"Get the flashlight. Now open the door." Tom's eyes widened. I stood back by my bunk and leveled the .270. Bob backed me up from the other corner of the room with his revolver. "Just swing it open and stay behind it. If he comes in we'll blast him." The door opened. Cold came in.

"Maybe he's waiting out there."

We never found a sign of that bear, but the next day we saw a beaver and figured Tom had startled it as it swam down the creek. Then, in standard beaver fashion, it dived and slapped the water with its tail. Unfortunately, the creek was so shallow that it couldn't get under, so it slapped and tried to dive again and again, right past poor Tom who wishes now it really had been a bear.

Mountain Lion Distribution

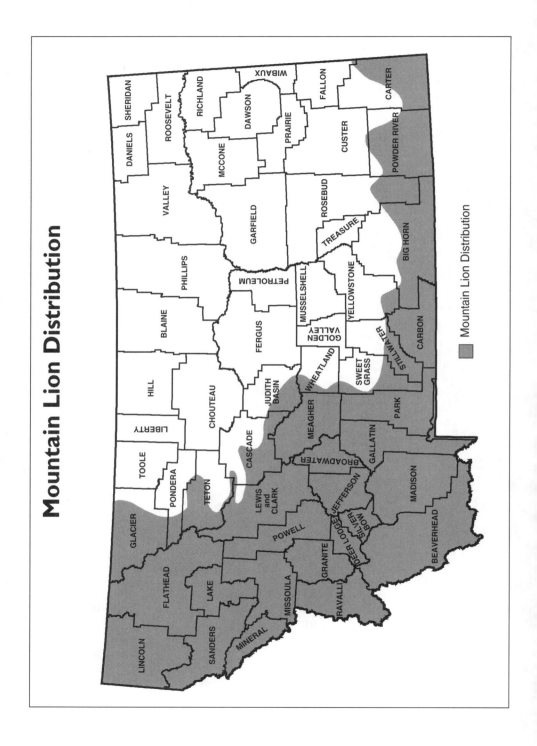

Mountain Lion Distribution

Mountain Lion

Felis concolor

Once considered vermin to be shot on sight, America's biggest wild cat has since been elevated to its richly deserved status as trophy big game animal. Shy, elusive and quiet as smoke, lions are the essence of stealth and mystery in the wilderness.

Fascinating Facts

- Cougars are the only wild cats that routinely kill prey much larger than themselves–often 5 times heavier, sometimes 8 times heavier. Lions weighing less than 120 pounds have been documented killing and dragging away 800-pound steers.
- More people have been attacked by mountain lions in North America during the past 20 years than the previous 80.
- Hunters have treed mountain lions by following their fresh tracks while barking like a dog.
- The legal take of Montana mountain lions was 51 during the 1971–72 season, 566 during the 1994–95 season.
- In 1962, the State of Montana paid $3,100 in lion bounties. It collected $137,320 in license fees during 1994.
- Wolf packs along the North Fork Flathead River have been documented killing several mountain lions during the last decade.
- Cougars rarely get rabies, but more than 60 percent of those in Montana carry trichinosis. Their flesh must be thoroughly cooked to be safe for eating.

Local Names
Lion, cougar, puma, panther, painter, cat

Size
Males weigh 125 to 250 pounds, stretch to 9 feet from nose to tail tip, and stand 3 feet at the shoulder. The heaviest ever documented weighed 275 pounds field dressed. Females vary from 75 to 150 pounds, stand just under 3 feet, and measure 6 to 7 feet.

Coat and Color
Kittens are spotted, but adults are uniformly pale brown-yellow or tawny with black tipped tail, black spots on either side of muzzle, and black on the backsides of ears. The muzzle front, inner ear hairs, chest, and inside rear legs are pale tawny to white. The coat is dense, uniformly short-haired, and sleek.

A mountain lion snarls while sitting on a rock above the snow.

Voice and Communication

Mountain lions are mostly silent. Kittens mew, adults whistle, chirp, purr, growl, snarl when angry, and wail and scream like oversized house cats when mating. Males and females claw trees and scrape up small piles of debris over dung and urine to mark territories. Males also back up to trees and rocks to squirt urine cat-style and scent mark their territories.

Senses

Cougars have excellent eyesight and hearing, but don't depend on their noses nearly to the degree wolves, bears, or even deer do. They are primarily sight hunters, patiently and cautiously waiting and watching before stalking in for the kill or slinking away to escape danger.

Tracks and Sign

The soft-footed, lightweight mountain lion doesn't lay tracks willy nilly across the countryside the way deer do. Unless ground is soft or snow covered, most prints never show. Retractable claws don't even contribute a few scuff marks. When you do find a track, it is distinctive, showing four toes above a rounded triangular pad with three lobes at the rear edge, one indentation at the middle front. These lobes and indentations only show in a good, detailed print, but even blurred prints can be identified by their size, usually 3 inches front to back and 3 to 4 inches side to side. The lynx track can be nearly as big, but usually doesn't show the lobed pad; besides, lynx are extremely rare in Montana.

Mountain lion tracks. Above, front, 3" long and 3½" wide; below, rear, 3" long and 3" wide.

A walking lion strides 12 to 16 inches and trots with about 24 inches between prints. The long tail sometimes drags in deep snow.

Lion scat looks much like dog droppings, often with long, tapering ends and much hair in them. They are frequently, but not always, covered in typical cat fashion.

Reproduction and Young

Since cougars do not depend on seasonally available vegetation to rear their kittens, they are free to reproduce at any time, and they do; however, in Montana the peak birthing period is summer. After being kicked out of mama's care at 18 months of age, youngsters wander until they find an unclaimed territory before breeding, generally between 20 and 36 months of age. Males are promiscuous and couple with all receptive females they discover within their vast territories. When a male finds a receptive female he travels with her for several days to two weeks. They mate many times during that period, accompanied with considerable howling and screeching. After about 92 days, 1 to 6 kittens (usually 2 to 4) are born under a ledge, root mass, in a cave, or some other sheltered spot. Females may leave for several days, returning after they make a kill.

Kittens begin predator-play at 10 days of age and have been documented killing deer while as young as 6 months. Normally, however, they must practice stalking and killing until 15 months old before becoming self-supporting. They weigh about 12 pounds and are 3 months old when weaned. After that, they follow their dam and eat what she kills, learning as they watch. Most mother-young separation occurs in spring and summer when small game is abundant. This increases the young cats' chances for catching enough to eat while honing hunting skills. Littermates often travel together during their first winter without mama and are prone to attack humans, livestock, and other taboo prey until they "learn the ropes." Young lions must travel until they find an unclaimed territory. Territorial males will permit new females to set up home ranges within their terrain, but not new males. This often forces them out of saturated wilderness habitats and into human-populated areas.

Habitat

Historically, cougars lived from coast to coast and from central Canada to nearly the tip of South America, so it is not surprising that they adapt to a wide variety of habitats. In Montana, this includes everything from wet forests in the northwest to brushy draws, river bottoms, and rocky buttes in the eastern plains. Lions are currently found in 46 of 56 Montana counties. As long as prey (most especially mule deer and whitetails, but also bighorn sheep, elk, rabbits, and other small game) is abundant and cover is available for stalking, hiding, and rearing young, mountain lions will thrive. We used to think these cats required vast wilderness to survive, but since becoming game animals with regulated harvest, they've increased in numbers and now live around ranches, farms, and even suburbs.

Home Range

Grazing animals can share abundant forage and live in herds. Mountain lions must guard a limited supply of prey species from other lions; thus, they are highly territorial, especially the males who, in addition to protecting their food, seek to control as many females as possible. They accomplish this by roaming as many as 25 miles per night in territories from 30 to 350 square miles. These ranges overlap territories of several females, which roam much smaller areas, usually 20 to 50 square miles in Montana. These territories are not static but, based on mutual avoidance, fluctuate seasonally. When one male smells or sees sign of another, he tends to shift away from that area, thus avoiding direct confrontation. It is uncommon, though not unusual, for these cats to meet and fight to the death. Old males will kill and eat juveniles and kittens. Home ranges shrink when prey is abundant or concentrated, such as on winter range, and expand when prey is scarce or widespread, such as on summer range.

Lions are more abundant in mountainous western Montana than in eastern counties.

Prey Species

Like most mammalian predators, cougars kill and eat whatever they have to or can most easily capture, but they are particularly adapted to take mule deer and whitetails. Studies in western states have proven that deer make up 64- to 77-percent of the mountain lion's diet. Old deer and bucks appear most vulnerable. Biologists in Montana calculate that cougars kill on average one deer or elk every 15 to 19 days in summer, every 6 to 9 days in winter. Elk are less often taken, but a big lion can leap on a mature, 6-point bull elk, sink its claws into its nose, wrench the head back and break the animal's neck. They also kill bighorn sheep, domestic sheep, cattle, horses, porcupines, coyotes, mice, beavers, and anything else they can lay their claws on.

Daily Patterns

Because of their shifting prey base, cougars may be the least predictable of all big game animals. They wander freely through their home ranges unless camped near a

A mountain lion lies on rocks atop a snowy ridge in the Rocky Mountains.

kill (which they'll usually revisit until they eat it or it's stolen by scavengers). They hunt mostly at night, but sometimes by day. Serious students and dedicated lion trackers can learn a specific cat's route through its territory and predict when it will return to a general area (often several days to a week), but the casual hunter has no clue. This is why following scenting hounds is the only dependable hunting tactic.

Rutting Behavior

Because mountain lions have no seasonal mating period, they exhibit virtually no unique rutting behavior. Males patrol and scent mark their home ranges, remaining alert for the sight or scent of females nearing estrus. Then the pair hunt and rest together for up to two weeks, mating frequently and noisily.

Trophy Dimensions

Like bears, cougars are scored based on length and width of skull. The world's record B&C cat totaled 16$\frac{4}{16}$ inches and was taken near Tatlayoka Lake in British

Atop a rocky ridge, this mountain lion seems curious about something below.

Columbia in 1979. Montana's biggest B&C registered cougar scored $15^{11}/_{16}$ and was taken near Darby in 1953. It ranks 10th in an eight-way tie.

Because skull size is difficult to appreciate, most hunters consider length and weight to be important measures. A male stretching 8 feet or more is considered big, a 9-footer huge. Anything over 200 pounds is also a big cat. Most B&C records from Montana were taken in west central counties like Missoula, Mineral, and Lewis and Clark.

Hunting Tactics

As already mentioned, turning scenting hounds onto a cat track is the only reliable method of seeing one. Hunters ride horses, trucks, or snow machines along roads and trails while scanning for tracks. The dogs lope alongside or ride in boxes with their sharp noses protruding and sniffing. Good hounds will sound off when they catch a whiff of cat. Once a trail is discovered, hunters determine which way the cat was headed, how recently it passed, and what their chances are of catching it. If

OFFICIAL SCORING SYSTEM FOR NORTH AMERICAN BIG GAME TROPHIES

Records of North American
Big Game

BOONE AND CROCKETT CLUB®

250 Station Drive
Missoula, MT 59801
(406) 542-1888

COUGAR AND JAGUAR

Kind of Cat: _____

Minimum Score:	Awards	All-time
cougar	14-8/16	15
jaguar	14-8/16	14-8/16

SEE OTHER SIDE FOR INSTRUCTIONS	Measurements
A. Greatest Length Without Lower Jaw	
B. Greatest Width	
FINAL SCORE	

Exact Locality Where Killed: _____

Date Killed: _____ Hunter: _____

Owner: _____ Telephone #: _____

Owner's Address: _____

Guide's Name and Address: _____

Remarks: (Mention Any Abnormalities or Unique Qualities)

I certify that I have measured this trophy on _____ 19_____

at (address) _____ City _____ State _____
and that these measurements and data are, to the best of my knowledge and belief, made in
accordance with the instructions given.

Witness: _____ Signature: _____

B&C Official Measurer

I.D. Number

Reprinted courtesy of the Boone and Crockett Club, 250 Station Dr., Missoula, MT 59801, 406-542-1888

INSTRUCTIONS FOR MEASURING COUGAR AND JAGUAR

Measurements are taken with calipers or by using parallel perpendiculars, to the nearest **one-sixteenth** of an inch, without reduction of fractions. Official measurements cannot be taken until the skull has air dried for at least 60 days after the animal was killed. All adhering flesh, membrane and cartilage must be completely removed **before** official measurements are taken.

A. Greatest Length is measured between perpendiculars parallel to the long axis of the skull, without the lower jaw and excluding malformations.

B. Greatest Width is measured between perpendiculars at right angles to the long axis.

FAIR CHASE STATEMENT FOR ALL HUNTER-TAKEN TROPHIES

FAIR CHASE, as defined by the Boone and Crockett Club®, is the ethical, sportsmanlike and lawful pursuit and taking of any free-ranging wild game animal in a manner that does not give the hunter an improper or unfair advantage over such game animals. Use of any of the following methods in the taking of game shall be deemed **UNFAIR CHASE** and unsportsmanlike:

   I.   Spotting or herding game from the air, followed by landing in its vicinity for the purpose of pursuit and shooting;

   II. Herding, pursuing, or shooting game from any motorboat or motor vehicle;

   III. Use of electronic devices for attracting, locating, or observing game, or for guiding the hunter to such game;

   IV. Hunting game confined by artificial barriers, including escape-proof fenced enclosures, or hunting game transplanted for the purpose of commercial shooting;

   V.   Taking of game in a manner not in full compliance with the game laws or regulations of the federal government or of any state, province, territory, or tribal council on reservations or tribal lands;

   VI. Or as may otherwise be deemed unfair or unsportsmanlike by the Executive Committee of the Boone and Crockett Club.

Were dogs used in conjunction with the pursuit and harvest of this animal?

                    Yes _____   No _____

If the answer to the above question is yes, answer the following statements:

   1. I was present on the hunt at the times the dogs were released to pursue this animal.
      True _____   **False** _____
   2. If electronic collars were attached to any of the dogs, receivers were not used to harvest this animal. **True** _____   **False** _____

I certify that the trophy scored on this chart was taken in **FAIR CHASE** as defined above by the Boone and Crockett Club. In signing this statement, I understand that if the information provided on this entry is found to be misrepresented or fraudulent in any respect, it will not be accepted into the Awards Program and all of my prior entries are subject to deletion from future editions of *Records of North American Big Game* and future entries may not be accepted.

Date: _____ Signature of Hunter:_____
                         (Signature must be witnessed by an Official Measurer or
                         a Notary Public.)

Date: _____ Signature of Notary or Official Measurer:_____

Reprinted courtesy of the Boone and Crockett Club, 250 Station Dr., Missoula, MT 59801, 406-542-1888

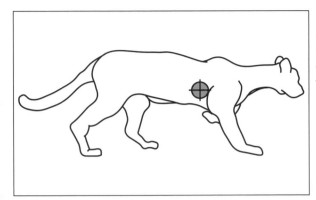

Shot Placement:
Broadside shot.
Aim for the center of the chest just behind the bend of the front shoulder; this should penetrate the lungs.

everything looks good, they turn the hounds loose and try to keep up. Some chases run a few hundred yards, but most unravel for hours, sometimes days, as the dogs decipher confusing trails and back trails and cats seek refuge in steep canyons, along fallen timber, and through hell holes of deep snow and blow downs. Cats may tree, leap out, and tree again and again. Sometimes they disappear in high, dense branches. Sometimes rain washes out trails or deep snows turn hunters back. Dogs may be lost for days.

One advantage of treeing cats is the chance to study them for sex and size. Toms generally have much wider and more massive heads than females. Females and small males can be left alone.

Though it doesn't happen often, a few cats are tracked down by unaided hunters in fresh snow. Others are serendipitously spotted and shot during still hunts, usually for other game, although virtually all Montana big game hunts are ended before the cat season begins.

Recommendations for Loads and Rifle Cartridges

Since most lions are taken after a long chase with dogs, most shots are close. To save carrying weight and leave both hands free for pulling themselves up hills, many hunters carry handguns in .357 Mag., .41 Mag. and .44 Mag. Others like short, handy lever-actions in .30–30. Pretty much any caliber will work. This is a good chance to use a muzzleloader, but be mindful of the wet conditions in the northwest after October.

Coyote

Canis latrans

The coyote is a varmint that is gaining respect as a challenging game animal. Wily, wary, and suspicious, coyotes have thrived despite a hundred years of intense persecution. Though no longer bountied, they remain fair game at any season and add spice to any big game hunt. Their pelts usually earn enough cash to cover gas expenses for week-long big game hunts, too.

Fascinating Facts

- After the demise of the wolf, coyotes became the dominant canine predator in the West, often adopting pack hunting techniques to take down deer and pronghorns.
- Despite their strong carnivorous nature, coyotes are quite omnivorous, consuming anything from wild berries to grasshoppers to power themselves through hard times.
- Coyotes do indeed "team up" with badgers to hunt ground squirrels and prairie dogs. While the badger goes down the hole, the coyote waits by the exit to nab any fleeing rodents.
- Two coyotes howling together can sound like a half-dozen, three like a small war party.
- Coyotes can run as fast as 40 mph.

Local Names
Song dog, 'yotes, dog, *%&!!*# stock killers

Size
Nowhere near the size most people imagine, adult coyotes average 20 to 40 pounds with the rare exception hitting 55 pounds. They stand about 2 feet at the shoulder and measure 3½ to 5 feet from nose to tail tip. An old dog has a deep but narrow chest reminiscent of a greyhound. Coyote snouts are much narrower and more pointed than a wolf's.

Coat and Color
Coyotes may appear dark or light, often with yellow or even reddish tints. Generally they are grizzly gray above and buff to nearly white under the neck, chest, and belly. Long, black-tipped guard hairs cover dense gray underfur on the back and down the sides. Legs, muzzle, and backs of ears are reddish or buff. Its tail is 12 to 16 inches long and black-tipped. Most mature animals have a ruff of extra-long guard hairs atop their backs between their shoulders.

*In snowy, sagebrush habitat, a coyote displays a bloody face
after feeding on an elk carcass.*

Voice and Communications

Coyotes are highly vocal, barking, yipping, and howling. A barking coyote has usually sensed something amiss. Soprano yipping and howling denote a multitude of things—pack cohesion, locating one another, territorial defense, etc. Dominant males usually howl at a slightly lower pitch than females and young. Knowledgeable hunters can howl to coyotes and bring them in for close shots.

Coyotes also use scent, primarily urine and dung, to mark territories.

Senses

Olfactory power is the coyote's strong suit, but hearing and vision aren't far behind. Let a coyote get your wind and he's gone. Let him hear you, and he may stick around to decipher the noise or blow out of there, depending on past experience. If he sees you move, he'll stare if inexperienced, but otherwise flee. A motionless person, particularly one partially obscured by ground or vegetation, is nearly invisible to coyotes. I've sat on a grassy hillside while wearing a blaze-orange vest and called coyotes within 80 yards.

Tracks and Sign

Medium-sized dog tracks in the wilds are usually coyote prints. Paw prints show claws just in front of the four toes and are between 2 and 2½ inches long and 1½ to 2 inches wide. Wolf tracks are more than 4 inches long. The rear of a coyote's heel pad is indented to show three lobes much like a cat track, but the front apex of the pad, unlike the cat print, is not indented; it comes to a rounded point. Stride is about 14 inches. During a run, the hind feet strike ahead of the front feet, all four fairly close together, while there are several feet between the clumps. Scat is cylindrical, dog like, often filled with hair, and usually black or gray.

Coyote tracks. Above, front, 2½" long; below, rear, 2¼" long.

Reproduction and Young

Coyotes pair up for mating and often stay together for years, sharing in raising the pups. Breeding is in February, and whelping is 63 days later in April. The female usually cleans out an old badger den, digs a new den, or finds a rock crevice for the nursing den, remaining in it with the pups for the first few days while the male brings food. Later, both parents hunt to supply the growing brood, which can vary from 2 to 19 pups, but is usually around 8. The lower the coyote population and the greater the prey base in a given area, the larger the litter size.

Within three weeks of birth, the pups are playing outside the den and taking solid food. After two months they are weaned and the den abandoned as they roam and learn to hunt with their parents. The family may break up by fall or stay together until late winter. Pups often run together for a year. Family units hunting together make up the packs sometimes seen tackling adult deer. I watched such an attack in the Gravelly Range years ago. Six coyotes took down a doe mule deer and polished her off in one night.

Habitat

Hey, the coyote isn't fussy. From dense conifer forests to bleak short-grass plains, if there's something to catch and eat, there's a coyote to catch and eat it. Densest populations are in mountain foothills and plains.

Home Range

In productive country a coyote may live out its entire life within a few square miles. When food is scarce it might be forced to wander over 100 square miles to fill its belly. Individuals have been recorded moving 400 miles beyond their initial capture sight. A mated pair will defend the heart of its territory from other coyotes, challenging them with howls, bristling and charging if they come too close, and driving them off.

A coyote stalks rodents in a mountain meadow during September.

Prey

As already mentioned, coyotes will eat nearly anything, but normally they concentrate on the most abundant small mammals like ground squirrels, rabbits, and
mice. They readily take red fox, mink, and other furbearers. Where necessary or
convenient, they key on deer and pronghorns, especially fawns, and domestic
sheep. Road kills, gut piles, garbage, barnyard chickens, upland game birds,
grasshoppers, crickets, and anything else is fair game.

Daily Patterns

Largely crepuscular and nocturnal, coyotes lay up during midday and rise near
dusk, often howling to begin the hunt. At dawn, they generally howl again before
retiring. It's almost as if they're letting their quarry know the working hours. More
likely, they're letting the competition know the boundaries. Of course, during fall and
winter you're likely to see them about at any hour, especially mousing in grassy
meadows. They will curl up in deep grass, atop a knoll or badlands butte, at the head
of a ditch or draw down which they can disappear in a wink, or on a ridgetop in
woods. They go to water daily in heat and drought.

Rutting Behavior

Coyotes don't rut like ungulates, but they pair up and run together from late January
on. Sometimes you'll see them playing like puppies. Imitate a howling dominant male
in a pair's territory at this season and you will likely bring the local male running.

Shot Placement:
Broadside shot.
Aim for the center of the chest just behind the bend of the front shoulder; this should penetrate the lungs.

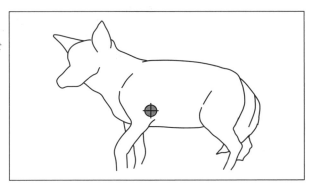

Trophy Dimensions

There is no official record list for trophy coyotes. Generally, any large, fully furred male or female with a deep chest weighing 30 pounds or more is considered big. Because pups of the year are the most gullible, they make up the bulk of the annual hunter harvest.

Hunting Tactics

By far and away the most productive technique is to slip into good coyote country and squeal like a frightened jackrabbit or cottontail. Where these calls are overused, mimic a stressed woodpecker or wounded fawn. In summer and early fall, the frantic yipping of a puppy brings older dogs running. The key to calling success is setting up within hearing and without alerting resident coyotes to your presence. Try not to skyline yourself. Slip over hills and ridges at their low points and crawl into position. Keep the wind in your face unless you're pretty well scent-proofed with something like a Scent-Lok charcoal-lined suit. You might place deer urine, coyote urine, glandular deer scent, or some sort of trapping lure scent 20 yards to either side of your position and directly at your feet to further fool approaching coyotes. For a visual lure, suspend a few light feathers or fur from thread tied to a stick or limb. Then start wailing on that call and see what develops. Call softly at first in case something is close. Blow about a minute, then rest for 2 or 3 minutes. Call more loudly for another minute, then rest again and keep a sharp watch. Coyotes have been known to run right over callers. Listen for paws hitting the ground behind you. Calling sequences can vary from 10 minutes to 30, but most dogs respond within 15 minutes.

To stop a coyote for a standing shot, bark at it. Some hunters simply yell "Hey!" but this can send an experienced dog running without a second look. Less popular ways to pursue song dogs include tracking after a fresh snow, glassing and stalking in open country, and howling to call them in. Many are taken incidentally to other big game hunting. Pelts have been fetching up to $25 in recent years.

Recommendations for Loads and Rifle Cartridges

Any centerfire rifle caliber will suffice, but centerfire .22s, 6mms, and .25s are best.

Region 1

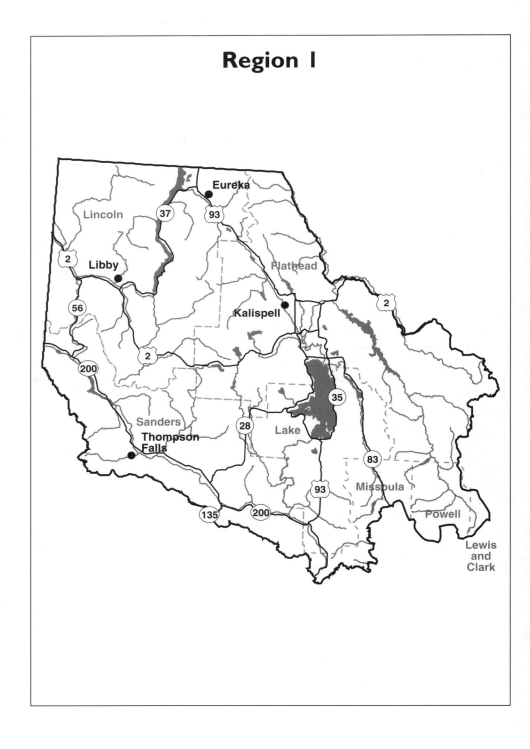

Region 1

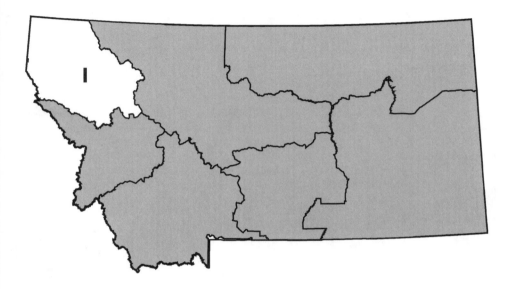

This is the place for intimate, close-range hunting in dense forest cover. Extensive high mountain wilderness areas provide physically challenging hunting, while thousands of miles of logging roads accommodate older or less physically fit hunters. In most places, terrain is steep, cover is thick, and game is difficult to see. Sign reading and tracking are important skills, and you'll use your ears as much as your eyes. Shifting mountain breezes foil many hunts, and it is often wet, cloudy, and cool during the fall and spring hunting seasons. Watch out for the protected wolves and grizzlies throughout the area. Access is wonderful, as most land in the region is public.

Game Species & Numbers

Whitetails are the bread-and-butter animal here, common at nearly all elevations. Elk are fairly common, though not as abundant as in Regions 2, 3, and 4. Mule deer are uncommon and limited to mid- and high elevations. Although no one has firm numbers of black bear and lion populations, densities of both species are probably higher in Region 1 than in any other region. Because of the dense cover and abundance of wetland habitat, moose densities are also quite high. There are several herds of mountain goats and sheep scattered across the high mountains, and they provide consistent hunting for lucky permit winners. There is no antelope hunting at all here, although there is a nice little herd worth viewing at the National Bison Range west of St. Ignatius.

Region 1
White-tailed Deer Distribution

LINCOLN

FLATHEAD

SANDERS

LAKE

MISSOULA

POWELL

LEWIS and CLARK

White-tailed Deer Distribution, Region 1

Region 1
Mule Deer Distribution

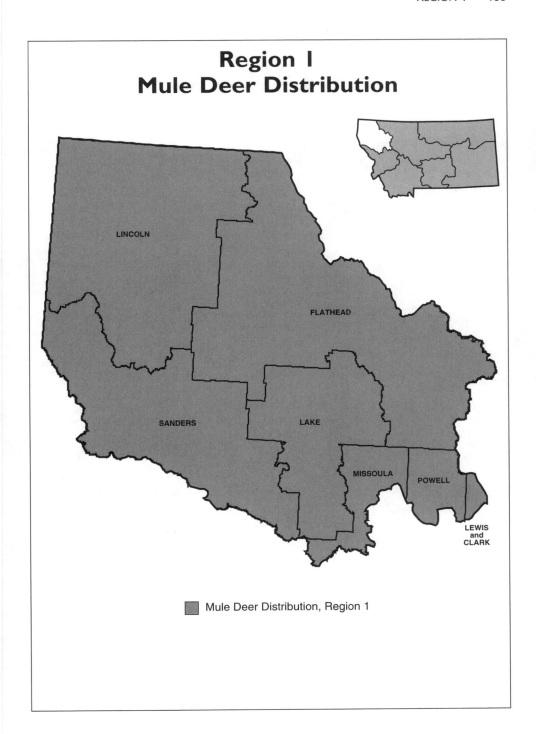

LINCOLN

FLATHEAD

SANDERS

LAKE

MISSOULA

POWELL

LEWIS
and
CLARK

Mule Deer Distribution, Region 1

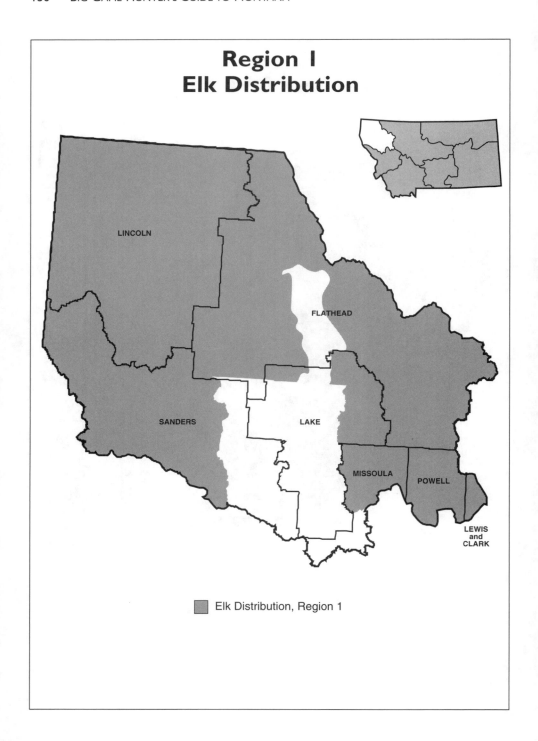

Region 1
Elk Distribution

LINCOLN

FLATHEAD

SANDERS

LAKE

MISSOULA

POWELL

LEWIS
and
CLARK

Elk Distribution, Region 1

Region 1
Moose Distribution

LINCOLN

FLATHEAD

SANDERS

LAKE

MISSOULA

POWELL

LEWIS
and
CLARK

Moose Distribution, Region 1

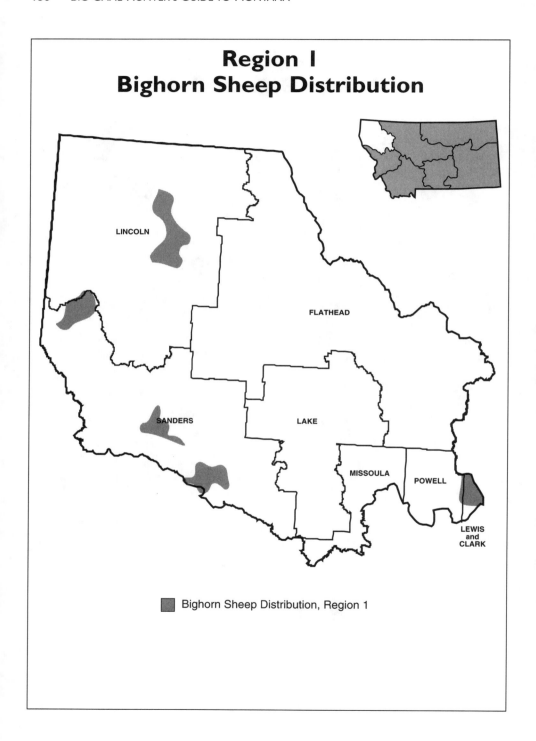

Region 1
Bighorn Sheep Distribution

LINCOLN

FLATHEAD

SANDERS

LAKE

MISSOULA

POWELL

LEWIS
and
CLARK

Bighorn Sheep Distribution, Region 1

Region 1
Mountain Goat Distribution

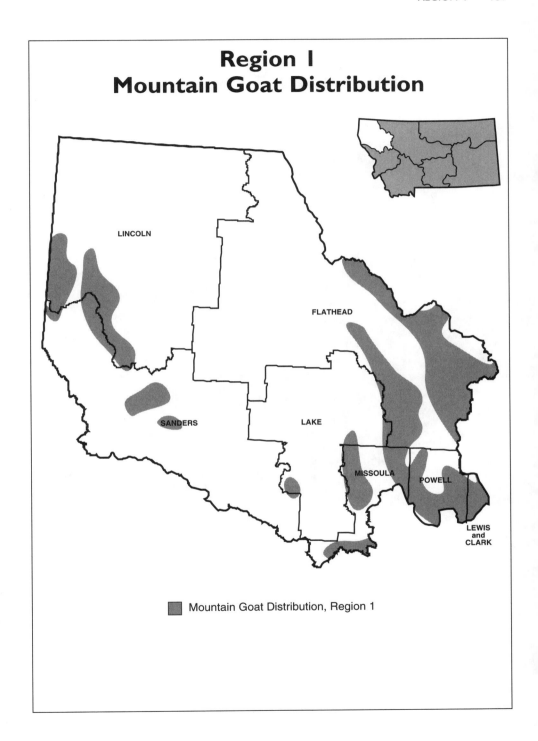

LINCOLN

FLATHEAD

SANDERS

LAKE

MISSOULA

POWELL

LEWIS and CLARK

Mountain Goat Distribution, Region 1

Region 1
Black Bear Distribution

LINCOLN

FLATHEAD

SANDERS

LAKE

MISSOULA

POWELL

LEWIS
and
CLARK

Black Bear Distribution, Region 1

Region 1
Mountain Lion Distribution

Mountain Lion Distribution, Region 1

Harvest Trend (1992–1996)

Species	Success Rate	Harvest	Hunters
Deer	60%	Mule bucks 1,130–3,208 Mule does 220–940 Whitetail bucks 7,900–10,000 Whitetail does 5,800–8,450	27,789–30,708
Elk	12%	Bulls 700–1,400 Cows 500–1,200	14,000–17,500
Moose	73%	Bulls 154–188 Cows 48–136	243–272
Bighorn Sheep	87%	Rams 12–48 Ewes 19–46	59–99
Mountain Goat	54%	Billies 16–23 Nannies 9–23	46–50
Cougars & Bears—No harvest statistics available			

Physical Characteristics

The essential description of Region 1 is mountainous and heavily forested with many streams, rivers, and lakes. Nine distinct mountain ranges in the region top out between 5,000 and 7,000 feet. The highest point is 8,890 feet in the Bob Marshall Wilderness to the east; Snowshoe Peak in the Cabinet Mountains to the west reaches 8,738 feet. The lowest point in the region (and the entire state) is 1,862 feet on the Kootenai River at the Idaho border. Glacier National Park, with its dramatic peaks, borders the northeast side of the Region and is, of course, closed to all hunting.

Because of the abundant moisture, most mountains here are heavily forested. Rainforests cover the north slopes and protected mid-elevation valleys with huge, old growth Douglas firs, western red cedars, western hemlocks, western larch (called tamaracks locally), and white pines. Lodgepole pines form extensive stands on drier, higher sites and old burns. Ponderosa pines cover drier south slopes. Engelmann spruce, subalpine fir, and alpine larch stand like sentinels on the high peaks and glacial cirques. Lush, often impenetrable, understory brush includes ninebark, *ceanothus*, spirea, huckleberry, oceanspray, mountain maple, and *syringa* to name a few. Elk, deer, and moose forage on these plants.

All of Region 1 was heavily glaciated during the last ice age. Though many mountain slopes exceed 60 percent, they are thickly forested. The highest peaks are barren, chiseled, and dramatic, surrounded by alpine meadows and dotted with cirque lakes. The only extensive level, open areas are in the Flathead River Valley above and below Flathead Lake. Narrower strips of flat, open land line many river valleys throughout the region. Virtually all valley land belongs to private farms, ranches, or home sites.

In recent years, the Kalispell and Flathead Lake area has been ravaged by home development. This is one of the fastest growing areas in Montana and a playground for retirees, vacationers, skiers, and second-home builders. Finding a place to hunt amid the new roads and houses isn't easy. Fortunately, the bulk of the hills and mountains are National Forest, State Forest, or timber company lands open to hunting.

Thousands of small streams, hundreds of large creeks, and several small rivers drain the mountains. The Flathead, Kootenai, and Clark Fork Rivers gather the waters and carry them west/northwest into Idaho and on to the Pacific Ocean. At 28 miles long and 8 miles wide, Flathead Lake is the largest lake in the state. Numerous smaller lakes dot the valleys and mountains. Koocanusa, Hungry Horse, and Noxon Reservoirs are the largest reservoirs in the region. It is possible to boat hunt their shores.

Four wilderness areas—the Bob Marshall Wilderness, Great Bear Wilderness, and Mission Mountains Wilderness in the east and the Cabinet Mountains Wilderness in the west—provide nonmotorized, backcountry, high mountain hunting for horsepackers and backpackers. Many outfitters operate in these areas. The Flathead Indian Reservation surrounding the south end of Flathead Lake covers 1,242,969 acres, but is closed to big game hunting. The amount of Block Management Land in the area is deceptive because it is mostly Plum Creek Timber Company land.

Land Use

Logging is the number one industry in Region 1. There are literally thousands of miles of logging roads through the forests providing good access—sometimes too good. Most are open to motor vehicles, but some are closed to protect sensitive areas from excessive pressure. Closed roads provide convenient foot, horse, and bicycle access into largely undisturbed areas for excellent hunting. Closed roads are clearly marked with locked gates. To avoid the disappointment of being turned back from a planned hunting area by a closed road, call the appropriate Forest Service office and request its road closure list and map before your hunt. Also, beware of huge logging trucks in active logging areas. These areas are usually, but not always, posted. Try to stay out of them. Yield the right of way to oncoming trucks; they weigh several tons and cannot easily stop, so pull well off the road. Never park on narrow, active logging roads; find an unused pullout and park completely off any logging road, active or not.

The clearcuts that have resulted from decades of logging can provide good or dismal hunting, depending on the size of the regrowth. Fresh cuts are barren. Cuts from 3 to 10 years old are favored feeding sites for elk, deer, and bears. They usually provide a good mix of forage plants and are open enough for productive glassing. When young foliage grows too dense and too high, hunting success drops. The best clearcuts are small ones located next to mature forests in which game can hide. Watch the edges at dawn and dusk for feeding game. Still-hunt dense forest cover at midday for bedded game.

Small scale ranching is the second most obvious use of the land. Most river valleys are given over to cattle and haying. Bottomland alfalfa fields lure whitetails year round and hungry elk in winter. In addition, you'll find orchards and some small grain farms in the Flathead Valley.

Weather

Despite the high mountains and its extreme northern location, Region 1 is actually the mildest in the state, with winter temperatures 10 to 15 degrees warmer on average than in northeast Montana. The moderate temperatures are due to Pacific low pressure weather fronts that blow in from Washington and Idaho and fill the valleys. The rim of the Continental Divide on the east edge of Region 1 and traditional midcontinent high pressure weather hold Arctic cold fronts out most of the time.

The maritime weather that flows into Region 1 also brings considerable moisture, making this the wettest place in Montana. Valleys accumulate about 16 inches of precipitation annually, and mountaintops often endure more than 150 inches, mostly as snow. Hunters should expect extended rainy periods mixed with snow beginning anytime in September. October can be wet, but it's more likely to break warm and sunny for days on end. Usually, traditional winter drizzle and snow sets in sometime in November. Expect endless days of clouds, fog, rain, and snow, but rarely extreme cold. Snow often melts about as fast as it falls at lower elevations. Wet, heavy snows up to 5,000 feet often frustrate mountain lion hunters who lose the track or get stuck in slush too wet for snowmobiles and too deep for tires. Waterproof boots, pants, and jackets are essential. Expect late season temperatures in the teens to 40s, but come prepared for the odd cold snap that could hit −30° F.

Public Lands and Acreages

Region 1 National Forests	Forest Size (not all acres necessarily within Region 1)
Flathead National Forest	2,350, 508 acres
Kaniksu National Forest	468,500 acres in Montana
Kootenai National Forest	2,245,000 acres
Lolo National Forest	2,091,944 acres

Region 1 Wilderness Areas	Size (not all acres necessarily within Region 1)
Bob Marshall Wilderness	1,009,356 acres
Cabinet Mountains Wilderness	94,272 acres
Great Bear Wilderness	285,701 acres
Mission Mountains Wilderness	73,877 acres

Block Management Acres	865,000 acres (mostly Plum Creek Timber Co. land)

Region I
Mountain Ranges

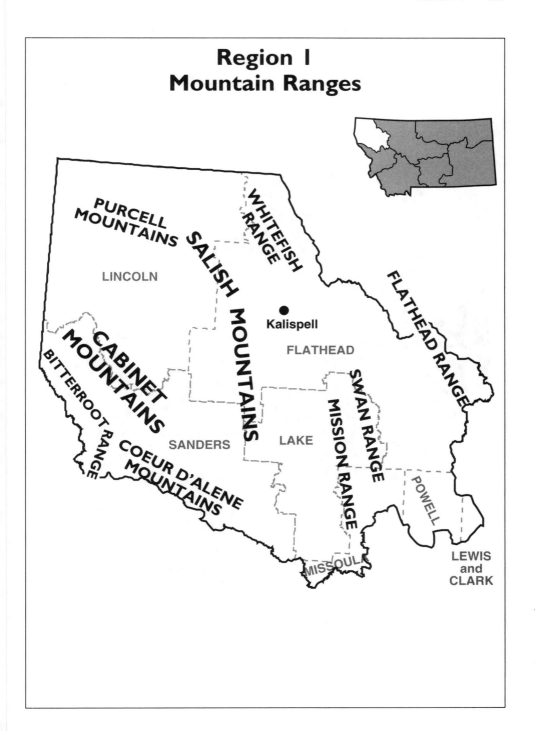

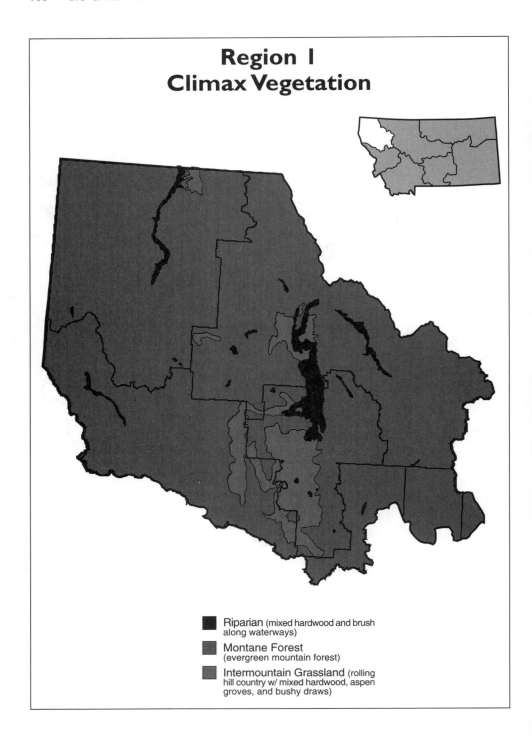

Region 1
Climax Vegetation

Riparian (mixed hardwood and brush along waterways)

Montane Forest (evergreen mountain forest)

Intermountain Grassland (rolling hill country w/ mixed hardwood, aspen groves, and bushy draws)

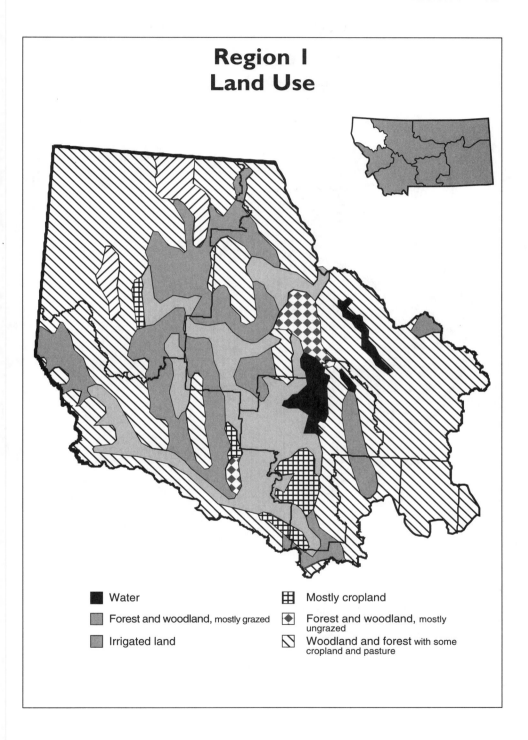

Region I
Land Use

Water

Forest and woodland, mostly grazed

Irrigated land

Mostly cropland

Forest and woodland, mostly ungrazed

Woodland and forest with some cropland and pasture

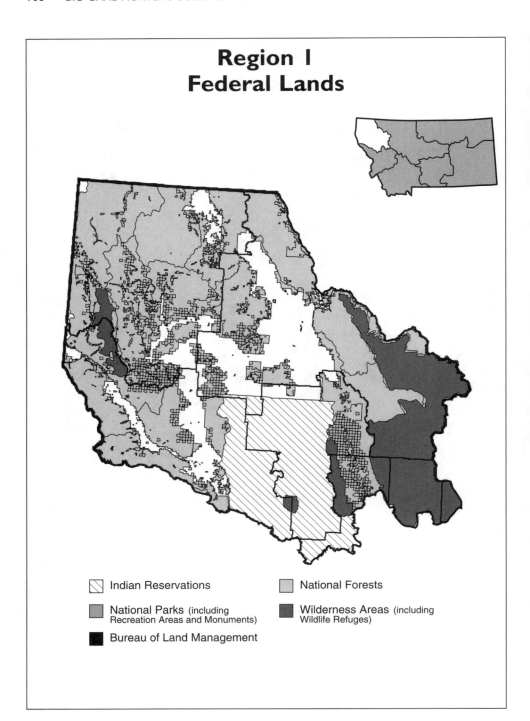

Region 1
Federal Lands

Indian Reservations

National Forests

National Parks (including Recreation Areas and Monuments)

Wilderness Areas (including Wildlife Refuges)

Bureau of Land Management

REGION I HIGHLIGHTS

Yaak Valley & Libby Area

There are no yaks in the Yaak River valley, but there may be more whitetails and black bears here than in any other part of Montana (HD 100). This is wet coniferous forest with lots of places to hide and suitable habitat from the river valley to the mountaintops for deer and bears. And it's almost all public land; narrow strips of private land along the river are too small to worry about.

You reach the Yaak country from the south via the Yaak River road which takes off from US 2 northwest of Troy. From the north, you can come in via Sullivan Creek Road, which starts near the west shore of Lake Koocanusa, but to get to the west shore road you must take State Route 37 west out of Eureka, follow it along the east shore of the lake to the bridge, and then cross the bridge and go north up the west side road to Sullivan Creek. If this sounds complicated, buy a map and start practicing your pathfinding skills. The entire region is a mass confusion of winding roads that'll have a novice lost within minutes. Pay attention to your compass, and don't be afraid to ask directions. If that isn't confusing enough for you, try going down the South Fork Yaak River via Pipe Creek Road north of Libby to South Fork Yaak River Road, which eventually dumps you onto the Yaak River Road. Whew. Any and all of this country is not only prime real estate for whitetails, but also for black bears and grizzlies, so be careful.

When the snow falls deep, and it can, the deer migrate a little, and that's mostly downslope. They suffered a major population decline after the brutal '96 winter which piled snow 12 feet deep at the Kalispell airport and reduced Region 1 big game populations by about half. But the whitetails already show signs of bouncing back. A good fawn crop in 1998 promises better hunting for the next few years. Hunter success is considered quite good for heavily forested mountain country–usually about 55 percent.

Black bear hunters should glass clearcuts and high country huckleberry patches in fall. In spring they should walk closed logging roads and glass grassy hillsides. This is just about the best black bear area in the state, and hunter success is high.

Surprisingly, the Yaak has some good mule deer, too. You find them in pockets and usually higher up the mountains on south- and west-facing slopes. Because most folks find whitetails easier to hunt, some muley bucks live long enough to grow quite hefty antlers. Biologists suspect at least a partial migration toward the lower slopes along Lake Koocanusa; some muleys have taken up residence close to the east side of the lake. In the mountains beyond, whitetails again dominate. The west side of the Fisher River drainage southeast of Libby (HD 103) also hosts some mule deer. But, really, muleys are just a sideshow here. Here, the whitetail is king, and this species makes up about 85 percent of the annual deer harvest in HD 100.

Elk, on the other hand, are almost a novelty in HD 100. Region 1 is the poorest elk producer in the state. In the best years, fewer than 400 are taken in HD 100, and in recent years the annual kill has been under 150. Hunter success is less than 10 percent.

This early spring meadow is typical grazing habitat of black bears, offering the dandelions that are particularly favored by bears.

Predictably, all the deer in the area support a healthy cougar population, one of the highest in the state. Harvest levels have risen dramatically over the past ten years and are now at historic highs. In short, the Libby country is a great place to hunt whitetails, black bears, and cougars.

Eureka to North Fork Flathead River

HDs 101, 102, and 110 east and south of Eureka are a mixed bag for whitetail, black bear, and cougar. HD 110 in the northeast corner of Region 1 has suffered significant elk, deer, and moose losses to wolf packs coming out of Canada and Glacier National Park. Because the wolves moved into territory that was flush with game but no other wolves, they prospered. Now it appears they may be stabilizing or declining, and game might have a chance to recover. Cougars are currently declining here, which could be due to direct competition from and harassment by wolf packs, which have been documented killing cougars. During the 1997 season, the local FWP biologist checked 10 elk and heard of about 8 more coming out of the district. He noted, however, that several of them were good sized bulls. Hunter success on elk here has

The Yaak Valley supports a healthy cougar population. Here, a rock, probably warmed by the sun, provides a resting place for a mountain lion.

been running about 5 percent. Grizzlies also reside in this district; if that makes you nervous, go somewhere else.

The Whitefish Range, split down its crest between HDs 101 and 110, has a good population of mule deer (for Region 1) that stay high early, then migrate down to the southwest slopes within spitting distance of US 93. As the season runs through most of November, you've a good chance of catching them in the foothills. If you bowhunt early, try the highest basins, which are a mix of spruce, fir, whitebark pine, and sub-alpine meadows above 5,500 feet. Plenty of logging roads penetrate into the White-fish Range from both sides, and there is an extensive trail system, too.

Abundant black bears in this mountain range and throughout Region 1 may suffer decreased population for the near future because of a major berry failure in 1998. This forced the bears into lowland, settled areas where they got into trouble with people. Many had to be killed, and the 1998 hunter take is expected to be higher than usual, as well.

HD 102 is another area you don't want to hunt elk in. Success rates hover around 5 percent, and most bulls are young when taken. People pick them off from the extensive system of logging roads in the Salish Range south of Eureka. Whitetails do well here, however, especially along major creek drainages like Fortine, Pinkham, and Wolf. Hunter success rates in HD 102 and 101 are in the 45 percent range, and that's darn good in thick, forested mountain habitat. There are some big bucks, too.

Thompson Falls Area

Thompson Falls south of Libby sits on the Clark Fork River with the rugged Cabinet Mountains on the north and the Coeur D'Alene Range to the south. For some reason, elk hunting here (HD 121) is significantly better than up north. The old wildfire of 1910 opened a lot of the forest, which grew back in shrubs. These brush-lands still harbor elk. In fact, the annual kill is double HD 100, and the success rate is triple. Most years this is the best elk district in Region 1, and because of the steep terrain and thick brush, quite a few bulls grow old and big. Walking the old gated logging roads can be quite productive. A local joke, more fact than fiction, states that these old roads are the only flat places for elk to lie down.

Whitetails are about as strong here as they are to the north, and the hunter success rate usually averages about 55 percent—a good figure to base a hunt on. The Cabinets, with their extensive backcountry centered around the small Cabinet Mountains Wilderness, also kick out several really good mule deer each year, but the rock-and-ice high country they hide in is tough to reach and hunt. As most outfitters camp outside the wilderness, this would be a great place for a couple of young, tough backpacking hunters to make a true wilderness mule deer hunting adventure. Look for the old bucks in the highest, remotest regions, and hunt early before the snow flies. This area also can get a lot of heavy snow, though the woods here are slightly drier and more open than HD 100—which may have something to do with the higher success rates. Again, hunting opportunities abound all around Thompson Falls, as most of the district is public forest land.

The showcase species for the Thompson Falls area is bighorn sheep. The herds roaming the high country above the Thompson River east of town yield several 180-inch and better rams each year. Sheep districts 121, 122, and 124 are the hot spots. About 35 ram licenses were issued in 1998, but there was fierce competition for them.

Swan Valley

Because this valley (HD 130) is unusually broad and gentle for Region 1, it gets a lot of hunting pressure. The bulk of the land is public and in either state or national forest. Access is via State Route 83 south out of Kalispell or north out of the Blackfoot Valley.

The riparian deciduous brush, wetlands, and low forest support one of the best whitetail herds in the Region. Fully 85 percent of all deer harvested in this region are whitetails, and a lot of them are taken out of the Swan every year. There's been a lot of logging here over the years, and there are plenty of roads to prove it. This easy access made hunting all too efficient years ago, but today many roads are closed to

This mature Rocky Mountain bighorn ram stands on a rocky outcrop at the edge of a spruce forest.

vehicle traffic to provide security for grizzlies. For the hiker or biker, these closed roads make great ribbons into open habitat for accessible, undisturbed whitetail hunting. While it will take a few more years for the herds to recover from the winter of 1996, this is still one of the best places in Montana to hunt whitetails.

Mule deer live in isolated pockets atop the Flathead Range on the east side of the Swan Valley, sticking mostly to heavy timber on the east side until heavy snows force them lower on the west side. They drop only as low as they have to in order to find food and move about freely. You must hunt stealthily in the heavy forest to take this particular brand of mule deer.

The Swan is not noted for its elk, but the small population is slowly growing under fairly conservative management. Only brow-tined bulls may be taken. There is no cow harvest except during the early archery season. Bulls in this district have lots of secure cover in which to hide, so they tend to grow old, leading to impressive antler growth. Some good elk racks come out of HD 130 each year.

The opposing view: a Rocky Mountain bull elk with 6×6 antlers walks away.

The Bob Marshall Wilderness

Everyone who knows the Bob Marshall Wilderness calls it simply "The Bob." And those who hunt it come mainly for the elk. It is a vast, rugged wilderness straddling the Continental Divide southeast of Kalispell and northwest of Helena. It runs more than 100 miles north to south (counting the Great Bear Wilderness to the north and the Scapegoat to the south). You don't hunt here casually, and just getting in is a major undertaking. Often, you ride 25 miles by horse just to reach your base camp. For this reason, hunters tend to be repeat customers, often families that have been hunting from the same camps for generations, and outfitters who have their established areas. Very few pioneers go through the trouble of putting together the necessary livestock, tents, and gear to tackle the Bob on their own. Backpack hunting is a logistical nightmare. If you go in more than a few miles, you'll spend three days to a week packing out an elk. And there are always grizzlies to contend with. They can destroy a camp in seconds–or a hunter in a heartbeat.

While there are some big mule deer in the high country and whitetails along the rivers, few hunters bother with them. Locals don't want the hassle of butchering and packing out deer when they need to concentrate on getting their elk. They can always hunt deer later and closer to town. Non-residents, of course, take big bucks when they see them, but they, too, are concentrating on elk, saving serious deer hunting for afterward.

The Bob is probably the second best elk hunting spot in Region 1, right behind the Thompson Falls area. Bulls are high and scattered, but there is very little hunting pressure, so they grow big. The rifle season is open during the rut, too, which makes for increased excitement and success. Because biologists have noted a slow decline in elk numbers in the Bob, spike hunting has recently been stopped. Now only brow-tined bulls may be taken. Wildfire control since the 1930s has let forests grow more dense in the wilderness. While these trees provide increased security for elk, they also reduce forage, and elk need lots of high quality forage to produce those big antlers.

Depending on what part of the Bob you're in, the bull to cow ratio varies from 15 to 35 bulls per 100 cows. Fully 72 percent of bulls are branch-antlered, and between 13 and 16 percent have 6 points or more.

A few people pursue black bears here, but there are much easier places to hunt them. Also, there are grizzlies to worry about. Mountain goats provide limited hunting in HDs 140, 141, 142, 150, and 151. Thirteen licenses were available in 1998. There is no bighorn sheep hunting in the Bob on the Region 1 side. Moose live in nearly every drainage, but they are widely dispersed. Bulls can and do grow big here and they provide a wonderful wilderness hunting experience for those lucky enough to draw the few available permits—17 in 1998.

Some outfitters head into the Bob for lions and take a handful each year, but the area's quota is almost never filled. In summary, the Bob is the ultimate wild Rocky Mountain hunting adventure, a slice of America the way God made it. But it is also a major challenge best met by men and women who have the necessary equipment, experience, and common sense to handle it.

REGION 1 HUB CITIES
Libby

Population–2,800 • Elevation–2,066

Libby is located in a beautiful valley surrounded by the grandeur of the 2.5 million-acre Cabinet Mountain Wilderness. The blue-green Kootenai River borders the north edge of town. The Kootenai National Forest (over 2 million acres) provides extensive public hunting land in some of the most beautiful and rugged country in northwest Montana.

Lincoln County, whose habitat consists of montane forest, is first in the state in commercial lumber and wood products. Libby has a host of fine restaurants, motels, and services, and its people are known for their friendliness.

ACCOMMODATIONS: LIBBY

The Caboose Motel, West US 2 / 293-6201 / 28 rooms / Hunters and dogs welcome, $5 pet fee. / Very reasonable rates

Sandman Motel, US 2 West / 293-8831 / 16 units / Hot tub, cable, microwaves, and refrigerators in each room / Hunters and dogs welcome, $5 pet fee / Very reasonable rates / Your hosts are John and Christine Heinlein

Super 8 Motel, 448 West US 2 / 293-2771 / 42 units / Cable, indoor pool / Hunters and dogs welcome, $5 fee / Rates reasonable

Venture Motor Inn, 443 US 2 West / 72 rooms / Cable, indoor pool, exercise room, adjoining restaurant / Hunters welcome and dogs allowed / Rates reasonable

ACCOMMODATIONS: TROY

Tamarack Lodge, 32885 South Fork Road / 295-4880, toll free 888-295-1822 / Offers lodging, meals, and guided hunts for blue, ruffed, and spruce grouse / Hunts in the 2.25 million acre Kootenai National Forest / Also has sporting clays course. Hosts are Bill and Judy McAfee

Overdale Lodge, 1076 Overdale Lodge Road / 295-4057 / Two-story, 5 bedrooms / Fully equipped kitchen / Overlooks a pond and a lake—a beautiful, secluded setting / Hunters and dogs welcome / Hosts are Jim and Mary Jackson

CAMPGROUNDS AND RV PARKS

Big Bend RV Park, 13 miles from Libby on SR 37 / 792-7277 / 25 tent, 25 RV sites / Water, electric, sewer, dump / 10 acres on lake / Restaurant and bar

Mountain View Conoco, 2 miles west of Libby on US 2 / 293-4942 / 5 tent, 20 RV sites / Water, electric, sewer, dump, shower, laundry, store.

RESTAURANTS

Treasure Mt. Casino & Restaurant, 485 US 2 W / 293-8763

Beck's Montana Cafe, 2425 US 2 West / 293-6686 / Open 8AM–10PM daily / Specializing in broasted chicken / Thursday night prime rib special

4B's Restaurant, 442 US 2 / 293-8751 / Open 24 hours

Henry's Restaurant, 407 West 9th / 293-7911 / Family restaurant.

MK Steakhouse, 9948 US 2 South / 293-5686 / Open for dinner 6 days, closed Mondays / Beautiful log building/ Cocktails, specializing in steaks and prime rib

Venture Inn Restaurant, 443 US 2 West / Open 6AM–11PM / Family restaurant

VETERINARIANS

Treasure Valley Veterinary Clinic, 845 US 2 West / 293-7410 / Doug Griffiths, DVM

SPORTING GOODS, GUNS, & GUNSMITHS

Frank's Guns & Custom Ammo, 113 Woodland Road / 293-3635

Doug Johnson Gunsmith, 1325 Chase Cut Off Road, Troy / 295-4958

Highline Sports, Libby Shopping Center / 293-8178

Libby's Sport Center, 116 East 9th / 293-4641 / Complete hunting supplies and licenses

TAXIDERMISTS

Bear Creek Ventures Taxidermy, 190 Three Corner Road / 293-9682

Dumont Taxidermy, 3707 Kootenai River Road / 293-6776

Frontier Custom Taxidermy, 268 Taylor Road / 293-7158

Kootenai Country Bed & Breakfast, 264 Mack Road / 293-7878

Libby Creek Taxidermy, 9615 US 2 South / 293-4689

Pine Creek Taxidermy, Troy / 295-4989

Pioneer Taxidermy, 2243 US 2 West / 293-6041

Schad Brothers Taxidermy, 364 North Milnor Lake Road, Troy / 295-5828

Milfred & Amy L Siefke, 264 Mack Road / 293-7878

Wildlife Recapture Taxidermy, 3 Mile Marker State Route 37 / 293-7878

MEAT PROCESSORS

Fred's Meats, 6718 Pipe Creek Road / 293-4273

AUTO REPAIR

Auto Haus, 808 Hwy 2 West / 293-4351

Carr's Towing, 4063 Hwy 2 South / 293-3988

AIR SERVICE

Libby Airport, Keith Kinden / 293-9776

MEDICAL

St. John's Lutheran Hospital, 350 Louisiana Avenue / 293-7761

FOR MORE INFORMATION

Libby Area Chamber of Commerce
905 West 9th Street
P.O. Box 704
Libby, MT 59923-0704
406-293-4167

Kootenai National Forest
506 U.S. Hwy 2 West
Libby, MT 59923
406-293-6211

Eureka

Population–1,100 • Elevation–2,400

Situated in a broad agricultural valley surrounded by mountains and forests, Eureka is part logging, part farming (Christmas trees are a major crop), and part tourist town. Lake Koocanusa on the impounded Kootenai River lures fishermen and summer recreationists, so there are plenty of facilities and services for such a small town. The surrounding Kootenai National Forest provides miles of public hunting for elk, whitetails, black bear, and cougar.

ACCOMMODATIONS
Huckleberry Hannah's, 3100 Sophie Lake Road / 888-889-3381
Willow Fire Lodge, 1866 West Road / 888-406-3344
Ksanka Motel, US 93 & SR 37 / 296-3127
Lake Koocanusa Elk & Guest Ranch, Rexford / 889-3809

CAMPGROUNDS & RV PARKS
Frontier Bar, Rexford / 296-3951

RESTAURANTS
Valley Pizza Steakhouse, US 93 North / 296-2738
Bullwinkles, Dewey Avenue / 296-3932
Three CCCs Restaurant, US 93 at Canada Border / 889-3654
Point of Rocks Restaurant, US 93 South, Olney / 881-2752
4 Corners Restaurant, US 93 & SR 37 / 296-2444
Sophie's Emporium, Dewey Avenue / 296-2893
Sunflower Bakery & Coffeehouse, 312 Dewey Avenue / 296-2896
TJs Restaurant, US 93 & SR 37 / 296-3174

VETERINARIAN
Mountain Vista Veterinary, 551 SR 37 / 296-2564

SPORTING GOODS, GUNS, & GUNSMITHS
Green Mountain Sports, 800 US 93 North / 296-2566
Grave Creek Service, US 93 & SR 37 / 296-2416

TAXIDERMISTS
Hoof & Claw Taxidermy & Art Studio, Hwy 93 North / 296-2797.
Wolf Taxidermy, 1711 MT Highway 37 / 296-2591

MEAT PROCESSORS
Baney Meats, Osloski Road / 296-2611

AUTO REPAIR
Gibbon's Garage, 11th Street & US 93 / 296-2141

AIR SERVICE
North Lincoln County Airport, Fred King / 296-2738

MEDICAL SERVICES
Prompt Care Clinic, 1200 US 93 South / 296-3145

FOR MORE INFORMATION
Tobacco Valley Board Of Commerce
P.O. Box 186406
Eureka, MT 59917
889-4636

Kalispell

Population–26,000 • Elevation–2,959

Kalispell and its sister communities of Columbia Falls and Whitefish represent one of the fastest growing areas in Montana. Nearby Flathead Lake and Glacier National Park and a relatively mild winter climate provide much of the allure. Kalispell is a regional trade center with large shopping malls, numerous stores and dozens of motels, hotels, lodges, and restaurants. It is located in the broad Flathead Valley surrounded by the Flathead National Forest. The Salish Mountains lie to the west and the Whitefish and Swan Mountains to the east. Montane forest covers the bulk of the mountains while the valley is devoted to housing, pastures, and farm fields with some riparian habitat.

ACCOMMODATIONS

Blue and White Motel, 640 East Idaho Street / 755-4311 / 107 rooms, sauna, hot tub, pool, and restaurant / Dogs allowed in rooms / Rates moderate

Kalispell Super 8, 1341 1st Avenue East / 755-1888 / 74 rooms / Dogs allowed in smoking rooms only / Rates moderate

CAMPGROUNDS AND RV PARKS

Rocky Mountain "Hi" Campground, 5 miles east of Kalispell on Rt 2 / 755-9573 / Open year-round / 20 tent and 70 RV spaces / Full facilities including laundry and store

Spruce Park RV Park, 3 miles east, Junction US 2 and 93 on SR 35 at Flathead River / 752-6321 / Open year-round / 60 tent and 100 RV spaces / Full facilities including laundry and store

RESTAURANTS

Bulldog Steak House, 208 1st Avenue East / 752-7522 / Spirits, beer, fine steaks, and salads / Steamed shrimp is their specialty

Que Pasa Restaurant, 75 Woodland Park Drive / 756-8776 / Open 7AM–10PM daily / Serving breakfast, lunch, and dinner / Fine Mexican food, beer, wine, and margaritas

Fred's Family Restaurant, 1600 Hwy 93 / 257-8666 / Open 5:45AM–11PM daily / Serving breakfast, lunch, and dinner

VETERINARIANS

Animal Clinic, 1408 City Airport Rd / 755-6886 / 24-hour service

Ashley Creek Animal Clinic, 3251 Hwy 93 South / 752-1330 / 24-hour service

SPORTING GOODS, GUNS, AND GUNSMITHS

Snappy Sport Center, 1400 Hwy 2 East / 257-7525 / Open 7 days

Sportsman and Ski Haus, Junction of Hwy 2 and 93 / 755-6484

Brass & Bullets Inc., 2703 Hwy. 93 S / 752-4867.

Kalispell Army Navy Store Inc., 327 Main Street / 752-7575

Montana Rifleman, 2593 Hwy 2 East / 755-4867

Powder Horn Trading Post, 2052 Hwy 2 East / 752-6669
St. John's Gun Shop, 95 West Reserve Drive / 752-2577
Jim's Gun Shop, 246 Railway Street, Whitefish / 862-2274
Forthofer Gunsmithing & Knife, 5535 Hwy 93 South, Whitefish / 862-2674

TAXIDERMISTS
Arrowhead Taxidermy, 2412 US 2 East / 257-7026
Adventures in the Wild, 5895 US 93 South / 862-4096
Alpine Custom Taxidermy / 752-2709
Bicknell's Taxidermy, 192 Bernard Road / 756-7505
Critter Factory Taxidermy, 1406 Foothill Road / 756-3048
Great Northern Taxidermy, 240 Liahona Lane / 257-7281
Masterpiece Taxidermy, 3024 MT Highway 35 / 257-0037
The Montana Taxidermist, 2668 Hwy 2 East / 752-4504
Wildlife West, 17 Magstadt Lane / 756-9378
Montana Wildlife Museum Taxidermy, Hwy 2 West, Columbia Falls / 892-2591
Ron West Taxidermy, 1688 Monte Vista Drive, Columbia Falls / 892-2060
Tolar's Taxidermy, 111 Midway Drive, Columbia Falls / 892-9378
Whitefish Taxidermy, 5895 US 93 South, Whitefish / 862-4096

MEAT PROCESSORS
Creston Processing, 4239 MT Hwy 35 / 752-6880
Custom Meats, 1860 Voerman Road, Whitefish / 862-7854
Lower Valley Processing Co., 2115 Lower Valley Road / 752-2846
Vandevanter Meats Inc., 180 Trap Road, Columbia Falls / 892-5643

AUTO REPAIR AND RENTAL
Conoco Car Care Center, 229 3rd Avenue / 755-3797
Avis, Glacier Park International Airport / 257-2727
National Car Rental, Glacier Park International Airport / 257-7144

AIR SERVICE
Glacier Park International Airport, 4170 Hwy 2 East / 257-5994

MEDICAL
Kalispell Regional Hospital, 310 Sunnyview Lane / 752-5111

FOR MORE INFORMATION
Kalispell Chamber of Commerce
15 Depot Loop
Kalispell, MT 59901
406-752-6166

Fish, Wildlife & Parks–Region 1 Office
490 North Meridian
Kalispell, MT 59901
406-752-5501

Flathead National Forest
1935 3rd Avenue East
Kalispell, MT 59901
406-758-5200

Thompson Falls

Population– 1,300 • Elevation– 2,463

Thompson Falls is a small, friendly town in northwestern Montana on the banks of the Clark Fork River. Timber and agriculture are the dominant industries of the area. The beautiful Cabinet Mountains are to the east of Thompson Falls and the Bitterroot Mountains frame the western border. These vast mountain ranges of the Lolo National Forest provide countless acres of public land for great hunting opportunities. The mountains are covered in forest.

ACCOMMODATIONS

Falls Motel, 112 South Gallatin / 827-3559 / 22 rooms / Dogs allowed, $10 per dog, per night / Rates very reasonable

Rimrock Lodge, Hwy 200, 1 mile west of town overlooking the Clark Fork River / 827-3536 / Cable, restaurant / Dogs allowed / Rates moderate

Black Bear Bar & Hotel / 827-3951

CAMPGROUNDS AND RV PARKS

Riverfront RV Park, 1 mile west on Hwy 200 / 827-3460/ 3 tent and 10 RV sites / Full facilities / Motel units recently added

Birdland Bay RV Park, Blueflag Rd / 827-4757

RESTAURANTS

Broomtown Cafe, 915 Main Street / Open for breakfast, lunch, and dinner

Rimrock Lodge, Hwy 200, 1 mile west / 827-3536 / Beautiful dining room overlooking the Clark Fork River / Open for breakfast, lunch, and dinner / Fine food and western hospitality

Bell's Café, Black Bear Hotel / 827-3270

VETERINARIANS

Thompson Falls Lynch Creek Vet. Clinic, 1 mile east on Hwy 200 / 827-4305

SPORTING GOODS, GUNS, & GUNSMITHS

Krazy Ernie's, 602 Main Street / 827-4898

Tom's Sporting Goods, 1002 Main Street / 827-4096

TAXIDERMISTS

Stan's Taxidermy & Gifts, 2742 Hwy. 200 / 827-4040

Masterpiece Taxidermy, Hwy. 200 E / 827-3170

MEAT PROCESSOR

Revais Meats, 3miles west of Dixon / 246-3588

AUTO REPAIR

Ken's Auto Repair, Hwy 200 East / 827-3940

Doug's Autos & Towing, 4890 Hwy. 200 / 827-4387

Tim's Auto, 1015 Main / 827-3516

AIR SERVICE
County airstrip, Frank Barbeau / 827-3536

MEDICAL
Clark Fork Valley Hospital, in Plains, 22 miles east / Emergency, call 911
Thompson Falls Medical Clinic, Pond Street / 827-4442
Dr. Lovell, D.O., 907 Main / 827-4307

FOR MORE INFORMATION
Thompson Falls Chamber of Commerce
P.O. Box 493
Thompson Falls, MT 59873.
827-4930

Region I Guides and Outfitters

Outfitter Services by Species and Specialty

A	Elk, deer, bear, antelope	F	Mountain lion	I	Moose
B	Deer & antelope	G	Sheep	L	Drop Camps
WT	Whitetail deer	H	Mountain goat	M	Tent Camps

A **Gary Abbey**
Glacier Outfitters
3242 Back Road
Ronan, MT 59864
406-657-2142

AF **Richard Birdsell**
The Northern Rockies Outfitter
P.O. Box 2443
Columbia Falls, MT 59912
406-758-6649

AFG **Lee Bridges**
HI Mountain Trails Outfitters
WT P.O. Box 389
Eureka, MT 59917
406-889-3652

AFH **Virgil Burns**
WT Bob Marshall Wilderness Ranch
Box 24
St. Ignatius, MT 59865
406-745-4466

AB **Mike Canavan**
FG Bull River Valley
HI 239 Shalom Drive
WT Libby, MT 59923
406-293-8666

AG **Gerald Carr**
HI Cabinet Mountain Outfitters
WT P.O. Box 766
Plains, MT 59859
406-826-3970

AB **Mike Cheff**
FH Cheff Guest Ranch
4274 Eagle Pass Trail
Charlo, MT 59824
406-644-2557

ABI **William Jr. Crismore**
Lazy JR Outfitters
P.O. Box 1038
Libby, MT 59923
406-293-9494

ABF **Brent Fitchell**
Elk Creek Outfitting
20 W. Elk Creek Rd.
Heron, MT 59844
406-847-5593

AB **Larry Frost**
FG Rafter H Outfitting
I P.O. box 159
Eureka, MT 59917
406-292-2104

AB **Bruce Funk**
WT Running Waters Ranch
2115 Riverside Road
Bigfork, MT 59911
406-755-2041

A **Kirk Gentry**
Spotted Bear Ranch
115 Lake Blaine Drive
Kalispell, MT 59901
406-755-7337

A	Elk, deer, bear, antelope	F	Mountain lion	I	Moose
B	Deer & antelope	G	Sheep	L	Drop Camps
WT	Whitetail deer	H	Mountain goat	M	Tent Camps

AG   **Ellen Hargrave**
Hargrave Cattle & Guest Ranch
Thompson River Valley
Marion, MT 59925
406-858-2284

AF
WT   **Steve Hawkins**
Hawkins Outfitters
P.O. Box 187
Eureka, MT 59917
406-296-2642

ABF
GI   **David Hayward**
Kootneai High Country Hunting
Box 1428
Eureka, MT 59917
406-889-HUNT

AF
GH   **Wayne Hill**
Wayne Hill Outfitting
Box 592
Noxon, MT 59853
406-847-5563

AG
HI
WT   **Len Howells**
Silver Bow Outfitters
500 East Fisher Road
Libby, MT 59923
406-293-9497

BF
WT   **James P. Landwehr**
Glacier Fishing Charters
375 Jensen Road
Columbia Falls, MT
406-892-2377

BFG
HI   **Cameron Lee**
Skyline Outfit, Inc.
& Wilderness Lodge
P.O. Box 391
Hungry Horse, MT 59919
406-387-4051

AFG
HI   **Shawn Little**
Snowy Springs Outfitters
P.O. Box 686
Kalispell, MT 59903
406-755-2137

AF   **Jerry Malson**
Jerry Malson Outfitting & Guiding
22 Swamp Creek Road
Trout Creek, MT 59874
406-847-5582

ABF
IWT   **William McAfee**
McAfee Outfitting & Lodge
27744 Yaak River Road
Troy, MT 59935
406-295-4880

AWT   **Mark Moss**
Salmon Forks Outfitters
475 Elk Park Road
Cloumbia Falls, MT 59912
406-892-5468

AWT   **Cecil L. Noble**
Lion Creek Outfitters
610 Patrick Creek Road
Kalispell, MT 59901
406-755-3723

A	Elk, deer, bear, antelope	**F**	Mountain lion	**I**	Moose
B	Deer & antelope	**G**	Sheep	**L**	Drop Camps
WT	Whitetail deer	**H**	Mountain goat	**M**	Tent Camps

AFG **Doug Peterson**
HI Bull River Outfitters
WT Bull River, Box 227
Noxon, MT 59853
406-847-2641

ABF **Mike Robinson**
GHI Thunder-Bow Outfitters
WT P.O. Box 1194
Condon, MT 59826
406-754-2701

ABG **Tim Reishus**
HI High Country Outfitters
WT P.O. Box 1608
Noxon, MT 59853
406-847-2279

AFG **Jerry C. Shively**
IWT Flat Iron Outfitting
3 Golf Course Road
Thompson Falls, MT 59873
406-827-3666

ABF **Glenn E. Smith**
GHI 5/S Outfitting & Guide Service
366 Swamp Creek Road
Trout Creek, MT 59874
406-827-4908

AFG **Jeff Smith**
HWT Bullseye Outfitting
49 Vermillion Road
Trout Creek, MT 59874
406-827-4932

ABF **Richard Wayman**
HI Big Salmon Outfitters
1316 Mink Lane
Ronan, MT 59864
406-676-3999

A **Harry Williams**
Williams Outfitters
1905 Foothills Road
Kalispell, MT 59901
406-257-2027

ABF **Jeryl Williams**
GHI WW Outfitters, Inc.
P.O. Box 249
Darby, MT 59829
406-821-3622

AGH **Richard K. Willis**
IWT Rus Willis & Associates Inc.
710 Bull River Road
Noxon, MT 59853
406-847-5597

AGH **Harry T. Workman**
IWT Buckhorn Ranch
P.O. Box 84
Eureka, MT 59917
406-889-3762

AFG **E. Neven Zugg**
IWT Koocanusa Outfitters
23911 Hwy 37
Libby, MT 59923
406-293-7548

Region 2

Region 2

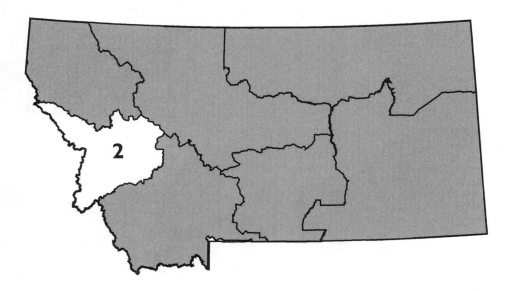

Region 2 is a mixed habitat region similar to Region 1 in the north, but drying to habitats similar to Region 3 in the east and south. Steep, dense, fairly wet mountain forests pervade the northwest corner and west edge. Drier forests occupy the central and eastern regions. You'll also find high, rocky mountains and wilderness and flat to rolling dry grassland/ranchland valleys. Take your pick of close, dense-cover hunting or open country roaming, rugged mountains or gentle valleys. Gaining permission to hunt private land is a challenge, but there's plenty of public land. There is a good mix of road access in some places, foot and horse access in others.

Game Species and Numbers

Region 2 is one of the best elk producers in the state, with good numbers in the mountain forests throughout. Whitetails are found throughout in the moist, western conifer mountains and in valley riparian zones. Mule deer populations are higher than in Region 1, with numbers increasing toward the southeast in foothills, grasslands, and high mountains. Extremely limited pronghorn hunting is available by permit in district 215 north of Butte. Several bighorn and mountain goats herds are found in the highlands. Moose, cougar, and black bear are widespread, though densities in these drier mountains are not as high as in the wet forests of the northwest.

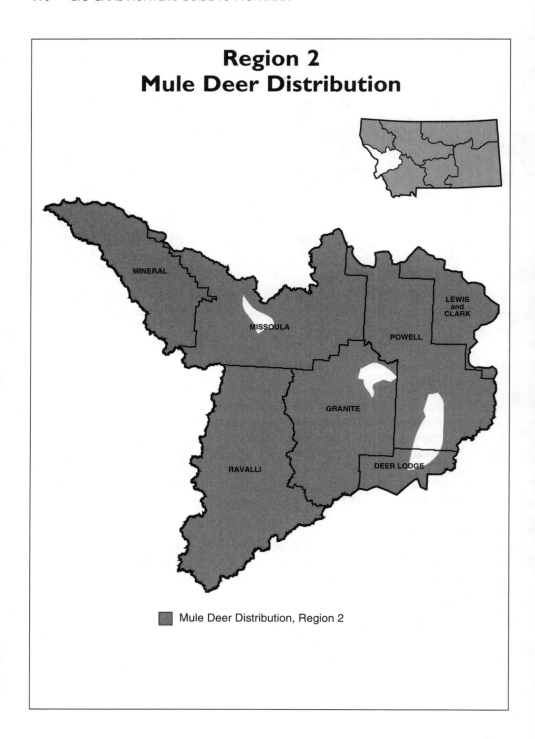

Region 2
Mule Deer Distribution

MINERAL

LEWIS
and
CLARK

MISSOULA

POWELL

GRANITE

RAVALLI

DEER LODGE

Mule Deer Distribution, Region 2

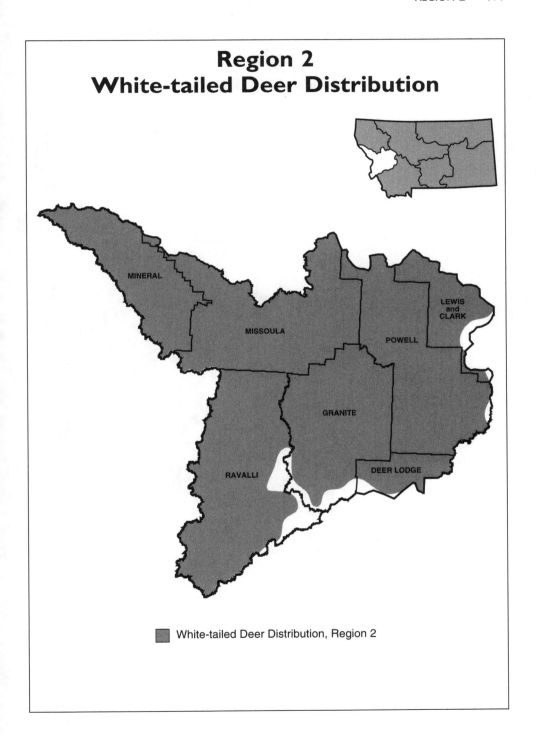

Region 2
White-tailed Deer Distribution

White-tailed Deer Distribution, Region 2

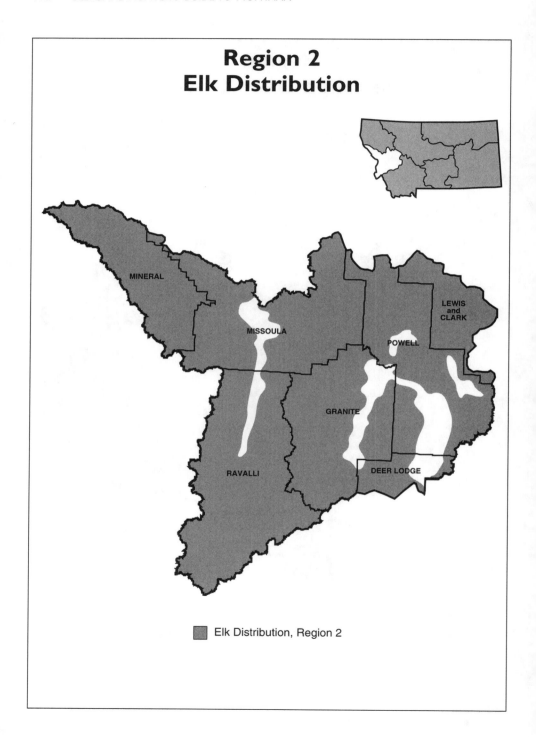

Region 2
Elk Distribution

MINERAL

MISSOULA

LEWIS
and
CLARK

POWELL

GRANITE

RAVALLI

DEER LODGE

Elk Distribution, Region 2

Region 2
Moose Distribution

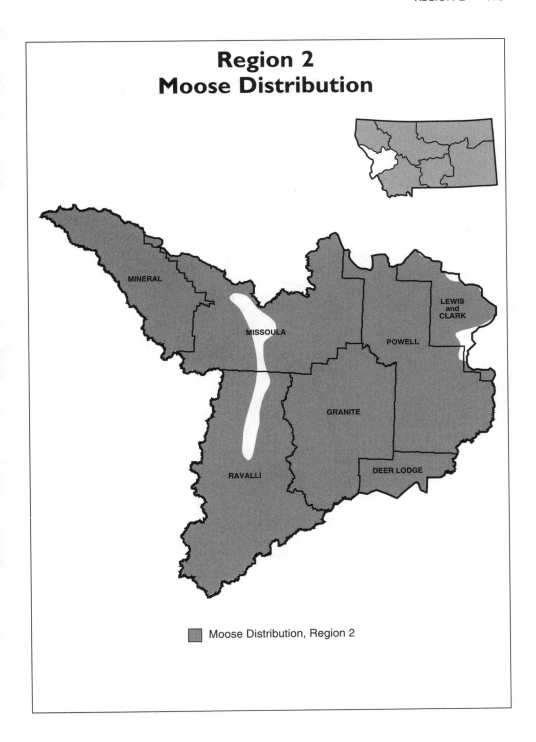

Moose Distribution, Region 2

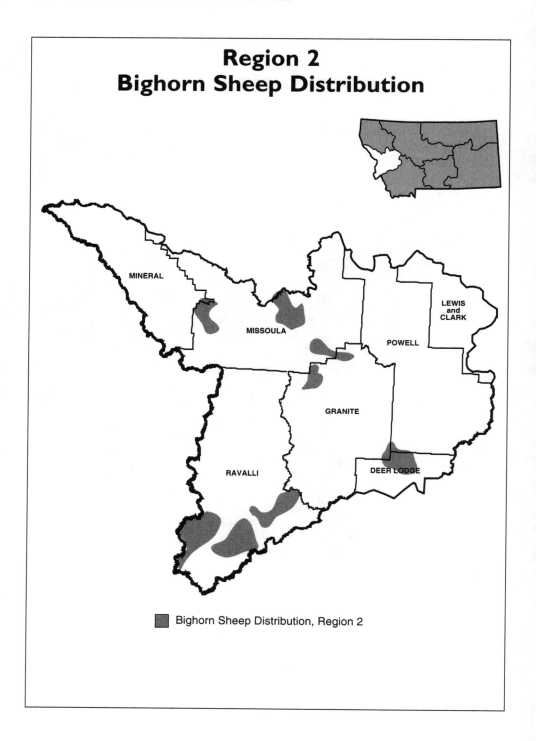

Region 2
Bighorn Sheep Distribution

Bighorn Sheep Distribution, Region 2

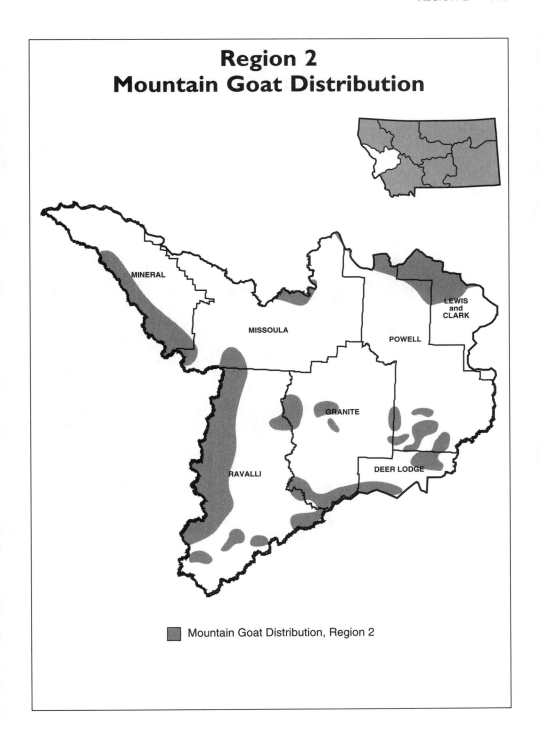

Region 2
Mountain Goat Distribution

Mountain Goat Distribution, Region 2

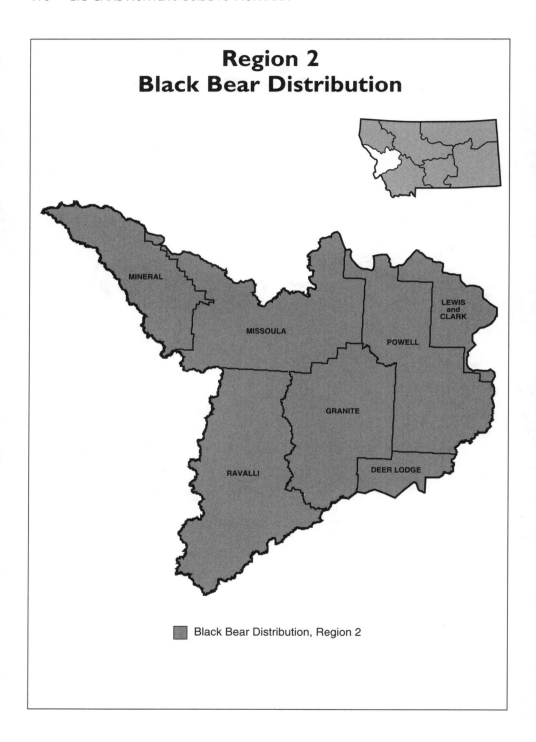

Region 2
Black Bear Distribution

MINERAL

LEWIS and CLARK

MISSOULA

POWELL

GRANITE

RAVALLI

DEER LODGE

Black Bear Distribution, Region 2

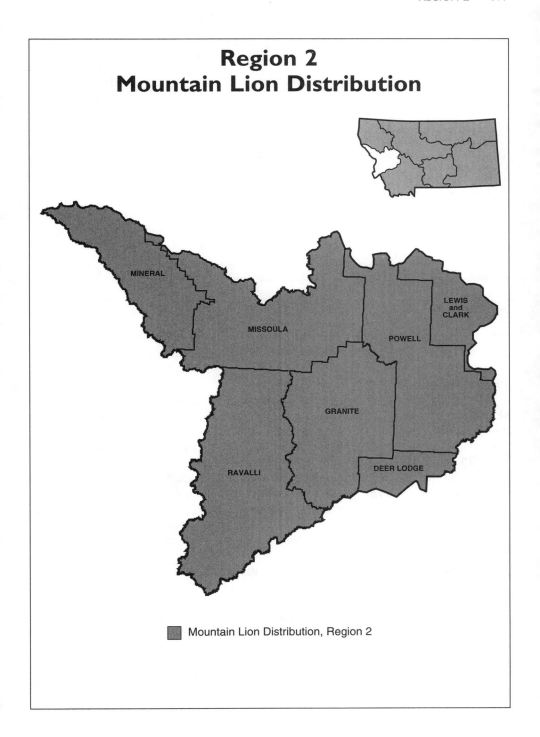

Region 2
Mountain Lion Distribution

Mountain Lion Distribution, Region 2

Harvest Trend (1992–1996)

Species	Success Rate	Harvest	Hunters
Deer	49%	Mule bucks 2,410–4,500 Mule does 548–1,500 Whitetail bucks 5,500–6,086 Whitetail does 3,800–5,900	26,715–30,542
Elk	21%	Bulls 2,300–2,900 Cows 1,800–4,100	27,000–28,000
Moose	90%	Bulls 54–66 Cows 6–19	75–82
Bighorn Sheep	87%	Rams 26–36 Ewes 43–54	77–101
Mountain Goat	72%	Billies 14–25 Nannies 4–23	29–75
Pronghorn	100%	Bucks 2–5 Does 2–8	2–13

Cougars and Bears—No harvest statistics available

Physical Characteristics

The Bitterroot Mountains form a sharp wall of steep, forested, mixed-conifer slopes and barren, rocky peaks reaching 8,000 to 10,157 feet along the Idaho border and western edge of Region 2. As much as 100 inches of annual precipitation has been recorded on the higher peaks, most of it as snow. In northwest Mineral County, the Bitterroots, here within the Lolo National Forest, are similar to the thickly forested mountains in Region 1. Logging roads penetrate the ridges and forests on both sides of Interstate 90, which cuts northwest up the only major valley in the area. There is considerable de facto wilderness in the Great Burn area on the Idaho border accessible via horse and foot trails from Forest Service Road (FR) 250 (Trout Creek Road) south of Superior and FR 343 (Fish Creek Road) south of Tarkio. This has long been a prime elk, black bear, and moose area.

Farther south along the crest of the Bitterroots, 248,893 acres of the Selway-Bitterroot Wilderness lie within Montana and the Bitterroot National Forest in a narrow strip extending from just south of Lolo nearly to the southwest tip of the state. The bulk of the Selway-Bitterroot lies in Idaho, but big game crosses freely both ways. Outside of the rugged wilderness, 70 percent of the Bitterroots' slopes are considered moderate to steep. West of Darby, a famous jump-off town for wilderness hunters, ridges rise 5,000 feet in as few as three horizontal miles. South- and west-facing slopes are dry with open stands of pine and grassland below 5,000 feet. Fully three-fourths of the mountains are forest covered.

The dry, flat Bitterroot valley in the rain shadow of these mountains gets just 13 inches of precipitation each year. Highways, small towns, farms, ranches, and ranchettes make most of the valley off-limits to all but a few hunters with permission. Stevensville, Victor, Hamilton, and Darby are the principal valley towns, and US 93 is a major thoroughfare. Whitetails along the cottonwood-lined Bitterroot River and bordering alfalfa fields are the main game. At the north end of the valley near Missoula, housing development has changed the character of the land. North of Missoula is the 31,479 acre Rattlesnake Wilderness with peaks as high as 8,620 feet.

The north-south tending Sapphire Range—extending into each of the Lolo, Bitterroot, and Deerlodge National Forests—rises gradually east of the Bitterroot valley, its foothills forming a typical dry mountain steppe habitat covered in a mix of grass, sage, and other shrubs. Better road access is available here than in the Bitterroots. Mule deer begin to replace whitetails in this higher, drier habitat. Junipers, ponderosa pines, Douglas firs, and lodgepole pines march in roughly that sequence up the higher hills, which eventually rise to 7,000- and 9,000-foot peaks. In the south, the Sapphires merge with the northeast-southwest tending Anaconda Range and the Continental Divide. Here, you'll find the 157,874 acre Anaconda-Pintler Wilderness with its deep canyons, dark forests, and rocky peaks reaching to 10,793 feet. Lots of logging roads in the southern Sapphires push right against the wilderness boundary. The Sula State Forest in this area provides hunting on relatively gentle terrain.

Northeast of the Sapphires open the Rock Creek and Philipsburg valleys with the John Long Mountains between them. The bulk of this area is privately owned. In the northwest corner of Granite County is the 28,184-acre Welcome Creek Wilderness, accessible via logging roads southeast of Missoula and FR 102 (Rock Creek Road).

The dry Garnet Range east of Missoula and north of I-90 is a mix of private and BLM land with a significant parcel within the Clearwater State Forest. Much of it is high, rugged, and unroaded. Open valleys radiate east and north into the Nevada Creek and Blackfoot River valleys, an extensive grassland/ranching district. This is a good place to hunt whitetails and mule deer if you can get on private land. State Route 200 runs through the north end of the valley.

North of SR 200, the Rockies rise quickly again. The Lolo and Helena National Forests assume management, so you are again free to hunt. The Region 2 border bumps up against the Bob Marshall Wilderness in northern Powell County. FR 131 up Lodgepole Creek is the closest access. Farther east on SR 200 is Lincoln, the town made famous by the Unabomber. The high mountains on the Continental Divide north of town have been saved for wildlife and hunters as the Scapegoat Wilderness, accessible from an elaborate trail system off numerous Forest Service roads in the area. Logging roads provide considerable easy forest access around Lincoln.

The private grasslands bordering I-90 from Butte to Drummond are good for mule deer and whitetails, if you can get on. South and west of I-90, the Flint Creek

Range rises within the Deerlodge National Forest to over 10,000 feet. It hosts glacial mountain lakes, mountain goats, and sheep along with mule deer, elk, and black bears. Forest Service roads penetrate from the north and south; a surprising number run along the Continental Divide north of Butte and east of Deer Lodge.

Land Use

Logging and mining are major activities in the forests and mountains, ranching and farming in the valleys, with considerable suburban development around Missoula and in the Bitterroot Valley. There are big mines operating in Butte and Anaconda, many smaller ones deep in the mountains, and lots of abandoned shafts and ghost towns. Be courteous to loggers, staying off active logging roads whenever possible and pulling well off roads to let those behemoth logging trucks by. While moving cattle from higher summer range to lower winter range, ranchers often drive herds down public roads. If you come upon a cattle drive, slow to a crawl and proceed when the herd parts or the cowboys move it out of your way. Don't honk and scream and get the little doggies (not to mention the cowboys) stirred up. Watch also for overloaded hay trucks and give 'em room.

Weather

Pacific weather moderates the climate in Region 2, much as it does in Region 1. Expect rainy periods in September, a pleasant, sunny Indian summer in October, and the start of low pressure winter rains in November. Temperatures are generally mild by comparison to eastern Montana at all seasons. In September, expect temperatures between 30 and 70 degrees, depending on elevation. The higher you are, the more it rains. It can snow on the higher peaks at any time. By October, be prepared for temperatures falling into the single digits, but more realistically, expect high 20s to high 50s. By November, there is potential for below-zero cold, but anticipate lows in the teens and highs in the mid 40s. Wind is possible, but not usual except on the tops of divides.

Public Lands and Acreages

National Forests in Region 2	Forest Size (not all acres necessarily within Region 2)
Bitterroot National Forest	1,650,310 acres
Deerlodge National Forest	1,195,000 acres
Flathead National Forest	3,630,210 acres
Helena National Forest	975,100 acres
Lolo National Forest	2,100,000 acres

Wilderness Areas in Region 2	Size (not all acres necessarily within Region 1)
Anaconda-Pintler Wilderness	41,134 acres
Welcome Creek Wilderness	28,135 acres
Rattlesnake Wilderness	33,000 acres
Scapegoat Wilderness	239,936 acres
Selway-Bitterroot Wilderness	1,337,910 acres
Block Management Acres	**300,000 acres**

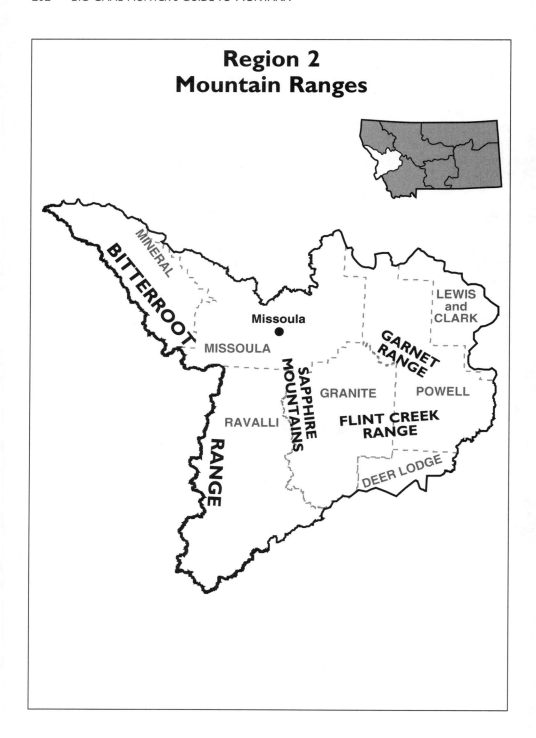

Region 2
Mountain Ranges

Region 2
Climax Vegetation

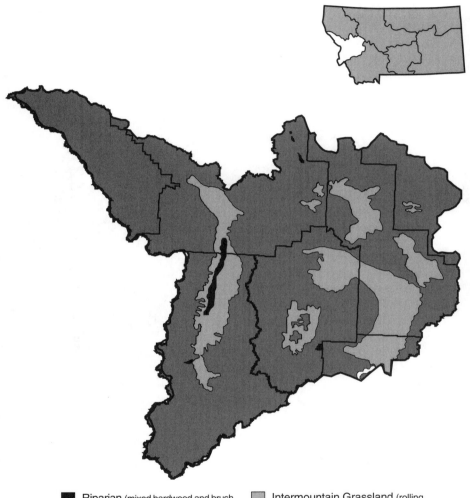

Riparian (mixed hardwood and brush along waterways)

Montane Forest (evergreen mountain forest)

Intermountain Grassland (rolling hill country w/ mixed hardwood, aspen groves, and bushy draws)

Shrub Grassland (sage brush and brush habitat)

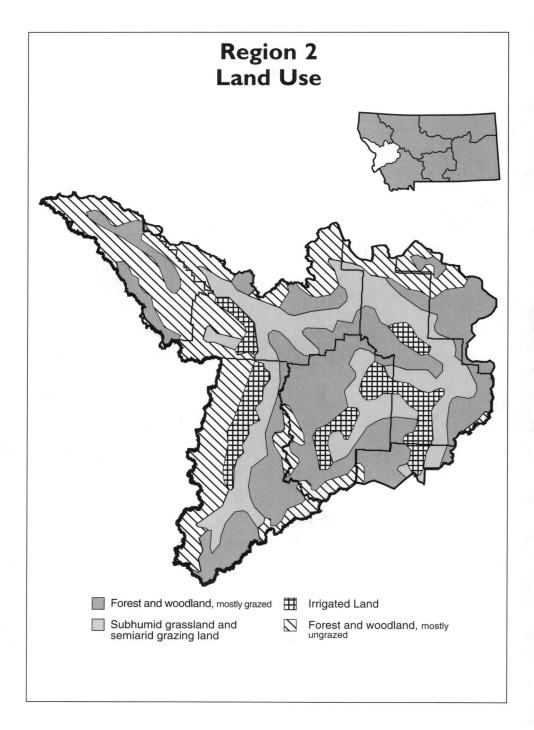

Region 2
Land Use

Forest and woodland, mostly grazed

Subhumid grassland and semiarid grazing land

Irrigated Land

Forest and woodland, mostly ungrazed

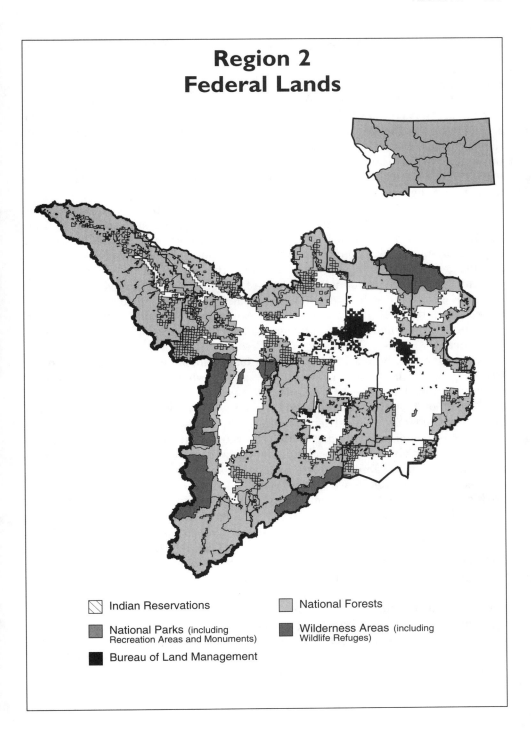

Region 2
Federal Lands

Indian Reservations

National Forests

National Parks (including Recreation Areas and Monuments)

Wilderness Areas (including Wildlife Refuges)

Bureau of Land Management

REGION 2 HIGHLIGHTS

Lower Clark Fork River

The Clark Fork River valley from Missoula to St. Regis and then up the I-90 corridor to Idaho is perhaps the most productive elk, whitetail, black bear, and cougar area in Region 2. The west and south sides (HD 202) are much more productive than the north and east sides (HDs 200 and 201). Both elk and whitetails are spread throughout the high country near the Idaho border during the early season, coinciding with the elk bugle/rut period. The populations make this a popular bowhunting district. Logging road access is good—perhaps too good—throughout most of 202, as the DeLorme *Montana Atlas*, Lolo National Forest, and area topographical maps clearly show. There are substantial unroaded areas along the state line south of Trout Creek Road, east of Forks off Fish Creek Road, and as far south as Lolo Pass. Most hunters day-hunt or work out of roadside camps. Those who horse or backpack deep into the area can find solitude and often undisturbed game.

This has been a traditionally good area for branch-antlered bulls. In the 1980s, sex ratios were about 20 bulls per 100 cows. That slipped to 10:100 in the early 90s but worked back up to 15:100 in 1997. Late season snows and cold temperature push deer and elk low, forcing them to move and feed more—increasing hunter success dramatically.

Near the valley bottom, whitetails grow fat on alfalfa fields, but big bucks often roam the high country, too. This is a superb area in which to take a mature, heavily antlered whitetail, but forest cover is dense.

Like all of Region 2, this is part of the Southwest Montana Antlered Buck Mule Deer Area; validate your deer license for one of the districts here, and you cannot use it to hunt mule deer anywhere else. Mule deer are scattered in pockets throughout this area, both high and low. Local hunters who've discovered them often take good bucks, but they aren't about to reveal their secret spots.

Because of the wet, dense forests here, black bear and mountain lion numbers are higher than elsewhere in Region 2, but not as high as in most parts of Region 1. Some 70 lions and an equal number of black bears were taken in 1997. Finally, there is one bighorn sheep herd with between 100 and 150 head in the Petty Creek drainage (HD 203) west of Missoula and north of Lolo. In 1997, 478 hunters applied for 5 tags there. Should you receive a tag, though, the chances for taking a B&C ram are good, as this is a healthy herd.

Blackfoot River Valley

A mix of forested hills, bordering mountains, rolling pastures and hay fields, and riverside brush make this a consistent whitetail producer. The lower half of the valley from Missoula to the Clearwater Junction (State Route 83) is as good as the lower Clark Fork for whitetails. SR 200 runs through the heart of this area. From SR 83 east, the valley opens, and mule deer become more common, as do elk. Most of this area

A sizable population of mountain lions lives along the lower Clark Fork.

is privately owned, some leased to hunters, but much of it can still be accessed if you ask local ranchers for permission well ahead of the seasons. Because of landowner concerns over safety, HD 290 south of Ovando is archery only for deer, and the season stretches from September 5-December 15. Hunters can use their deer A license or apply for a deer B license. The hitch is that virtually all of the land within this district is private, and you must obtain hunting permission. The FWP's Aunt Molly Wildlife Management Area (WMA) is one exception. It has 1,200 acres open to archers. Take Rd. 111 west off SR 141 to the Blackfoot River. Farther north off SR 200 on the North Fork Blackfoot River is the 2,000-acre Blackfoot Waterfowl Production Area administered by the US Fish and Wildlife Service. This public area is also open to bowhunting for deer and elk.

Elk hunting in this same area is restricted, as well as in parts of the bordering districts 298 and 299, which are virtually all private lands. Hunters must apply for special A-7 permits good for antlerless elk only in these districts. Anyone who applies for one of these licenses gets one; however, you must have permission to hunt private land in order to use the license, and the A-7 license is valid only for the district and season marked on it. A-7 license holders may not hold a general elk license nor hunt elk anywhere else in the state. In a portion of HD 290, hunters are restricted to bows or slug shotguns.

Displaying 6×6 antlers, a bull elk walks along a sagebrush ridge in the foothills of a dry western range.

Another unique hunt in the Blackfoot Valley is the 200 Series Districts Special Youth Whitetail Hunt. In 1998, 200 antlerless whitetail permits for youths 12–14 years old were available through drawing.

For more traditional and less confusing hunting, try the early season deer and elk hunt in the Scapegoat Wilderness north of Lincoln and Ovando (HDs 280 and 281). This option is popular with many outfitters and quite a few do-it-yourselfers who have horses and attendant gear. The rifle season starts in mid-September and runs through November. This is a chance to rifle hunt bugling bulls. As the wilderness is big and far from roads, backpack hunting is not recommended, though you're certainly welcome to try it. Remember, it takes a strong person about a week to pack a boned elk about 10 miles.

Easier elk and deer hunting can be had on the Blackfoot-Clearwater Wildlife Management Area (District 282) south of Seeley Lake off SR 83. This is a mix of Forest Service, state school, Plum Creek Timber Co, and FWP lands, and has the single largest elk herd (800–1,000 wintering elk) in the Blackfoot Valley. Because the terrain is relatively flat and open, hunters formerly flocked to the area and overhunted it. Now, hunting for both deer and elk is by special permit only for rifle hunters. Apply by June 1 for one of the limited permits. Archers can hunt on their regular licenses during the early September to mid-October seasons for whitetails, mule deer, and elk, both sexes.

HD 291, south of Helmville in the Garnet Range, has a special permit mule deer buck hunt limited to 200 permits in 1998. This is an effort to reduce overharvest and raise the age and trophy quality of muley bucks in the area. Since its inception about 10 years ago, average age of harvested bucks has crept up from 1½ to 4½ years.

The best black bear hunting in the Blackfoot is up around Seeley Lake. In recent years, the lion harvest in the Blackfoot has been about 30-40 annually. A mountain goat herd in the Scapegoat Wilderness (HD 280) has been entertaining a couple of hunters in each of the last few seasons. Herds are rebuilding after lows in the late 1960s. A bighorn herd along the lower Blackfoot (HD 283) was opened for one (1!) lucky hunter in 1997.

Bitterroot Valley

Despite the cancerous spread of housing throughout the once lovely Bitterroot Valley south of Missoula, some excellent whitetail hunting still exists there for those who gain access on the mostly small parcels of private land. Tiring of deer eating their ornamental yard plants, many homeowners welcome hunters. Others do not. A few fishing access sites along the river are surrounded by enough FWP land (65 to 650 acres) to accommodate bowhunting. Get maps of these accesses from the Missoula FWP office. The Lee Metcalf National Wildlife Refuge north of Stevensville offers a generous bowhunting season for deer from September 5–January 15. Call the refuge at 406-777-5552 for complete information, or mail them at PO Box 254, Stevensville, MT 59870.

A special permit season (September 12–20 in 1998) on antlerless whitetail is available in the valley (HD 260) for restricted weapons—slug-only shotgun and muzzleloader—but it is restricted to non-FWP lands, and the Lee Metcalf NWR is off-limits; in other words, the hunt is primarily on private lands, and you'll have to knock on some doors to participate. In 1998, 150 permits were available allowing for up to 2 deer B licenses; applications were due by June 1. Call the Missoula FWP office for details, 406-542-5500.

Farther south in the valley remain some larger traditional ranches and more open country, but you must make connections to get on. Begin early. Much of the settled lower valley (HD 260) is open to special permit archery, muzzleloader, or shotgun slug only hunting over a long season stretching into January. Additional B doe licenses are often sold. Contact the Missoula FWP office at 406-542-5500 for complete and current information. Whitetail bucks can and do grow quite large in this district.

Moose numbers are relatively high on the west slope of the Bitterroots. This bull moose provides a view from the rear in an open area amidst evergreen forest.

West Slope and Selway-Bitterroot Wilderness

The face of the Bitterroot Range (HDs 240 and 250) rises like a wall on the west side of the Bitterroot Valley and is not very productive. Rocky, steep, and covered with conifers, it provides hard living for big game and is not noted for abundance or trophy quality, compared to the gentler parts of Region 2.

There are fair numbers of whitetails on the lower slopes near the valley. Do your homework, and you might waylay an old mossy horn feeding in the valley and hiding in the higher forest. Mule deer numbers are low, and no doe hunting has been allowed for some eight years. This is not great mule deer habitat, but some good bucks do roam the upper ends of the rugged creek drainages that cut west to east through the mountains. They stick to the high end and high ridges between drainages until snow forces them low. Hunt high in early season.

Two types of elk seem to call the Bitterroot face home. One sticks to the lower slopes year round. The other migrates to the high country for summer, then moves down when snow and cold force them. Because the upper country is so remote and hard to reach, it harbors a few good bulls. Many of them drift between Montana and Idaho. Terrain and hunting are tough, but you should find plenty of isolation.

One thing the rugged canyon slopes do provide is mountain goat habitat. HDs 240 and 250 are divided into 11 different goat hunting districts. In 1998, 14 permits were available for the entire area. The goats stick to the high north and east ridges and faces until deep snow pushes them south and down.

A native sheep herd persists in the Sheephead and Watchtower Creek area (HD 250 along the Idaho border). Two or three permits have been available in recent years. Rams do not grow exceptional horns here.

In 1998, there were 10 moose tags available in HDs 240 and 250. Numbers of this largest deer are relatively high for the limited habitat.

Bear and cougar hunting are relatively difficult along the face due to limited road access, steep terrain, and dense conifer forests. Populations are fair.

Sapphire Mountains

The Sapphire Mountains on the east side of the Bitterroot Valley are much more productive than the west-side Bitterroots. Slopes are more gradual, and there are more grasslands and meadows with nutritious winter browse like sage, bitterbrush, and bunch grasses on important south- and west-facing slopes where winds and sun melt snow free. This is one of the best parts of Region 2 for mule deer, although herds have been down in recent years. For this reason, mule deer buck hunting is restricted here under the Southwest Antlered Buck Mule Deer regulations. Validate your tag to hunt muley bucks in one of the several areas here, and you cannot hunt muley bucks anywhere else in the state. Additionally, in HDs 261 and 270 you must apply for a limited permit to hunt mule deer bucks or does. Loss of winter range to housing gets much of the blame for declining mule deer herds here, and that is likely to only get worse. It's a sad commentary on land use planning in the West.

The Sapphires are also one of the better elk areas in Region 2. Consequently, there is considerable hunting pressure. During the general season, only brow-tine antlered bulls may be harvested. A-7 antlerless permits are available via drawing in HDs 204, 261, and 270. Apply before June 1 for A-7 permits. Remember, these permits are valid only on certain private ranchlands in Region 2. You must have permission to hunt one of these ranches before you can use the A-7 tag. Contact FWP in Missoula (406-542-5500) for current and complete information.

HD 270 is tops for moose, with 10 licenses issued in 1998, compared to 2 in HD 261. Road access is good throughout much of 270 and slightly less in 261 and 204. There are sheep and goat herds in the upper reaches of the East Fork Bitterroot River (HD 270) which takes in a bit of the Continental Divide and Anaconda-Pintler Wilderness. Five goat and 2 sheep tags were offered in 1998.

Looking down from a rocky prominence, a mature bighorn ram displays fully curled and broomed horns. B&C class sheep can be found in the mountains surrounding the Rock Creek drainage.

Rock Creek Sheep

Rock Creek, a famous trout fishing stream that drains the east side of the Sapphires, much of the Anaconda Range to the southeast, the John Long Mountains, and part of the Flint Creek Range, is famous for its monster bighorn rams. The lower end of the creek (HD 210) had 10 either sex and 15 ewe-only tags in 1998, while upper Rock Creek (HD 216) had 12 and 20 respectively. Odds for drawing one of the coveted ram tags were about 1 in 81 in HD 210 and an unbelievable 1 in 116 in HD 216. Don't hold your breath. Anyone lucky enough to get one of these tags had better be prepared to hunt hard for as long as the season lasts. It's a once-in-a-lifetime chance to take a B&C ram.

John Long Mountains

This little known range east of Rock Creek resembles the Sapphires and has similar opportunities for elk, though it's not quite as good for mule deer. The better deer and elk are on average found toward the south where private ranchland and more open pastures prevail. There is some Block Management land in this area (about 15,000 acres in 1998), mostly in the foothills where cow elk and whitetails are what you're most likely to find. As many of the Block Management areas require advanced written permission from the landowner or FWP, do your planning well ahead of time. Some are open to daily walk-in hunting and others have a daily sign-in box, but don't depend on finding these where and when you need them. Advance scouting is important.

Flint Creek Range

Elk hunting is surprisingly good in this unheralded island of mountains north of Anaconda, east of Philipsburg, west of Deer Lodge, and south of I-90. Access via Forest Service roads from State Route 1 is good. Many old logging roads penetrate fairly deeply into the high mountains, and lots of trails branch from them. Nearly all of the mountains are public land within the Deerlodge National Forest. Mule deer hunting is not as good as the elk chasing, but fair. There are some decent bucks hiding out in the unroaded high country, but few true monsters.

There's a nice little band of sheep in the southeast corner of these mountains (District 213), and it's producing some excellent rams. Drawing one of the 4 or 5 available permits, of course, is the biggest hurdle; would you believe one chance in 100?

Mountain goats are a similar story. Two permits were sold in 1998, and about 40 times that many hunters applied for them. Moose hunters fared a little better; they had 7 bull and 4 cow tags to fight for, and about 235 entered the fray.

Montana State Prison Ranch at Deer Lodge

This may be the only place where people are eager to get into prison. Behind the old Montana State Prison in Deer Lodge (a tourist stop) are 23,000 acres of grassland sloping up toward the Flint Creek Range, comprising deer and elk district 212. Archers can hunt on 18,000 acres, rifle hunters get 5,300 acres. The bow benders can stalk mule deer, whitetails, and elk from early September through early October, then again from late October through January 1. And that's not all. In order to control deer herd numbers, they can purchase up to 5 extra B licenses for does. Because much of the archery hunting area borders town and the prison, all hunters must enter through the prison administration building! Now there's a unique start to a hunt.

Rifle hunters work the far west edge of the property, so they don't need to go through the front door. Maps and rules for both hunts are available from the Region 2 FWP office in Missoula, 406-542-5500, and from the prison (should you happen to be stopping in).

Region 2 Hub Cities
Superior

Population–1,200 • Elevation–2,740

Mineral County is along the Montana-Idaho border. Eighty-two percent of the land in the county is federally owned and provides abundant recreational and hunting opportunities. The famous Clark Fork River runs through the center of the county, and the Bitterroot Mountains and the Lolo National Forest comprise most of the land. Terrain consists of montane forest.

Superior, the largest town in Mineral County, is on the banks of the Clark Fork, 57 miles northwest of Missoula.

Accommodations
Bellevue Motel, 110 Mullan Road East / 822-4692 / 22 rooms / Dogs welcome / Rates very reasonable
Budget Host Big Sky Motel, 103 4th Avenue East / 822-4831 / 24 rooms / Dogs welcome / Rates very reasonable

Campgrounds and RV Parks
St. Regis Campground, 2 miles west of St. Regis and 16 miles west of Superior / 649-2470 / 25 tent and 75 RV spaces / Full facilities including showers, laundry, and store

Restaurants
Rock 'n' Rodeo, 102 River Street / 822-3040
4-Aces, 104 West Mullan Road / 822-3181
JG's Family Restaurant, 204 East 4th Avenue / 822-4967

Veterinarians
Closest in Missoula, 60 miles south:
Missoula Veterinary Clinic, 3701 Old 93 South / 251-2400 / 24-hour emergency service
Pruyn Veterinary Hospital, 2501 Russell / 251-4150 / 24-hour emergency service

Sporting Goods, Guns & Gunsmithing
Castle's Westgate, 302 South River / 822-4801
Abbey's Trustworthy Hardware, 106 East Mullan Road / 822-4602

Meat Processors
Superior Meats, Inc., 569 East Mullan Road / 822-4209
Diamond S Meats, 432 Mullan Road / 822-4702

TAXIDERMISTS
Gerald Stroot, 569 East Mullan Road / 822-4209

AUTO REPAIR
Dave Beck, 321 West Mullan Road / 822-3207
Carl's Auto Repair, 35 Diamond Road / 822-4691
Schneider Auto Service, 109 River / 822-4811

AIR SERVICE
County Airstrip, Gerald Geske / 822-4917

MEDICAL
Mineral Community Hospital, Brooklyn and Roosevelt / 822-4841

FOR MORE INFORMATION
Superior Area Chamber of Commerce
Box 483
Superior, MT 59872
406-822-4891

Missoula

Population– 43,000 • Elevation–3,200

Missoula is located in a broad valley in western Montana. It is at the center of five scenic valleys: the Flathead to the north, Frenchtown to the west, Bitterroot to the south, Blackfoot to the northeast, and Hellgate to the east. The Clark Fork River flows through the center of town and is joined by the famous Bitterroot River from the south. Home to the University of Montana, Missoula is a major retail and cultural center of western Montana. Habitat consists of montane forest, grassland, and agricultural fields.

ACCOMMODATIONS

Bel Aire Motel, 300 East Broadway / 543-7183 / 52 rooms / Dogs allowed in smoking rooms, $5 fee / There is one nonsmoking room in which dogs are allowed / Rates moderate

Days Inn/Westgate, Rt 93 and I-90 / 721-9776 / 69 rooms / Dogs allowed, $5 fee / Restaurant on premises / Rates moderate

4B's Inn North, 4953 North Reserve / 542-7550 / 67 rooms / Dogs allowed / Restaurant on premises / Rates moderate

4B's South, 3803 Brooks / 251-2665 / 79 rooms / Dogs allowed / Restaurant on premises / Rates moderate

CAMPGROUNDS AND RV PARKS

Missoula El-Mar KOA, Reserve Street exit, 1½ miles south / 549-0881 / 36 tent and 164 RV spaces / Open year-round / Full facilities, including hot tub and store

Out Post Campground, I-90 exit 96, 2 miles north on Rt 93 / 549-2016 / 10 tent and 35 RV spaces / Open year-round / Full facilities

RESTAURANTS

4B's, located at 4B's motels north and south / 542-7550, 4B's North; 251-2665, 4B's South / Open for breakfast, lunch, and dinner

Finnegan's Family Restaurant, 700 East Broadway / 542-2752 / Open 24 hours, 7 days for breakfast, lunch, and dinner

McKay's on the River, 1111 East Broadway / 728-0098 / Restaurant/lounge open 7 days for breakfast, lunch, and dinner / Unique antique gun display / Steaks, prime rib, and seafood

New Pacific Grill, 100 East Railroad Avenue at the old Northern Pacific Railroad station / 542-3353 / Open 7 days for lunch and dinner / Casual dining / Fresh seafood and beef

Paradise Falls, 3621 Brooks / 728-3228 / Restaurant, lounge, casino open 6AM–2AM for breakfast, lunch, and dinner / Steaks and baby-back ribs

VETERINARIANS
Missoula Veterinary Clinic, 3701 Old 93 South / 251-2400 / 24-hour emergency service
Pruyn Veterinary Hospital, 2501 Russell / 251-4150 / 24-hour emergency service

SPORTING GOODS, GUNS, & GUNSMITHS
Bob Ward and Sons, 2300 Brooks / 728-3220 / Open 7 days
Sportsman's Surplus, Temperaturer's Shopping Center / 721-5500 / Open 7 days
Black Sheep Discount Sporting Goods, 1010 North Avenue West / 721-2218
Lock, Stock & Barrel, 1615 Montana Street / 543-7830
Brainard Gunsmithing, 818 Woody Street / 549-3249
Gart Sports, 2640 N Reserve Street / 542-2112
Sportsman's Surplus/Hi Country, 2301 Brooks Street / 721-5500
Barrel Shop, 566 Blodgett View Drive / 363-0583

TAXIDERMISTS
Bear Paw Taxidermy, 311 South Avenue / 542-2238
Bitterroot Taxidermy Studio, 707 Ronan Street / 728-0999
Buckhorn Taxidermy, 805 Sherwood Street / 721-4759
Holst Taxidermy, 3418 Helena Drive / 251-5484
Second Nature Taxidermy, Bonner, MT / 244-5404

MEAT PROCESSORS
H&H Meats, 1801 South Avenue West / 549-1483
Lolo Locker, Hwy 93 South & Caras Lane / 273-3876

AUTO RENTAL
Avis, Missoula International Airport / 549-4711
Hertz, Missoula International Airport / 549-9511
National, Missoula International Airport / 543-3131

AUTO REPAIR
Ram Towing and Repair, 3402 Grant Creek Road I-90 at Reserve Street / 542-3636 or 800-870-3634 / 24-hour auto and diesel repair
Skip's Orange Street Sinclair, 400 West Broadway / 549-5571 / Open 7 days

AIR SERVICE
Missoula International Airport, Hwy 93 north of town / 728-4381 / Delta, Horizon, and Northwest airlines

MEDICAL
Community Medical Center, 28227 Fort Missoula Road / 728-4100
St. Patrick Hospital, 500 West Broadway / 543-7271 / 24-hour emergency services / Life flight

FOR MORE INFORMATION

Missoula Chamber of Commerce
825 East Front Street
Missoula, MT 59802
406-543-6623

U.S. Forest Service
Northern Region Office
200 East Broadway, Box 7669
Missoula, MT 59807
406-329-3511

BLM–Missoula Field Office
3255 Fort Missoula Road
Missoula, MT 59804-7293
406-329-3914

Fish, Wildlife & Parks–Region 2
3201 Spurgin Road
Missoula, MT 59804
406-542-5500

Lolo National Forest
Building 24, Fort Missoula
Missoula, MT 59804
406-329-3750

Hamilton

Population–2,800 • Elevation– 3,600

Hamilton is a retirement and resort community located in the beautiful Bitterroot Valley. The Bitterroot Mountains form the western border of the valley, and the Sapphire Mountains are to the east. The famous blue-ribbon Bitterroot River runs north through the valley. Logging and log home manufacturing are the main industries of Ravalli County.

ACCOMMODATIONS

Best Western, 409 South 1st / 363-2142

City Center Motel, 415 West Main / 363-1651

Deffy's Motel, 321 South 1st / 363-1244

Bud & Shirley's Motel & Restaurant, Main Street, Darby / 821-3401 71 rooms

Wilderness Motel & RV Park, 308 South Main, Darby / 821-3405 / 12 rooms, 8 with kitchens

Sula Campground & Store, 7060 Hwy 93 South of Darby / 821-3364 / Four 2-bedroom cabins, RV Park, restaurant

Bitterroot Motel, 408 South 1st Street / 363-1142 / 10 rooms / Dogs welcome / Rates very reasonable

Sportsman Motel, 410 North 1st Street / 363-2411 / 18 rooms / Dogs allowed in smoking rooms only / Rates very reasonable

Comfort Inn of Hamilton, 113 North 1st Street / 363-6600 / 64 rooms / Restaurant / Dogs allowed, $5 charge / Rates moderate

CAMPGROUNDS AND RV PARKS

Angler's Roost, on Bitterroot River 3 miles south on Rt 93 / 363-1268 / 15 tent and 60 RV spaces / Open year-round / Full facilities, including cabins, store, gun and tackle shop, hunting licenses, and gas

RESTAURANTS

BJs, 900 North 1st / 363-4650

The Edge, 140 Bitterroot Plaza / 375-0007 / Open 24 hrs

The Stone Pony, 310 South 1st / 375-0381

Coffee Cup Cafe, 500 South 1st Street / 363-3822 / Home-style cooking and pastry / Breakfast served all day

4B's Restaurant, 1105 North 1st Street / 363-4620

Spice of Life Restaurant, 163 South 2nd Street / 363-4433 / The Bitterroot's finest bar and grill

SPORTING GOODS, GUNS, & GUNSMITHS

Bob Ward and Sons, 1120 North 1st Street / 363-6204

Bitterroot Trading Post, 1010 1st Street / 363-2525

Jarvis Gunsmithing, 1123 Cherry Orchard Loop / 961-4392

Mike's Gunsmithing, 156 Denali Street / 363-3233
Mountain Outfitters-Sporting, 205 Main Street / 363-1560

VETERINARIANS
Basin Veterinary Service, 58 Roaring Lion Road / 363-4579
Bitterroot Veterinary Clinic, 1116 North 1st Street / 363-1123

TAXIDERMISTS
Big Sky Taxidermy Studio, 1984 1st / 363-5780
Rose Taxidermy, Main Street, Darby / 821-3231
Rocky Mountain Taxidermy, Hwy 93, Florence / 273-6697
Trautman Taxidermy, 378 Harlan Creek Road, Darby / 821-4923
The Taxidermist, 18300 US 93 N, Florence / 549-6671

MEAT PROCESSORS
Hamilton Pack, 2464 Hwy 93 North / 961-3861
Darius Badgley, 3609 Eastside Hwy, Stevensville / 777-5684

AUTO REPAIR
Mildenberger Chevrolet, 1717 North 1st / 363-4110
Bell-McCall Ford, 300 West Main / 363-2011
Al's Car Care Center, 324 South 1st Street / 363-3700

AIR SERVICE
Ravalli County Airport / 363-3833

MEDICAL
Marcus Daly Hospital, 1200 Westwood Drive / 363-2211

FOR MORE INFORMATION
Bitterroot Valley Chamber of Commerce
105 East Main
Hamilton, MT 59840
363-2400

Bitterroot National Forest
1801 North First Street
Hamilton, MT 59840
406-363-7167

Anaconda

Population–10,700 • Elevation– 5,331

Anaconda, a town built by copper magnate Marcus Daly, was once home to one of the largest copper smelters in the world. Anaconda is bisected by the Flint River and sits in the middle of the Flint Creek Valley.

Deer Lodge County is comprised of montane forest and intermountain grasslands. Georgetown Lake and the Anaconda-Pintler Wilderness are located in the western part of the county.

ACCOMMODATIONS

Georgetown Lake Lodge, Restaurant and Lounge, Denton's Point Road / 563-7020 / 11 rooms / Dogs allowed / Rates moderate

Seven Gables Inn Restaurant and Lounge, Georgetown Lake / 563-5052 /10 rooms and one cabin that sleeps 8 / Dogs allowed / Very reasonable rates

Trade Winds Motel, 1600 East Commercial / 800-248-3428 / 24 rooms / Kitchenettes available / Dogs allowed / Rates moderate

CAMPGROUNDS AND RV PARKS

Georgetown Lake KOA, 14 miles west on MT 1, 2 miles south at lake / 563-6030 / Open year-round / 10 tent and 48 RV spaces / Full services except for sewer / Store and laundry

RESTAURANTS

Barclay II Supper Club, 1300 East Commercial / 563-5541 / Open for dinner / Italian food

Georgetown Lake Lodge, Denton's Point / 563-7020

Granny's Kitchen, 1500 East Commercial / 563-2349

VETERINARIANS

Anaconda Veterinary Clinic, 1501 East Park / 563-2440

SPORTING GOODS

Don's Sport Center, 1310 East Commercial / 563-3231

Rainbow Sporting Goods, 605 East Park / 563-5080

TAXIDERMISTS

Capp's Taxidermy, 213 East Park Street / 563-7659

Daybreak Taxidermy, 108 Stewart Street / 797-3552

MEAT PROCESSORS

Rocky Mountain Meats, 1515 East Commercial Street / 563-6328

AUTO REPAIR

Anaconda Automotive, 1400 East Commercial / 563-8126

Air Service
Bowman Field, Warm Springs, MT (contact John McPhail) / 563-8112 or
563-9984

Medical
The Community Hospital of Anaconda, 401 West Penn / 563-5261

For More Information
Anaconda Chamber of Commerce
306 East Park Avenue
Anaconda, MT 59711
406-563-2400

Deer Lodge

Population–3,378 • Elevation–4,688

The friendly community of Deer Lodge is in the heart of a beautiful mountain valley in southwestern Montana, bisected by the Clark Fork River. The Deerlodge National Forest borders the western part of the county, and the Helena National Forest is to the east. Deer Lodge is situated on Interstate 90 and is home to the state prison and the Grant-Kohrs Ranch National Historical Site. Timber and agriculture are the main industries. Terrain consists of intermountain grassland and montane forest.

ACCOMMODATIONS

Western Big Sky Inn, 210 North Main, Deer Lodge / 846-2590
Downtowner Motel, 500 4th Street / 846-1021
Deer Lodge Super 8, 1150 North Main Street / 846-2370 / 54 rooms / Dogs allowed in smoking rooms only, $5 per dog / Rates very reasonable
Scharf Motor Inn, 819 Main Street / 846-2810 / 44 rooms / Dogs allowed / Restaurant on premise / Rates very reasonable

CAMPGROUNDS AND RV PARKS

Riverfront RV Park, Garrison Mtn, off I-90, 10 miles north / 800-255-1318 / Open year-round / 12 tent and 16 RV spaces / Full facilities including store

RESTAURANTS

4B's Restaurant, I-90 interchange / 846-2620 / Breakfast, lunch, and dinner / 24 hours
Country Village, I-90 interchange / 846-1442 / Open 7:30AM–9PM, 7 days
RJ's Steakhouse and Casino, 317 Main / 846-3400 / Open for dinner 7 days a week
Scharf's Family Restaurant, 819 Main / 846-3300 / Serving breakfast, lunch, and dinner 7 days a week / Family style dining

VETERINARIANS

Clark Fork Veterinary Clinic, 390 North Frontage Road / 846-1925 / Paul Bissonette, DVM / 9AM-5PM M–F, 9AM–1PM Sat.

SPORTING GOODS

River's Edge Sporting Goods, 101 Milwaukee Avenue / 846-2926
Ace Hardware, 506 Second Street / 846-2461

MEAT PROCESSOR

Zachery Game Processing, 706½ Maryland Avenue / 846-3070 or 846-3532

AUTO REPAIR

Riverside Service Center, 228 Mitchell / 846-3113

AIR SERVICE

County Airstrip, Ralph Besk / 846-2238 or 846-1771

MEDICAL

Powell Co. Memorial Hospital, 1101 Texas Avenue / 846-1722
Deer Lodge Clinic, 1101 Texas / 846-2212

FOR MORE INFORMATION:

Powell County Chamber of Commerce
P.O. Box 776
Deer Lodge, MT 59722
406-846-2094

Lincoln

Made infamous by the Unabomber, Lincoln would prefer its fame hinge on its friendly citizens or its proximity to some of Montana's finest big game hunting. This is a jump-off city for the surrounding Helena National Forest along the Continental Divide, the Scapegoat Wilderness to the north, and the southern end of the Bob Marshall Wilderness beyond. There is good elk, mule deer, and whitetail hunting nearby in the Blackfoot Valley. For decades, logging and ranching have powered the local economy, but hunting tourism dollars are contributing more each year.

Lincoln's Main Street is State Route 200, a major route between Missoula and Great Falls, and virtually every business is on this highway. They don't even bother to list addresses in the local phone book.

ACCOMMODATIONS

Blue Sky Motel / 362-4450 / A fireplace in every room!
Leepers Motel / 362-4333 / Separate units in woods just off Highway
Lincoln Lodge, Sleepy Hollow Lane off Hwy 200 / 362-4395
Three Bears Motel / 362-4355
Snowy Pine Inn / 362-4481

RESTAURANTS

Garland's Town & Country / 362-4244
Lambkin's Restaurant / 362-4271
Lumberjack Inn / 362-4001
Pit Stop Restaurant / 362-4848
Rainbow Café / 362-4543
Scapegoat Eatery / 362-4272
Seven-Up Ranch Supper Club / 362-4255
Stonewall Steakhouse / 362-4696
Mom's Café / 362-4480

SPORTING GOODS, GUNS AND GUNSMITHS

Grizzly True Value Home Center / 362-4995
Mountain Sports / 362-4849

TAXIDERMISTS

JR's Taxidermy Studio / 362-4282

GAME PROCESSOR

Aaron Custom Meat Cutting, 4x4 Road / 362-4461

AUTO REPAIR

Pete's Towing & Repair / 362-4528
Lincoln Auto Repair / 362-4186

AIR SERVICE
Lincoln Airport / 362-9530

MEDICAL
Blackfoot Valley Medical Services / 362-4603

FOR MORE INFORMATION
Lincoln Chamber of Commerce
Box 985
Lincoln, MT 59639
362-4949

Region 2 Guides and Outfitters

Outfitter Services by Species and Specialty

A	Elk, deer, bear, antelope	F	Mountain lion	I	Moose
B	Deer & antelope	G	Sheep	L	Drop Camps
WT	Whitetail deer	H	Mountain goat	M	Tent Camps

AB
H
James Anderson
Monture Outfitters
Box 112
Ovando, MT 59854
406-793-5618

AF
GI
Bob Batterton
Thunder Mountain Outfitters
9959 West Fork Road
Darby, MT 59829
406-349-2920

AF
H. Earl Butler
Butler Outfitters
P.O. Box 701
Darby, MT 59829
406-821-4546

AF
Joe Cantrell
Joe Cantrell Outfitting
Box 443
Silverton, ID 83867
208-753-4501

A
WT
Steven Copenhaver
Copenhaver Outfitters, Inc.
45 Coopers Lake Rosd
Ovando, MT 59854
406-793-5547

AI
Todd Earp & Fred Daigle
Hole in the Wall Outfitters
Box 326
Alberton, MT 59820
406-523-6145

AF
GH
WT
Dan J. Ekstrom
L. Diamond E Ranch
P.O. Box 885
Clinton, MT 59825
406-825-6295

A
Arnold D. Elser
Wilderness Outfitters
3800 Rattlesnake Drive
Missoula, MT 59802
406-549-2820

ABF
GHI
Vaughn Esper
Under Wild Skies
Lodge & Outfitters
P.O. Box 849
Philipsburg, MT 59858
406-859-3000

AFG
HI
WT
Jeff Freeman
JM Bar
23945 Bonita Road
Clinton, MT 59825
406-825-3230

AFG
HI
WT
Tom Henderson
Bitterroot Outfitters
1842 Hwy 93 South
Hamilton, MT 59840
406-363-0403

AHI
Mary Faith Hoeffner
K Lazy Three Ranch
P.O. Box 247
Lincoln, MT 59639
406-362-4258

A	Elk, deer, bear, antelope	F	Mountain lion	I	Moose
B	Deer & antelope	G	Sheep	L	Drop Camps
WT	Whitetail deer	H	Mountain goat	M	Tent Camps

GH
WT **Bob Hogue**
Big M Outfitters
St. Rt. 1, Box 519
Philipsburg, MT 59858
406-859-3746

HI **Chris O'Brien**
Lightning Creek Outfitters
1424 Skalkaho Road
Hamilton, MT 59840
406-363-0320

F
WT **Jack Howser**
Muleshoe Outfitters
& Guide Service
2404 Antelope Gulch
Anaconda, MT 59711
406-563-4218

H
WT **Jack Rich**
Double Arrow Outfitters/
Rich Ranch
P.O. Box 495
Seeley Lake, MT 59868
406-677-2317

WT **Tom Ode**
Montre Face Outfitters
P.O. Box 27
Greenough, MT 59836
406-244-5763

WT **Raymond Rugg**
Rugg's Outfitting
50 Dry Creek Road
Superior, MT 59872
406-822-4240

BHI **Dave Lindquist**
High Country Connection
321 Cooper Loop
Hamilton, MT 59840
406-821-3389

ABF
HI
WT **Daniel Shoemaker**
Rocky Mountain Adventures, Inc.
2050 Little Sleeping Child Road
Hamilton, MT 59840
406-363-0200

FG **Thomas McGlaughlin**
Thunder Mountain Outfitters
9959 West Fork Road
Darby, MT 59829
406-349-2920

AFH
WT **Mike Smith**
Bartlett Creek outfitters
1190 Quinlan Road
Deer Lodge, MT 59722
406-693-2433

GH
WT **Bill Mitchell**
Bill Mitchell Outfitters
364 McCarthy Loop
Hamilton, MT 59840
406-363-4129

AFG
HI
WT **Russ Smith**
Smith & Baker Outfitting Co.
P.O. Box 88
Philipsburg, MT 59858
406-859-3948

A	Elk, deer, bear, antelope	F	Mountain lion	I	Moose
B	Deer & antelope	G	Sheep	I	Drop Camps
WT	Whitetail deer	H	Mountain goat	M	Tent Camps

AFG	**William White**
HI	Rocking W Outfitters
WT	Box 507
	Darby, MT 59829
	406-821-3007

Region 3

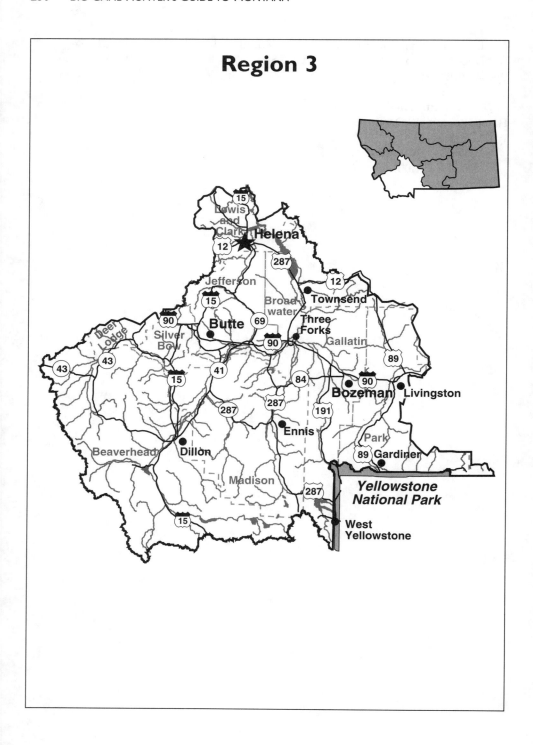

Region 3

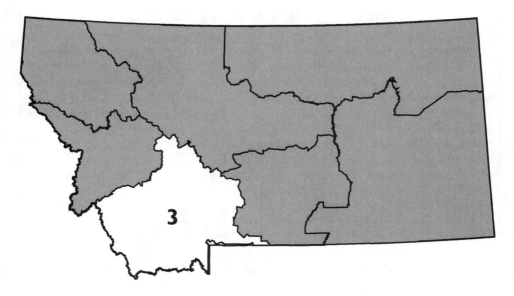

To many, Region 3 is quintessential Montana—broad grassland valleys punctuated by dramatic, towering mountain ranges. It is a beautiful place to hunt all of Montana's big game, but especially the mountain species. Millions of acres fall under Forest Service management and are open to public hunting. There is also a fair amount of open BLM public land in the region and, as of 1998, 300,000 acres under Block Management. This has created what may be the region's biggest drawback—too many hunters. A lot of locals from Helena, Bozeman, Butte, and Billings hunt the region, and nonresidents flock in because of all the public land. Partly due to hunting pressure, there are more mule deer hunting restrictions here than anywhere else in the state. It's also getting tougher to get permission to hunt private land. Logging and mining access roads penetrate many mountain canyons, but in many ranges, hunters must scramble up steep slopes and ridges for the best hunting. There are extensive horse and foot trail systems through the high mountains and wilderness areas.

Game Species and Numbers

This is the best elk region in Montana, yielding both the greatest number of animals each season and the highest hunter success rates. Mule deer hunting is also good, but increasing hunter pressure and population declines in recent years have reduced muley harvest sharply. Hunters who validate their deer A tags for certain southwest districts cannot hunt mule deer elsewhere. Still, there are big bucks hiding out in undisturbed ranchland and high wilderness mountains. Whitetails are consistent in valley

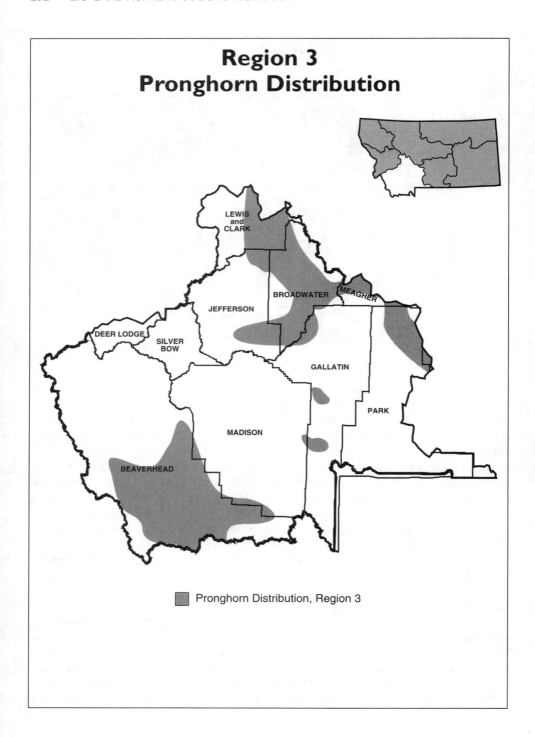

Region 3
Pronghorn Distribution

Pronghorn Distribution, Region 3

Region 3
White-tailed Deer Distribution

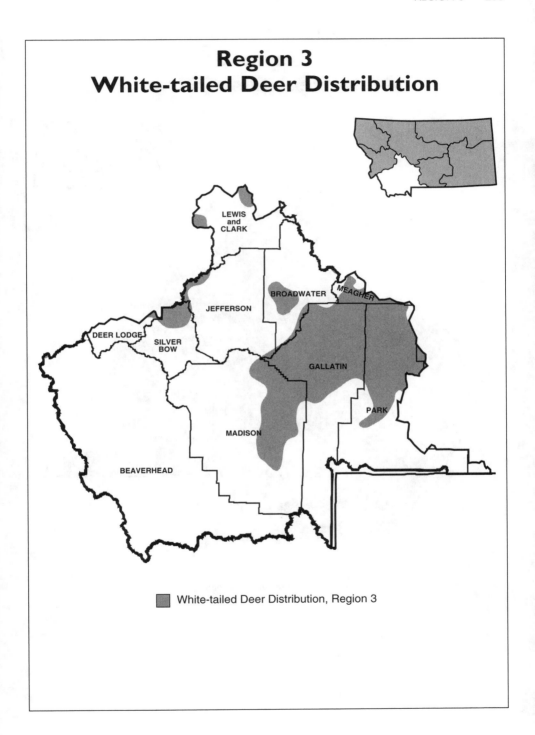

White-tailed Deer Distribution, Region 3

Region 3
Mule Deer Distribution

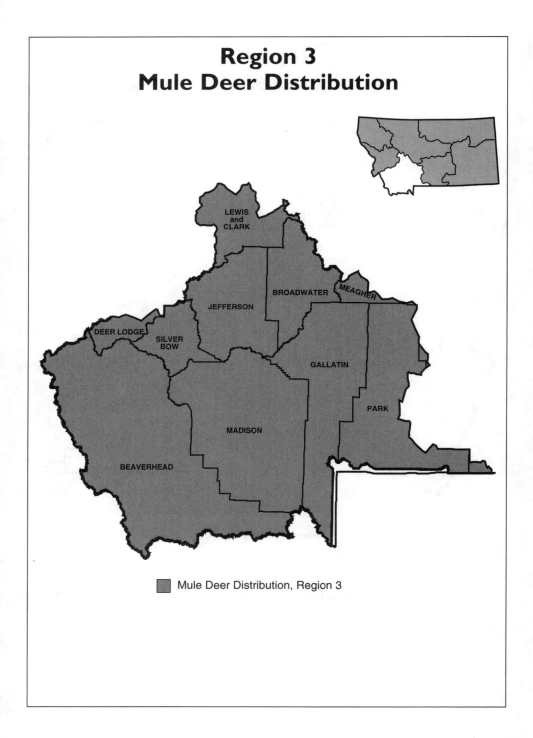

Mule Deer Distribution, Region 3

Region 3
Elk Distribution

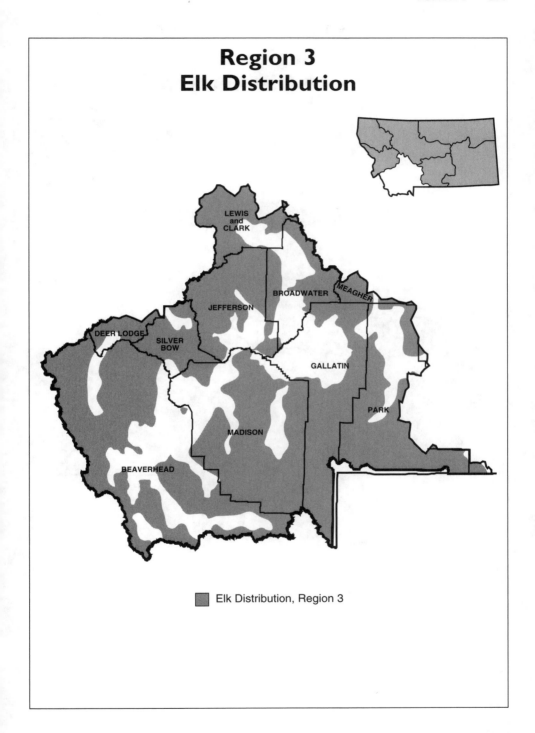

Elk Distribution, Region 3

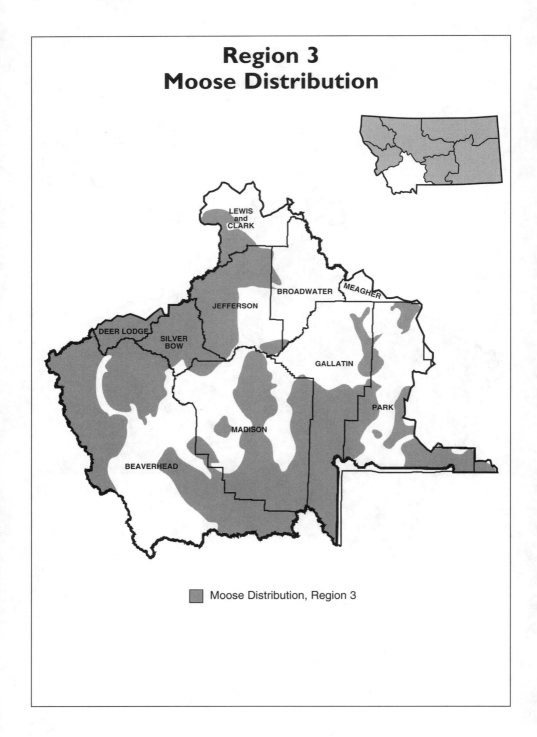

Region 3
Moose Distribution

Moose Distribution, Region 3

Region 3
Bighorn Sheep Distribution

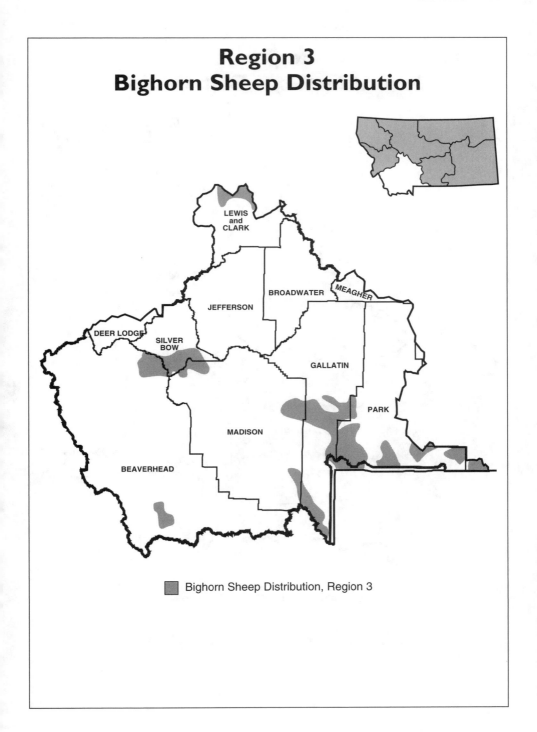

Bighorn Sheep Distribution, Region 3

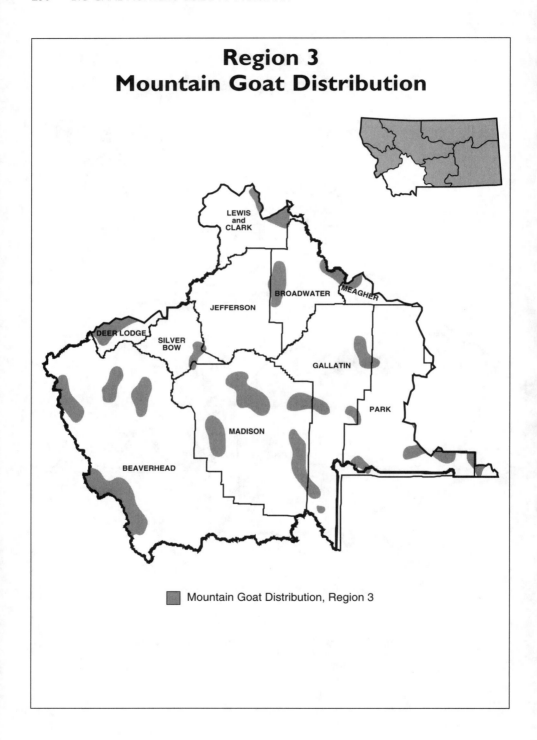

Region 3
Mountain Goat Distribution

Mountain Goat Distribution, Region 3

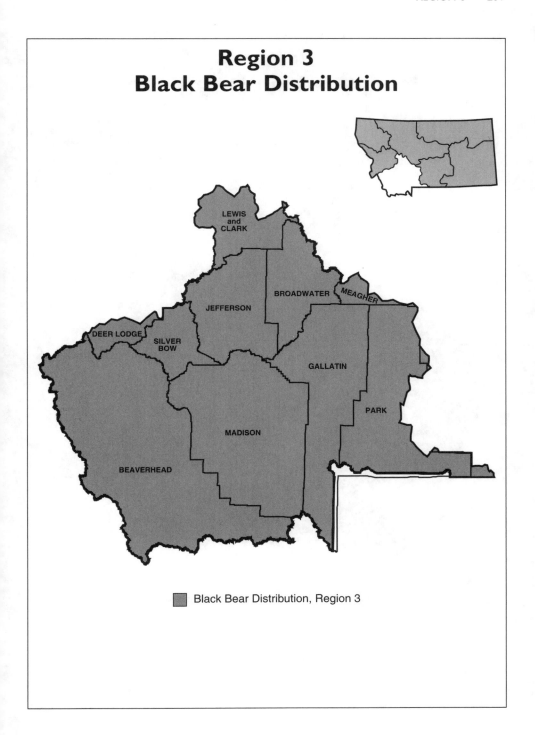

Region 3
Black Bear Distribution

LEWIS and CLARK

BROADWATER

MEAGHER

JEFFERSON

DEER LODGE

SILVER BOW

GALLATIN

PARK

MADISON

BEAVERHEAD

Black Bear Distribution, Region 3

Region 3
Mountain Lion Distribution

Mountain Lion Distribution, Region 3

riparian habitat, but hunting opportunities are limited unless you get on private property. Much of the best antelope hunting is on private land, too. Due to the size of the region and all its mountains, it produces more moose than any other region. Until recently, it was also the top producer of bighorn sheep, but die-offs in recent years have set back at least two herds. Mountain goat hunting is limited but consistent. Black bears and cougars are widespread but not as common as in Regions 1 and 2. Grizzlies, and recently wolves, have expanded from Yellowstone and should be anticipated in most mountain habitats. Always be careful.

Harvest Trend (1992–1996)

Species	Success Rate	Harvest	Hunters
Deer	51%	Mule deer 8,549–18,400 Whitetail deer 6,673–8,998	31,187–39,446
Elk	32%	Bulls 3,500–7,000 Cows 4,000–9,000	36,000–50,000
Moose	91%	Bulls 193–282 Cows 90–104	340–380
Bighorn Sheep	37%	Rams 18–49 Ewes 0–33	157–280
Mountain Goat	74%	Billies 67–89 Nannies 32–50	113–161
Pronghorn	35–79%	Bucks & does 1,905–3,984	3,353–5,763
Cougars and Bears—No harvest statistics available			

Physical Characteristics

All of Region 3 lies east of the Continental Divide and is a pleasant mix of broad, grassy, mountain valleys punctuated with dramatic, often isolated, mountain ranges, many climbing to 10,000, 11,000, and even 12,000 feet. Typical alpine and subalpine habitats at these extreme elevations include steep rock faces and cliffs, talus slopes, snow patches, small glaciers, tundra basins, and stands of spruce, subalpine fir, and scattered white bark pines. Lower down are extensive forests of lodgepole, Douglas fir, and aspens mixed with sagebrush and grass parks and providing wonderful foraging areas for elk, mule deer, and black bear. Lower slopes are clothed in sagebrush, some extensively. Wherever slopes mellow and flatten, marshy areas support willows and moose.

Aside from the mountains of the Continental Divide, which curve west and south before turning sharply east, interior ranges tend mostly north-south or northwest-southeast with creeks cutting east-west canyons into their slopes. Game likes to hide in the moister, thicker forests on the shady north-facing sides of these canyons.

Mountain creeks gather into famous trout rivers like the Big Hole, Beaverhead, Jefferson, Madison, and Gallatin that flow through broad grassy valleys, and sometimes narrow, rocky, constricted canyons. The latter three rivers join at Three Forks just north of I-90 to create the Missouri River, which flows north toward Helena, the state capital, and out through the narrow Gates of the Mountains at the northwest corner of the Big Belt Mountains.

Human development is gobbling up wildlife habitat and hunting land not only around bustling communities like Bozeman but also in isolated valleys like the Madison. Huge, ostentatious houses now stand where cattle and mule deer once grazed, where cowboys herded, and where hunters stalked. Wealthy actors, tycoons, and retired businessmen are buying working cattle ranches and converting them into off-limits private retreats. Fortunately, some new owners are wise enough to share their newly captured resources with the local citizenry through some sort of limited access hunting program.

Some of the region's mountains have been saved as wilderness. On the western fringe atop the Anaconda Range, the Anaconda-Pintler Wilderness (also described in Region 2) protects high mountain habitat used by sheep, mountain goats, mule deer, elk, moose, black bears, and cougars. Atop the Madison Range, the Lee Metcalf Wilderness protects similar habitat. It is a conglomerate of four separate units: the Spanish Peaks in the north Madison Range, the Taylor-Hilgard in the south Madison, Bear Trap Canyon on BLM land north of Ennis Lake, and the Monument Mountain section abutting the northwest corner of Yellowstone National Park. Much of the vast Absaroka-Beartooth Wilderness south of Livingston and east of US 89 falls within the boundaries of Region 3. This is the highest and arguably most rugged mountain wilderness in Montana. Northeast of Helena at the north end of the Big Belt Mountains is the small Gates of the Mountains Wilderness. In addition to these official wilderness areas, there are several isolated, unroaded mountain areas just as wild, and suitable for tough hunters under backpacks or atop good horses.

Land Use

Because of limited rainfall, timber doesn't grow as fast or as big in this region as in Region 1. Nevertheless, logging is still big business. Watch for logging trucks, and try to stay out of active logging areas. There are also various mines scattered throughout the mountains. Don't block a road leading into a mine. Also, don't park so you block a field or pasture gate. Cattle ranching is big in the valleys, particularly north and south of Dillon and west of Bozeman. Watch for cattle drives on roads and even highways. Slow down early and watch for directions from the herders. Generally, you try to "part the sea" of cattle by easing through with your vehicle. Don't honk and shout unless directed to by the cowboys.

Near Bozeman and other towns where you notice Montana's once beautiful hills and valleys being polluted by suburban development, shed a tear for what was and drive on to the few green pastures that remain.

Weather

Since all of Region 3 falls east of the Continental Divide, the climate is continental, meaning wicked Arctic cold fronts settle in. Luckily, moderating chinook winds can also blow in. Up on the high peaks, however, and around Yellowstone National Park, things can get cold and snowy enough to close some roads by late September. November is potentially snowy and deadly anywhere, so beware. I've seen the thermometer shivering at –15°F in mid-November in the Gravelly Range.

Because of mountain rain shadows, Region 3 valleys average only 12 inches of moisture a year. The crests can catch as many as 60 inches, most of it snow. Early summer is the rainy period. Mountain afternoon thundershowers are common and linger into September. It is often windy, and we're talking sustained 25 to 30 mph all day with gusts to 50 mph. I've had tent guy ropes snapped by October winds along the Madison River. Don't be surprised if it snows as early as mid-September, especially in the high elevations. These early snows usually melt within a week or two, but by late October snow can stay for the duration. Hunt prepared for the worst and hope for the best.

Public Lands and Acreages

National Forests in Region 3	Forest Size (not all acres necessarily within Region 3)
Beaverhead National Forest	2,100,000 acres
Custer National Forest	2,446,130 acres
Deerlodge National Forest	1,195,000 acres
Gallatin National Forest	1,735,412 acres
Helena National Forest	975,100 acres
Wilderness Areas in Region 3	**Size (not all acres necessarily within Region 3)**
Absaroka-Beartooth Wilderness	944,060 acres
Anaconda-Pintler Wilderness	41,134 acres
Gates of the Mountains Wilderness	28,562 acres
Lee Metcalf Wilderness	248,944 acres
Block Management Acres	**600,000 acres**

Region 3
Mountain Ranges

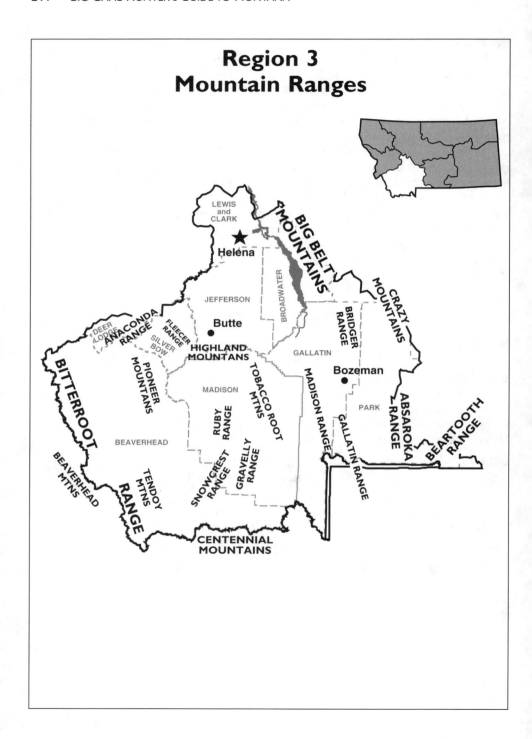

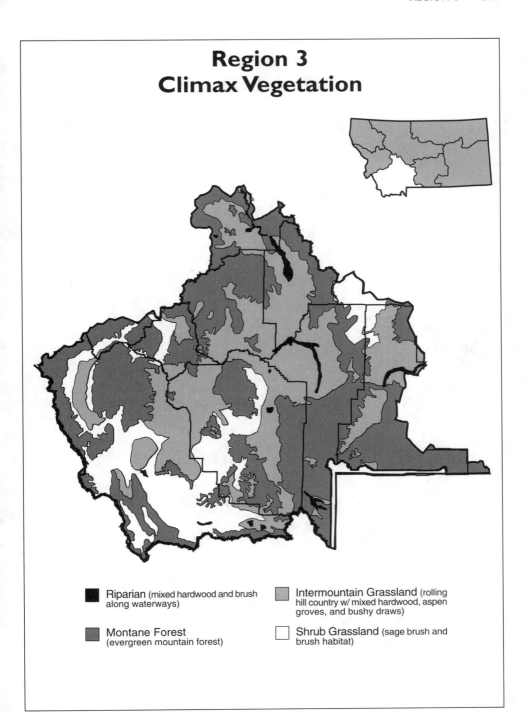

Region 3
Climax Vegetation

Riparian (mixed hardwood and brush along waterways)

Montane Forest (evergreen mountain forest)

Intermountain Grassland (rolling hill country w/ mixed hardwood, aspen groves, and bushy draws)

Shrub Grassland (sage brush and brush habitat)

Region 3
Land Use

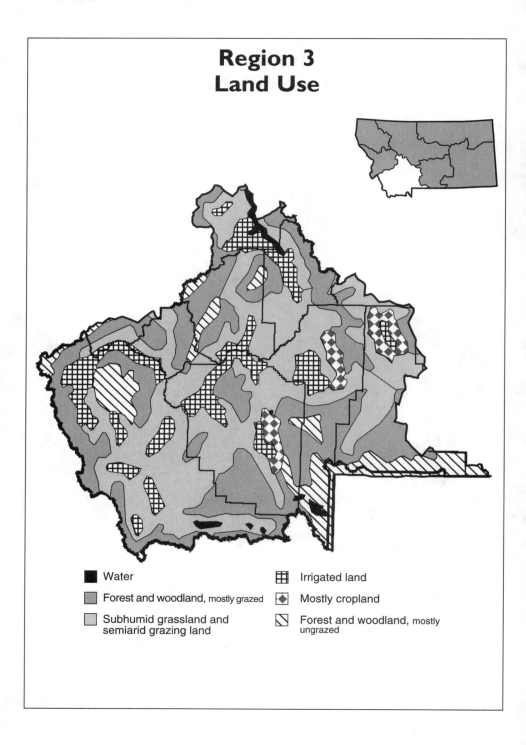

Water

Forest and woodland, mostly grazed

Subhumid grassland and semiarid grazing land

Irrigated land

Mostly cropland

Forest and woodland, mostly ungrazed

Region 3
Federal Lands

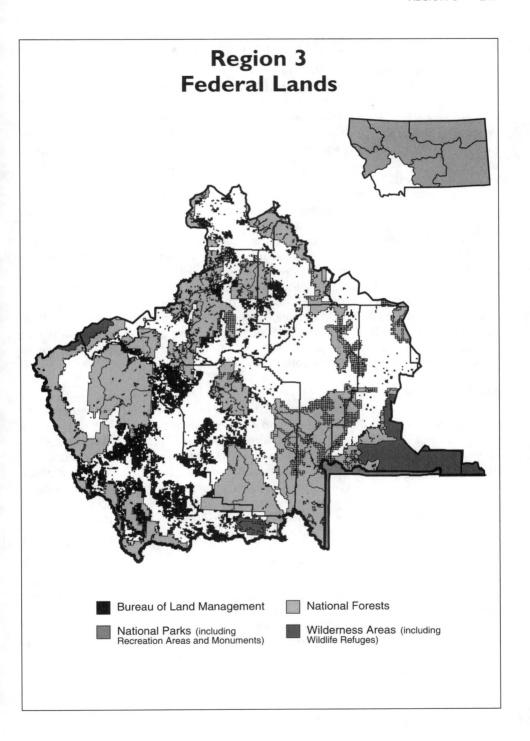

■ Bureau of Land Management   National Forests

National Parks (including
Recreation Areas and Monuments)   Wilderness Areas (including
Wildlife Refuges)

REGION 3 HIGHLIGHTS

Gardiner Late Season Park Elk Hunt

The most famous elk hunt in Montana has taken place each winter for decades near Gardiner (HDs 313 and 314, south ends), where the Yellowstone River flows out of Yellowstone Park. Here deep winter snows drive hungry Park elk north toward lower elevations and winter browse. In order to control this population of elk that is essentially off-limits during the regular fall seasons, Montana FWP sells special permits for either four-day or two-day hunts conducted between Jan. 3 and Feb. 15. In 1998, 105 permits, restricted to branch-antlered bulls or antlerless elk, were sold for four-day hunts. Fully 2,660 permits were sold for two-day hunts for antlerless elk only. This is the mechanism by which the National Park controls its northern elk herd while washing its hands of all blood.

Predictably, this is not the most aesthetically pleasing elk hunt going. Extreme cold and the temptation to concentrate one's efforts along the Park boundary invite crowding and conflict. Before hunts were broken into short segments, huge crowds would compete in what became known as "the firing line." If you can handle deep snow and temperatures to –30°F, this might be the hunt for you. To get away from the crowds, hunt well back from the fence, tracking elk that have moved out at night. Early heavy snows will also move elk out of the park during the general season; you can expect heavy crowds then, as well. Applications for the late season hunts must be made by June 1. Contact FWP for complete details.

Special Youth Elk Hunt

Youth 12–14 years of age can apply for one of five any-elk permits valid for HD 314, the east slope Gallatin Range and west Yellowstone River Valley between Livingston and Gardiner, and five more permits good in HD 393 north of Livingston. These permits are valid during the general season throughout their respective districts and during an extended season (usually in foothills where wintering herds concentrate) that stretches into mid-December. This gives ten lucky young hunters extra chances to take their first elk. Applications are due June 1. Successful applicants will receive complete instructions and descriptions of the hunting area.

Gallatin Range

The Gallatin Range between Bozeman and Yellowstone Park sees lots of hunting pressure, but remains a good place to find an elk. Hunting success is largely weather dependent. Elk are high and scattered early, often on midlevel slopes after the second week of the season, and often on private valley ranchland late in the season after snow has pushed them down. This makes late season hunting frustrating unless you have permission to be on private land. Hunting in the south near Yellowstone is often futile in the first half of the season but can be excellent later if snows push the herds out. Timing is everything.

In mid-September, this spike bull elk in Yellowstone National Park is still in velvet.

Don't look to the Gallatins if you're after a mule deer. This has always been rather poor mule deer habitat, and populations in the late 1990s are depressed. You'll do better in the Madisons, Gravellys, Crazies, Big Hole basin, and the Yellowstone Valley.

Spanish Peaks Sheep

The Spanish Peaks in the Madison Range southwest of Bozeman might be your best bet for attempting to take a bighorn ram (HD 301). First, permits are unlimited, so you don't have to luck out in one of those lousy odds drawings. Second, there is no quota, so you don't have to quit hunting just because someone else got lucky. Third, the season is six days long, so with good planning, you should have enough time to find your ram. Fourth, the hunt is held in early September, so the weather should be good.

A hunter glasses for sheep in the Spanish Peaks. (Photo by Craig Carns)

The downside is that there are only about 180 sheep roaming a large wilderness area, rams do not grow huge horns here, and some 150 hunters compete against you to find them. Usually it takes dedicated hunters three to five years to explore the range and figure out the sheep before they take a ram. To save money and frustration, you might want to "hunt" the area with backpack and binocular only for a few years, then buy the license when you have the country and its rams figured out. Once you take a sheep, you must wait seven years before trying again.

Madison Range and Bridger Range Goats, Moose, Lions, and Bears

The high, rugged Madison Range is also home to quite a few goats. Look to HDs 324–328 and 362. A total of 48 tags were available here in 1998, but nearly 750 folks tried for them. Wise hunters scout the range before they ever apply for a tag. By the time they finally draw one, they know the goats and their habits intimately. Summer backpack trips are a great way to start.

Displaying full winter pelage, a Rocky Mountain goat stands at the edge of a mountain cliff.

Moose are not as common as goats but are increasing in HDs 307–310. Thirty-four permits were doled out in 1998, most for bulls.

The Madisons are not the equal to Region 1 for black bears. Nevertheless, they get plenty of hunting pressure. The best hunting is near Yellowstone, but you have to be extra cautious not to misidentify a grizzly. Lions are increasing throughout the range, and more houndsmen are taking up the challenge. It is rare that a hunter even sees a cougar that hasn't been treed by dogs, but every year a few get lucky, almost always while elk or deer hunting.

The Bridgers north of Bozeman aren't quite as well known as the Madisons, but they take quite a bit of hunting pressure off the bigger mountains. This is a great place for elk hunting, but most of it is on private lands, and access is difficult to get. Locals from Bozeman have things pretty well in hand. Although the higher spine of the Bridgers falls within the Gallatin National Forest, its elk seem to prefer the private land foothills where they find both solace and nearby crop fields to raid. None of these areas were in the Block Management Program in 1998, either; if you wish to hunt elk in the Bridgers, get to know a landowner. In a north portion of HD 393, which includes the east side of the Bridgers, there is a special antlerless elk hunt during the last week of the regular season. This is to alleviate pressure on private ranch lands where most of the cows hang out at this late date, so you'd better have permission on private land before trying this hunt. If you do gain access, it's a great way to fill the freezer with delicious meat.

Mule deer hunting can be pretty good in HD 312, a large HD that takes in the west side of the Bridgers, but in order to hunt buck mule deer in the Bridger Mountains portion of this HD, you must apply by June 1 for a special permit. In 1998, 50 permits were up for grabs. Study current regulations or call FWP for complete information year by year. With so few buck hunters scattered through the area, this can be a fine way to enjoy an uncrowded hunt.

Weapons Restricted Areas

In case you were still laboring under the impression Montana was the wild open West, read this: Due to human population and housing, portions of several HDs in Region 3 fall under restricted weapons regulations. While hunting deer and elk in portions of HDs 301, 311, 312, and 393 (Gallatin Valley), you may use only shotgun, traditional handgun, muzzleloader, or archery equipment. This Gallatin Valley season is also an extended season, running from October 25–January 15 in the 1998 regulations. It offers one additional antlerless whitetail deer B license, and the deer A license remains valid for antlerless whitetails after the end of the general season for these districts if you were unable to fill it.

On several Yellowstone River islands in HDs 315, 317, and 393 near Livingston, only archery gear may be used for deer and elk. Pick up a detailed description and map of the Gallatin Valley restricted area at Bozeman license agents or the Bozeman FWP office (406-994-4042).

South of Dillon on the Poindexter Slough area (HD 331), only shotguns, muzzleloaders, traditional handguns, and bows may be used during the general season. No extra tags are offered.

The Townsend Special Management Area (HD 391) is restricted to archery, shotgun, traditional handgun, and muzzleloader. That same restriction applies to several areas within HDs 380 and 343 near Helena, including the Scratchgravel Hills, Muskrat Valley near Boulder, Prickly Pear Creek in Helena Valley, and portions of the Canyon Ferry WMA. For complete descriptions of all these area boundaries, contact the Helena Area Resources Office at 406-444-4720.

Always carefully and completely read annual deer and elk hunting regulations for such restrictions, as they are liable to pop up any year.

Highland Mountains

Due south of Butte, the Highland Mountains rise to 10,000 feet and provide good hunting for a herd of between 800 and 900 elk. Open stands of Douglas fir, subalpine

*Hoping to stimulate bulls
in the basins below to
bugle back, an elk hunter
bugles from a ridge.*

fir, and lodgepole pine on north- and east-facing slopes are mixed with extensive areas of grass and sage meadow. This does not provide the highest security cover for elk, but it makes hunting easier. Most of the land lies within the Deerlodge National Forest or Bureau of Land Management (to the southwest). Over the years, there has been considerable mining in these mountains, so there are quite a few roads. Access is considered good, yet there remains enough rugged, high, unroaded territory on the east side to make backcountry hunting via backpack or horseback viable. Some outfitters work the area. Despite the relatively easy access, some fair-sized bulls are in there. As is the case with most mountain elk, snow pushes herds low and concentrates them. During the open, early season they are high and scattered. Wet summers and lush summer growth permit them to remain high longer as they are in better condition and considerable forage remains under the forest canopy.

There is potential for big mule deer bucks in the Highlands, but hunting pressure is too intense for many to escape to old age, so don't come here expecting a monster muley. Two permits are available for mountain goats. The sheep herd, formerly strong and large, was hit hard by lung worm and pneumonia in 1996 and fell from 350 animals to just 50. This is the tragic legacy of domestic sheep grazing in the West—introduced diseases that hang around in the soil for decades to infect native bighorns.

Moose are thriving in this range, as there is good moose habitat throughout the area. In 1998, 16 permits were available. A herd of about 350 pronghorn roam on private and BLM ground on the south end of the range. They periodically put out nice 14-inch to 15-inch bucks.

Access the Highlands via Moose Creek road east of Melrose (I-15, exit 93), Moose Creek Road (exit 99), or Highland Drive (FR 84) south out of Butte.

Fleecer Range

Southwest of Butte and west of I-15, the Fleecer Range within the Beaverhead National Forest (HDs 319 and 341) supports an abundant, highly migratory herd of elk. FWP controls about 60,000 acres of land in this area that provide excellent winter forage for the elk. When snows deepen, usually during the last half of the November elk season, scattered bands that had been roaming the high country along the Continental Divide drop down toward the Big Hole Valley near Wisdom on State Route 43. There are several sections of state school land in this area mixed with private ranch lands, but because of elk depredations, many ranchers do welcome hunters. The standard approach is to knock on doors and ask until you make the right connection. There were Block Management lands in this area in 1998, too.

The mule deer population in the Fleecers is fair, but there is no outstanding trophy potential due to a long history of meat hunting in the area. You can't expect a high and wide 4x4 when you shoot them as fork horns. Farther south in the Big Hole Valley, mule deer are scarce.

Big Hole Moose Bonanza

Because much of the Big Hole Valley (HDs 323, 302, 327, and 326) surrounding State Route 43 is low, swampy, and thick with willows, it's one of the top three moose producers in the state. The big deer cause considerable consternation among ranchers when they raid haystacks in winter, so you can generally ask about and gain hunting permission on the mostly private land in the area where your odds for a big bull are excellent. Limited permits only, of course. Applications must be in by May 1. It is suggested you scout the area and make landowner contact before applying for a license.

Interstate Elk West of Wisdom

There is so much cover in the Big Hole River valley that elk actually summer in it, then migrate west into the mountains for winter. Trouble is, the bunch south of Wisdom actually goes into Idaho and becomes inaccessible to Montana hunters. This happens about one year out of five and is quite a management problem for FWP. In past years, they've tried opening the rifle season early in order to get the herd reduction they've needed. Recently, they've been opening a limited permit antlerless hunt a week before the general season. A total of 600 permits were available in 1998. As a hunter, your best chance might be during the early bow season in September when bulls will be bugling and both sexes are fair game. You might want to make arrangements with a river valley rancher to hunt private property at this season. Work the edges where timber meets meadows. There are quite a few Block Management areas in district 321, too, most operating under a three-day registration schedule. Call the Butte (406-494-1953) or Dillon (406-683-9305) FWP field offices for specifics. Be forewarned: this area receives heavy hunting pressure from the Missoula and Kalispell areas. It can be crowded by Montana standards.

Disappearing Pronghorns in the Big Hole

Elk aren't the only critters that migrate in the Big Hole valley. A herd of about 600 antelope in the valley (HD 321) traditionally move about 50 miles toward the drier, more open Bannack area (HD 329) southeast of the Big Hole Divide. There is extensive BLM land around Bannack, but you could hunt here before the migration and find few antelope until the Big Hole herd migrates in. It's important to stay abreast of the migration if you hunt either district; antelope move well ahead of any major snows.

Boulder Horseshoe Elk

East of Butte and I-15, south of Boulder, north of I-90, and west of State Route 69 in Jefferson County, a range of mountains arcs like a horseshoe, and on this horseshoe live some 650 elk that provide pretty good hunting (HDs 350 and 370). The west side of the horseshoe is the eastern edge of the Boulder Mountains; the east side is known as the Bull Mountains. The valley between them is drained by Whitetail Creek. This entire area is rather special because it retains some of the old-fashioned Montana character. Hard-working ranchers generally grant hunting rights to polite hunters who stop to visit and request permission. In addition, in 1998, more than 37,000 acres of private land within the arms of the mountains was open under the Block Management Program; there is also considerable BLM land in the foothills. Hunter access is superb.

The elk hunting is good because the general season is limited to brow-tined bulls only, unless you draw one of the 325 antlerless permits. This means spikes survive to become at least rag horns. Also, several areas in the mountains contain unusual outcroppings of vertical granite that create a labyrinth of alleys and cloistered avenues in which elk can hide and through which vehicles cannot drive. You see these along I-90 near the Continental Divide southeast of Butte. This rugged terrain increases bull survival. Post season sex ratios are around 15 bulls per 100 cows.

Access into the area via old mining and logging roads is good. The only fly in the ointment might be the controversy over ATV hunting in the south of this area. Few things spoil the illusion of a wild, "got it all to myself" hunt than ATVs, especially when they are used more for joy riding and road hunting than simple transportation to the jump-off hunting spot. ATV use is under review and might someday be curtailed.

In addition to elk, a good moose herd is found in both districts with some big bulls. Five bull tags were offered in 1998. Mule deer are depressed here as elsewhere

A beautiful bull elk with 6×6 antlers.

in Region 3, but populations are still judged fair. Whitetails are rare despite the name of the creek. Several hundred antelope range the valley and foothills. Fifty either sex and fifty doe tags were available in 1998.

Elkhorns

The highest hunter densities in the state of Montana have been recorded in the Elkhorn Mountains, HD 380 southeast of Helena. There are many roads through the area, so pressure on elk and mule deer is intense. It got so bad a decade ago that biologists were counting one bull elk per 100 cows on the wintering grounds. To solve the overharvest problem, FWP instituted special permit hunting only for branch antlered bulls. Currently, they're issuing 100 of these permits each year for HD 380. But hunting pressure is still intense because on the general elk license you can hunt spike bulls as long as they don't have a second point longer than four inches. These details are difficult to detect in many hunting situations, so enough bulls escape to keep the population at reasonable levels. Today there are about 15 bulls per 100 cows in the herd, and the average age of branch antlered bulls is 5 to 6 years. Several 9- to 10-year-olds are killed by hunters every year, and at that age they can be quite impressive.

The south and west sides of the range are drier and have a more open forest. The higher elevations and north and east slopes are wetter and more densely covered in spruce, fir, and lodgepole pine. Naturally, the elk move to the thicker timber when pressed.

Considering all the hunters roaming the Elkhorns, mule deer hunting is excellent for smaller bucks. HD 380 has the highest mule deer harvest in Region 3 most years. It's a productive area with the potential to produce some buster bucks, but with all the competition from hunters, few bucks ever grow old enough to produce trophy antlers. This is a meat hunt.

Whitetails are practically an afterthought here. You'll find a few in the lower drainages and especially along the Missouri and Boulder river valleys. Most are on private land. The area is not noted for trophy quality, but there's always the odd, good buck around.

Big Belts

The majority of the Big Belt Mountains lies within Region 3 in HDs 390–392. An estimated 3,000 elk call this home. Most of HD 390 on the south end of the range is in private ownership, including a Ted Turner ranch. The result is that of the three HDs, hunter access in HD 390 is lowest and bull size is highest. Lots of outfitters work this area. Nearly all elk in 390 and 391 winter on private land. Most landowners allow hunters to take cows to reduce depredation problems and control the population, but they reserve bulls for paying clients. If you want to take a bull from either of these units on public land (Helena National Forest), hunt early while the elk are still in the high timber. There are a lot of roads in both districts, so you'll have to look for isolated, dog hair timber where the elk should be hiding out.

In HD 392, there are fewer roads and more backcountry, including the Gates of the Mountain Wilderness in the north end of this rather long district. Major access into the region is via Canyon Ferry Road and the York Road, both heading east out of Helena. The York-Nelson Road takes off north from York Road and branches east and west along Beaver Creek. North of that drainage is the Gates of the Mountains Wilderness. Nearly all elk in 392 winter on public ground, so late season hunting can be excellent if the snow isn't too deep. Most bulls taken in the Big Belts are young.

The mule deer situation here is similar to the Elkhorns: lots of young bucks in HDs 390 and 391, and slightly older bucks in 392 because of the more limited access. The southern ranges are more productive than the more heavily forested northern end of these mountains. Hunting pressure is fairly intense in HD 392. A few folks pack into the Gates of the Mountains Wilderness each year, probably for both elk and deer.

The mountain lion population here and in the Elkhorns is stable or decreasing. They get a lot of hunting pressure, and the quota fills every year. The Big Belts have the highest lion quota in Region 3.

Gravelly, Snowcrest, and Centennial Ranges

One of the most productive elk ranges in all of Region 3 includes parts of HDs 323, 324, and 330 in the Gravelly, Snowcrest, and Greenhorn Ranges south of Ennis on the west side of the Madison River (US 287). Roads may be impassable late in the season, particularly the Gravelly Range Road. The ranges lie almost entirely within the Beaverhead National Forest. The coniferous habitat is quite open with lots of sage/grass parks, and hunters see lots of elk, which keeps them coming back for more. Because the area is so easy to hunt, it is popular with nonresidents (30 percent of the annual hunters here) who can set up camps and do-it-themselves with reasonable odds for success. About 25 percent of hunters take an elk each year, and the vast majority of the bulls are young 5-pointers (2- to 3-year-old raghorns) or better. A few really good bulls are taken each year, thanks to considerable migration from Yellowstone National Park and the Centennial Mountains in Idaho. Yes, that's a long way to travel, but they do it, especially late in the season when they head for wintering grounds on the Blacktail Wildlife Management Area and Rob Creek Wildlife Management Area. These are foothills grasslands managed by FWP for elk and deer wintering habitat. Both are open for hunting, as are virtually all such FWP game winter ranges in the state.

Only in HD 330 do the majority of elk winter on private land where access is difficult. Hunter success in this district is some 6 percent poorer than in HDs 323 and 324, too.

Although the Centennials, which run east-west and form the border with Idaho, seem a long way from the Gravellys, elk trade freely between the two ranges, crossing the open, high mountain Red Rock River and Centennial Valley usually at night in a matter of a few hours. And because the Idaho elk season is held earlier than Montana's, a few big bulls are able to escape by high-tailing it to Montana, then turning back into Idaho when the Montana late season opens. Many of these wily survivors eventually head for the low slopes of the Snowcrest Range when late season snows fall, so the later you hunt, the better your odds for finding a big bull.

Elk hunting in the Centennials themselves is less predictable than in the Gravellys. The elk may be there, they may be in Idaho, or they may be over east in Yellowstone. Unless you've hunted here often enough to get a feel for migration patterns, you might be frustrated. Snowstorms are usually a good time to hunt the Centennials as elk should be moving through then.

FWP biologists have counted more than 8,500 elk wintering around the Gravelly and Snowcrest Ranges, so the pre-season elk herd could easily be as high as 12,000. No wonder so many people hunt here. If you don't mind crowds and like a young bull, this might be your hunt.

Tobacco Root Mountains

Northwest of Ennis and southwest of Three Forks, the small Tobacco Root Mountains (HDs 333 and 320) provide limited hunting for elk and deer. Only 150 to 300 elk are taken here each year, compared to 1,000 to 1,400 in the Gravelly complex. The range is fairly rugged, access is poor, and the elk herd is relatively small. About

*A herd of pronghorn does walks away from camera
across a grassy plain in September.*

20 percent of elk hunters are successful, and most bulls taken are 2- and 3-year-olds. The deer harvest is split about evenly between mule deer and whitetails. Some 2,000 elk hunters work the Roots each season, compared to about 5,000 in the Gravellys.

Madison Valley Pronghorn Migration

While Region 3 is but a blip on the pronghorn hunting radar compared to eastern Montana, the intermountain valleys do hold resident herds that provide limited hunting for lucky permit winners. In the Madison Valley south of Ennis (HD 360), as in most grassland valleys, nearly all antelope hunting falls on private land, further complicating the issue. One must make landowner contact or find a suitable Block Management area before hunting. Nevertheless, the Madison provides some quality pronghorn hunting each year—with a twist. Biologists have discovered that this valley actually gains antelope as the season progresses. Apparently, animals from Idaho are migrating into the valley to winter. The timing of this migration is impossible to predict, but with the season stretching into early November, odds are good that hunters can find additional quarry late in their hunt. Of course, delaying the taking of a buck always risks finding one with a missing horn or two, as pronghorns shed their outer horn sheaths in late October and November. About 70 percent of HD 360 hunters are successful. In 1998, 400 tags were available.

REGION 3 HUB CITIES
Butte

Population–34,800 • Elevation–5,750

For many years, Butte was a booming mining center. Located at the crossroads of Interstates 15 and 90, Butte is now a diversified commercial city. The habitat in Silver Bow and Jefferson Counties is primarily montane forest. The Beaverhead National Forest forms the western part of the county, and the Deerlodge National Forest is east and north of the county.

ACCOMMODATIONS
Town House Inns of Butte, 2777 Harrison Avenue / 494-8850 / 150 rooms / Dogs allowed, $5 fee / Rates moderate
War Bonnet Inn, 2100 Cornell Avenue / 494-7800 / 134 rooms / Dogs allowed, $10 fee / Restaurant on site / Rates expensive

CAMPGROUNDS AND RV PARKS
Fairmont RV Park, 17 miles west of Butte off I-90 / 797-3535 / 84 RV spaces / Full facilities including showers, laundry, store, and cabins

RESTAURANTS
4B's Family Restaurant, 1905 Dewey and Rocker Interchange / 494-1199
Perkins Family Restaurant, 2900 Harrison Avenue / 494-2490 / Open 24 hours
The Uptown Cafe, 47 East Broadway / 723-4735 / One of the finest restaurants in Montana

VETERINARIANS
Animal Hospital, 2330 Amherst Avenue / 494-4044
Butte Veterinary Service, 6000 Harrison Avenue / 494-3656

SPORTING GOODS, GUNS, & GUNSMITHS
Bob Ward and Sons, 1925 Dewey / 494-3445
Fran Johnson's Sports Shop, 1957 Harrison Avenue / 782-3322
Bugs & Bullets Sport Shop, 1210 Harrison Avenue / 782-6251
Jim's Custom Gun Works, 105 North Parkmont / 494-1747
John's Log Cabin Guns, 2205 Amherst Avenue / 494-2127
Shooter Shop, 221 North Main Street / 723-3842

TAXIDERMISTS
Atcheson Taxidermy, 3210 Ottawa Street / 782-0569
Kivela's Taxidermy, 445 East Park Street / 723-8533

MEAT PROCESSORS
Western Meat Block, 800 Dewey / 494-4319

AUTO REPAIR

Mark's Sinclair, 1200 South Montana, 3 blocks north of I-90 / 723-3351 / Open
7 days

AIR SERVICE

Bert Mooney Field, Harrison Avenue South / Delta (Sky West), 494-4001 /
Horizon, 494-1402

MEDICAL

St. James Hospital, 400 South Clark Street / 782-8361

FOR MORE INFORMATION

Butte Chamber of Commerce
2950 Harrison Avenue
Butte, MT 59701
800-735-6814, Ext. 10

BLM–Butte Field Office
106 North Parkmont, Box 3388
Butte, MT 59701-3388
406-494-5059

Fish, Wildlife & Parks
Butte Area Resource Office
1820 Meadowlark Lane
Butte, MT 59701
406-494-1953

Helena

Population–24,569 • Elevation–4,157

Helena is the capital of Montana. It is a thriving commercial center, bordered on the west by the Helena National Forest. The Missouri River flows east of town. The Big Belt Mountains and the Gates of the Mountains Wilderness Area are east of the Missouri. A number of reservoirs along the river provide outstanding hunting and recreational opportunities. The habitat is comprised of montane forest and inter-mountain grasslands.

ACCOMMODATIONS

Aladdin Motor Inn, 2101 East 11th Avenue / 443-2300 or 800-541-2743 / 13 rooms, indoor pool, sauna, steam, health club / Dogs allowed, $5 fee / Rates moderate

Days Inn, 2001 Prospect Avenue / 442-3280 / Dogs allowed with $40 deposit, smoking rooms only / Rates moderate

Lamplighter Motel, 1006 Madison / 442-9200 / Large units, 13 with kitchens, suites with up to 4 bedrooms / Dogs allowed, $4 per day (no dogs left unattended in rooms)

Super 8 Motel, 2201 11th Avenue / 443-2450 / Dogs allowed with $25 deposit in smoking rooms only

CAMPGROUNDS AND RV PARKS

Helena KOA, 3 miles north of city limits on Montana Avenue. 458-5110 / Open year-round / Full service, including laundry and store

RESTAURANTS

Frontier Pies, 1231 Prospect Avenue / 442-7437 / Family dining, specialty pies / Open 7AM–10PM daily

The Pasta Pantry, 1220 11th Avenue / 442-1074

Windbag Saloon and Grill, 19 South Main / 443-9669

VETERINARIANS

Big Sky Animal Clinic, 1660 Euclid Avenue / 442-0980 / Gary Erickson, DVM / 24-hour emergency service

Animal Center Veterinary Clinic, 1301 Cedar Street / 442-3160; if no answer, 442-7094 / Arla Barkemeyer, Julie Kappes, Ed Newman, George Bates, DVMs / 24-hour emergency service

SPORTING GOODS, GUNS, & GUNSMITHS

Bob Ward and Sons, 1401 Cedar Street / 443-2138

Cross Currents (an Orvis Full-Line Dealer), 326 North Jackson Street / 449-2292

Capitol Sports and Western Wear, Hustad Center / 443-2978

Montana Outdoor Sports, 708 North Last Chance Gulch Street / 443-4119

Mountain Man Pawn Shop, 1230 Euclid Avenue / 443-3363

Frontier Gun Shop, 3280 Green Meadow Drive / 442-4533

TAXIDERMISTS

Montana Trophy Mounts, 7350 Green Meadow Drive 458-5840
Trails West Taxidermy, 3280 Green Meadow Drive / 443-0022

MEAT PROCESSORS

Elk Horn Processing, 1622 Prospect Avenue / 443-5422.
Rocky Mountain Processing, 5275 North Montana Avenue. 458-5905

AUTO REPAIR AND RENTAL

Prestige Service Center, 1140 11th Avenue / 442-2724
Al Rose Garage and Wrecking Service, 2801 North Cook / 442-9965 or 442-3400
/ 9AM–6PM Mon–Sat
Hertz Rent-a-Car, at the Helena Regional Airport / 442-8169

AIR SERVICE

Helena Regional Airport, 2850 Skyway Drive / 442-2821 / Serviced by Delta and
Horizon / Charter service available

MEDICAL

St. Peter's Community Hospital, 2475 Broadway / 442-2480

FOR MORE INFORMATION:

Helena Area Chamber of Commerce
201 East Lyndale Avenue
Helena, MT 59601
406-442-4120

Helena National Forest
2880 Skyway Drive
Helena, MT 59601
406-449-5201

Fish, Wildlife & Parks
State Office
1420 East 6th Avenue
P.O. Box 200701
Helena, MT 59620-0701
406-444-2535

Fish, Wildlife & Parks
Helena Area Resource Office
930 Custer Avenue West
Helena, MT 59620-0701
406-444-4720

Townsend

Population–1,635 • Elevation–3,833

Known as the "First City on the Missouri," Townsend is located on US 287 between Three Forks and Helena. It is 5 miles south of Canyon Ferry Lake and 1 mile east of the Missouri River. There is a great deal of public land around the lake. The vegetation consists of intermountain grasslands and montane forests.

ACCOMMODATIONS

The Bedford Inn, 3 miles north of Townsend on Hwy 287 / 266-3629 / 5 units in a large home / Dogs allowed

Mustang Motel, Hwy 287 / 266-3491 / 22 units / Dogs allowed, but they cannot be left unattended

Lakeside Motel, Hwy 287 / 266-3461 / 12 units / Dogs allowed for a $10 deposit, some housekeeping units

CAMPGROUNDS AND RV PARKS

Road Runner and Fireside RV Campground, 2 miles east of Townsend on Hwy 12 / 266-9900 / Showers, laundry, phone, hook ups, tent spots, and pull-through

Goose Bay Marina RV Park, Hwy 287 on the east side of Canyon Ferry Lake / 266-3645 / Sanitary dump, tent camping, store, showers, propane, ice, beer

RESTAURANTS

Jasper's Pub and Pizza, North 287 / Lunch and dinner

A&W Townsend, North 287 / 266-3814 / Open year-round with drive-up and inside seating / Good sandwiches for lunch and dinner

Horseshoe Family Dining, 550 North Front Street / 266-3800 / Unbeatable breakfasts / Open all week for breakfast, lunch, and dinner

Deep Creek Restaurant, 11 miles east of town on Rt 12 / 266-3718 / Gourmet dining in a rustic log cabin / Excellent Sunday brunch

VETERINARIANS

Elkhorn Vet Clinic, Rt 287 just north of town / 266-5794 / Erik Sorensen, DVM / The clinic also boards dogs

TAXIDERMISTS

Townsend Taxidermy, 128 North Maple Street / 266-3361

MEAT PROCESSING

R Family Meats, 4010 MT Hwy 284 / 266-3512

AUTO REPAIR

Valley Sales / 266-5207

Townsend Muffler and Welding / 266-3935

AIR SERVICE

City/County Airport, one mile east of town, contact Vern Spanfill / 266-3218

MEDICAL

Townsend Community Hospital, on North Oak near the center of town /
266-3186

FOR MORE INFORMATION:

Townsend Chamber of Commerce
Box 947
Townsend, MT 59644
406-266-3911

Bozeman

Population–25,000 • Elevation–4,793

Known for its blue-ribbon trout fishing and great skiing, Bozeman is a rapidly growing resort and college town. There has been a recent population boom, resulting in crowded conditions and high prices. In spite of this, Bozeman has a lot to offer the sportsman. There is still a small-town atmosphere with big city amenities: good air service, shopping, fine restaurants, and outdoor activities. The surrounding habitats include montane forests and intermountain plains. The Gallatin Valley economy is based on agriculture. Bozeman is bordered by the Bridger Mountains northeast of town, the Gallatin National Forest and Gallatin Range to the south, and the Madison Range to the southwest.

ACCOMMODATIONS
Days Inn, 1321 North 7th Avenue / 587-5251 / 80 rooms, cable, continental breakfast / Dogs allowed, $25 deposit / Moderate rates

Fairfield Inn, 828 Wheat Drive / 587-2222 / 57 rooms, 12 suites w/kitchenettes / Continental breakfast, pool, and jacuzzi / Dogs allowed, no restrictions / Rates moderately expensive

Holiday Inn, 5 Baxter Lane / 587-4561 / 178 units, restaurant, bar, pool and jacuzzi, cable / Dogs allowed, but not unattended in rooms / Rates expensive

Super 8, 800 Wheat Dr / 586-1521 / 108 rooms, cable / Dogs allowed, no restrictions / Budget rates

The Bozeman Inn, 1235 North 7th Avenue / 587-3176 / 45 rooms, outdoor pool, sauna, cable / Mexican restaurant and lounge / Dogs allowed for a $5 fee / Moderate rates

CAMPGROUNDS AND RV PARKS
Bozeman KOA, 8 miles west on US 91 / 587-3030 / Open year–round / 50 tent and 100 RV spaces / Full services including laundry and store

RESTAURANTS
Boodles Restaurant, 215 East Main / 587-2901 / Highly recommended

Bacchus Pub and Rocky Mountain Pasta Co., 105 West Main / 586-1314 / Breakfast, lunch, dinner. / **Bacchus Pub,** 7AM–10PM; Sandwiches, burgers, salads, soups, and daily special entrees; moderate prices / **Pasta Company,** 5:30PM–10PM; Fine dining, pasta and seafood; expensive

John Bozeman's Bistro, 242 East Main / 587-4100 / International and regional specialties / Breakfast and lunch moderate, dinner expensive

Mackenzie River Pizza Company, 232 East Main / 587-0055 / Mon–Sat 11:30AM–10PM, Sun 5–9PM / Fancy pizzas, pasta, salad / Moderate prices

O'Brien's, 312 East Main / 587-3973 / Mon–Sun 5PM–9PM / Continental cuisine / Expensive

Mint Bar and Cafe, 27 East Main, Belgrade / 388-1100 / Great steaks and seafood / Superb bar / Good selection of single malt scotches

Crystal Bar, 123 East Main / 587-2888 / Open every day / Beer Garden / Will pack lunches for hunters / Reasonable

Spanish Peaks Brewery, 120 North 19th / 585-2296 / Mon–Fri for lunch 11:30AM–2:30PM, Mon–Sun, dinner 5:30–10:30PM, Sat–Sun, brunch 11AM-2PM / Italian cuisine, microbrewed ales / Moderate to expensive

VETERINARIANS

All West Veterinary Hospital, 81770 Gallatin Road / 586-4919 / Gary Cook, Honor Nesbet, David East Catlin, DVMs / 24-hour emergency service

Animal Medical Center, 216 North 8th Avenue (behind Kentucky Fried Chicken) / 587-2946 / Sue Barrows, DVM / Emergency service

SPORTING GOODS, GUNS, & GUNSMITHS

Bob Ward and Sons, 2320 West Main / 586-4381

Powder Horn Sportsman's Supply, 35 East Main / 587-7373

The River's Edge, 2012 North 7th Avenue / 586-5373

David Gentry Custom Gunmaker, 314 North Hoffman Street / 388-4867

Julian Nagorski Gunsmith, 23 West Main Street / 388-6934

Bullet Hole, 515 West Peach Street / 586-9355

Guns Galore, 2622 West Main Street / 586-7772

TAXIDERMISTS

John Berger Taxidermy, 705 South Church / 586-4244

Bridger Canyon Taxidermy, 8860 Bridger Canyon Road / 582-1029

Field and Stream Taxidermy, 1202 Ludwig Lane / 388-4647

MEAT PROCESSORS

Yellowstone Sausage Co., 803 North Wallace Avenue / 587-9385

Budget Game Processing, 4110 Thorpe Road, Belgrade / 388-4691

The Meat Shoppe, 722 North Rouse / 526-6328

AUTO RENTAL

Budget Rent-A-Car of Bozeman, Gallatin Field / 388-4091

Avis Rent-A-Car, Gallatin Field / 388-6414

Hertz Rent-A-Car, Gallatin Field / 388-6939

AUTO REPAIR

College Exxon Service, 723 South 8th Avenue / 587-4453

Frank Manseau Auto Clinic, 715 East Mendenhall / 586-4480

E.J. Miller Service and Towing, 28373 Norris Road / 587-0507

Air Service

Gallatin Field Airport, 8 miles west of Bozeman / 388-6632 / Served by Delta, Horizon, and Northwest Airlines / Charter service available

Medical

Bozeman Deaconess Hospital, 915 Highland Boulevard / 585-5000

For More Information

Bozeman Chamber of Commerce
1205 East Main
P.O. Box B
Bozeman, MT 59715
800-228-4224

Gallatin National Forest
10 East Babcock Avenue/Federal Building
P.O. Box 130
Bozeman, MT 59771
406-587-6701

Fish, Wildlife & Parks–Region 3 Office
1400 South 19th Avenue
Bozeman, MT 59718
406-994-4042

Livingston

Population–6,700 • Elevation–4,503

Livingston is located in southcentral Montana, on the big bend of the Yellowstone River, 53 miles north of Yellowstone National Park and 25 miles east of Bozeman. It is in the lovely Paradise Valley, surrounded by the Absaroka-Beartooth Wilderness, and the Gallatin, Bangtail, and Crazy Mountain Ranges. Livingston is a hospitable western town. Its hotels, motels, and bed and breakfasts have over 600 rooms, and there are many fine restaurants.

Livingston is the county seat of Park County. Here, as in several other counties in Montana, the Great Plains and the rolling foothills give way to the Rocky Mountain Front. There are campgrounds, scenic areas, and fishing accesses along the Yellowstone River. Some of the best trout fishing in the country is found here in the rivers, small streams, spring creeks, and lakes.

ACCOMMODATIONS

The Murray Hotel, 201 West Park / 222-1350 / Located downtown, next to Dan Bailey's Fly Shop / Newly renovated, deluxe, turn-of-the century hotel / 40 charming guest rooms with or without adjoining baths / The Winchester Cafe, The Murray Bar, and large lounge are adjoining / Dogs allowed / Reasonable rates

Paradise Inn, P.O. Box 684 / 800-437-6291 / Off Interstate 90, Exit 333 / 42 rooms, all ground floor / Lounge, indoor pool, jacuzzi, and restaurant / Dogs allowed, some restrictions / Reasonable rates

Parkway Motel-Budget Host, 1124 West Park Street / 222-3840 / Reservations: 800-727-7217 / Interstate 90, Exit 333 / 28 rooms, 8 kitchenettes, 3 two-bedroom rooms / Dogs allowed, $3 charge / Reasonable rates

Livingston Inn and Campground, Box 3053-A, Rogers Lane. Interstate 90, Exit 333, ½ block north / Motel: 222-3600; 16 rooms / Campground: 222-1122; 26 hook-ups, pull-through spaces, showers, and laundry / Reasonable rates

Chico Hot Springs Lodge, Pray, Montana / 333-4933 / Located 23 miles south of Livingston on US 89 / Inn has 50 rooms, motel has 24 rooms / 4 cabins, 3 cottages with kitchens, log house with kitchen, 2 condos with kitchens / Mineral hot springs pool / Chico Inn gourmet dining room / Poolside Grill, Saloon / Dogs allowed, $2 charge / Moderate rates

Yellowstone Motor Inn, 1515 West Park / 222-6110 / Indoor parking and indoor pool / Dogs allowed; $5 fee

RESTAURANTS

Winchester Cafe and Murray Bar, 201 West Park / 222-1350 / Downtown Livingston / Full-service restaurant—breakfast, lunch, dinner, and a Sunday brunch / Homemade desserts, espresso, fine wine selection

Chico Inn, Pray / 333-4933 / 23 miles south of Livingston on US 89 / Fine
dining, reservations recommended / Great wine list / Poolside Grill has great
homemade food, bar

Stockman, 118 North Main Street / 222-8455 / Bar and restaurant / Lunch and
dinner—steaks, prime rib, seafood, and burgers

Livingston Bar and Grill, 130 North Main Street / 222-7909 / Antique bar /
Steak, seafood, and buffalo burgers

The Sport, 114 South Main Street / 222-3533 / bbq ribs, chicken, burgers, cocktails, and wine

Martin's Cafe, 108 West Park Street / 222-2110 / Open 24 hours, 7 days / Carry-
out, breakfast specials, smorgasbord on Sundays

VETERINARIANS

Colmey Veterinary Hospital, P.O. Box 521 / 222-1700 / Duane Colmey, DVM /
½ mile south of Livingston on US 89 / Pet food, supplies, grooming, kennel

Shields Valley Veterinary Service, Rt 85 Box 4321 / 222-6171 / Donald Smith,
DVM

SPORTING GOODS, GUNS, & GUNSMITHS

Heckman Specialties, 223 South B Street / 222-8618

Dan Bailey's Fly Shop, 209 West Park Street / 222-1673 or 800-356-4052 / Flies,
fishing equipment, clothing, and accessories

George Anderson's Yellowstone Angler, Rt 89 South, P.O. Box 660 / 222-7130 /
Flyfishing specialties, outdoor clothing

Yellowstone Gateway Sports, 1106 West Park St. #22. 222-5414 / Guns, shells,
clothing, and accessories

TAXIDERMISTS

Bob's Taxidermy Studio, 621 East Park Street / 222-3941

Sasquatch Taxidermy, 1 Pronghorn Drive / 222-5890

Wildlife Artistry, 101 Star Road / 222-0732

MEAT PROCESSOR

Livingston Meat Company, 206 South 11th / 222-0760

AIR SERVICE

Mission Field, east of Livingston / 222-6504

AUTO RENTAL AND REPAIR

Livingston Ford-Lincoln-Mercury, 1415 West Park Street / 222-7200 / All
models, 4-wheel-drive, and vans

MEDICAL

Livingston Memorial Hospital, 504 South 13th Street / 222-3541

FOR MORE INFORMATION
Livingston Area Chamber of Commerce
Depot Center, Baggage Room
212 West Park Street
Livingston, MT 59047
406-222-0850

Gardiner

Population–600 • Elevation–5,314

Gardiner is the northern gateway city to Yellowstone National Park and has services out of proportion to its population. More than a million people pass through each year, yet the town retains a raw, western atmosphere, not a kitchy, touristy one. Hunters see Gardiner more as the gateway to the northern Absaroka Mountains and headquarters town for hunting the Yellowstone elk herd during the late season. The town sits on a bench above the Yellowstone River and is split in two by it. Most services and facilities line US 89 and the short Park Street downtown. Because this is the only vehicle access to the Park during winter, most businesses are open year-round. Elk and pronghorns commonly graze and sleep in the town's streets and yards.

ACCOMMODATIONS
Absaroka Lodge, US 89 at Yellowstone River Bridge / 848-7414, 800-755-7414
Best Western Motel, US 89 / 848-7311, 800-828-9080
Blue Haven Motel, Box 952 / 848-7719
Comfort Inn, 107 Hellroaring Drive / 848-7536, 800-228-5150
Hillcrest Cottages, 200 Scott Street / 848-7353, 800-970-7353
Jim Bridger Court, US 89 / 848-7371
Maiden Basin Inn, #4 Maiden Basin Drive / 848-7080, 800-624-3364
Motel 6, 109 Hellroaring Drive / 848-7520, 800-466-8356
Town Café & Motel, Park Street / 848-7322
Westernaire Motel, US 89 South / 848-7397
Yellowstone River Motel, Park Street / 848-7303, 888-797-4837
Yellowstone Super 8, US 89 South / 848-7401, 800-800-8000
Yellowstone Village Inn, 1102 Scott Street West / 848-7417, 800-228-8158

CAMPGROUNDS & RV PARKS
Rocky Mountain Campground, Jardine Road / 848-7251

RESTAURANTS
Town Café, Park Street / 848-7322
Cecil's Restaurant, Park Street / 848-7561
Yellowstone Mine (in Best Western) / 848-7336
Ranch Kitchen, US 89, Corwin Springs / 848-7891

SPORTING GOODS, GUNS, & GUNSMITHS
Flying Pig Pawn Shop, 233 Main / 848-7510
Frontier Mercantile, Outpost Mall / 848-7473
Park's Fly Shop, Hwy 89 / 848-7314

TAXIDERMIST
Wildlife Preservations, North of Gardiner / 848-7675

MEAT PROCESSOR
Claude Long / 848-7248

AUTO REPAIR
Tire Iron, Hwy 89 / 848-7090

AIR SERVICE
Sagebrush Aero, Inc., Bill Chapman / 848-7794.

MEDICAL
Yellowstone Park Medical Service, Mammoth Hot Springs / 307-344-7965

FOR MORE INFORMATION
Gardiner Chamber of Commerce
Box 81
Gardiner, MT 59030
406-848-7971

West Yellowstone

Population–2,000 • Elevation–6,666

West Yellowstone began as an entrance city to Yellowstone National Park in 1907 and a Union Pacific tourist rail line depot in 1909, so it is by long tradition a tourist town with plenty of trinket shops and the usual high-priced supplies and services for the outdoor life. In winter, it's a snarl of exhaust fumes and snowmobiles as revelers embark for their winter rides to Old Faithful. The town is also a hub for some of the finest trout fishing in North America, and the venerable Bud Lilly's Fly Shop still stands on the corner of 39 Madison Avenue to provide equipment, flies, guides, and advice. The terrain surrounding the town is flat as a table and covered in lodgepole pines. Ravens perching on power poles and dead pine snags are often the only wildlife stirring, but plenty of elk, moose, bears, mule deer, mountain goats, bighorn sheep, and bison are a short distance away in the Park and in the Gallatin Range north of town. There are motels and restaurants to fit every taste and budget, only some of which are listed here. A central reservation number (800-521-5241) can be used to reserve rooms in any of the motels that belong to the local Chamber of Commerce. Due to all the tourist traffic, even during the cold months, it's wise to book a room early.

ACCOMMODATIONS
Alpine Motel, 120 Madison Avenue / 646-7544
Al's Westward Ho, 16 Boundary Street / 646-7331, 888-646-7331
Lazy G Motel, 123 Hayden Street / 646-7586
Best Western Desert Inn, 133 Canyon Avenue / 646-7376, 800-528-1234
Brandin Iron Motel & RV Park, 201 Canyon / 646-9411, 800-217-4613
Crow's Nest Motel, 608 US 20 / 646-7873
Pine Shadows Motel, Hayden & US 20 / 646-7541, 800-624-5291

CAMPGROUNDS
KOA Campground, west of West Yellowstone / 646-7606
Hebgen Lake Lodge, Motel, and Tent Campground, US 287 / 646-9250
Hideaway RV Camp, corner of Gibbon Avenue / 646-9049

RESTAURANTS
Three Bears Restaurant, 217 Yellowstone Avenue / 646-7811
Gringo's Chuckwagon (Mexican), 13 Canyon St.
Running Bear Pancake House, 538 Madison / 646-7703
Silver Spur Café, 111 Canyon Street / 646-9400
Rustler's Roost (in Big Western Pine Motel), 234 Firehole Avenue / 646-7622
Trapper's Inn, 315 Madison Avenue / 646-9375

VETERINARIANS
West Yellowstone Veterinary Service, 125 Geyser / 646-7886

White and White Veterinary Hospital, Gibbon Avenue / 682-7151

Sporting Goods, Guns, & Gunsmiths

Canyon Street Exxon & Mini Mart, 215 Canyon Street / 646-7614 / Sells hunting licenses
Eagles Market, 3 Canyon / 646-9300
Madison River Outfitters, 117 Canyon / 646-9644
Smith & Chandler, 121 Yellowstone / 646-7841

Taxidermist

Fish West Taxidermy, North West Yellowstone / 646-9232

Auto Rentals

Big Sky Car Rentals / 646-9564, 800-426-7669
Budget Rent-A-Car / 646-7882, 800-231-5991
Yellowstone Car Rental / 646-9332

Auto Repair

Randy's Auto Repair, 429 Yellowstone Avenue / 646-9353
Canyon Street Exxon & Mini Mart, 215 Canyon / 646-7614
Yellowstone Automotive, 555 Yellowstone Avenue / 646-4074

Air Service

Closed after September; use Bozeman

Medical

Medical Clinic, 236 Yellowstone Avenue / 646-7668

For More Information

West Yellowstone Chamber of Commerce
Box 458
West Yellowstone, MT 59758
406-646-9691

Three Forks

Population—1,200 • Elevation—4,081

Lewis & Clark were the first white men to see the three forks of the Missouri River where the Madison, Gallatin, and Jefferson Rivers joined to form the mighty Mo. Today the folks living in the I-90 hamlet of Three Forks enjoy that view year-round. They also find themselves smack in the center of some great big game hunting with whitetails in the river bottoms, mule deer and pronghorns in the grasslands, and elk, black bear, sheep, goats, and cougars in the surrounding mountains. This is a great jump-off point for hunters who find mountains and game in every direction. US 287 runs through town north to south. There's also lots of historical information at nearby Missouri Headwaters State Park and at the Headwaters Heritage Museum on Main Street.

ACCOMMODATIONS
Sacajawea Inn, 5 North Main Street / 285-6515, 800-821-7326 / Delightful old hotel circa 1910, beautifully restored
Broken Spur Motel, 124 West Elm / 285-3237, 800-354-3048
Fort Three Forks Motel, Hwy 287 & I-90 / 285-3233, 800-477-5690
Perren Park Hotel, 114 Main Street / 285-3457

CAMPGROUND
Three Forks KOA Kampgrounds / 285-3611 / Open through October / Showers, tents sites, RV sites

RESTAURANTS
Historic Headwaters Restaurant, Main Street / 285-4511
The Longhorn Café, US 287 / 285-4106
Prairie Schooner, US 287& I-90 / 285-6948
Steer In, US 287 & I-90 / 285-6694

VETERINARIANS
Headwaters Veterinary, 11370 US 287 / 285-6672
Three Forks Veterinary Hospital, 223 North Railroad Avenue / 285-3225

SPORTING GOODS, GUNS, & GUNSMITHS
Ace Hardware, Main Street / 285-6666

TAXIDERMIST
Old Town Taxidermy, 310 Old Town Road / 285-4575

MEAT PROCESSOR
Milligan Canyon Meats, 269 Cottonwood Road Cardwell / 285-3112.

AUTO REPAIR
GMC Truck Agency, 304 1st Avenue West / 285-3253

M & W Motor Machine, 304 1 Avenue W / 285-3253
Tim's Diesel and Auto Repair, 285-3828.
Tocci Repairs & Welding, South of Three Forks / 285-4063

AIR SERVICE
Pogreba Field / 285-3431

MEDICAL
Three Rivers Clinic, 223 1st Avenue East / 285-3251

FOR MORE INFORMATION:
Three Forks Chamber of Commerce
Box 1103
Three Forks, MT 59752
406-285-4880

Ennis

Population–790 • Elevation–4,927

Ennis is located on the banks of the famous blue-ribbon Madison River. It is a small ranching and tourist community situated in a broad valley between the Gravelly and Tobacco Root Mountains to the west and the Madison Range to the east. Nearby are montane forests and intermountain and shrub grasslands.

ACCOMMODATIONS

Riverside Motel, 346 Main Street / 682-4240, 800-535-4139 / Open May– December / Cabins, some with kitchens / All have cable, refrigerator, picnic table, and gas grill / Located on the Madison River, only 12 miles from a bird hunting preserve / Hunters and dogs are welcome, $3 per dog / Reservations are necessary / Your host is Robert Hines

The Sportsman's Lodge, P.O. Box 305 / 682-4242 / 18 lodgepole pine cabins, 11-unit motel / Cable, restaurant, and lounge on premises / Dogs allowed, $5 per dog / Reservations recommended

CAMPGROUNDS AND RV PARKS

Elkhorn Store and RV Park, ½ mile south on Hwy 287 / 682-4273 / Open year- round / 12 tent and 13 RV spaces / Full facilities except for laundry

RESTAURANTS

Continental Divide Restaurant, Downtown Ennis / 682-7600 / Open for dinner summer through midfall / One of Montana's finest restaurants / Your hosts are Jay and Karen Bentley

Ennis Cafe / 682-4442 / Breakfast, lunch, and dinner

Kathy's Wild Rose Restaurant / 682-4717

VETERINARIANS

White and White Veterinary Hospital and Supply, 5098 Hwy 287 / 682-7151

Douglas B. Young, DVM / 682-7956

SPORTING GOODS, GUNS, & GUNSMITHS

True Value / 682-4210

TAXIDERMISTS

Jordan Creek Taxidermy, Ennis Trade Center / 682-4135

Altimus Taxidermy, P.O. Box 701 / 682-7141

MEAT PROCESSOR

Restvedt & Son Meat Market / 682-7306

AUTO REPAIR

D&D Auto / 682-4234

AIR SERVICE
Ennis Airport, 8 miles south of town / Contact Madison Valley Aircraft / 682-7431

MEDICAL
Madison Valley Hospital / 682-4274 / Emergency, 682-4222

FOR MORE INFORMATION
Ennis Chamber of Commerce
P.O. Box 297
Ennis, MT 59729
406-682-4388 (If no answer try Ed Williams, Chamber President, 682-4264)

Dillon

Population–3,991 • Elevation–5,057

Dillon is a friendly college town located in southwestern Montana, surrounded by four mountain ranges—the Beaverhead, Tendoy, Centennial, and Pioneer. The famous blue-ribbon Beaverhead River flows through Dillon. The Big Hole River flows west to east across the northern part of the county. These two rivers join and eventually become part of the Missouri River.

Beaverhead County is Montana's largest producer of cattle and is one of the largest counties in the nation, with an area larger than Connecticut and Rhode Island combined. Much of the surrounding terrain is covered by grass and sagebrush.

ACCOMMODATIONS

Sundowner Motel, 500 North Montana / 683-2375 / 32 rooms, cable / Dogs allowed / Reasonable rates

Super 8 Motel, 550 North Montana / 683-4288 / 46 rooms, cable / Refrigerators and microwave ovens in some rooms / Dogs allowed / Reasonable rates

Town House Inns of Dillon, 450 North Interchange / 683-6831 / 46 rooms, cable / Laundry, indoor pool / Dogs allowed in rooms for a $3 fee

CAMPGROUNDS AND RV PARKS

Beaverhead Marina and RV Park, 20 miles south on I-15, exit 44 on Clark Canyon Reservoir / 683-5556 / 2 tent and 31 RV spaces / Full facilities including docks, gas, and boat ramp

Skyline RV Park, 3 miles north of Dillon on Hwy 91 / 683-4903 / 5 tent, 38 RV spaces / Full facilities

RESTAURANTS

Anna's Oven, 120 Montana Street / 683-5766 / 7AM–4PM / Breakfast and baked goods

Buffalo Lodge, I-15 20 miles south of Dillon at Clark Canyon / 683-5088 / Open 10:30AM–9PM / Features burgers and steaks

Lion's Den, 725 North Montana / 683-2051 / 11AM–10PM / Steak, prime rib, cocktails

The Mine Shaft, 26 South Montana / 683-6611 / 11AM–11PM / Wide variety of steaks

Town Pump, 625 North Montana / 683-5097 / Open 24 hours for breakfast, lunch, and dinner

VETERINARIANS

Veterinary Hospital, 935 South Atlantic / 683-2385 / Dr. Knorr and Dr. Nelson

SPORTING GOODS, GUNS, & GUNSMITHS

Hitchin Post Sporting Goods, 125 North Montana / 683-4881

Big Buck Sporting Goods, 124 North Montana Street / 683-4881
Blacktail Gunsmithing, 4225 Anderson Lane / 683-2153
Riflesmith, Inc., 105 Mill Street, Sheridan / 842-5814,

TAXIDERMIST
Trout and Trophy, 323 North Montana Street / 683-9749

MEAT PROCESSORS
Beaverhead Meats, 610 North Montana Street / 777-5684

AUTO REPAIR
B&L Auto Repair, 250 North Railroad / 683-6733
Dillon Auto Repair, 624 East Glendale / 683-5214

AIR SERVICE
Iverson Aviation / 683-4447 / Call for information

MEDICAL
Barrett Memorial Hospital, 1260 South Atlantic / 683-2323

FOR MORE INFORMATION
Dillon Chamber of Commerce
Box 425
Dillon, MT 59725
406-683-5511

Beaverhead-Deerlodge National Forest
420 Barrett Street
Dillon, MT 59725-3572
406-683-3900

BLM–Dillon Field Office
1005 Selway Drive
Dillon, MT 59725-9431
406-683-2337

Region 3 Guides and Outfitters

Outfitter Services by Species and Specialty

A	Elk, deer, bear, antelope	F	Mountain lion	I	Moose
B	Deer & antelope	G	Sheep	L	Drop Camps
WT	Whitetail deer	H	Mountain goat	M	Tent Camps

AB
F
Frank Anderson
Climbing Arrow Outfitters
31000 Francis Road
Belgrade, MT 59714
406-388-4845

AB
WT
Rob Arnaud
Arnaud Outfitting, Inc.
P.O. Box 478
Gallatin Gateway, MT 59730
406-763-4235

AB
HI
WT
Tim Beardsley
Beardsley Outfitting & Guide
P.O. Box 360
Ennis, MT 59729
406-682-7292

AG
H
Storn Bishop
Willow Ranch
Box 667
Ennis, MT 59729
406-682-4641

AH
WT
John C. Cargill
Cargill Outfitting
40 Cedar Hills Road
Whitehall, MT 59759
406-494-2960

AFG
HI
Gregory Doud
Sphinx Mountain Outfitting
Box 111
Cameron, MT 59720
406-682-7336

ABF
GHI
WT
David Duncan
Canyon Creek Guest Ranch
P.O. Box 126
Melrose, MT 59743
800-291-8458

AB
Wade Durham
ICR Outfitters
P.O. Box 234
Cameron, MT 59720
406-682-7223

AFG
HI
Dave Ellingson
Canyon Creek Ranch, LLC
3645 Holmes Park Road
Lincoln, NE 68506
402-489-5982

A
Kent D. Grimm
Jake's Horses
5645 Ramshorn
Gallatin Gateway, MT 59730
406-995-4630

A
WT
John Hanson
John Hanson MTI
5210 Foster Lane
Belgrade, MT 59714
406-388-6789

AB
FI
Brad Hanzel
S&W Outfitters
P.O. Box 160502
Big Sky, MT 59716
406-995-2658

A	Elk, deer, bear, antelope	F	Mountain lion	I	Moose
B	Deer & antelope	G	Sheep	L	Drop Camps
WT	Whitetail deer	H	Mountain goat	M	Tent Camps

AG
HI **Lee Hart**
Broken Hart Ranch
73800 Gallatin Road
Gallatin Gateway, MT 59730
406-763-4279

ABG
HI **Thomas M. Heintz**
Medicine Lake Outfitters
Box 3663
Bozeman, MT 59715
406-388-4938

AG **James L. Hubbard**
Yellowstone Outfitters
& Guide School
18 Hill Street
Bozeman, MT 59715
406-848-7755

AB
HI **Leland Keele**
Buffalo Jump Outfitting
P.O. Box 649
Ennis, MT 59729
406-682-7900

ABG
HI
WT **Russ Kipp**
Montana High Country Tours
1036 East Reeder
Dillon, MT 59725
406-683-4920

ABI **William Knox**
Curry Comb Outfitters
Box 70
Dell, MT 59724
406-683-4784

AB **Max Lapham**
Lapham Outfitters
Box 795
Jackson, MT 59736
406-834-3134

AGH
WT **Stephen Luckey**
Four Six Outfitters
3640 Heeb Lane
Manhattan, MT 59741
406-282-7917

AHI
WT **Donna McDonald**
Tate's Upper Canyon Ranch
Montana City R1, Box 841
Clancy, MT 59634
406-842-5775

A **Robert McNeill**
Diamond Hitch Outfitters
3405 10 Mile Road
Dillon, MT 59725
406-683-5494

A
WT **Ralph Mersdorf**
Elk Horn Hot Springs,
Home of Trail Creek Lodge
Box 514
Polaris, MT 59746
406-834-3434

ABI
WT **Mel W. Montgomery**
Centennial Outfitters
P.O. Box 92
Lima, MT 59739
406-276-3463

A	Elk, deer, bear, antelope	F	Mountain lion	I	Moose
B	Deer & antelope	G	Sheep	L	Drop Camps
WT	Whitetail deer	H	Mountain goat	M	Tent Camps

AG **Charles A. Page**
HI Pioneer Outfitters
WT 400 Alder Creek Road
Wise River, MT 59762
406-832-3128

AF **Mike Parsons**
WT Crow Creek Outfitters & Guides
314 Hwy 285
Toston, MT 59643
406-266-3742

ABG **Gordon Patton**
HI Willow Springs Outfitters
WT 1525 Hwy 287 North
P.O. Box 591
Cameron, MT 59720
406-682-4884

AB **Dan Reddick**
FG Wapiti Basin Outfitters
2755 Outlaw Drive
Belgrade, MT 59714
406-388-4941

AB **Larry Richtmyer**
F Battle Creek Outfitters
199 South Fork Ray Creek
Townsend, MT 59644
406-266-4426

A **Keith Rush**
Lakeview Ranch
Monida Star Rt
Lima, MT 59739
406-276-3300

AB **Fordon Sampson**
WT Mossy Horn Outfitters
375 Parrot Ditch Road
Whitehall, MT 59759
406-287-5652

A **Terry Throckmorton**
Bar Six Outfitters
1975 Sullivan Lane
Dillon, MT 59725
406-683-4005

A **Jim Walma**
Buffalo Horn Ranch
13825 Country Road
Meeker, CO 81641
970-878-5450

AB **Dave Warwood**
H Bridger Outfitters
15100 Rocky Mountain Road
Belgrade, MT 59714
406-388-4463

AG **Robert W. Wetzel**
HI RW Outfitter
P.O. Box 471
Manhattan, MT 59741
406-284-6562

AH **Jeffrey Wingard**
Wolfpack Outfitters
Box 472
Ennis, MT 59729
406-682-4827

Region 4

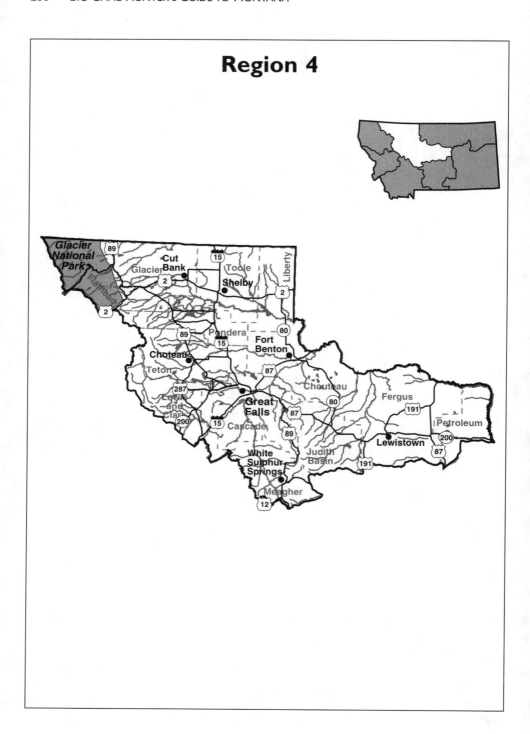

Region 4

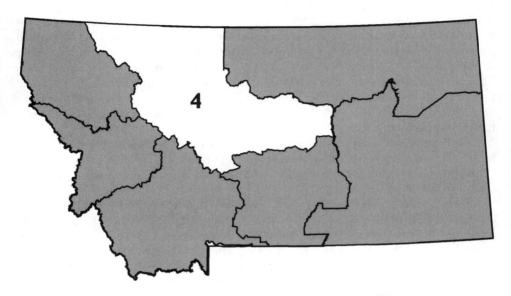

Region 4's terrain varies widely from wilderness mountains to agricultural plains and accommodates hunting via backpack, horsepack, or vehicle. All Montana big game species are represented. This is where most of the antelope and deer hunting takes place. For other species, concentrate on the Continental Divide, Big Belt Mountains, Little Belt Mountains, Castle Mountains, and Big Snowy Mountains. The downside of Region 4 for visiting hunters is the preponderance of private land. Happily, leased hunting is not the rage in Region 4, and nearly a million acres of Block Management lands take the sting out of the lack of public land. Ranchers, particularly those far from population centers, still grant hunting permission to polite strangers who knock and ask. It takes some effort to locate landowners and get to know them, but it's worth it for both the hunting and the friendships that often develop. Realize, however, that a few ranches are leased to outfitters and a few charge trespass fees. There are a few chunks of BLM land in the Judith Mountains, along the Musselshell River and Missouri River in the east, and a spattering of state school lands large enough to warrant a hunt. A serious hunter willing to do a bit of prospecting should find a good place to hunt; just do the homework early. Don't knock on a ranch house door at dawn of opening morning and expect to get in.

Game Species & Numbers

Region 4 ranks behind only Regions 6 and 7 in mule deer production, the bulk of the deer living on the plains east of the mountains. It's also the state's fourth most productive antelope region. Populations of both species were at record or near record highs in the early 1990s but have been declining due to intentional intense harvest and several years of drought and subsequent poor fawn survival, especially in the popular Missouri Breaks. Mule deer and whitetails in agricultural areas did not suffer the dry years as much as did the plains deer; river bottom whitetails enjoyed the benefit of irrigated crops and flowing water. Traditionally, deer, and to a lesser degree pronghorns, have rebounded quickly from population lows, sometimes doubling their numbers in as little as two years. Spring and summer of 1998 were ideal for forage production. Wildlife managers are expecting mule deer and pronghorns to turn the corner and start increasing, but hunters will see the production shortage of the mid-1990s for several more years.

Elk hunting in the western forests, Little Belt Mountains, Snowy Mountains, and Judith Mountains is good enough to make this the third best elk region in the state. Elk have not suffered from drought the way deer have. Seasons are liberal, and lots of cow permits are being offered.

For bighorn sheep, Region 4 is usually the second or third most productive region, ranking behind Regions 1, 2, and 3 in mountain goat harvest. Moose are uncommon. Black bears are stable in suitable forest habitat and provide a consistent, stable harvest. Mountain lions are increasing, and so are harvest quotas, but the big cats aren't nearly as common as they are in the wetter forests west of the Divide. Quite a few local hunters maintain hound packs to hunt them, as do several outfitters catering to nonresidents.

Harvest Trend (1992–1996)

Species	Success Rate	Harvest	Hunters
Deer	74%	Mule bucks 9,400–11,620 Mule does 3,900–5,120 Whitetail bucks 3,820–5,309 Whitetail does 4,201–5,100	28,163–31,086
Elk	26%	Bulls 1,700–2,000 Cows 2,200–3,550	17,000–19,000
Moose	50%	Bulls 2–4	5–6
Sheep	76%	Rams 17–38 Ewes 5–58	25–111
Mountain Goat	95%	Billies 6–14 Nannies 5–14	20–26
Pronghorn	39–76%	All sexes 1,322–5,468	1,997–7,523
Cougars and Bears—No harvest statistics available			

Region 4
Pronghorn Distribution

GLACIER

FLATHEAD

TOOLE

LIBERTY

PONDERA

TETON

CHOUTEAU

LEWIS
and
CLARK

CASCADE

FERGUS

PETROLEUM

JUDITH
BASIN

MEAGHER

Pronghorn Distribution, Region 4

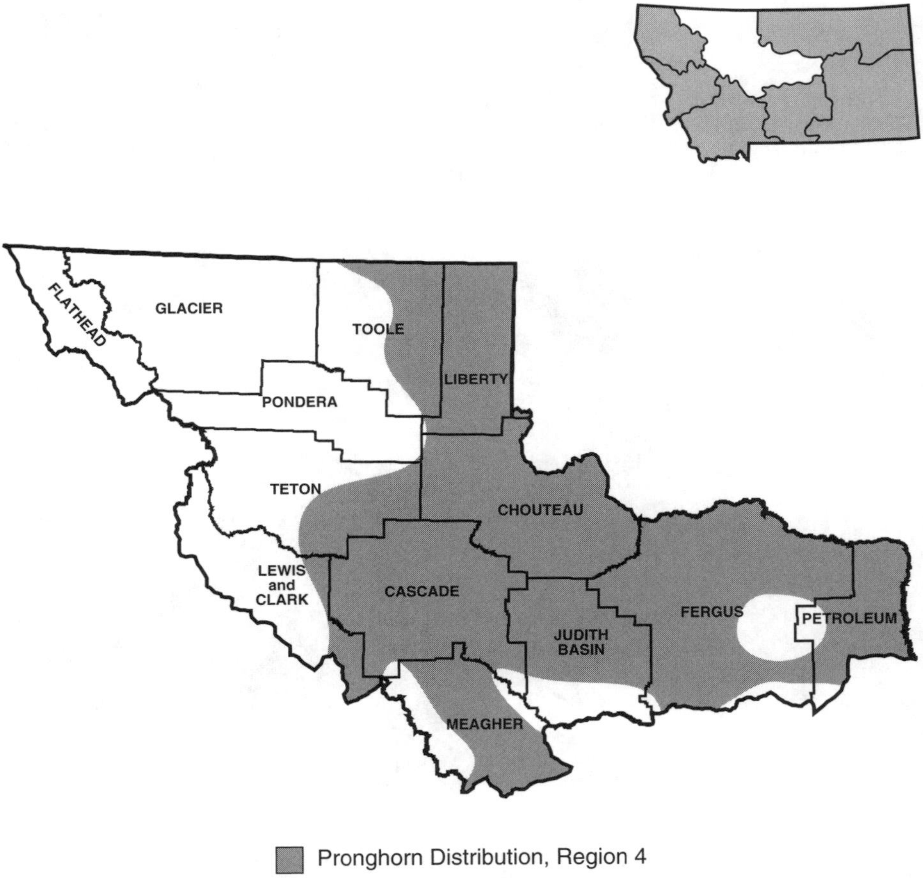

Region 4
White-tailed Deer Distribution

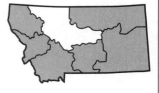

White-tailed Deer Distribution, Region 4

Region 4
Mule Deer Distribution

Mule Deer Distribution, Region 4

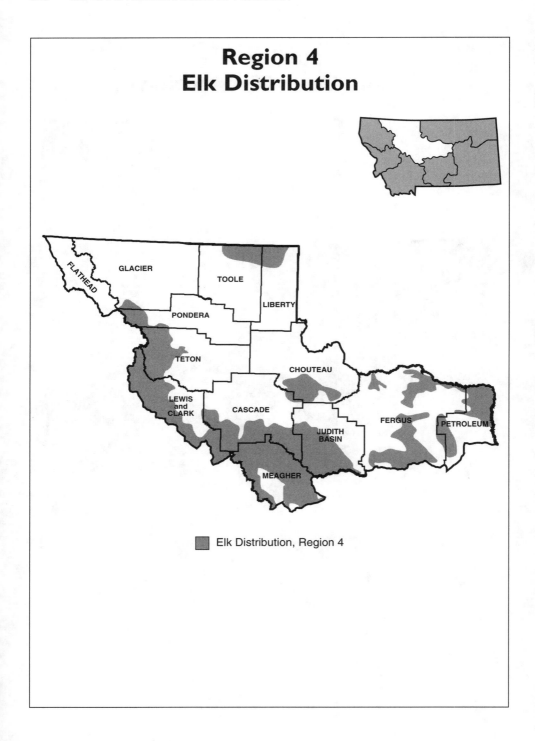

Region 4
Elk Distribution

GLACIER

FLATHEAD

TOOLE

PONDERA

LIBERTY

TETON

CHOUTEAU

LEWIS and CLARK

CASCADE

JUDITH BASIN

FERGUS

PETROLEUM

MEAGHER

Elk Distribution, Region 4

Region 4
Moose Distribution

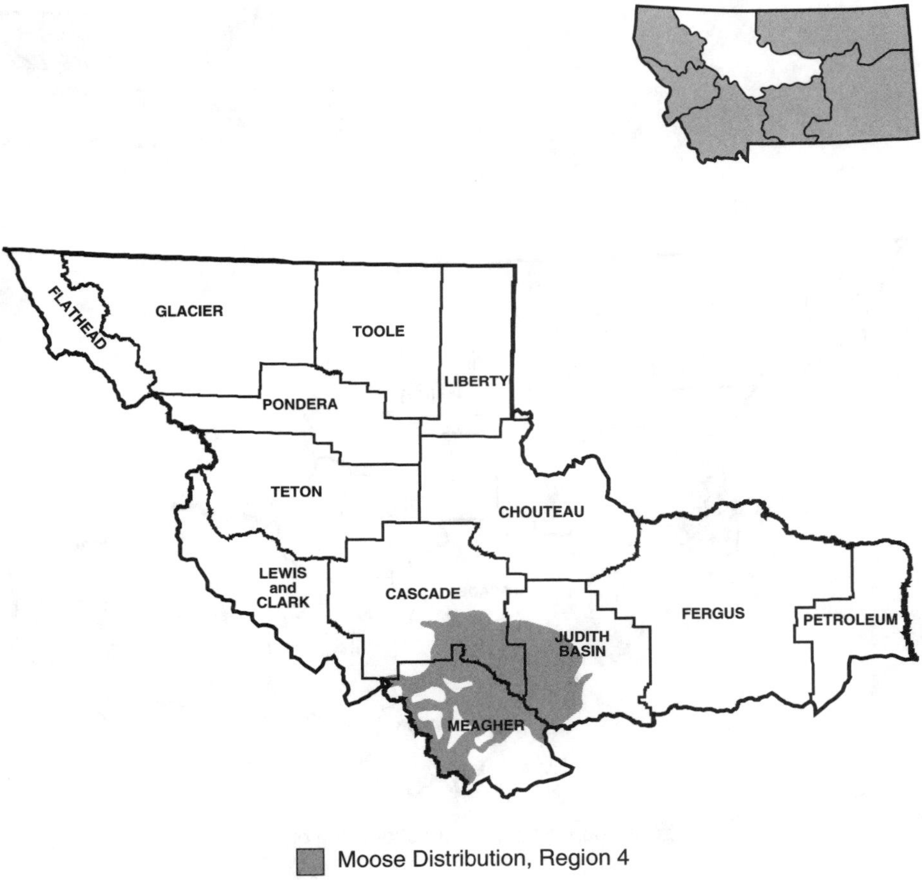

GLACIER

FLATHEAD

TOOLE

LIBERTY

PONDERA

TETON

CHOUTEAU

LEWIS and CLARK

CASCADE

JUDITH BASIN

FERGUS

PETROLEUM

MEAGHER

Moose Distribution, Region 4

Region 4
Bighorn Sheep Distribution

Bighorn Sheep Distribution, Region 4

Region 4
Mountain Goat Distribution

Mountain Goat Distribution, Region 4

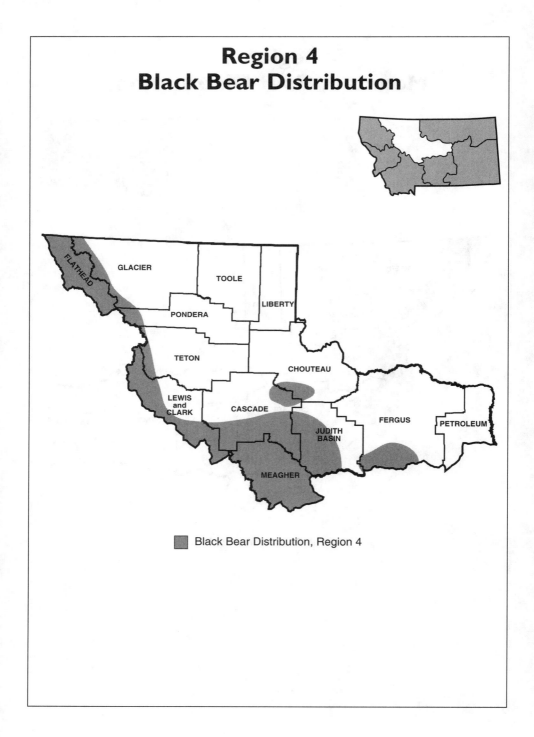

Region 4
Black Bear Distribution

Black Bear Distribution, Region 4

Region 4
Mountain Lion Distribution

Mountain Lion Distribution, Region 4

Physical Characteristics

From the conifer forested Continental Divide on its western border, Region 4 quickly plunges to typical high plains terrain across its northern half. Here, from the Missouri River north to Canada, flat to broadly rolling land is intermittently cut and broken with grassy to brushy runoff draws or coulees that lead to small rivers like the Marias, Teton, and Sun which drain east and south into the Missouri. Dryland wheat-fields mixed with native grasslands sweep mile after mile over most of this area, nearly all privately owned. Only isolated sections of state school lands and BLM lands provide public hunting. The Sweet Grass Hills rise to 6,983 feet in extreme northern Liberty County. There is extensive oil and gas development north of Shelby and north and south of Cut Bank. In the northwest corner of the region, the 1,525,712-acre Blackfeet Indian Reservation abuts the east edge of Glacier National Park. Here the Milk River runs northeast into Canada before dropping back into Montana for a long run across the top tier of counties and hitting the Missouri just below Fort Peck Reservoir.

Hundreds of small dams create ponds throughout the plains landscape. Tiber Dam on the Marias River east of Shelby backs up Lake Elwell, the largest body of water in the region. The high benchlands between I-15 and US 89 are a mix of irrigated farmland and broken runoff coulees. You will find more irrigated farmland in the Sun River Valley from Great Falls west to the mountains.

The highest, wildest, most extensive public land in the region sprawls north to south in the Bob Marshall Wilderness and Lewis and Clark National Forest astride the Continental Divide. This rugged mountain landscape begins at the southeast corner of Glacier National Park, stretches about 85 miles south, and varies between 9 and 22 miles wide—plenty of room for backcountry horsepack hunting for all the usual suspects, particularly as there are more than 1,000 miles of maintained horse trails. This is also grizzly country; they are both dangerous and off-limits, so stay out of their way and take precautions not to attract them to camp. Be certain you can tell them from any black bears you plan to shoot. Wolves also roam the mountains and are fully protected. Don't mistake one for a coyote.

The spine of the Rockies rises rugged and stark to a towering 9,362 feet, with most peaks ranging from 7,000 to 8,000 feet high. The valley of the North Fork Sun River divides the mountains in a wide, sloping, forested valley. The Sun River Game Preserve, created in 1913 by the Montana legislature to save declining big game, covers 199,661 acres from the North Fork and South Fork Sun Rivers west to the top of the Continental Divide. It is closed to hunting.

Douglas firs, lodgepole pines, whitebark pines, spruce, and fir trees at the highest elevations are short and thick, sometimes twisted and leaning because of the winds. They grow taller and narrower at lower elevations, with lodgepole pine dominating. There are some aspen patches, ponderosa pines, and grassland meadows. Because of the drying winds, true grasslands begin at about the 5,000-foot level.

Land Use

There is some logging in the mountains, considerable gas and oil well development around Cut Bank and Sunburst, irrigated farming west of Great Falls, but far and away the dominant land use in Region 4 is dryland wheat farming, with cattle grazing a strong second. The folks who work the land here are tough, hardy, proven survivors, often dating back several generations on the land. They don't suffer fools lightly, but go out of their way to help the unfortunate. They'll pull you out of a mud hole, drive you into town for spare parts, provide you with a few gallons of gas to get you home, and help you drag out a buck. Treat them with respect and an open friendliness because that's how they'll treat you.

Weather

Lying behind the rain shadow of the Continental Divide, Region 4 falls within the grip of continental weather. That means hot summers and icy winters. September through November hunting seasons can see anything from 80°F heat to below-zero cold, rain and mud to dust or snow. More than once I've been snowed on during early October antelope hunts. The warm Pacific air masses that sneak over the Continental Divide and pick up speed as they plunge downslope are know as chinook winds. They bring temperature relief in winter, sending temperatures soaring up as much as 50 degrees in an hour. Big game wintering on the lower slopes are often saved from starvation when chinooks melt deep snows. With major Arctic cold fronts and Gulf warm fronts colliding over the central U.S., this part of Montana registers high winds regularly. Gales of 20 to 35 mph are common. They're no fun to hunt in, but often you have no choice.

The highest mountains in the region collect up to 65 inches of moisture a year, 80 percent of it snow. The plains are lucky to get 12 inches of precipitation a year, and most comes as spring rains and summer thundershowers. The region passes through cycles of drought that create large game losses, as do hard, snowy winters. But during mild winters and wet summers, mule deer and antelope thrive and quickly reach supersaturated levels, necessitating increased hunter harvest to placate ranchers and farmers trying to save some feed and hay for their cattle. During such years, extra doe and fawn B licenses are sold in large numbers.

Public Lands and Acreages

National Forests in Region 4	Forest Size (not all acres necessarily within Region 4)
Lewis & Clark National Forest	1,843,469 acres
Helena National Forest	975,100 acres

Wilderness Areas in Region 4	Size (not all acres necessarily within Region 4)
Bob Marshall Wilderness	1,009,356 acres
Scapegoat Wilderness	239,936 acres
Gates of the Mountain Wilderness	28,562 acres

Block Management Acres	940,000 acres

Region 4
Mountain Ranges

FLATHEAD

GLACIER

TOOLE

LIBERTY

ROCKY MOUNTAIN FRONT

FLATHEAD RANGE

PONDERA

TETON

LEWIS and CLARK

CHOUTEAU

Great Falls

HIGHWOOD MOUNTAINS

FERGUS

PETROLEUM

CASCADE

JUDITH BASIN

JUDITH MOUNTAINS

LITTLE BELT

MOUNTAINS

BIG SNOWY MOUNTAINS

LITTLE SNOWY MOUNTAINS

MEAGHER

BIG BELT MOUNTAINS

CASTLE MTNS

Region 4
Climax Vegetation

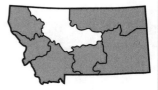

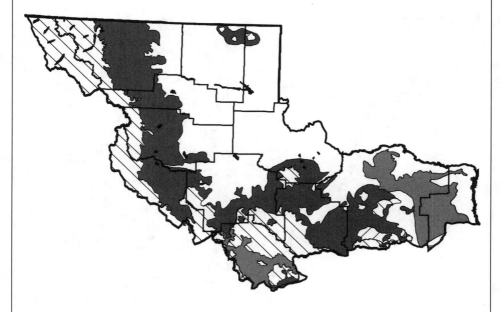

■ **Riparian** (mixed hardwood and brush along waterways)

◻ **Montane Forest** (evergreen mountain forest)

▨ **Plains Forest** (isolated evergreen mountain and hill forest in grassland)

◻ **Plains Grassland** (prairie grass)

▨ **Shrub Grassland** (sage brush and brush habitat)

■ **Intermountain Grassland** (rolling hill country w/ mixed hardwood, aspen groves, and bushy draws)

Region 4
Land Use

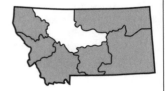

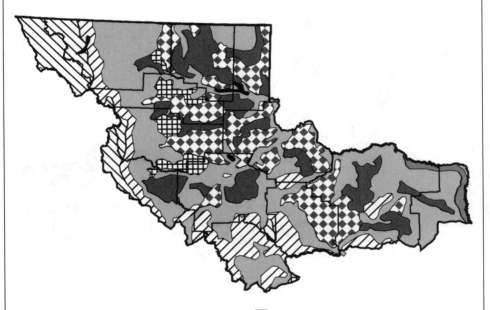

■ Water	⊞ Irrigated land
■ Cropland with grazing	◆ Mostly cropland
■ Open woodland, grazed	◣ Forest and woodland, mostly ungrazed
▨ Subhumid grassland and semiarid grazing land	▨ Forest and woodland, mostly grazed

Region 4
Federal Lands

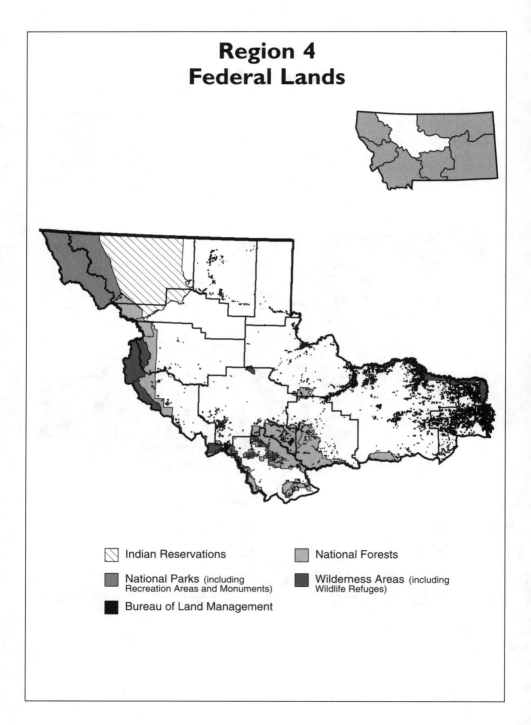

Indian Reservations

National Forests

National Parks (including
Recreation Areas and Monuments)

Wilderness Areas (including
Wildlife Refuges)

Bureau of Land Management

REGION 4 HIGHLIGHTS

Little Belts

US 89 runs through the heart of this broad range of spruce and fir covered mountains that are home to an elk herd quite accessible to the hunting public (HDs 416, 454, 448, 432, and 418). Because it is quite accessible via logging roads, 4-wheel-drive trails, and major highways and is relatively close to population centers, it is managed for maximum elk production rather than maximum trophy production. Most bulls taken are 1½-year-old spikes and brow-tines or 2½-year-old rag horns with three to five points. Only about 15 percent of the annual take are older than that. Nevertheless, there is enough dense forest escape cover that the occasional lucky bull escapes to grow truly massive antlers. One scoring 387 B&C points was taken in the mid-1990s. Generally one B&C bull comes out of the Little Belts about every five years. Don't expect to be the one to take him.

The good news is that when snows push the elk lower, they end up on the fringes of the forest and bordering private land and remain mostly accessible except on the south and southwest sides where quite a bit of private land is leased by outfitters. Even here, though, hunting pressure pretty well evens out distribution. Hunt the borders between National Forest and private land and you should do well. Cow elk may be taken in many of the area's districts during the last two weeks of the season; consult current regulations.

As is the case in most densely forested habitat, mule deer numbers are at low densities compared to the plains. Overall, the Little Belt herd has been in a slow decline, but it hasn't suffered the major setbacks the plains populations have in recent years. A good fawn crop in 1998 could start the rebound. At best, expect to find a young, light-horned 4×4. There is enough escape cover, however, that a surprise B&C buck is taken every four or five years. There's something for you to dream about.

Whitetails in small numbers prowl the lower forest, having worked their way up plains river corridors.

Moose are scattered widely through most suitable riparian habitats throughout the Little Belts, and hunters lucky enough to draw one of the limited permits have taken several B&C heads in recent years.

Big Belts

Elk are doing well in this range (HDs 445, 455, and 456) east of Helena, too. Only the north and east edges are within Region 4; the bulk are in Region 3. There is more of a problem getting access when snow drives them onto private foothills, though; the south and east slopes are pretty well leased up by outfitters. In an attempt to reduce human disturbance and hold more elk on the National Forest for hunters, FWP was considering imposing travel restrictions on some roads in the area. Though the range is rather narrow, it is long enough and high enough to provide enough escape cover that a few bulls escape to achieve decent antler growth, but most are killed as raghorns and spikes. In 1998, a brow-tine only regulation was tried to

An elk hunter/guide leads his pack string out of a mountain valley surrounded by pine and fir forest. Note the antlers on the first pack horse.

improve the age structure of the bull herd, which gets knocked back to between 10 and 12 per 100 cows at the end of each season. Mule deer and moose in the Big Belts are similar to populations in the Little Belts.

Castle Mountains

The Castles rise like an island east of White Sulphur Springs and south of the Little Belts (HD 452). The elk herd here was intentionally reduced in 1997 to address landowner concerns about depredation. Some 400 to 500 roamed the forest in 1998. Although wintering elk drop on to private land, much of which is either leased or reserved for old friends and family, enough elk remain within the boundaries of the Lewis and Clark National Forest to provide fair hunting. Expect small bulls. There are some mule deer scattered through the mountains, but rarely anything impressive. Moose are only now establishing themselves in the range.

Sun River Front Range

Though the east front of the Continental Divide (HDs 442, 424, and 422) looks wild and empty, it is not a fecund producer of big game. The land is just too steep, too high, and too rocky. As a result, backcountry hunters may scour the wilderness for days and never see a mule deer or elk, and if they do, chances are it's no world's

*Atop an open, rocky promontory, a hunter glasses in the Sun River area
west of Choteau for elk and mule deer.*

record. The critters find living hard in this harsh land, and they are just too scattered
across too much high country. In the early season they move to and stay as high as
they possibly can, even ranging above treeline. However, when harsh weather and
deep snow push them down, it can seem as if the lower slopes harbor an embarrass-
ing richness of game. Catching that weather, however, is a major guessing game.
Some years it never happens. And when it does, the animals often end up on private
land where access is not great.

On the bright side, because this country is so inaccessible, hunting pressure is
light and the odd buck or bull can grow to old age, producing massive antlers, even
if they aren't quite wide or long enough to make the book. And riding or hiking this
high, lonesome country has more than enough appeal for some hunters to offset the
relative paucity of game. It's wonderful country to hunt. You come into it from the
Sun River Road via Willow Creek Road northwest of Augusta on State Route 21.
Another entry point is Canyon Road along the Teton River northwest of Choteau. In
the south try the August Ranger Station Road which merges with the Benchmark
Road, ending at a National Forest Service campground on the South Fork of the Sun
River. Head southwest out of Augusta on the Elk Creek Road and catch the Lewis and
Clark National Forest boundary at the base of Lone Chief Mountain. Horse- and foot-
trails lead west and north from there. Fork south off Elk Creek Road on the Hay

Coulee Road, then turn west on the Dearborn Canyon Road which leads to trails up the Dearborn River and Falls Creek.

Another problem with hunting this region is the Sun River Game Preserve, a huge area on the east face closed to all hunting for decades by legislative decree. Many wildlife biologists who've studied this area would like to see that changed because generations of elk have learned to stay within the refuge where they stagnate. The result is inferior body and antler condition as well as little or no use of better foraging lands outside the refuge. Despite the protection the Preserve provides, the Sun River elk herd suffers chronically low reproductive success. In particularly deep snow years, hunters can catch some of these animals as they move out onto the Sun River Wildlife Management Area, a foothills grazing land managed by FWP and open to hunting. This area borders the south of the Sun River Road. You can also reach it from the southeast on the Augusta Willow Creek Road. It's a good mule deer wintering area, too.

One species that does get to hunt the Preserve is the cougar. The big cats are doing well in the area and they attract lots of attention. But when they move into the foothills to take advantage of clustered wintering herds, houndsmen jump on them. The area's annual harvest quota can be filled within a matter of days.

Learning to hunt the Sun River portion of the Bob Marshall and Scapegoat Wildernesses in this area can be time consuming. Outfitters and local horsemen have established long traditions of setting their camps in the same places year after year. There are only so many good campsites near water and forage to go around, and, while it's a free country, you might not want to be the greenhorn who "stole" old Jim Bob's traditional campsite. If you have a yearning to explore this area, it might be wise to begin with a few summer scouting trips. Otherwise, stick to the late-season flanks and foothills.

Rocky Mountain Front—North

HD 415 in the extreme northwest corner of Region 4, tight against Glacier National Park and the southwest border of the Blackfeet Indian Reservation, provides very limited mule deer bowhunting early in the season. This high country near the Continental Divide is mule deer summer range, and early snows move them out quickly. By the start of the rifle hunt in October, there isn't much left up there.

Elk in 415 take considerable pressure during the first week of the season as locals try to get their hunting done before winter weather closes in. Elk here trade in and out of the Park and across the divide into Region 1. The herd is static, but a few bulls each year attain antler growth in the 330 to 340 inch B&C range. Book heads are rare.

In HD 441 just to the southeast, elk are doing well in the Teton River drainage all the way to the Divide. The Bob Marshall Wilderness portion of 441 is open to antlered bull hunting on the general license, but hunting outside the Wilderness is by limited permit only. Twenty-five bull permits and 125 antlerless permits were available in 1998. Access the area via Canyon Road west of Choteau off US 89. Canyon Road forks up the Middle Fork Teton and South Fork Teton Rivers. Trails leave from the road-ends in both places. To get into the area farther north, take the road that leaves from the northwest corner of Bynum on US 89 west toward the Blackfeet ruins and the Blackfeet Wildlife Management Area. Trails begin at the end of the road just inside the National Forest boundary. There are some 500 elk in this district, and they roam from the Teton River north to the Reservation.

Mule deer in 441 are in good shape, too, though the hunting doesn't get good until mid-October as the deer begin to filter out of the high country toward lower wintering grounds. During the first two weeks of the general season, deer A licenses are valid for mule deer bucks. After that, they are valid for mule deer bucks only within National Forest lands in order to reduce the harvest on the more open wintering grounds. The buck to doe ratio in 441 is as good as 30 to 40 bucks per 100 does, an outstanding proportion. Trophy hunters will be interested in the special late season mule deer permits which are valid from about November 9–29, offering a prime chance to catch an old buck in the foothills. True B&C trophies are rare, but 150- to 170-class bucks can be found here.

The Great Wheat Desert

Much of the uplands from Great Falls north to Canada and from the western foothills east to Region 6 (HDs 400–406) are dedicated to dryland wheat and barley farming. In many places, mile after mile of these grain fields limits game habitat. Where breaks and coulees interrupt the fields, mule deer and whitetails find a place to hide. Most of this vast region holds "meat and potatoes" deer—small, young bucks. Watch for CRP fields if you hunt this area. The grass is a favorite hiding place for both types of deer.

The best deer habitat across this region lies along the Teton, Marias, and Missouri Rivers. Riparian woods and brush and some irrigated fields make for traditional whitetail habitat. Lake Elwell on the Marias is surrounded by a belt of Bureau of Reclamation land open to public hunting and has a pretty good number of mule deer and whitetails associated with draws and coulees feeding into it. This public land is mostly fenced and signed and sees a lot of hunting pressure. In addition, a large Block Management area borders the south edge of the reservoir and continues some 10 miles downstream, taking in the productive Marias River valley. This is a great place for deer.

Very little outfitting occurs in this vast farming area, and knocking and asking still works to get hunting permission, although many farmers are beginning to charge for upland bird hunting. Antelope are scattered throughout this area in suitable habitat. They've even introduced a new herd over west in the grassy foothills of the Front Range in HD 441. Antelope were never here 30 years ago, but they're here now. However, no hunting is allowed yet.

Sweet Grass Hills

These three, large, separated buttes and attendant breaks, coulees, and draws near the Canadian border in northeast Liberty County provide some of the best mule deer, whitetail, and elk habitat in the Region. There are 25 to 30 mule deer bucks per 100 does here, and quite a few of those bucks will sport 150–170 inches of antlers.

This muzzleloader hunter admires a 4×5 point buck taken from snowy mixed woods.

Then there are the elk, some 350 to 400 head working the wooded buttes and brushy draws. Elk hunting is by permit only (HD 401). Bull–cow ratios are about 30–100, and there's a good chance for a trophy. These hills also harbor some of the better antelope in the region. In 1998, there were about 3 per square mile, but in good years populations reach as high as 5. You can still get on the predominantly private lands to hunt them, and the area has a large number of acres in the Block Management Program, too. The Sweet Grass Hills are a long way from anywhere, but the hunting may make the drive worth it.

Highwood Mountains

The isolated Highwood Mountains east of Great Falls (HD 447) don't look impressive. They are a small island of conifer-covered peaks in a state full of more dramatic mountain chains. But they provide quality elk hunting out of proportion to their size. The Highwood herd is managed for trophy quality by restricting hunters via special permits. This limits hunting pressure and enables biologists to more carefully manage the harvest than they can with a general season. In 1998, for instance, 75 permits were allotted for either sex elk, which most hunters would use to take a

In mule deer, elk, and pronghorn habitat, a hunter rises to shoot amid rolling juniper and grassland hills.

bull. Another 450 permits were sold for antlerless elk hunting only. The antlerless harvest is what controls the population from growing too large for landowner tolerance. The either sex permits control bull harvest so that enough bulls escape to grow older than the typical 2 and 3 year olds found in most general season herds. This means your chances for finding a mature, large-racked bull in the Highwoods is excellent. For this reason, HD 447 elk tags are coveted. Anyone lucky enough to draw one expects to see lots of bulls and have a good chance to kill one. Usually between 50 and 60 percent of the bulls killed each season are 6 pointers; the second highest percent are 7 pointers! Anytime you're killing more 7 pointers than raghorns, you're in trophy elk country.

The mountains themselves, mostly within the Lewis & Clark National Forest, are covered in open stands of pine and Douglas fir at lower elevations, then lodgepole and limber pine in fairly dense stands higher up, and finally, near the 7,100-foot top of the range, spruce and fir. The interior of the range is surprisingly rugged, cut with steep, convoluted ridges and rimrock, creating lots of nooks and crannies where bulls take refuge once the shooting starts. When it snows significantly, herds move lower, often ending up on bordering private land, and then access becomes a problem. Many landowners charge daily trespass fees. At least one large ranch is closed to all hunting, period. So line up private land early if you plan to hunt late. Otherwise, get in early and hunt hard; this could be the bull of a lifetime.

Deer hunting in the Highwoods is pretty much wide open for either sex and either species under the general season with standard deer A licenses. Mule deer bucks are young and small, but fairly abundant when the population isn't depressed from hard weather as they have been in the late 1990s. There are whitetails in the drainages and foothills, as is the case throughout Region 4 and most of the rest of Montana. Hunting pressure is intense with Great Falls so close; consider this area a meat hunt for deer.

REGION 4 HUB CITIES
Cut Bank

Population–3,300 • Elevation–3,838

Cut Bank is an oil and gas town that sits on the Hi-Line at the eastern edge of the Blackfeet Indian Reservation. Most of Glacier County is comprised of Glacier National Park and the Indian reservation. Hunting is limited to the reservation or the small eastern part of the county that is privately owned. The habitat consists of inter-mountain grasslands on the reservation and plains grasslands in the eastern part of the county.

ACCOMMODATIONS
Glacier Gateway Inn, 1121 East Railroad Street / 800-851-5541 or 873-5544 / 19 rooms at the Inn, 9 more (budget) at another motel owned by the same people / Dogs allowed, $2.50 per dog / Some theme rooms, hot tub, free breakfast / Moderate prices / Your hosts are Irene and Keith Gustafson

CAMPGROUNDS AND RV PARKS
Riverview Campground, end of 4th Avenue Southwest / 873-5546 / Open year-round / 9 tent and 36 RV spaces / Full service except for sewer / Laundry and store

RESTAURANTS
Maxie's, 1159 East Railroad Street / 873-4220 / American fare / Prices moderate to expensive
Golden Harvest, Main Street / 873-4010 / 6AM–10PM / Breakfast, lunch, and dinner

VETERINARIANS
Northern Veterinary Clinic, 55 Santa Rita Hwy / 873-5604 / Gary Cassel, DVM

SPORTING GOODS, GUNS, & GUNSMITHS
Coast to Coast Hardware / 434-2104

TAXIDERMIST
Lone Pine Taxidermy, 15 3rd Avenue Southeast / 873-2088

AUTO REPAIR
Auto Tune Diagnostic Center, 1122 East Main / 873-2126
Northern Ford-Mercury, 120 West Main / 873-5541

AIR SERVICE
County Airstrip, Arnie Lindberg / 873-4722

MEDICAL
Glacier County Medical Center, 802 2nd Street Southeast / 873-2251

FOR MORE INFORMATION

The Cut Bank Chamber of Commerce
P.O. Box 1243
Cut Bank, MT 59427
406-873-4041

Shelby

Population–2,763 • Elevation–3,450

Shelby is a city with a colorful past and a bright future. It is located at the cross-roads of Interstate 15 and US 2 in the northern plains of the Hi-Line. The community is in the center of some of the best grain producing land in the nation. Shelby has many conveniences, and its warm and friendly people enjoy a great quality of life in this unique western atmosphere.

ACCOMMODATIONS
Crossroads Inn, 1200 West Hwy 2 / 434-5134 / 52 units, cable, coin operated laundry, continental breakfast / Dogs allowed in smoking rooms only
O'Haire Manor Motel, 204 2nd Street South / 434-5555 / 40 rooms, cable, coin operated laundry, hot tub / Dogs allowed in rooms, $5 a night / Hosts are Kevin and Elaine Mitchell
TownHouse Inn, 50 Frontage Road / 434-2212 / 72 rooms, cable, coin laundry / Dogs allowed in smoking rooms, $5 a night

CAMPGROUNDS AND RV PARKS
Lewis and Clark RV Court, North on Hwy 91 / 434-2710 / 65 spaces, water and electric hookups, showers, dump, laundry, store

RESTAURANTS
Pat's Diner, 742 Oilfield Avenue / 434-5452 / Open 6AM–10PM, 7 days / Serving fine home-cooked meals
Sports Club Lounge and Dining Room, 210 Main / 434-7224 / Open for dinner / Great steaks
Town Pump Travel Plaza and Restaurant, I-15 and Hwy 2 / 434-5491 / Open 24 hours

VETERINARIANS
Marias Veterinary Clinic, East of Shelby / 434-5176 / Clark Hardee, DVM

SPORTING GOODS, GUNS, & GUNSMITHS
Coast to Coast Hardware, 175 Main Street / 434-2104
Pamida, 1950 Roosevelt Hwy / 434-2377

TAXIDERMISTS
Moss Taxidermy, 800 10th Street. S / 434-2136

MEAT PROCESSOR
D&E Meats, Etheridge / 339-2635

AUTO REPAIR
Appley Repair, 902 Birch Avenue / 434-2915

AIR SERVICE
County Airstrip, Jerry Larson / 434-2462

MEDICAL
Toole County Hospital, 640 Park Drive / 434-3200

FOR MORE INFORMATION
Shelby Chamber of Commerce
Box 865
Shelby, MT 59474
434-7184

Fort Benton

Population–660 • Elevation–2,600

Fort Benton is 44 miles northeast of Great Falls on US 89. It is the county seat of Choteau County and the gateway to the upper Missouri River. There are 50 miles of beautiful scenery, fishing, and big game, upland bird, and waterfowl hunting along the waterway. The Teton and Marias Rivers come in from the north. The Shonkin Sag area in the southwest has a 500 foot deep, mile-wide, U-shaped valley along the Square Butte and the Highwood Mountains. Once a huge river, it is now a series of shallow lakes and scattered farms and ranches. In Choteau County, the Missouri River leaves its valley to form deep canyons and high eroded walls known as the Missouri Breaks. The Highwood Mountains in the southern area of the county, part of the Lewis and Clark National Forest, are surrounded by intermountain grassland. The majority of the county is plains grassland and crops.

ACCOMMODATIONS
Pioneer Lodge, 1700 Front Street / 622-5441 / 9 rooms / Reasonable rates / No dogs
Fort Motel, 1809 St. Charles / 622-3312 / 11 rooms / Dogs allowed, $2 per day / Reasonable rates

OUTFITTERS
Perry Hunts and Adventures, P.O. Box 355, Fort Benton, MT 59442 / 622-5336

RESTAURANTS
3-Way Cafe, 2300 St. Charles / 622-5681 / Breakfast and lunch, 7AM–3PM
Banque Club, 1318 Front Street / 622-5272 / Dinner and spirits, 5PM–1AM
CJ's Diner, 1402 Front Street / 622-5035 / Breakfast and lunch, 7AM–3:30PM

VETERINARIANS
Animal Medical Center, P.O. Box 1105 / 622-5027
Benton Vet Clinic, 999 St. Charles Avenue / 622-3732

SPORTING GOODS
Coast to Coast, 1422 Front Street / 622-5042 / Guns and ammunition

TAXIDERMISTS
Fort Benton Taxidermy, 2305 St. Charles Street / 622-5629

MEAT PROCESSOR
L&R Meat Co., 1310 Front / 622-5512

AUTO REPAIR
Fort Benton Motor, 2520 St. Charles Street / 622-5131

AIR SERVICE
County Airstrip, Rick Zanto / 622-5249

MEDICAL

Missouri River Medical Center, 1501 St. Charles Street / 622-3331

FOR MORE INFORMATION

Fort Benton Chamber of Commerce
406-622-3864

Lewistown

Population–6,051 • Elevation–3,960

Lewistown, 128 miles northwest of Billings and 105 miles west of Great Falls, is nestled at the foot of the Judith, Moccasin, and Big Snowy Mountains, along Big Spring Creek. This hub of central Montana is in the exact center of the state. It is a trading center for the ranchers and farmers in the area.

Lewistown is the county seat of Fergus County. Fergus County, like most of central Montana, produces beef cattle and grain products in the form of wheat and barley. The county is large and has a wide variety of terrain and vegetation, including mountains with montane forest and intermountain grassland, and rolling hill country with shrub and plains grasslands. Both are interspersed with ranch and farmland. The northern boundary of Fergus County is the Missouri River. The Judith River and its tributaries flow north into the Missouri River system. The county has numerous other creeks and small streams with mixed types of habitat along their water courses.

ACCOMMODATIONS

Mountainview Motel, 1422 West Main Street / 538-3457 or 800-862-5786 / Reservations suggested / 31 rooms, 3 kitchenettes, 1 house (day or week) / Dogs allowed / Reasonable rates / Your hosts are Jim and Virginia Woodburn

Yogo Park Inn, 211 East Main / 538-8721 or 800-437-PARK / Reservations suggested / 124 rooms, dogs allowed / Moderate rates / Golden Spike Lounge and Yogo Steak House

B&B Motel, 420 East Main / 538-5496 / 36 rooms, kitchenettes / Dogs allowed / Reasonable rates

OUTFITTERS

Montana Outdoor Expeditions, 76370 Gallatin Road, Gallatin Gateway, MT 59730 / 763-4749 or 580-1799 / Upland gamebird and big game hunting / Call for reservations / Bob and Patti Griffith

Pigeye Basin Outfitters, Peter B. Rogers, HCR 81, Box 25, Utica, MT 59452 / 423-5223 / Pete also has a private pheasant preserve / Accommodations and meals / Call for reservations

RESTAURANTS

Main Street Bistro, 122 West Main Street / 538-3666 / Daily specials 5:30AM–10PM / Closed Mondays

Sportsman Restaurant and Casino, top of the hill / 538-9053 / Dining, 6PM–10PM / Lounge, 8AM–2AM

4 Aces Casino and Restaurant, 508 1 Avenue North / 538-9744 / A great breakfast

VETERINARIANS
Lewistown Veterinary Service, Fairgrounds Road / 538-3663 / Dr. Visscher
The Animal Hospital, 801 Northeast Main Street / 538-3663 / Doug Anderson, DVM

SPORTING GOODS, GUNS, & GUNSMITHS
The Sports Center, 320 West Main Street / 538-9308 / Hunting and fishing headquarters / 8:30AM–6PM
Don's Sports, 2nd Avenue South / 538-9408

TAXIDERMISTS
Lewistown Taxidermy, Gill's, RR1, Box 1669 / 538-9388
Judith Mountain Taxidermy, 223½ West Main Street / 538-9700

MEAT PROCESSORS
Hilger Meat Processing / 538-2619
Snowy Mountain Meats, 612 1st Avenue South / 538-5932
Bill's Meat Service, Joyland Road / 538-3337
Denton Meats, 105 5 South, Denton. / 567-2281

AUTO REPAIR AND RENTAL
Dean Newton Olds, 519 West Broadway / 538-3455

AIR SERVICE
Lewistown Airport, Big Sky Airlines. Daily service / 538-3264

MEDICAL
Central Montana Medical Center, 408 Wendall Avenue / 538-7711

FOR MORE INFORMATION
Chamber of Commerce
P.O. Box 818
Lewistown, MT 59457
406-538-5436

BLM–Lewistown Field Office
Airport Road, Box 1160
Lewistown, MT 59457
406-538-7461

White Sulphur Springs

Population–1,002 • Elevation–5,200

White Sulphur Springs is located halfway between Yellowstone and Glacier National Parks on US 89 and US 12. The town is named for the mineralized, thermal waters located in the city park. The heated water is used in the Spa Hot Springs Motel's pool. White Sulphur Springs sits in a high mountain valley with the Big Belt, Little Belt, and Castle Mountains surrounding its perimeter.

It is a full-service community and the county seat of Meagher (pronounced "marr") County. There is a wealth of recreational opportunities, wide open spaces, and thousands of areas to explore in the Lewis and Clark and Helena National Forests. The headwaters of the Smith River are in the Castles and the Little Belts, and the river flows through the county to meet the Missouri at Ulm. The Smith is a famous floating river that passes through 61 miles of beautiful natural canyons cut in limestone formations. Although Meagher County is surrounded by mountains, the valley is vast and flat with shrub grasslands and croplands.

ACCOMMODATIONS
The Tenderfoot Motel, 301 West Main Street / 547-3303 / Reservations only, 800-898-3303 / 20 units, kitchenettes / Dogs allowed / Reasonable rates
Spa Hot Springs Motel, 202 West Main Street / 547-3366 / 21 rooms / Dogs allowed / Reasonable rates

CAMPGROUNDS AND RV PARKS
Conestoga Campground, 815 8 Avenue West / 800-898-3303

RESTAURANTS
The Truck Stop Cafe, 511 East Main Street / 547-3825 / Full menu, 5:30AM–10PM
Dori's Cafe, 112 East Main Street / 547-2280
The Connection, 547-9994 / Steaks, seafood, and cocktails
Mint Bar, 27 East Main Street / 547-3857

VETERINARIANS
William H. Shendel, DVM, 404 East Hampton / 547-3857
Elkhorn Vet Clinic / 547-3980 / Eric Sorenson, DVM

SPORTING GOODS, GUNS, & GUNSMITHING
Lone Wolf Sporting Goods Stores, 105 West Main / 547-2176

TAXIDERMIST
Great Outdoor Taxidermy, 603 East Washington / 547-2331

MEAT PROCESSOR
Pierce Meat Cutting, 415 E Main Street / 547-3467

Auto Repair
Berg Chevrolet Garage, 11 West Main Street / 547-3514

Air Service
Airport, south of White Sulphur Springs / 547-3511 / Prop aircrafts and small jets

Medical
Mountain View Memorial Hospital, 16 West Main Street / 547-3384

For More Information
Chamber of Commerce
P.O. Box 370
White Sulphur Springs, MT 59645
547-3366

Great Falls

Population– 55,000 • Elevation–3,333

Great Falls is located in northcentral Montana at the confluence of the Missouri and Sun Rivers. It is Montana's second largest town and home to the famous Charlie Russell Museum. The Lewis and Clark National Forest lies to the south and the rest of the surrounding area consists of intermountain and plains grasslands. Agriculture is one of the main industries of the county.

ACCOMMODATIONS

Budget Inn, 2 Treasure State Drive / 453-1602 / 60 rooms / Dogs allowed, grassy area / Rates moderate

Comfort Inn, 1120 9th Street South / 454-2727 / 64 rooms / Dogs allowed in smoking rooms only, $5 charge, grassy area / Spa / Rates moderate

Edelweiss Motor Inn, 626 Central Avenue West / 452-9503 / 20 rooms / Hunters and dogs welcome, grassy area / Rates very reasonable

Super 8 Lodge, 1214 13th Street South / 727-7600 / 117 rooms / Dogs allowed, grassy area / Rates moderate

TownHouse Inn, 1411 10th Avenue South / 761-4600 / 108 rooms / Dogs allowed, $5 charge per dog / Grassy area, pool, restaurant / Rates moderate

CAMPGROUNDS AND RV PARKS

Dick's RV Park, ½ mile east off exit 278 on 10th Avenue South / 452-0333 / Open all year / 10 tent and 140 RV spaces / Showers, laundry, and store

Great Falls KOA Campground, southeast edge of town at 10th Avenue South and 51st / 727-3191 / Open all year / 22 tent, 116 RV spaces / Showers, laundry, store, and cabins

RESTAURANTS

4B's, 4610 10th Avenue South / 727-3366 / Open 24 hours

Elmer's Pancake and Steak House, 1600 Fox Farm Rd, next to Budget Inn / 761-2400 / Open 6AM–10PM for breakfast, lunch, and dinner

El Comedor Mexican Restaurant, 1120 25th Street South / 761-5500 / Open 7 days, 11AM–11PM for lunch and dinner / Imported beers

Jaker's Steak, Ribs, and Fish House, 1500 10th Avenue South / 727-1033 / Open for lunch and dinner

VETERINARIANS

Rocky Mountain Medical Center, 1401 Northwest Bypass / 727-8387 / 24-hour emergency service

Skyline Veterinary Clinic, 15th Street North, Junction Havre Hwy and Bootlegger Trail / 761-8282 / 24-hour emergency service

SPORTING GOODS, GUNS, & GUNSMITHS

Big Bear Sports Center, 121 Northwest Bypass / 761-6400

Prairie Sporting Goods, 802 2nd Avenue North / 452-7319
Scheel's Sports, 1200 10th Avenue South #3, Holiday Village Shopping Center /
    453-7666 / Licenses, ammo, guns, complete line of hunting supplies

TAXIDERMISTS
Archer's Den & Taxidermy, 1520 River Drive North / 452-1921
Wildlife Reproductions, 2020 2nd Avenue North / 771-7729
Kent's Taxidermy, 801 Central Avenue West / 771-1717
Trophy Taxidermy, 911 Central Avenue West / 452-1951

MEAT PROCESSORS
Chaons Game Processing, 400 4th Avenue South / 761-2855
House of Meats, 608 14th Street North / 727-7849

AUTO RENTAL AND REPAIR
Budget, Great Falls International Airport / 454-1001
Hertz Rent-A-Car, Great Falls International Airport / 761-6641
Carl's Exxon, 2300 10th Avenue South / 761-1342 / Open 7 days / Towing
Westgate Exxon, 416 Smelter Avenue Northeast / 452-1271 / Open 7 days /
    Towing

AIR SERVICE
Great Falls International Airport, 15 South / 727-3404 / Serviced by Northwest,
    Delta, and Horizon airlines

MEDICAL
Columbus Hospital, 500 15th Avenue South / 727-3333
Montana Deaconess Medical Center, 1101 26th Street South / 761-1200

FOR MORE INFORMATION
Great Falls Chamber of Commerce
P.O. Box 2127-A
Great Falls, MT 59403
406-761-4436

Fish, Wildlife & Parks–Region 4 Office
4600 Giant Springs Road, P.O. Box 6610
Great Falls, MT 59406-6610
406-454-5840

BLM–Great Falls Field Office
812 14th Street North
Great Falls, MT 59401
406-727-0503

Lewis and Clark National Forest
1101 15th Street North, P.O. Box 869
Great Falls, MT 59403
406-791-7700

Choteau

Population–1,741 • Elevation–3,800

Choteau is a friendly ranching community located near the eastern edge of the Rocky Mountain Front. Southeast of town is the Freezeout Lake Waterfowl Refuge, noted for its outstanding duck and goose hunting. The Boone and Crockett Club has a ranch northeast of town, and the Pine Butte Swamp stretches west of town from the plains to the mountains across a wetland. One of the largest dinosaur sites, "Egg Mountain," is southwest of town. Tours of the dinosaur fields are available.

ACCOMMODATIONS

Western Star Motel, 426 South Main Avenue / 466-5737 / 18 rooms, cable, coin laundry next door / Dogs allowed, $5 per night / Rates reasonable

Big Sky Motel, 405 South Main Avenue / 466-5318 / 12 rooms, dogs allowed for a $5 charge

Hensley 287 Motel / 466-5775 / Dogs allowed in rooms / Rates reasonable

RESTAURANTS

Circle N, 925 North Main Avenue / 466-5331 / Lunch and dinner / Prime rib on weekends

John Henry's Pizza, 215 North Main Avenue / 466-5642 / Lunch and dinner

Log Cabin Drive-in, 102 South Main Avenue / 466-2888 / 6AM–6PM daily

VETERINARIANS

Double Arrow Veterinary Clinic, North of Choteau / 466-5333 / Robert Lee, DVM

SPORTING GOODS, GUNS & GUNSMITHS

Birds in Flight, 15 North Delaware Street, Conrad / 278-5886

TAXIDERMISTS

Artistic Taxidermy Studio, 119 1st Northwest / 466-2922

MEAT PROCESSOR

5-D Processing, 302 7th Avenue Southwest / 466-2061

AUTO REPAIR

Dirke's Chevrolet-Pontiac-Oldsmobile-GMC Trucks, 302 South Main Avenue / 466-2061

AIR SERVICE

Choteau Flying Service, east of Choteau / 466-2968

MEDICAL

Teton Medical Center Hospital and Nursing Home, 915 4th Street Northwest / 466-5763

For More Information

Choteau Chamber of Commerce
Rt 2, Box 256
Choteau, MT 59422
406-466-5332

Region 4 Guides and Outfitters

Outfitter Services by Species and Specialty

A Elk, deer, bear, antelope
B Deer & antelope
WT Whitetail deer

F Mountain lion
G Sheep
H Mountain goat

I Moose
L Drop Camps
M Tent Camps

A	**Gary Anderson** Deep Creek Outfitters Box 270 Ulm, MT 59485 406-866-3316
A	**Edward Arnott** The Homestead Ranch Utica, MT 59452 406-423-5301
A	**Liz Barker** Fork Creek Outfitters P.O. Box 329 Augusta, MT 59410 406-562-3672
A	**Clayton Barkhoff** Beaver Creek Outfitters RR 1, Box 1732 Lewistown, MT 59457 406-538-5706
AB FG	**William Brown** Chase Hill Outfitters Rt. 236, P.O. Box 849 Lewistown, MT 59457 406-538-5706
A WT	**Doug Caltrider** Avalanche Basin Outfitters Box 17 White Sulphur Springs, MT 59645 406-547-3962

AFG WT	**Lee Carlbom** Sun Canyon Lodge P.O. Box 327 Augusta, MT 59410 406-562-3654
AB WT	**Andy Celander** Tri Mountain Outfitters Box 229 White Sulphur Springs, MT 59645 406-547-2977
AF WT	**Donald DeGroft** Rawhide Guide Service P.O. Box 451 White Sulphur Springs, MT 59645 717-528-8170
AB FG	**Bruce Delory** Bear's Den Outfitters, Inc. Box 941 Livingston, MT 59047 406-222-0746
AB WT	**Thomas E. Elliott** N-Bar Land & Cattle Co. Grass Range, MT 59032 406-428-2497
AB FI	**Shane Erickson** God's Country Outfitters P.O. Box 265 Lincoln, MT 59639 406-362-3070

A	Elk, deer, bear, antelope	F	Mountain lion	I	Moose
B	Deer & antelope	G	Sheep	L	Drop Camps
WT	Whitetail deer	H	Mountain goat	M	Tent Camps

BG
WT Leo M. Faber
Faber Ranch
P.O. Box 554
Big Sandy, MT 59520
406-386-2266

A Kelly Flynn
Hidden Hollow Hideaway
P.O. Box 233
Townsend, MT 59644
406-266-3322

AB John R. Fritz
Cow Creek Outfitters
Box 280
Chester, MT 59522
406-432-2755

AF
WT William Galt
Birch Creek Outfitters/Think
Wild
P.O. Box 618
White Sulphur Springs, MT 59645
406-547-2107

AFG
HI
WT B.J. Gilchrist
Landers Fork Outfitters
P.O. Box 1247
Great Falls, MT 59403
406-761-3633

AB
FH
WT David Gill
Triple B Outfitters
616 W. Broadway
Lewistown, MT 59457
406-538-2177

ABF Matthew Balmes
Lepley Creek Ranch
1629 Simms Rd.
Cascade, MT 59421
406-521-8445

AG Allen J. Haas
A Lazy H Outfitters
Box 729
Choteau, MT 59422
406-466-5564

ABF
GHI
WT Rocky Heckman
Montana Safaris
P.O. Box 1044
Choteau, MT 59422
406-466-2004

ABH
WT John R. Hill
Hill Country Expeditions
P.O. Box 108
Geyser, MT 59447
406-735-4484

A Richard Jackson
Great Divide Guiding &
Outfitting
P.O. Box 315
East Glacier, MT 59434
406-266-4487

AB
WT Dwayne Kiehl
Flatwillow Creek Outfitters
Box 40
Winnett, MT 59087
406-429-5601

A Elk, deer, bear, antelope	**F** Mountain lion
B Deer & antelope	**G** Sheep
WT Whitetail deer	**H** Mountain goat
I Moose	
L Drop Camps	
M Tent Camps	

AFG Dick Klick Bar L Ranch
Box 287 Beyond All Roads
Augusts, MT 59410
406-562-3589 or 406-467-2771

ABF Dave Kozub
WT Montana Wilderness Outfitters
Rt. 1, Box 1802A
Lewistown, MT 59457
406-538-6516

AB Doug Landers
FG Elk Ridge Outfitters
Rt. 1, Box 218
Wilsall, MT 59086
406-578-2379

AF Dennis LeVeque
WT DL Elk Outfitters, Inc.
282 - 10 Mile Rd.
Cascade, MT 59421
406-468-2642

AF Dick Lyman
WT Dick Lyman Outfitters
20 Truly Loop
Great Falls, MT 59405
406-736-5645

AF Mike McCormick
WT Sunset Guest Ranch
50 Cutoff Rd.
Helmville, MT 59843
406-793-5574

ABF Barb & Rob McDonough
WT McDonough Outfitters
5545 Lewis & Clark Pass Rd.
Wolf Creek, MT 59648
406-235-4205

AB Keith Meckling
GF M&E Outfitters
Box 84
Winifred, MT 59489
406-462-5329

AF Ronald Mills
Ron Mills Outfitters
P.O. Box 2
Augusta, MT 59410
406-562-3335

AF David B. Moore
GI New West Outfitters
P.O. Box 6052
Helena, MT 59604
406-475-3218

AG Glen Nepil
WT Double R Outfitting & Guide
Service
Box 402
Big Sandy, MT 59520
406-378-3235

A Tag Rittel
Blacktail Ranch
Wolf Creek, MT 59648
406-235-4330

A	Elk, deer, bear, antelope	F	Mountain lion	I	Moose
B	Deer & antelope	G	Sheep	L	Drop Camps
WT	Whitetail deer	H	Mountain goat	M	Tent Camps

B   **Paul Roos**
North Fork Crossing & Paul Roos
Outfitters
P.O. Box 621
Helena, MT 59624
406-442-5489

AB   **Chad S. Schearer**
F   Central Montana Outfitters
Box 2002
Great Falls, MT 59403
406-454-1156

AG   **Lamonte J. Schuur**
Monte's Guiding & Mtn.
Outfitting
16 N. Fork Rd.
Townsend, MT 59644
406-266-3515

A   **Mike Simpson**
WT   Simpson Outfitters, Inc.
3747 Lewis Lane
East Helena, MT 59635
406-227-5277

AB   **Sarah Stevenson**
Circle Bar Guest Ranch
Utica, MT 59452
406-423-5454

AB   **Edwin W. Watson**
EW Watson & Sons Outfitting
7837 US Hwy 287
Townsend, MT 59644
406-266-3741

AF   **P.K. Williams**
GH   Belt Creek Outfitters
WT   741 E. Highwood Rd.
Belt, MT 59412
406-738-4281

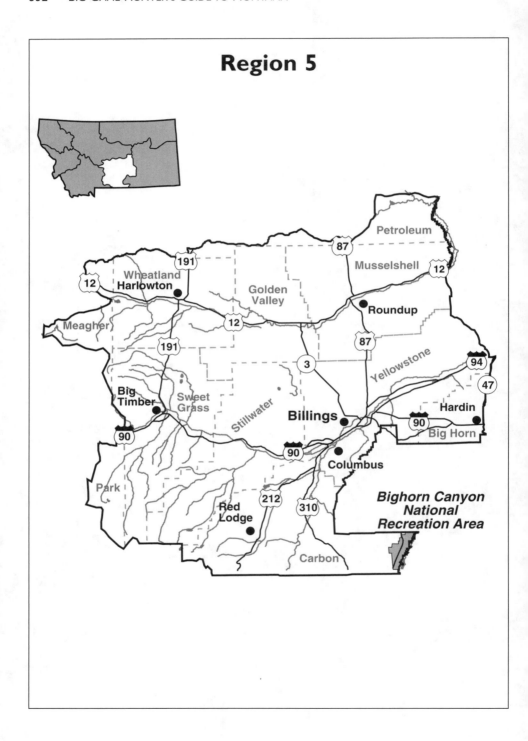

Region 5

Region 5

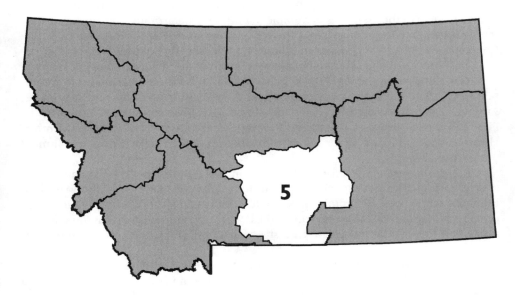

If you're traveling from the west, this is the last of the mountainous Montana hunting regions. It's the first if you're coming in from the east. As seen from I-90 west of Billings, the snow-capped peaks of the Absaroka Range rise to the blue heavens like a dream. But they're real enough, as your legs will tell you if you hunt them; you'll also encounter the Pryor Mountains and the east flank of the isolated Crazy Mountains. Unfortunately, these conifer-forested ranges under Forest Service management represent the bulk of public hunting available in the region. The rest consists of tamer, privately owned foothills and grasslands where cattle ranching and wheat farming predominate. The usual problems associated with gaining permission to hunt private land apply here, but ranchers living out of the river valleys and away from population centers are still big-hearted and likely to grant hunting permission to polite, sincere hunters who ask long before the season starts. Those who do get onto private land usually enjoy excellent hunting for mule deer, antelope, whitetails, and even elk. New "hobby" farm and ranch owners who have recently moved in from other states jealously guard their property and rarely grant hunting rights; this is one of the sadder developments in Montana. Fortunately, there are 750,000 acres under Block Management to offset this.

Game Species & Numbers

Region 5 has always been a consistent producer of mule deer and antelope on the grasslands and foothills, but recent winter storms and summer droughts have hurt reproduction of both these open-country species. Whitetails, common in riparian cover and adjacent cropland along the Yellowstone, Musselshell, and their tributaries, were also knocked back by the deep snow, extended cold, ice, and subsequent flooding. Each of these species is capable of bouncing back quickly, given easier winters and wet growing seasons, and the 1997 winter and 1998 spring were just that. Consult the Regional FWP office in Billings for the most recent prognosis.

Traditionally, the best antelope areas are north of the Yellowstone. Mule deer are common throughout the region in suitable habitat. Elk strongholds are in the mountains, but their numbers are increasing, and they are expanding into new areas. Among other places, elk now roam the Musselshell River, the Bull Mountains, the Pine Ridge southwest of Custer, and along Sweet Grass Creek near Big Timber. However, more than half of the elk hunting districts in the region are open to limited permit hunting only.

Though moose aren't abundant, due to limited habitat, they are expanding and showing up in the lower reaches of mountain drainages. One even stumbled into Billings a while back. Mountain lions are also increasing, though hunting for them remains under the quota system statewide. Black bears are stable within their limited range and under a quota system in districts 520 and 510, the Beartooth and Pryor Mountains.

There have been no sheep die-offs in the region. Unlimited permit hunting remains open under the quota system in districts 500 and 501 in the Absaroka and Beartooth mountains where a total of 3 rams may be taken and hunter success hovers in the 2-5% range. Limited permit hunters in district 503 (Pryor Mountains) usually enjoy 100% success. About a dozen to 17 mountain goats are harvested from four districts in the Beartooths. There are a few permits offered for the Crazy Mountains and northeast end of the Absarokas, too.

Region 5
Pronghorn Distribution

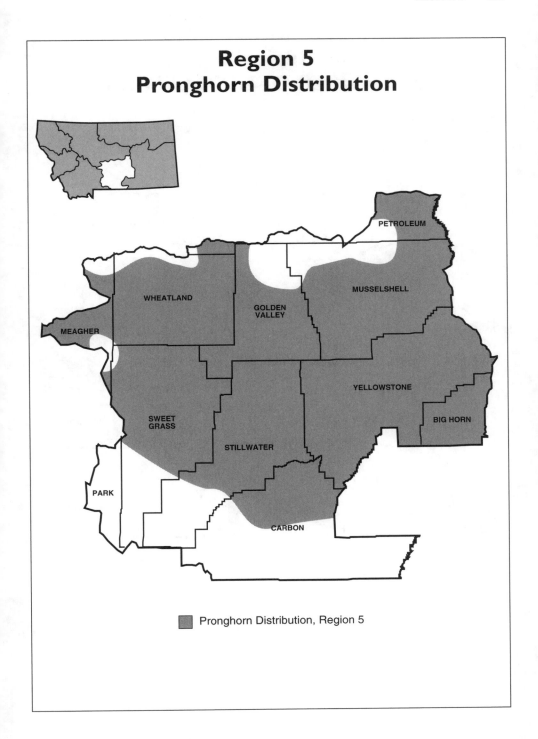

Pronghorn Distribution, Region 5

Region 5
White-tailed Deer Distribution

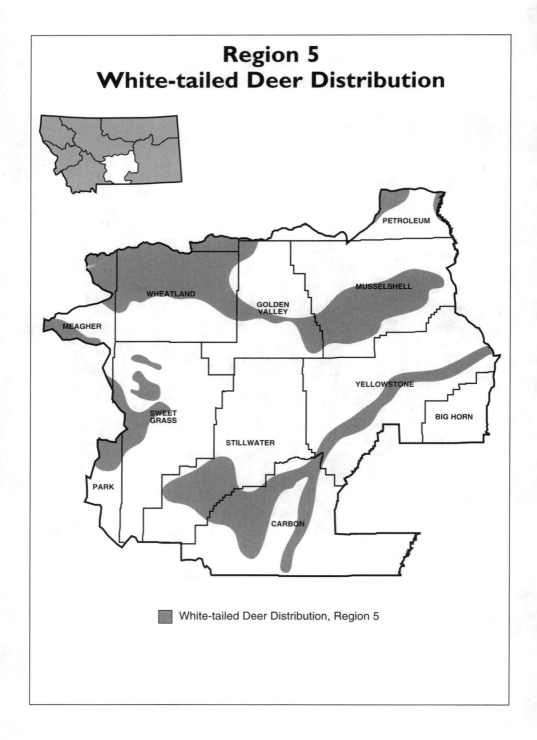

White-tailed Deer Distribution, Region 5

Region 5
Mule Deer Distribution

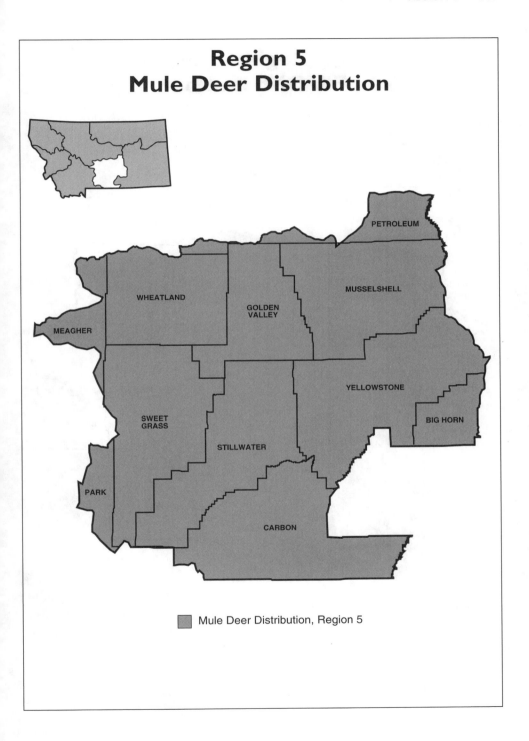

Mule Deer Distribution, Region 5

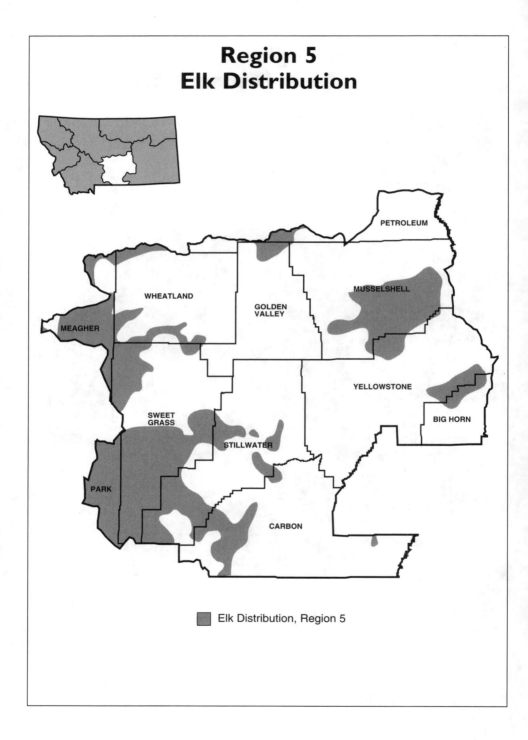

Region 5
Elk Distribution

PETROLEUM

WHEATLAND

GOLDEN VALLEY

MUSSELSHELL

MEAGHER

YELLOWSTONE

SWEET GRASS

STILLWATER

BIG HORN

PARK

CARBON

Elk Distribution, Region 5

Region 5
Moose Distribution

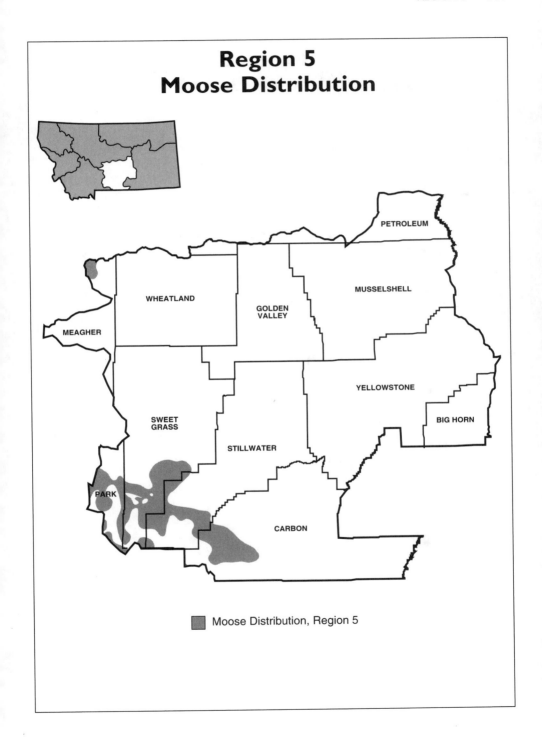

Moose Distribution, Region 5

Region 5
Bighorn Sheep Distribution

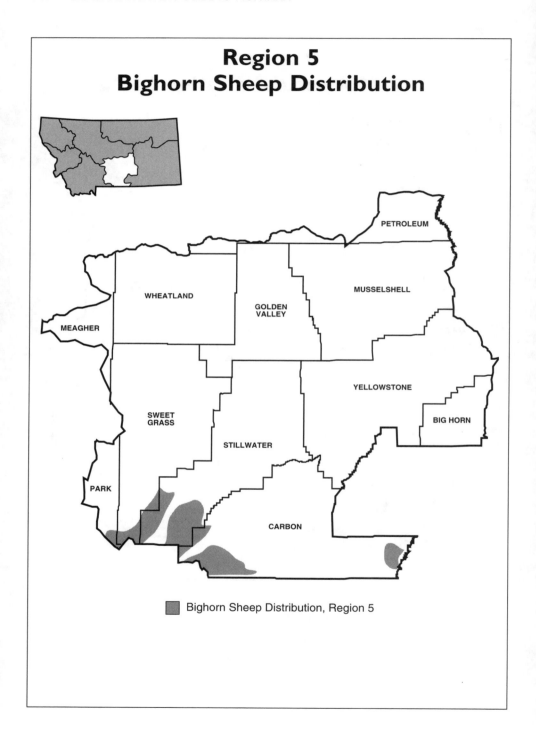

Bighorn Sheep Distribution, Region 5

Region 5
Mountain Goat Distribution

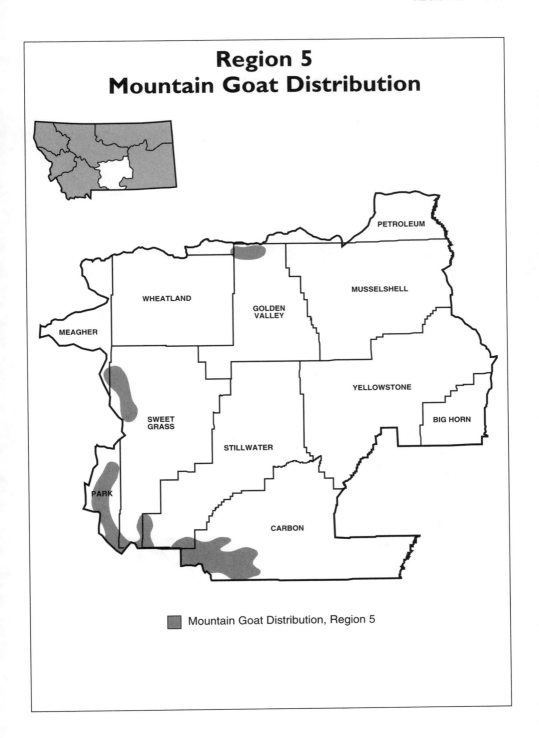

Mountain Goat Distribution, Region 5

Region 5
Black Bear Distribution

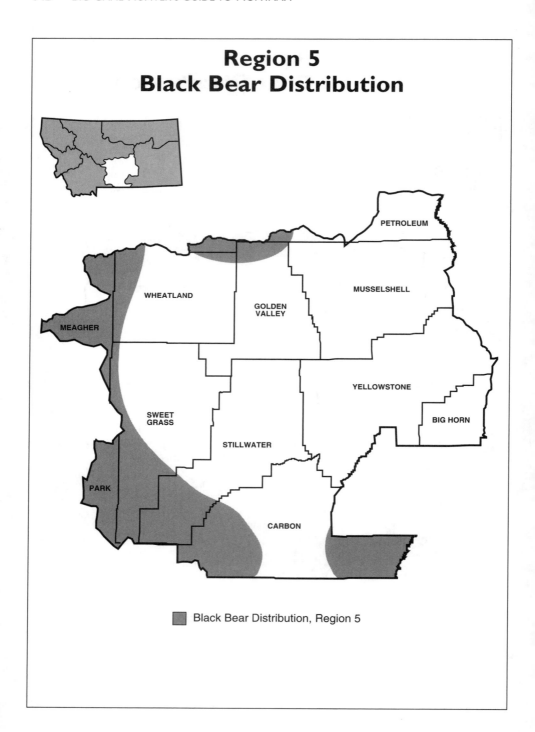

Black Bear Distribution, Region 5

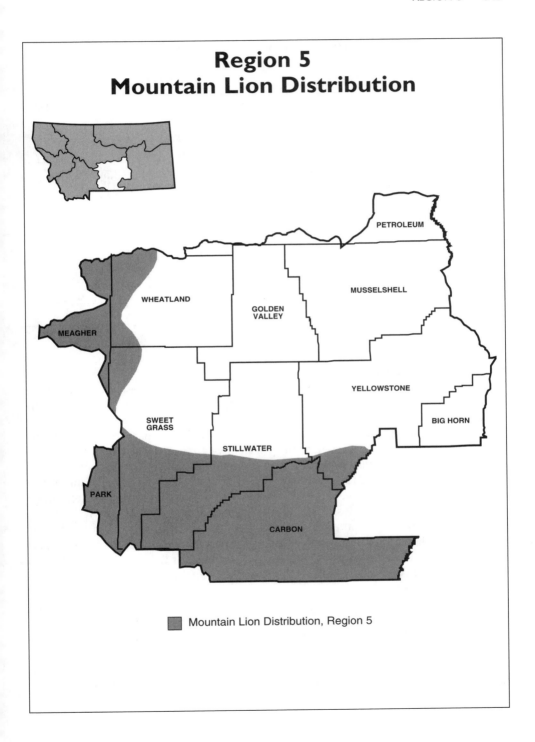

Region 5
Mountain Lion Distribution

Mountain Lion Distribution, Region 5

Harvest Trend (1992–1996)

Species	Success Rate	Harvest	Hunters
Deer	78%	Mule bucks 5,900–8,200 Mule does 2,300–6,100 Whitetail bucks 2,601–3,993 Whitetail does 2,200–2,810	18,432–22,013
Elk	25%	Bulls 340–550 Cows 300–980	3,500–5,000
Moose	81%	Bulls 16–24 Cows 4–6	33–35
Sheep	9%	Rams 4–7	48–71
Mountain Goat	84%	Billies 7–13 Nannies 1–7	17–19
Pronghorn	55%–100%	Bucks & does 4,666–9,335	6,074–8455
Cougars and Bears—No harvest statistics available			

Physical Characteristics

Rolling plains, lush river valleys, pine-covered hills and ridges, and some of the highest mountains in Montana make up this region. The Absaroka and Beartooth Ranges in the southwest corner stretch to 12,000 feet with many peaks above 10,000. That's alpine tundra habitat, home of snowfields, glaciers, talus slopes, pikas, and mountain goats. If you aren't physically capable of walking or horseback riding to such country, take heart. You can drive to it and at least look at it from the Beartooth Highway, US 212, south out of Red Lodge. The paved road, one of the most scenic drives in the nation, switchbacks from about 5,500 feet at Red Lodge to 10,000 feet in a few miles, topping out in Wyoming amid dwarf wild flowers, rocks, and dozens of glacial pothole lakes. Outfitters and properly outfitted individuals enter this land of mountain goats, bighorn sheep, elk, moose, cougars, and black bears (with some grizzlies and wolves spilling out from Yellowstone) from several Forest Service roads penetrating from the northeast and north as well as south from Cooke City.

East of the Beartooth Highway there is considerable low elevation BLM grassland and sage drained by the Clark's Fork of the Yellowstone River; you will find limited antelope hunting here. Looming on the eastern horizon are the 8,465-foot Pryor Mountains, with more bighorn sheep, elk, mule deer, and even some wild horses. The Crow Indian Reservation bordering the south and east of Region 5 is closed to big game hunting by nontribal members. The beautiful, rolling foothills between the

Absarokas and I-90 are prime ranchland and mule deer country, with whitetails in the crop fields and river valleys.

The Crazy Mountains, though isolated from other ranges, still rise to over 10,000 feet and boast elk, mule deer, mountain goats, and even a few moose. Antelope are quite common in the grasslands along their eastern flank. Elk have spilled down to the Musselshell, east along it, and along bordering hills as far as Lavina. The land between the Musselshell and the Yellowstone River to the south consists of plains and grasslands; coulees, breaks, and badlands; and hills covered in junipers and pines. Valleys support a few irrigated crops, dryland grain fields, hay fields, and cattle pastures. Toward the east side of the region bordering the Musselshell, the Bull Mountains rise to 4,700 feet. This is a gentle range clothed in pines and junipers with a nice population of elk and mule deer. Whitetails prance up from the river.

North of the Musselshell, the land is a combination of plains, hills, buttes, breaks, and draws—cattle and wheat country mostly with the forested Little Snowy Mountains and Big Snowy Mountains providing elevations to 8,500 feet and a bit of elk habitat on the northern border of the region.

The Yellowstone Valley is glorious in late September and early October with its ribbons of cottonwoods painted yellow. Whitetails hide in thick riverside brush, venturing out mornings and evenings to forage in lush alfalfa fields and grain stubble. They work their way up any wooded creek or ridge nearby and spread surprisingly far afield.

Land Use

Welcome to cattle and sheep country. Old working ranches are sprinkled across the region, with a mixture of grazing lands and wheat fields in the uplands. The fertile, flat, and heavily irrigated Yellowstone Valley grows corn, soybeans, sugar beets, and some alfalfa. It also offers the state's major travel routes, I-90 and a major railway, both busy and noisy by Montana standards. There are oil refineries in Laurel and Billings, livestock auction centers in Billings, and major shopping centers for a wide region.

A major rail route used to run up the Musselshell Valley, too, but that closed nearly 20 years ago. Ranching and irrigated farming fill the valley now, along with dying small towns. Roundup and Harlowton remain to serve local ranchers and farmers with basic services, and hunters are most welcome at local gas stations, groceries, restaurants and motels.

Many of the most beautiful mountain valleys on the Absaroka Front are playgrounds for the rich and famous. Other former working ranchlands throughout the region are falling to the same fate, and the hunting rights with them.

Weather

Chinook winds help moderate some of winter's harshest cold snaps, but by and large, Region 5 suffers bitter cold in the depths of winter. The hunting season weather is quite variable depending on elevation. On the Beartooth and Absaroka Ranges, snow squalls and big winds can hit anytime. It isn't unusual for snow to close the Beartooth Highway in September. As much as 60 inches of precipitation can fall in the high country each year, most of it as snow. Valleys may get as little as 7 to 13 inches, and most of that in spring and summer as thundershowers.

Out on the plains it can rain, snow, and blow, and sometimes even shine sunny and pleasant. Expect nearly anything. Ideally, you'll look at September temperatures in the mid 30s to mid 60s, October in the mid 20s to mid 50s, and November from the teens to high 30s. Winds up to 35 mph are not uncommon.

Public Lands and Acreages

National Forests in Region 5	Size (not all acres necessarily within Region 5)
Custer National Forest	2,446,130 acres
Gallatin National Forest	1,735,412 acres
Lewis & Clark National Forest	1,843,469 acres
Wilderness Areas in Region 5	**Size (not all acres necessarily within Region 5)**
Absaroka-Beartooth Wilderness	944,060 acres
Block Management Acres	**775,000 acres**

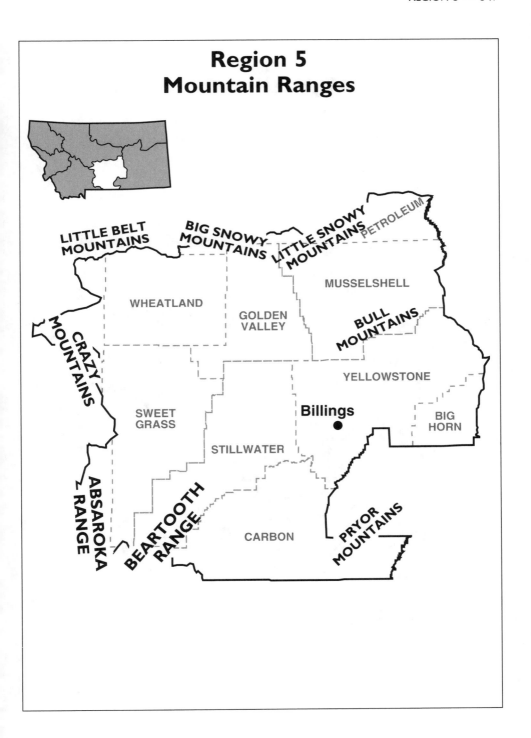

Region 5
Mountain Ranges

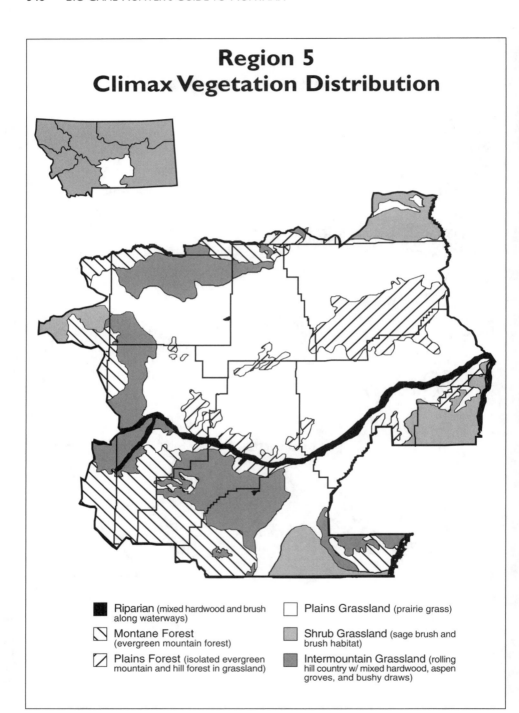

Region 5
Climax Vegetation Distribution

Riparian (mixed hardwood and brush along waterways)

Montane Forest (evergreen mountain forest)

Plains Forest (isolated evergreen mountain and hill forest in grassland)

Plains Grassland (prairie grass)

Shrub Grassland (sage brush and brush habitat)

Intermountain Grassland (rolling hill country w/ mixed hardwood, aspen groves, and bushy draws)

Region 5
Land Use Distribution

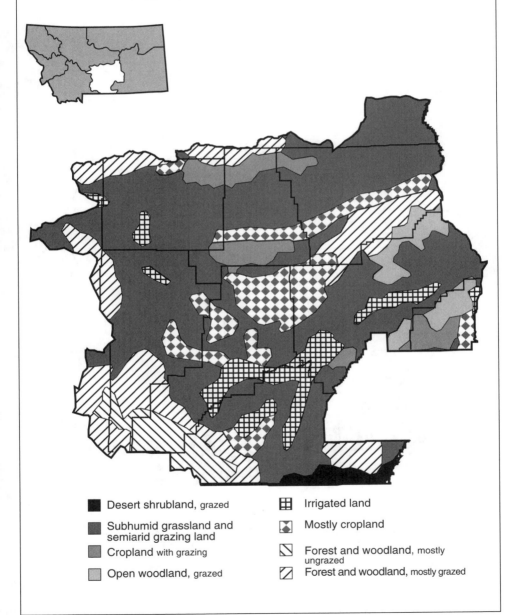

Desert shrubland, grazed

Subhumid grassland and semiarid grazing land

Cropland with grazing

Open woodland, grazed

Irrigated land

Mostly cropland

Forest and woodland, mostly ungrazed

Forest and woodland, mostly grazed

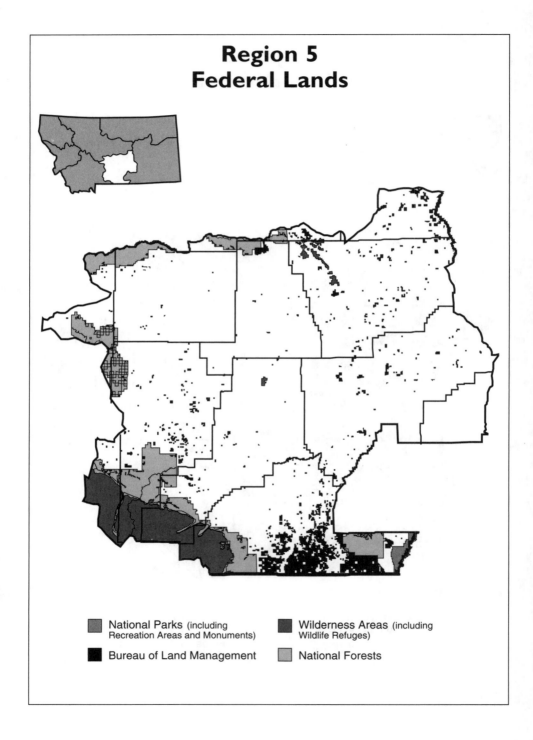

Region 5
Federal Lands

National Parks (including Recreation Areas and Monuments)

Bureau of Land Management

Wilderness Areas (including Wildlife Refuges)

National Forests

REGION 5 HIGHLIGHTS

Beartooths & Red Lodge Area

With the Custer National Forest and towering Beartooth Mountains on its back doorstep, Red Lodge would appear the perfect headquarters for any kind of Montana big game hunting. But don't rush to judgment. While there is excellent hunting for whitetails and elk, most is on private lands in the foothills and plains. These places are traditionally booked years in advance by friends and family. Billings is less than an hour drive, and locals take advantage of this. The high country itself is rugged and relatively unproductive. Big bulls are uncommon. The large hunting district 520, which encompasses most of the mountains in this area, is limited to brow-tined bull hunting only in some areas, branch-antlered bull hunting only in much of the north, and permit only hunting in the south. Special permits are available via drawing for antlerless elk in 8 subdistricts within HD 520. Essentially, elk hunting here is carefully controlled. You need to plan ahead, line up your hunting grounds, and apply by June 1 for those special permits, or else work hard for a bull. According to the local FWP biologist, during the early season, elk are in the low foothills where they launch raids on private alfalfa fields. The high country is steep and forested on its east face, then largely flat, open, alpine habitat on top.

Mule deer in 520 are in even worse shape, down 20 to 40 percent from long term averages. This could turn around with a few good weather years, but this has never been huge buck country. No doe hunting is currently allowed. The news is better in the Pryor Mountains (HD 510) where larger muley bucks have been taken in the past. An unlimited number of antlered mule deer permits were issued to hunters who applied for them by June 1 of 1998. With this permit, hunters were restricted to hunting mule deer in HD 510 only. The bad news is that the sex ratio has been as bad as 8 bucks per 100 does in recent years. Such numbers are not conducive to trophy buck production.

Whitetails are a different story. They're doing well in all the creek and river bottoms and associated agricultural lands in the foothills, and especially north and east of Red Lodge. There were some winter losses recently, but those are expected to be temporary. Irrigated cornfields along the lower Clark's Fork of the Yellowstone produce the biggest bucks. State Route 310 runs through this valley. Naturally, all the land is private, but there were nearly 4,000 acres along the Clark Fork enrolled in the Block Management Program in 1998. Archers can check out 8 FWP fishing accesses on the Stillwater River (SR 78 from I-90 to Absarokee, Stillwater River Road from Absarokee to Nye). Some of these may have enough suitable habitat for a whitetail hunt.

Black bears find HD 520 and 510 to their liking, but considerable hunting pressure keeps a tight quota lid on the area. Only 26 bears were allowed to be harvested during the spring 1998 season. Successful hunters had to present the hide and skull to a Region 5 FWP official for inspection and aging within 5 days of harvest. All bear

Guide Greg Metz fleshing a black bear hide.

hunters must be extra cautious about identifying their quarry because of Yellowstone grizzlies wandering into the region.

At the risk of this sounding like an unending litany of bad news, the report on bighorns in the unlimited sheep districts 500 and 501 is not good. Lamb production has been poor over the last few years in 501, so there are few rams in the herd now. Few have been taken in the past three years; the 1998 quota was just 3 rams. In HD 500, habitat is marginal, and sheep move in and out of Yellowstone; sometimes they're in HD 500 during the season, sometimes they aren't. The 1998 quota was a single ram. Fortunately, HD 503 sheep in the Pryors are doing better. Four rams were available via limited permit in 1998; odds for drawing a license were roughly 1 in 81.

One thing the steep Beartooth Range and its barren alpine uplands are good for is mountain goats. Much of HD 519 was burned during the fires of 1988, and the revitalized vegetation had fueled growth and health in resident goats. They're in their

At sunrise, a hunter shoots from a prone position on a rocky rim overlooking a deep canyon.

best shape in years. Areas that weren't rejuvenated by fire have stagnant goat populations. For the 1998 season, 19 licenses were available by lottery. Application deadline was May 1.

Now for the good news. Moose are doing well on the Beartooth face and drifting ever lower down its rivers and creek valleys. It takes a brutal winter to stop this long-legged browser. Licenses for 42 moose were sold in 1998 for HDs 512–516.

Mountain lions are also thriving in the Beartooths. More hunters are pursuing them each year. Of course, it takes a good pack of well-trained hounds to do the job —and a strong-legged, long-winded hunter.

In summary, if you want to hunt the Red Lodge-Beartooth area, plan to make a tough, isolated hunt for a smallish branched bull elk in high-country wilderness with stunning scenery, or work early to arrange a lowland hunt on private property where there are plenty of small bull and cow elk, lots of whitetails, and a few muleys. Your best bet for trophies are whitetails, moose, and mountain goats.

Yellowstone River Valley

The Yellowstone Valley throughout Region 5 is rather like Midwest farmland. Riparian deciduous trees and brush provide dense escape cover and irrigated corn, alfalfa, sugar beets, and wheat provide a banquet. It sounds like ideal whitetail habitat, and it is. Densities are consistently good with occasional losses to the midge-transmitted disease EHD which usually hits during hot, dry, late summers. Generally, herds bounce back quickly, though.

By Montana standards, this valley is heavily settled, yet it remains largely open to hunting to those who take time to meet and know the landowners. A few places are leased, but those who knock and ask eventually find a place.

If you're terribly shy, you can try floating the river and hunting the islands. This is somewhat risky because in many cases no one knows for sure which islands belong to which landowner. Over the years, meanders have mixed things up considerably, and by state law you are supposed to get permission before hunting private land. Reportedly, no one has been threatened or charged for trespass in recent years, but the issue could always come up. Plenty of locals simply float, beach, and hunt. You're on your own with this approach. Beware.

Musselshell River

Compared to the Yellowstone, the Musselshell is harder to access. This gentle, irrigated river valley is popular with outfitters and bowhunters who lease private land because of its trophy whitetail potential, especially from Melstone north to the Missouri. Fortunately, in 1998 there were two large areas of Block Management lands in this stretch. The leasing applies to adjacent uplands for mule deer and antelope, too. It's easier to gain hunting permission on the upper Musselshell farther west where there are still some enormous whitetail bucks and lots of Block Management Lands. EHD doesn't seem to hit here much, possibly because at the higher elevation early frosts kill the midges. Populations are consistently high. The valley here is generally low and flat to rolling without the dramatic bordering hills and breaks common to the Missouri.

The Uplands

The upland plains and dryland wheat fields between the Yellowstone and Musselshell and to the north of US 12 are almost entirely privately owned, but reasonably accessible to hunters who get out and press the flesh. Block Management lands are scattered nicely throughout the region, so it's relatively easy to find a place to hunt. Pronghorn numbers are highest in the west from the base of the Crazies south to Big Timber and east to State Route 3. South of the Bull Mountains and north of the Yellowstone east of SR 3, antelope densities are much lower. Mule deer numbers are currently down in both areas, but good fawn production in 1998 promises a brighter future. The Bull Mountains themselves (HD 590), while forested in pine, are almost entirely privately owned, but it is possible to gain trespass permission by

A mule deer hunter sits to shoot his rifle in a brushy draw.

knocking on doors. Start early as there's plenty of competition from Billings. All elk hunting is by limited permit only.

The Crazy Mountains, Little Belts, and Snowy Range

Region 5 encompasses the best elk range in the Crazy Mountains northwest of Big Timber (HD 580). These are the north and east sides where two roads provide the only public access. From the north, drive down the Cottonwood Creek Road in southeast Meagher County. Once it enters the Lewis & Clark National Forest, several old logging roads branch off it. There are lots of elk in this area—some 1,000 to 1,200 head! They are scattered and high during the early season, but late season cold and snow pushes them down to the north and east. Try to get them before they enter private land leased to outfitters. If you have a cow permit, some of these outfitters will let you on; if you've got a bull permit, they won't unless you're willing to pay.

To enter the Crazies from the east, take the Big Timber Canyon road west off US 191 north of Big Timber. It dead ends at a campground inside the forest. From here you must walk, and you can walk your boots off in lots of wild backcountry with no roads. It's a great place for the hunter who wants to get away from it all, but there

A mountain lion stalks across a rocky and weedy ridge during winter.

aren't as many elk as farther north. All bull and cow hunting here is by limited permit only. You might find the odd old buck mule deer here, too.

The eastern extension of the Little Belt Mountains lines the northwest corner of Region 5 (HD 540); the Belts here are covered mostly in ponderosa pines. Access is pretty good here starting from US 12 up several county and Forest Service roads leading north. You'll need a map to figure them all out; the DeLorme *Montana Atlas* is a good start. From the north, you come in via a long drive on the Judith River Road. The mule deer population is rather light here, elk are fair in the mountains, and there are some whitetails in the lower riparian zones. Antelope numbers are strong and getting stronger on the surrounding plains. There is quite a bit of elk hunting pressure here from the Billings crowd; crowding seems to be the story wherever logging roads provide easy access. Bull-cow sex ratios are fairly low, so don't expect any big bulls.

The Snowys (HD 511) have better elk hunting because it is all permit only. You actually apply under HD 411 since the bulk of the Snowys lie within Region 4. HD 411 elk permits are good for HD 530, too; however, only 75 bull licenses were issued in 1998. Don't expect a bull behind every bush; you should know this country and its elk before you tackle it. Altogether, these districts cover a lot of territory. The best access is via county roads from the southwest and north.

REGION 5 HUB CITIES
Big Timber

Population–1,557 • Elevation–4,100

Tucked between the Yellowstone and the Boulder Rivers and in the shadow of the Crazy Mountains to the northwest, is the town of Big Timber. It is located halfway between Bozeman and Billings off I-90. The Boulder River leads south into the spectacular Absaroka-Beartooth Wilderness. There are many Forest Service campgrounds in the area. In addition to hunting opportunities, fine fishing abounds here.

ACCOMMODATIONS

Big Timber Super 8 Motel, Interstate 90 and Hwy 1 / 932-8888 / 39 rooms / Dogs allowed with a $15 deposit / Reasonable rates

The Grand Hotel, Box 1242, McLeod Street / 932-4459 / Recently restored with high ceilings and Victorian atmosphere, 10 rooms / No dogs / Moderate rates / A hearty breakfast is included with your room

Lazy J Motel, P.O. Box 1096, on old Hwy 10 / 932-5533 / 15 rooms / Dogs allowed for a small fee / Reasonable rates

CAMPGROUNDS AND RV PARKS

Spring Creek Camp & Trout Ranch, 2 miles south on Rt 298 / 932-4387 / Open April 1–November 30 / 50 RV and 50 tent spaces / Full services

KOA Kampgrounds, east of Big Timber off I-90 / 932-6569

RESTAURANTS

Frye's Cafe and Lounge, Hwy 10 West / 932-5242 / Breakfast, lunch, and dinner

The Grand Hotel, 139 McLeod Street / 932-4459 / Breakfast, lunch, and dinner / Fine dining and full beverage service / Expensive but elegant

Country Pride Restaurant, Old Hwy 10 West / 932-4419 / Breakfast, lunch, and dinner

Timber Bar, 116 McLeod Street / 932-9211 / Breakfast, lunch, and dinner / 10AM–Midnight

VETERINARIANS

All Creatures Veterinarian Service, 21 North Bramble / 932-4324

SPORTING GOODS, GUNS, & GUNSMITHS

The Fort, Hwy 10 East / 932-5992 / Guns and ammunition

Bob's Sport Shop, 230 McLeod Street / 932-5464 / Guns and ammunition

Montana Armory Inc., 100 Centennial Drive / 932-4353

C Sharps Arms, Co., 100 Centennial Drive / 932-4443

TAXIDERMISTS

Montana Taxidermy Inc., Hwy. 10 West / 932-5246

Meat Processor
R&R Locker Plant, 209 East 1st Street / 932-5324

Auto Repair
Stetson Ford, 403 McLeod Street / 932-5732

Air Service
County Airstrip, Justin Ferguson / 932-4389

Medical
Sweet Grass Family Medicine, 5th Avenue and Hooper / 932-5920

For More Information
Sweet Grass Chamber of Commerce
Box 1012
Big Timber, MT 59011
406-932-5131

Harlowton

Population–1,049 • Elevation–4,167

Harlowton is located at the intersection of US 12 and US 191, 93 miles northwest of Billings. It is nestled among three mountain ranges near the geographic center of the state. The Graves Hotel and other buildings on Main Street still have the native sandstone of a frontier town. The Upper Musselshell Historical Society Museum on Central Avenue contains interesting memories of the local past.

US 12 follows the Musselshell River with its many sandstone buttes and cotton-wood bottomlands across the county. North of the river is intermountain grassland, and plains grassland grows on the south side. The agricultural land along the Musselshell is mainly irrigated crops. The rest of the agriculture in the county is dry-land farming.

ACCOMMODATIONS

Corral Motel, Junction US 12 and 191 east of Harlowton, P.O. Box 721 / 20 rooms, 3 kitchenettes / Dogs allowed / Reasonable rates

County Side Inn, 309 3rd Street Northeast, P.O. Box 72 / 11 rooms / Dogs allowed / Reasonable rates

Troy Motel, 106 2nd Avenue Northeast, P.O. Box 779 / 632-4428 / 7 rooms / Dogs allowed / Reasonable rates

RESTAURANTS

Cornerstone Inn, 11 North Central Avenue / 632-4600 / Breakfast and lunch

Wade's Cafe, 632-4533 / Open 7 days

VETERINARIANS

Holloway Veterinary Hospital, P.O. Box 274 / 632-4371

SPORTING GOODS, GUNS, & GUNSMITHS

Ray's Sports and Western Wear, Hwy 12 and Hwy 191 / 632-4320 / Guns, sporting equipment, clothing, and source for hunting guides and outfitters

AUTO REPAIR

Woltowick Auto Repair, 119 2 Northeast / 632-5591

AIR SERVICE

County Airstrip, Will Morris / 632-4545

MEDICAL

Wheatland Memorial Hospital, 530 3rd Street Northwest / 632-4351

FOR MORE INFORMATION

Harlowton Chamber of Commerce
P.O. Box 694
Harlowton, MT 59036
406-632-5523

Roundup

Population–1,088 • Elevation–3,184

Roundup is located 46 miles north of Billings on US 87 in a valley near the Musselshell River. Long known for its natural geographic design useful for rounding up livestock, one of the highlights of the year is the annual Roundup cattle drive, a truly western adventure lasting six days and five nights in August. Not a single motorized vehicle is used during the drive. Roundup is also famous for its Musselshell Valley Historical Museum, open May through September.

Roundup is the county seat of Musselshell County. The Musselshell River, named for the oblong mollusks found there, was an important waterway for the early fur traders and hunters. The river flows east through the county, turns north at Melstone, and carries on to Fort Peck Lake in the C.M. Russell National Wildlife Refuge.

The county has widely varied terrain and habitat. The Bull Mountains and the surrounding area, in the southern part of the county, is plains forest. Northern Musselshell County is plains grassland mixed with shrub grassland, and the river bottom is riparian habitat.

Accommodations
Big Sky Motel, 740 Main / 323-2303 / 22 rooms / Dogs allowed / Reasonable rates

Campgrounds and RV Parks
Ideal Motel and RV Park, 926 Main / 323-3371 / 10 rooms, 9 RV spaces, no tents / No dogs in rooms / Reasonable rates

Restaurants
Busy Bee, 317 1st Avenue West / 323-2204 / Diner, open 24 hours
Stella's Supper Club, 123 Hwy 87 North / 323-1166 / Good steaks / 11AM–10PM
Pioneer Cafe, 229 Main / 323-2622 / Full menu and spirits / 6AM–8PM
Arcade, 230 Main / 323-1304 / Bar and sporting goods

Veterinarians
Roundup Vet Clinic, 56 Tumbleweed Road / 323-2287

Sporting Goods
Enjoy Sports, 342 Main / 323-1977
Bull Mountain Trading, 136 Main / 323-1333

Meat Processor
Stratton's Butcher Block Inc., 37 Meat House Road / 323-1810

Auto repair
A&A, 102 2nd Street East / 323-1708

AIR SERVICE
County Airstrip, Orville Moore / 323-1011

MEDICAL
Roundup Memorial Hospital, 1202 3rd Street West / 323-2301

FOR MORE INFORMATION
Musselshell Valley Chamber of Commerce
P.O. Box 751
Roundup, MT 59072
406-323-1966

Hardin

Population–2,940 • Elevation–2,905

Hardin is located 46 miles east of Billings just off Interstate 90, and lies at the northern edge of the Crow Indian Reservation in southern Montana. Hardin has a multitude of attractions, including the gateway to the Bighorn Canyon Recreation Area, Yellowtail Dam, and the Bighorn River, a blue-ribbon water.

Hardin is the county seat of Big Horn County. The county is large, stretching from the Yellowstone River south to the Wyoming border, and from the Pryor Mountains in the east beyond Tongue River Reservoir. A large portion of the county is in the Crow Reservation. The major waterways are the the Bighorn River and the Little Bighorn River.

ACCOMMODATIONS

Super 8 Motel, I-90, Exit 495 / 665-1700. Peaceful, quiet atmosphere / Guest laundry, free coffee and toast / Non-smoking rooms available / Dogs with permission / Reasonable rates

Western Motel, I-90, Exit 495 or 497 / 665-2296 / Single or two-family units, room coffee / Dogs allowed with restrictions / Reasonable rates

American Inn, 324 Crawford / 665-1870 or 800-582-8094 / 42 units / Swimming pool, hot tub, coffee and toast / Dogs allowed with restrictions / Reasonable rates

CAMPGROUNDS

Grandview Campground, 1001 North Mitchell Avenue / 665-2489

Hardin KOA, north of Hardin / 665-1635

OUTFITTERS

Bighorn Hunting Lodge, P.O. Box 7578, Ft. Smith 59035 / 800-211-8530

RESTAURANTS

Merry Mixer, 317 North Center Avenue / 665-3736 / Restaurant and lounge / Breakfast, lunch, and dinner / Daily specials, wide selection of steaks

Purple Cow, Rt. 1, Box 1003 / 665-3601 / Family restaurant, homemade soups and pies / 7am–10pm.

Corner Pocket, 920 West 3rd / 665-2024 / Full bar / Handmade pizza and sandwiches

VETERINARIANS

Animal Care Center, ½-mile west of Hardin / 665-3456 / Call day or night / Boarding

Bighorn Veterinary Hospital, 1224 North Crawford Avenue / 665-2405 / Emergency, 665-1815 / 24-hour emergency care

SPORTING GOODS, GUNS, & GUNSMITHS
Bighorn Fly and Tackle Shop, 1426 North Crawford Avenue / 665-1321

TAXIDERMY
Bighorn Taxidermy, 115 ½ 13th Street East / 665-1760

AUTO REPAIR
Hardin Auto Company, 416 Center Avenue / 665-1211
Jay's Body Shop and Service Center, East of Hardin / 665-3969

AIR SERVICE
Hardin Airstrip, Larry Romine / 665-2301

MEDICAL
Big Horn County Memorial Hospital, 17 North Miles Avenue / 665-2310

FOR MORE INFORMATION
Hardin Chamber of Commerce
200 North Center Avenue
Hardin, MT 59034
406-665-1672

Columbus

Population–1,573 • Elevation–3,585

Columbus is located off Interstate 90, 40 miles west of Billings, where the Stillwater River meets the Yellowstone River. Columbus, the county seat of Stillwater County, offers a quiet, peaceful, and friendly atmosphere with full-service facilities. The town is situated along the Yellowstone at the foothills of the Beartooth Mountains. North of the river there are open foothills, grasslands, and cultivated fields.

ACCOMMODATIONS

Super 8 TownHouse Inn, 602 8th Avenue North / 322-4101 / 72 rooms / Kitchenette, spa, sauna, guest laundry, coffee and toast bar / Dogs allowed / Reasonable rates.

Riverside Cabins and Fly Shop, 44 West Pike / 322-5066 / 7 cabins, 3 with kitchens / Fishing guide service, licensing agent / No dogs in cabins and no smoking / Reasonable rates

RESTAURANTS

Town Pump, Exit 408, Interstate 90 and Hwy 78, 8th Avenue North / 322-5239. Lucky Lil's Casino, buffet breakfast, lunch, and dinner / Open 24 hours

Apple Village Cafe, I-90, Exit 408 / 322-5939 / Breakfast, lunch, and dinner

Branding Iron Cafe, downtown Columbus / 322-4690 / A taste of the Old West / 6AM–10PM, 7 days

VETERINARIANS

Cloverleaf Veterinarian Service, Frontage Road / 322-4581 / Kevin Homewood, DVM

SPORTING GOODS, GUNS, & GUNSMITHS

Stillwater Hardware, 508 Pike Street / 322-4436 / Guns, ammunition, and licenses

MEAT PROCESSOR

Stillwater Packing Co., north of Columbus / 322-5666

AUTO REPAIR

Ken's I-90 Repair / 322-4730

Bob Kem Auto Repair, 36 West Pike Avenue / 322-5996

AIR SERVICE

Columbus Airport, Rickman Field / 322-5974

MEDICAL

Stillwater County Hospital / 322-5316 / 24-hour emergency service

FOR MORE INFORMATION

Columbus Chamber of Commerce
440 East 5th Avenue North
Box 783
Columbus, MT 59019
406-322-4505

Billings

Population–81,151 • Elevation–3,567

Billings, located in the southcentral portion of the state, is the industrial, commercial, and agricultural hub of the region. Accommodations range from casual to elegant with over 3,000 rooms and 150 restaurants to meet every taste and budget.

Billings is the county seat of Yellowstone County. The Yellowstone River Valley covers a large portion of the county with riparian habitat along the waterway. The agricultural land fans out across the valley floor to the rimrocks and foothills. To the north are plains forest, plains grassland, and dryland farming.

ACCOMMODATIONS

Ramada Limited, 1345 Mullowney Lane / 252-2584, 800-272-6232 / Off I-90, Exit 446, one block south / The Best Rest in the West Lounge, continental breakfast / Dogs allowed / Reasonable rates

Kelly Inn, 5425 Midland Road / 252-2700 / Off I-90, Exit 446, three blocks east / 88 rooms, indoor whirlpool and sauna, continental breakfast / Dogs allowed / Reasonable rates

Motel 6, 5400 Midland Road / 252-0093 / Off I-90, Exit 446, 3 blocks east / 99 rooms / Dogs allowed / Reasonable rates

CAMPGROUNDS AND RV PARKS

Trailer Village, I-90 exit 447. 6 blocks north on South Billings Blvd / 248-8685 / Open year-round / 35 RV spaces / Full services

Billings Big Sky Campground & Trailer Court, 5516 Laurel Road / 259-4110

KOA Kampground, 547 Garden Avenue / 252-3104

Yellowstone River Campgrounds, 309 Garden Avenue / 259-0878

RESTAURANTS

Olive Garden Restaurant, 220 Grand Road / 652-1395 / Fine Italian dining, bar / Serving lunch and dinner, 10AM–11PM

Tiny's Tavern, 323 North 24th, Exit 450 / 259-0828 / Bar / Serving lunch and dinner, 10AM–11PM

Billings Club-Sports Pub, 2702 1st Avenue North, Exit 450 / 245-2262 / Serving lunch and dinner 10AM–11PM / Bar open until 2AM

VETERINARIANS

Moore Lane Veterinary Hospital, 50 Moore Lane / 252-4159 / Emergency 252-4159 or 656-1910 / Boarding services, office hours 8AM–Noon

Shepard-Huntley Animal Care Center, ½ mile east of Shepard / 373-6642

Excellent Dog Care, 10th West and Avenue B / 252-9499

SPORTING GOODS, GUNS, & GUNSMITHS

Big Bear Sports Center, 2618 King Avenue West / 652-5999 / Complete sporting goods store, guns, ammunition, clothing

Scheel's, 1233 24th Street West / 656-9220 / Complete sporting goods at affordable prices
Gart Sports, 100 24th St. West / 656-3888
Billings Gunsmiths, 1841 Grand Avenue / 256-8390
Butt's Gun Sales, 635 Wicks Lane / 252-8442

TAXIDERMISTS
Montana Taxidermy, 302 South 27th Street / 245-4161
Montana Wildlife Artistry, 222 North 17th Street / 256-9663
Horns Inc., 8101 Grand Avenue / 652-0550

MEAT PROCESSORS
4th Avenue Meat Market & Lockers, 117 North 25th Street / 252-5686
Project Meats, 6608 Hwy 312, Shepherd / 373-6315

AUTO RENTAL AND REPAIR
Budget Rent-A-Car, Logan International Airport / 259-4168
Hertz Rent-A-Car, Logan International Airport / 248-9151 or 800-654-3131
Custom Auto Repair, 4840 Laurel Road / 245-9912, Mobile 698-2897 / Complete repair service, American and foreign / 24-hour towing

AIR SERVICE
Logan International Airport, 245-9449 / The region's busiest airport / Seven airlines

MEDICAL
Deaconess Medical Center, 2800 10th Avenue North / 657-4000 / Full-service regional medical center
Billings Clinic, 2825 8th Avenue North / 238-2500 / 85 physicians / Over 25 specialists

FOR MORE INFORMATION
Billings Area Chamber of Commerce
and Visitor Center
815 South 27th St
Billings, MT 59107
406-245-4111, 800-735-2635

BLM–Montana State Office
222 North 32d Street
P.O. Box 36800
Billings, MT 59107-6800
406-255-2888

Custer National Forest
1310 Main Street, P.O. Box 50760
Billings, MT 59105
406-248-9885

Fish, Wildlife & Parks–Region 5 Office
2300 Lake Elmo Drive
Billings, MT 59105
406-247-2940

BLM–Billings Field Office
810 East Main Street
Billings, MT 59105-3395
406-238-1540

Red Lodge

Population–1,875 • Elevation–5,555

The majestic Beartooth Mountains form the backdrop for Red Lodge, the former summer camp of the Crow Indians. It is located on Rock Creek in the middle of a triangle formed by Billings, Cody, WY, and Yellowstone National Park, each approximately 65 miles away. Red Lodge offers a variety of lodging, including motels, condominiums, an historic hotel, and bed and breakfasts. There are two private campgrounds and numerous public campsites in the surrounding National Forests.

The county seat for Carbon County, Red Lodge is the starting point for what is arguably the most beautiful drive in America, the 69-mile Beartooth Highway that reaches a height of almost 11,000 feet as it climbs through the Beartooth Mountains to Yellowstone National Park. This highway is usually open from Labor Day to at least Memorial Day, depending on snow depth. Fine fishing can be found in nearby streams and mountain lakes. Red Lodge Mountain is a well-known ski area.

ACCOMMODATIONS

Red Lodge Super 8, 1223 Broadway / 446-2288 / 50 units, kitchenettes, indoor pool / Dogs allowed / Reasonable rates

Eagle's Nest Motel, 702 South Broadway / 446-2312 / 16 units, 2 with kitchens / Dogs allowed / Reasonable rates

Yodeler Motel, 601 South Broadway / 446-1435 / 22 rooms, in-room steam bath / Dogs allowed / Reasonable rates

Red Lodge Inn, 1223 South Broadway / 446-2030 / 12 units / Dogs allowed / Reasonable rates

CAMPGROUND

Perry's Camper Park, south of Red Lodge / 446-2722

RESTAURANTS

Bogart's Restaurant, 11 South Broadway / 222-1784 / Great atmosphere, bar, Mexican food, pizza, sandwiches, Italian dishes

Old Pitney Dell, south of Red Lodge / 446-1196 / Gourmet dining / Mon–Sat, 5–10PM

Red Lodge Cafe, 16 South Broadway / 446-1619 / Breakfast, buffalo burgers, homemade pie, soup / Full-service bar and lounge

The Pollard, 2 North Broadway / 446-0001 / Newly renovated, full-service restaurant and bar

VETERINARIAN

Red Lodge Veterinary Clinic, Rt 1, Box 4025 / 446-2815 / John Beud, DVM

SPORTING GOODS, GUNS, & GUNSMITHS

Outdoor Adventure, 110½ South Broadway / 446-3818

Sir Michael's Sport Shoppe, 21 North Broadway / 446-1613 / Hunting licenses

True Value Hardware and Variety, 101 North Broadway / 446-1847 / Hunting licenses

MEAT PROCESSORS
Franks Custom Meat Processing, 202½ South Broadway Avenue / 446-2566
Fred's Quality Meat Processing, 1 North Broadway Avenue / 446-3780

AUTO REPAIR
Horse Power Wagon Works, 104 Hauser / 446-1277
Miner Automotive Repair and Service, 24 North Oak Avenue / 446-1815

AIR SERVICE
County Airstrip, Amos C. Clark / 466-2537

MEDICAL
Billings Clinic, 10 South Oaks / 446-2412 / 8AM–5PM / Walk-in care available
Carbon County Memorial Hospital, 600 West 20th Street / 446-2345

FOR MORE INFORMATION
Red Lodge Chamber of Commerce
601 North Broadway Avenue
P. O. Box 988
Red Lodge, MT 59068
406-446-1718

Region 5 Guides and Outfitters

Outfitter Services by Species and Specialty

A Elk, deer, bear, antelope   F Mountain lion   I Moose

B Deer & antelope   G Sheep   L Drop Camps

WT Whitetail deer   H Mountain goat   M Tent Camps

AB **FH** **WT**	**Bob Bovee** Spring Creek Camp & Trout Ranch P.O. Box 328 Big Timber, MT 59011 406-932-4080
A	**Irving "Max" Chase** Point of Rocks Guest Ranch Rt. 1, Box 680 Emmigrant, MT 59027 406-848-7278 or 406-333-4361
ABF **GH**	**Pete Clark** Elkhorn Enterprises Slough Creek Outfitters Box 1437 Big Timber, MT 59011 406-932-4482
A	**Jack W.P. Davis** Flying Diamond Guide Service 12 Luccock Park Road Livingston, MT 59047 406-222-1748
A **WT**	**Paul Donohoe** Donohoe Outfitting Box 250 Nye, MT 59063 406-328-6293
AFH	**Charles G. Duffy** Wilderness Connection Cinnabar Basin Road, Box 674 Gardiner, MT 59030 406-848-7287

ABH	**Dave Egdorf** Last Stand Outfitters Star Rt., Box 2131 Hardin, MT 59034 406-665-3489
AF	**LeRoy Fatouros** Rawhide Guiding Service Box 252 Livingston, MT 59047 406-333-4756
A	**William R. Flanagan** Sugarloaf Mountain Outfitters Rt. 1, Box 2620 Absarokee, MT 59001 406-328-4939
A	**Thomas Francis** Elk Creek outfitters 4284 US Hwy. 89 S Livingston, MT 59047 406-222-3637
A	**David B. Gamble** Mountain Trail Outfitters Rt. 38, Box 2206 A Livingston, MT 59047 406-222-2534
AF	**J.O. Hash, Jr.** Black Butte Outfitters Box 171 Red Lodge, MT 59068 406-446-3097

A	Elk, deer, bear, antelope	F	Mountain lion	I	Moose
B	Deer & antelope	G	Sheep	L	Drop Camps
WT	Whitetail deer	H	Mountain goat	M	Tent Camps

AHI   **Chad Hoover**
Silver Creek Outfitters, Inc.
P.O. Box 171
Columbus, MT 59019
406-322-5872

AG   **Victor Jackson**
HI   Skyline Guest Ranch & Guide
Box 27
Belfry, MT 59008
406-664-3187 or 406-838-2380

AI   **Ronald Jarret**
WT   Hawley Mountain Guest Ranch
P.O. Box 1044
Big Timber, MT 59011
406-932-5791

ABF   **Edwin L. Johnson**
GHI   Montana Guide Service
WT   80 Mol Heron Road
Gardiner, MT 59030
406-848-7265

AFG   **Warren Johnson**
HI   Hell's A-Roarin' Outfitters
Box 399
Gardiner, MT 59030
406-848-7578

AFH   **Ray Keefer**
WT   Craxy Mountain Outfitters
P.O. Box 54
Clyde Park, MT 59018
406-686-4648

AG   **John A. Keenan**
Bugle Ridge Outfitters
P.O. Box 1060
Emigrant, MT 59027
406-848-7525

A   **James Langston**
Beartooth Ranch & JLX Outfitters
HC54, Box 350
Nye, MT 59061
406-328-6194

AG   **Bruce Malcolm**
Horse Creek Outfitters
Rt. 1, Box 683
Emigrant, MT 59027
406-333-4977

AB   **Garry McCutcheon**
Big Sky Flies & Guides
P.O. Box 4
Emigrant, MT 59027
406-333-4401

AFG   **Monte McLane**
HI   Running M Outfitters
WT   P.O. Box 1282
Big Timber, MT 59011
406-932-6121

AB   **M.J. Murphy**
Bull Mountain Outfitters
P.O. Box 286
Musselshell, MT 59059
406-947-3337

A	Elk, deer, bear, antelope	**F**	Mountain lion	**I**	Moose
B	Deer & antelope	**G**	Sheep	**L**	Drop Camps
WT	Whitetail deer	**H**	Mountain goat	**M**	Tent Camps

AG
HI   **Duane Neal**
Black Otter Guide Service
P.O. Box 68
Pray, MT 59065
406-333-4362

ABF
GH   **Scott Sallee**
Black Mountain Outfitters
P.O. Box 117
Emigrant, MT 59027
406-222-7455

A   **Randy Petrich**
Rising Son Outfitters
Rt. 38, Box 2190
Livingston, MT 59047
406-333-4624

AB   **Jim Schell**
Lone Willow Creek Guide Service
P.O. Box 775
Livingston, MT 59047
406-222-7584

AB   **Floyd Price**
F&M Ranch Outfitters
Box 17
Musselshell, MT 59059
410-778-1965 or 410-778-6412

AB
FI
WT   **Bob Shiplet**
Shiplet Ranch Outfitters
Box 58
Clyde Park, MT 59018
406-686-4696

AB   **Joyce Rehms**
Hanging "J" Ranch
P.O. Box 46
Livingston, MT 59047
406-222-5572

BF   **Vernon Smith**
Absaroka Outfitters
1828 Old Yellowstone Tr. S
Emigrant, MT 59027
406-848-7477

ABF
WT   **Chuck Rein**
Anchor Outfitting
HC 87, Box 2174
Big Timber, MT 59011
406-537-4485

AB
FI
WT   **Mike Story**
Story Cattle Co. & Outfitting
P.O. Box 55
Emigrant, MT 59027
406-333-4739

A   **Frank Rigler**
Slip 'N Slide Guide Service, Inc.
P.O. Box 970
Gardiner, MT 59021
406-848-7648

B   **Richard Watkins**
Trophies Plus Outfitters
641 W. Plainview Rd
Springfield, MO 65810
417-883-0808

A	Elk, deer, bear, antelope	**F**	Mountain lion	**I**	Moose
B	Deer & antelope	**G**	Sheep	**L**	Drop Camps
WT	Whitetail deer	**H**	Mountain goat	**M**	Tent Camps

AB   **Gilbert "Mac" White**
McFarland & White Ranch
Box 235
Two Dot, MT 59085
406-632-4868

ABF   **Thomas M. Wolfe**
GH   Paintbrush Trails, Inc.
RR1, Box 518
Nye, MT 59661
406-328-4158 or 406-446-2376

A   **Ronnie Wright**
WT   Beartooth Plateau Outfitters, Inc.
HCR 48, Box 1028
Roberts, MT 59070
406-445-2293 or 800-253-8545

Region 6

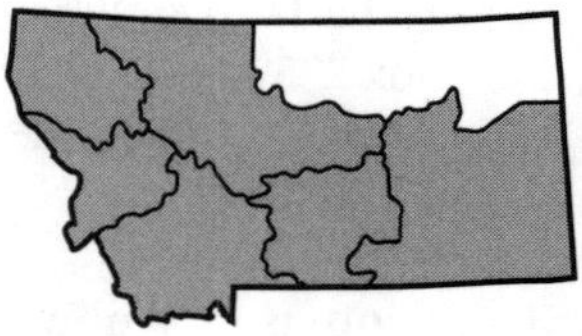

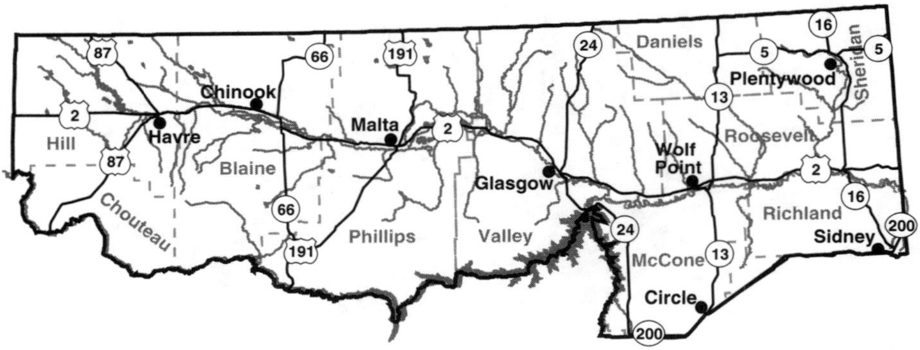

87
2
Hill
87
Chouteau

Chinook
66
Havre
Blaine
66
191
Phillips

191
Malta
2
Glasgow
Valley

24
Daniels
13
Wolf
Point
24
McCone
13
Circle
200

5
Plentywood
Roosevelt
2

16
Sheridan
5
Richland
16
Sidney
200

Region 6

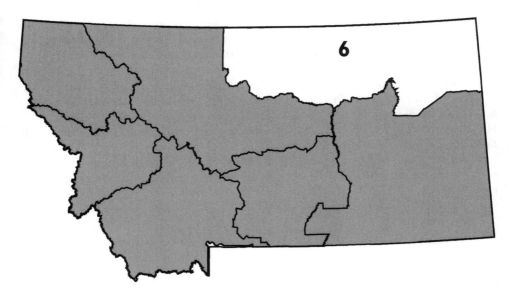

This region consists of mostly flat to rolling grasslands and wheat fields cut with steep, eroded ravines; creeks provide classic spot-and-stalk plains hunting. Binoculars and spotting scopes are important tools; you'll find more game by looking than walking or driving. Strong winds often make long-range shooting difficult; nevertheless, flat-shooting calibers are valuable—often essential. Shooting sticks and bipods are also useful. Grainfields often concentrate deer and elk at dusk and dawn, after which the animals slip into draws, canyons, and valley woods to bed. Access is good across most of the region, but much irrigated valley farmland is leased for trophy whitetail hunting. Make landowner contacts early and cultivate them for future hunts. For public hunting, try the large chunks of BLM land north of Glasgow and Malta, state school lands north and northeast of Glasgow, the C. M. Russell NWR, and BLM land along the refuge's north border. As of 1998, Region 6 had 900,000 acres in the Block Management Program, second highest in the state.

Game Species & Numbers

This seemingly bleak northeast corner of Montana has some of the best pronghorn and mule deer populations in the state, second only to Region 7. After reaching cyclic highs in the late 1980s and early 1990s, both species nose-dived, because of snowy winters and some summer drought. As of 1998, mule deer were rebuilding quickly, but pronghorn were still struggling. Whitetails didn't suffer as much from harsh weather; they were near all-time population highs before the 1996–97 winter and are expected to regain those numbers within the next year or two. Whitetails are also associated with CRP fields adjacent to pothole wetlands and wooded drainages throughout.

Thanks to the Missouri Breaks along the north side of C.M. Russell NWR, The Bears Paw Mountains, The Little Rockies, and a small section of badlands along the Milk River near the Canadian border, Region 6 has a growing elk herd, although hunting is by special, limited permit only. In 1805, Lewis & Clark saw the first live bighorn sheep ever reported to scientists scampering along the Missouri River Breaks. Predictably, unregulated subsistence hunting in the late 1800s extirpated this population, but thanks to hunter-funded reintroduction programs, the bighorns are back. Hunts are conducted annually in three districts, but odds for drawing limited ram tags are as low as 1 in 184.

There are no mountain goats, black bears or moose in the region, but a few cougars associated with the Little Rockies, Bears Paws, and Missouri Breaks are taken each year.

Harvest Trend (1992–1996)

Species	Success Rate	Harvest	Hunters
Deer	83%	Mule Deer 5,479–14,548 Whitetail bucks 7,608–10,301	16,589–21,454
Elk	30%	Bulls Cows	2,460–3,700
Sheep	97%	Rams 13–24 Ewes 0–12	13–38
Pronghorn	53–85%	Bucks & does 2,077–12,239	3,411–12,510
Cougars—No harvest statistics available			

Region 6
Pronghorn Distribution

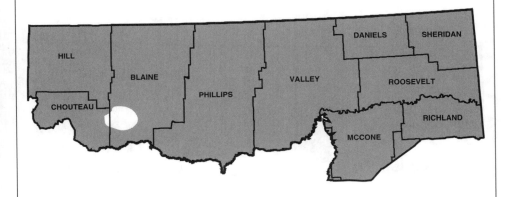

Pronghorn Distribution, Region 6

Region 6
White-tailed Deer Distribution

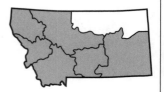

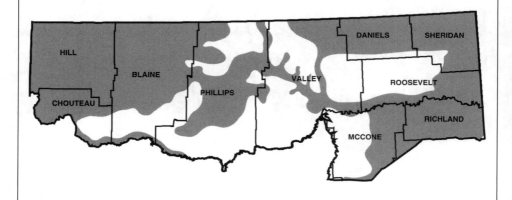

White-tailed Deer Distribution, Region 6

Region 6
Mule Deer Distribution

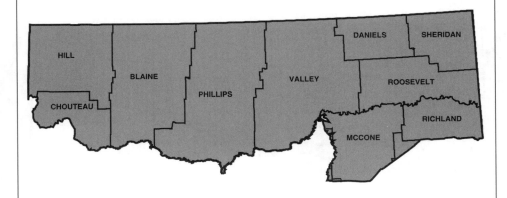

Mule Deer Distribution, Region 6

Region 6
Elk Distribution

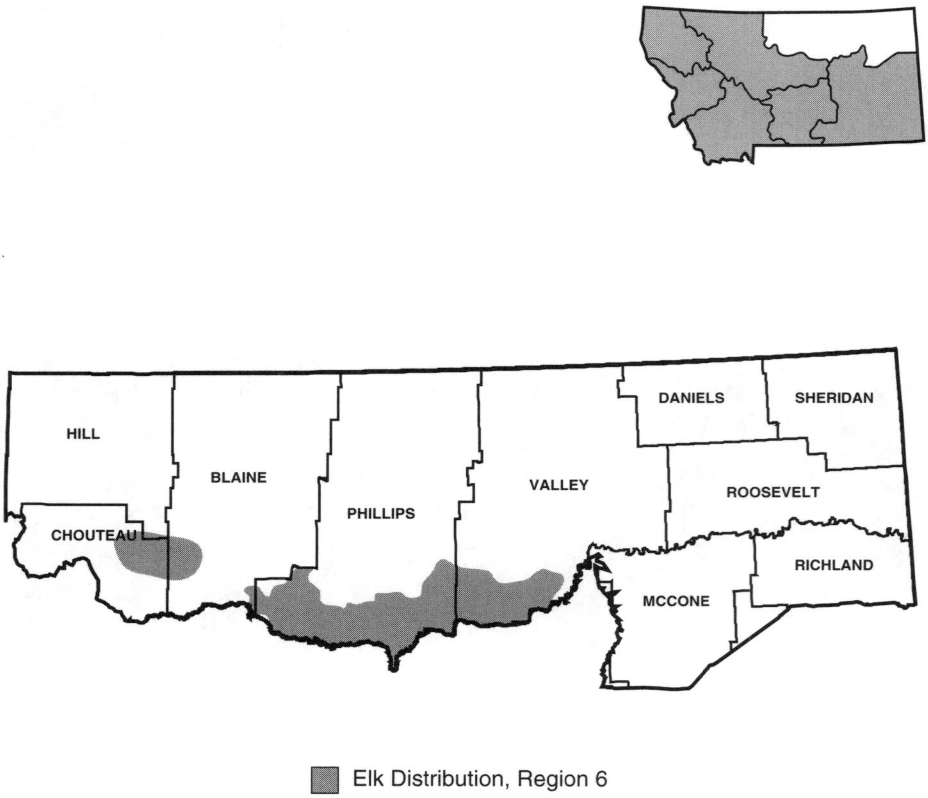

HILL

DANIELS

SHERIDAN

BLAINE

VALLEY

ROOSEVELT

CHOUTEAU

PHILLIPS

RICHLAND

MCCONE

Elk Distribution, Region 6

Region 6
Bighorn Sheep Distribution

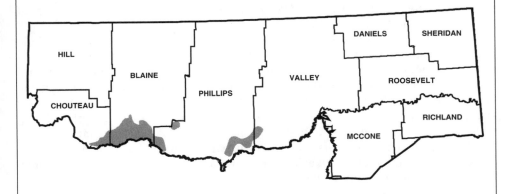

Bighorn Sheep Distribution, Region 6

Physical Characteristics

Thanks to the scouring effects of continental glaciers, the bulk of Region 6 is flat to gently rolling, save for a few small volcanic mountain ranges in the western half. The Bears Paw Mountains rise to 6,916 feet from a surrounding prairie base of roughly 2,800 feet. Most of the plains west of Havre are flat as a ballroom floor. The Little Rocky Mountains at the southeast corner of the Fort Belknap Indian Reservation climb rather quickly from 3,000 feet to a peak of 5,610 feet, then fall southward into the Missouri Breaks, which extend west to the confluence of the Judith River and east to Fort Peck Dam (and slightly beyond on the south side). Though the Missouri Breaks are not mountains, they drop so quickly from 3,000 feet to about 2,400 feet and are so cut with ravines, coulees, and badlands drainages that they feel like mountains and have much the same character for hunting. Like much of eastern Montana, Region 6 soils can turn to gumbo with the addition of small amounts of rain, so beware. Test all soils with your boots for this slippery, sticky, gumbo mud before venturing onto ungraveled roads with vehicles.

North and east of the Breaks, only a few stream courses and coulees break the level plain. The Larb Hills south of US 2 between Malta and Glasgow also lend a bit of relief to the landscape.

One of the most unusual geophysical regions in Montana is the glacial pothole country in extreme northwest Phillips County and near the North Dakota border in northeast Sheridan County. These natural basins with no outlets collect rain and snowmelt to hold water in an otherwise dry landscape. Though not a major big game habitat, their cattails, reeds, and rushes often provide cover for whitetails. When dry and choked with head-high vegetation, a glacial pothole can hide surprisingly big whitetail bucks that sneak out at night to frolic in nearby pastures and farm fields.

Antelope thrive on short-grass vegetation, wheat, and alfalfa. Mule deer feed on crops, but need the plum, chokecherry, and buffaloberry thickets in which to hide. They thrive in broken country, particularly the river breaks. Scattered stands of ponderosa pines and junipers blanket the highest ridges and mountains in this region. These coniferous trees are most common in the Little Rockies and western Missouri Breaks where they provide cover for elk and mule deer.

River bottoms always support cottonwoods, willows, and assorted other deciduous trees and shrubs, and this is the region's best whitetail habitat. Irrigated bottomlands along the Milk and Missouri south of Fort Peck provide a cornucopia of shelter and forage for whitetails, but numerous surprisingly small creeks throughout the region also support enough shrub growth to suit whitetails.

Towns are few and far between, as well as small. Many shown on road maps don't even have businesses to supply food or gas, so don't take crosscountry travel lightly. Much of the country between US 2 and the Missouri is a No-Man's-Land with no services. Glasgow is the largest community in the region, boasting but 3,600 souls.

Land Use

Cows, sheep, and wheat, folks. Cows, sheep, and wheat. And a few gas wells thrown in for good measure. That sums up Region 6. Oh, there are a few sugar beets grown in the Yellowstone Valley near Sidney, but most of those are outside of the Region 6 boundary. Some irrigated corn is cultivated along the Missouri and Milk, too, but most is cut for silage and fed to cattle. Irrigated alfalfa is a more common crop, and all hooved animals relish it.

Because livestock is critical to the survival of folks living in this remote part of America, be especially respectful of these and their needs. Watch for cattle on roads, especially at night, and report them at the nearest ranch house if possible. It goes without saying that you close all gates behind you, both going in and coming out, unless they have been pulled all the way back against the fence. This usually indicates the landowner wants that gate open so livestock can move between pastures or because they are out of those pastures entirely. Ask about gate etiquette on every private ranch and farm you hunt.

Should you find yourself behind or before a sheep or cattle drive on a public road, slow to a crawl and move ahead as the sea of animals parts before you, unless instructed otherwise by the cowboys in charge. Don't honk, shake your fists, and yell. This isn't New York.

Weather

This can be cold country. A late September or early October rain can turn to blowing snow in minutes, and temperatures can drop to near zero overnight. Generally, September and October are dry with crisp nights and clear days. This ideal weather can continue into November, but snow can also begin piling in deep drifts that stay through March. As in any part of Montana, be prepared for anything, particularly high winds that make even mild temperatures feel like below-zero conditions.

Average rainfall is about 12 inches, but it takes less than a quarter inch to make gumbo soils impassable.

Public Lands and Acreages

C.M. Russell National Wildlife Refuge	1,100,000 acres (not all acres necessarily in Region 6)
Block Management Acres	986,636 acres

Region 6
Mountain Ranges

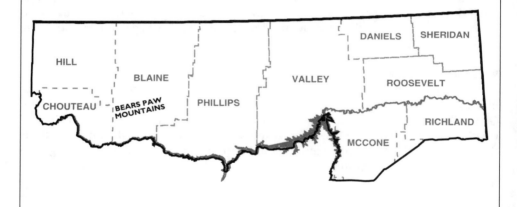

DANIELS

SHERIDAN

HILL

BLAINE

VALLEY

ROOSEVELT

CHOUTEAU

BEARS PAW MOUNTAINS

PHILLIPS

RICHLAND

MCCONE

Region 6
Climax Vegetation

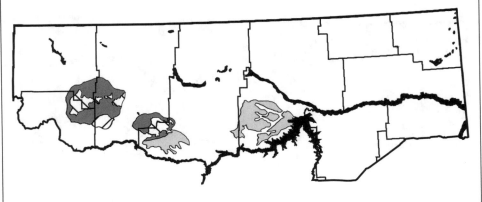

■ **Riparian** (mixed hardwood and brush along waterways)

◪ **Montane Forest** (evergreen mountain forest)

◪ **Plains Forest** (isolated evergreen mountain and hill forest in grassland)

☐ **Plains Grassland** (prairie grass)

▨ **Shrub Grassland** (sage brush and brush habitat)

▨ **Intermountain Grassland** (rolling hill country w/ mixed hardwood, aspen groves, and bushy draws)

Region 6
Land Use

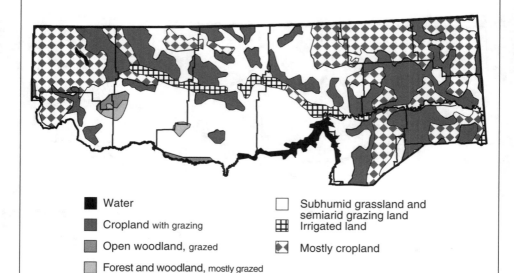

■ Water

■ Cropland with grazing

■ Open woodland, grazed

■ Forest and woodland, mostly grazed

☐ Subhumid grassland and semiarid grazing land

⊞ Irrigated land

◆ Mostly cropland

Region 6
Federal Lands

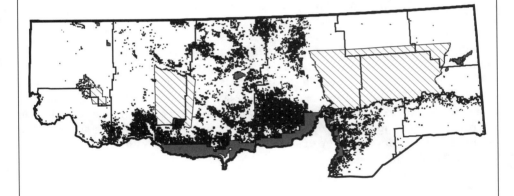

Indian Reservations

Bureau of Land Management

Wilderness Areas (including Wildlife Refuges)

Region 6 Highlights

Choteau County

Not much of Choteau County lies within Region 6, but the part that does—specifically, the Marias River north of Fort Benton and the Missouri River from US 87 downstream to just beyond the Judith River mouth—hunts well. In these river valleys hide some whitetails and mule deer, and given the remoteness of the area, you can generally get on the private lands by asking. Quite a bit of the Missouri Valley in the east is under BLM control, but the valley walls are steep and dry without the irrigated fields more common upstream, so there are fewer whitetails and more mule deer. Mule deer numbers south of the Bears Paw Mountains are at medium densities across a mix of dryland wheat fields and grasslands. Small groups of pronghorn are scattered throughout the county with perhaps the biggest concentration near Big Sandy on US 87. Whitetails throughout the county are also associated with big CRP grass fields and the pines in the Bears Paws. In 1998, there were some sizeable chunks of Block Management lands in the northeast corner.

Hill County

Just north of Choteau County, Hill County provides only fair numbers of antelope, due to too much farm ground and not enough big, open rangelands. Mule deer are at medium densities throughout. Most of the county is heavily cultivated with dryland wheat. The Bears Paws in the extreme southeast are the most rugged terrain and perhaps best for mule deer and whitetails. Don't expect any monster bucks; the country is just too open for them to hide long enough to grow old. Virtually all of the county is private, but ask and you shall receive. This is not the optimum destination for Montana hunting.

Blaine County

This big county east of Hill is much better for the hunter. About half of it is accessible as BLM ground, state school lands, and Block Management areas. In 1998, there were more than 300,000 acres in Block Management, and that's a heap of country. Most were north and south of Chinook. The southern end of the county (HD 680) takes in the Missouri Breaks, where there are enough elk to host a handful of permit only elk hunters; apply for the permits under HD 690 in the regulations. The breaks here are rugged and isolated with considerable timber—a great place to camp. By the way, this is bighorn sheep district 680, with a healthy herd running the breaks. In 1998, 15 ram tags were doled out to lucky drawing winners. There are some good mule deer here, too, and in 1998 you could take either sex with your deer A license. Mule deer in the rest of the county are in low to medium densities. Whitetails are associated with the Milk River in the north and the Bears Paw Mountains in the middle. The best antelope area lies between these mountains and the town of Chinook to the north.

Blue sky frames a mature pronghorn antelope buck with 14-inch horns walking along a shortgrass ridge.

Phillips County

Unfortunately, mule deer are in rough shape in this county, despite the extensive Missouri Breaks in the south, lots of BLM land scattered in sizable blocks throughout, and more than 200,000 acres in Block Management. Weather gets the blame, and hopefully herds may start rebounding any time. There is certainly ample opportunity to hunt them here.

Whitetails are doing a little better, mostly along the Milk River with its abundance of willows, cottonwoods, and irrigated fields. There's quite a bit of outfitter leasing here, but it's still possible for a prospecting hunter to meet the right landowner and secure access.

Much of the south and Larb Hills are too rugged and broken for pronghorn, but the sagebrush flats in other areas host the animals, which currently are at low numbers. A couple of wet summers and mild winters should help them recover quickly.

As with Blaine County, Phillips treats hunters to elk and bighorns in its rugged Missouri Breaks. Look for sheep in HDs 622 and 620. Elk are in HDs 621–623, all permit only hunts, which means hunting pressure is controlled and your odds for taking a good bull are good, if you can just draw the permit and then hunt hard.

Shooting over the back of a pronghorn decoy, a bowhunter draws his compound bow.

Valley County

Due east of Phillips County, Valley County provides similar habitat and similar game populations. Whitetails are abundant along the Milk River from the Phillips County line downstream to the Missouri east of Glasgow. And you can get on much of the predominantly private land just by asking. Several Block Management Areas include Milk River whitetail habitat. There were over 170,000 acres in Block Management in Valley County in 1998, many of them concentrated along the Milk River corridor.

There's considerable BLM and state land north of Glasgow and south bordering Fort Peck Reservoir, the latter prime area for mule deer and elk (HDs 631 and 632). Elk hunting is by special permit only, but those who draw one enjoy some of the most atypical elk hunting in the world. The elk wander up from the Missouri Breaks north across Willow Creek South Road and Stone House Road, across Willow Creek and out into barren, broken badlands country with nary a tree in sight. They use nooks and crannies in the landscape to hide and stay in that inhospitable terrain for days, unless disturbed. When pushed, they might run ten miles. This area is popular with bowhunters, who also must apply for special permits; there is no general elk season here.

Daniels County

This far northern county has extensive blocks of state school lands west of Scobey, with lots of dryland wheat, roads, and fences. Mule deer populations are fair, but pronghorn populations are poor. Whitetails are probably your best bet and are associated with the West Fork Poplar River in the southwest, adjacent CRP and croplands and the main fork of the Poplar to the south, and the land north of Scobey.

Sheridan County

There isn't much public land in Sheridan County, but the folks up there are so genuinely friendly that most hunters find plenty of places to stalk abundant whitetails just by asking. The land is flat to rolling and dotted with many reed-and-cattail filled wetlands where whitetails like to hide. This is wheat and barley country, and the deer forage on both. They also hide in the deep CRP grass. There's good whitetail habitat along the Big Muddy River valley. Mule deer become more common to the west. Reeds and cattails along the edges of big Medicine Lake create good whitetail habitat, too, as do the sandhill dunes southeast. Deer hunting is allowed within Medicine Lake National Wildlife Refuge; contact the manager at 789-2305 for complete information and a map detailing areas open to hunting.

Roosevelt County

Most of this county is taken up by the Fort Peck Indian Reservation. East of the reservation, there is surprisingly good whitetail and mule deer hunting associated with the Missouri River bluffs and coulees in the extreme southeast, as well as in scattered sandhills northwest of Culbertson. You can pick up hunting permission by asking in most places except the popular Missouri River bottoms where whitetail hunters have things pretty well leased up. Surprisingly, there were over 61,000 Block Management acres in this small corner of the county in 1998, providing plenty of places to hunt.

Richland County

This southern projection of Region 6 is virtually all in private ownership. Again, the concentration of whitetails along the Missouri has inspired serious whitetail hunters and outfitters to lease the prime real estate. The dry uplands, a mix of range and wheat fields, are rugged enough to hide some average mule deer and quite a few pronghorns. Access is a little tougher than in other parts of the region. Keep knocking on doors and asking around; there were four Block Management areas totaling nearly 37,000 acres in 1998.

*Still-hunting for deer
through a grove of young
cottonwood trees in a
Montana river bottom.*

McCone County

Dryland wheat farming is intense in the east, and cattle grazing predominates in the west. Predictably, whitetails are more common in the east, associated with the grain and bordering CRP fields, and mule deer do better in the rugged, broken western terrain draining toward the southeast arm of Fort Peck Reservoir. There are no elk in the county, and pronghorn numbers are low. Asking still gets you on many ranches, though a few are closed; more than 53,000 acres were in Block Management in 1998.

REGION 6 HUB CITIES
Havre

Population–10,500 • Elevation–4,167

Havre is located on the rolling plains of northcentral Montana. It is the largest town on the Hi-Line. The city of Havre is the focal point of commercial activity in the area and is home to Northern Montana College. The city is surrounded by the Milk River, golden wheat fields, and the rising peaks of the Bear Paw Mountains that tower several thousand feet above the plains. While providing excellent services, Havre still maintains the charm and friendliness that is the trademark of Montana.

ACCOMMODATIONS

Budget Inn, 114 9th Avenue / 265-8625 / 39 units, some with kitchenettes / Dogs allowed / Rates are reasonable

El Toro Motel, 521 1st Street / 265-5414 / 41 units, all with refrigerators and micro-ovens / Dogs allowed / Coin laundry / Very nice accommodations at reasonable rates / Your hosts are Norm and Sandy Larson

Super 8 Motel, 901 Hwy 2 West / 265-1411 / 64 units / Dogs allowed / Nice accommodations at reasonable rates

CAMPGROUNDS AND RV PARKS

Havre RV Park, 1465 1st Street / 265-8861 / 59 spaces / All season, full hook-up, tent space, free showers, deli, saloon, Conoco food and fuel store

Evergreen Campground, 2 miles west of Havre at Junction 87 / 22 full hook-ups, unlimited tent space, laundry, shower, dump

RESTAURANTS

Andy's Supper Club, 658 West 1st Street / 265-9963 / Open for lunch and dinner / Cocktails, steak and lobster

Duck Inn, 1300 1st Street / 265-6111 / Two restaurants / Mediterranean room has gourmet dining, cocktails / Main dining room open for breakfast, lunch, and dinner

4B's, 604 1st Street West / 265-9721 / Breakfast, lunch, and dinner

Naliuka's, 415 1st Street West / 265-5426 / Open 11AM–10PM, 7 days a week

VETERINARIANS

Bear Paw Veterinary Service, 5051 Hwy 2 East / 265-8901

Shambo Veterinary Hospital, 6751 West / 265-4514 / Frank Meiwald, DVM

SPORTING GOODS

Bing 'n Bob's Sport Shop, 316 3rd / 265-6124

Stromberg's Sinclair and E-Fish-Hunt Sports, 1200 1st Street / 265-3441

SPORTING GOODS, GUNS, & GUNSMITHS
Gun Corral, 220 3rd Avenue / 265-6945
R-New, 642 1st St. W. / 256-5057

TAXIDERMISTS
ASAP/Northern Taxidermy, 730 16th Street / 265-1514

MEAT PROCESSORS
Chippewa Cree Meats, RR1, Box 544, Box Elder / 395-4919

AUTO REPAIR
G and B Toyota, Hwy 2 West / 265-2205

AIR SERVICE
Havre City County Airport, Airport Road / 265-4671 / Serviced by Big Sky
    Airlines, 265-5494

MEDICAL
Northern Montana Hospital, 30 13th Street / 265-2211

FOR MORE INFORMATION
Havre Chamber of Commerce
P.O. Box 308
Havre, MT 59501
406-265-4383

BLM–Havre Field Station
1704 2nd Street West, Drawer 911
Havre, MT 59501-0911
406-265-5891

Fish, Wildlife & Parks
Havre Area Resource Office
2165 Hwy 2 East
Havre, MT 59501
406-265-6177

Chinook

Population–1,512 • Elevation–2,340

Chinook is a cattle town on the Hi-Line. The Milk River runs just south of town. The Chief Joseph Battlefield, where the Nez Perce Indians fought their final battle, is just 16 miles to the south.

Agricultural land and rangeland comprised of shrub grassland make up most of Blaine County's terrain. The northern part of the county is cattle country with rolling hills and coulees. The Bears Paw Mountains are in the southern region.

ACCOMMODATIONS
Chinook Motor Inn, 100 Indiana Avenue / 357-2248 / 38 rooms, restaurant, lounge, cable / Hunters welcome and dogs allowed in rooms / Reasonable rates

RESTAURANTS
Chinook Motor Inn, 100 Indiana Avenue / 357-2248 / Open 6AM–9PM for breakfast, lunch, and dinner
Pastime Lounge and Steakhouse, 326 Indiana Avenue / 357-2424 / Open for lunch and dinner

VETERINARIANS
Blaine County Veterinary Services, southeast of Chinook / 357-2279 / Roger Baxter, DVM

SPORTING GOODS, GUNS, & GUNSMITHS
Paulfon's Hardware, 420 Indiana Avenue / 357-3350
Paulsen Gun Stocks, Clear Creek Rt / 357-3403
Mile's Gun Hut, 12 north of Turner, Turner / 379-2661

TAXIDERMIST
Montana Tanning Co., 228 Indiana Street / 357-2258

MEAT PROCESSOR
Chinook Meats, East 9th Street / 357-3119

AUTO REPAIR
Jamieson Motor, 100 Pennsylvania Street / 357-2470

AIR SERVICE
Chinook Airport / 357-2429

MEDICAL
Sweet Medical Center, 419 Pennsylvania Street / 357-2294

FOR MORE INFORMATION
Chinook Chamber of Commerce
P.O. Box 744
Chinook, MT 59523
406-357-2313

Malta

Population–2,400 • Elevation–2,300

Malta is a small, friendly Hi-Line town located on US 2 in the center of Phillips County. Just east of town is the 15,500-acre Bowdoin National Wildlife Refuge. Malta also is adjacent to the 1.1-million-acre C.M. Russell National Wildlife Refuge. The Milk River runs through the center of town. Malta is one of the stops on the northern Amtrak route.

ACCOMMODATIONS

Edgewater Inn, Hwy 2 across from the Westside Restaurant / 654-1302 / 32 units, many with refrigerators / Cable, indoor pool, and sauna / No dogs allowed in rooms / Nice accommodations at reasonable prices

Riverside Motel, Hwy 2 West / 654-2310 / 21 units / Dogs allowed in some rooms / Reasonable rates

CAMPGROUNDS AND RV PARKS

Edgewater Campground, Hwy 2 West / 60 tent sites, 40 RV spots / Full hook-up facilities / Laundry, indoor pool, and sauna

RESTAURANTS

Westside Restaurant, Hwy 2 West / 654-1555 / Open 5AM–Midnight / Good food, good service, and good prices

Roger's Saloon and Chuck Wagon, 139 South 1st Avenue East / 654-9987 / Open for lunch and dinner / Good steaks / Bar and live music on weekends

Hitchin' Post Cafe, Hwy 2 East / Open 6AM–9PM for breakfast, lunch, and dinner

VETERINARIANS

Phillips County Veterinary Clinic, located 2 miles south of Malta on Hwy 191 / 654-1794

SPORTING GOODS, GUNS, & GUNSMITHS

Westside Sporting Goods, Hwy 2 West / 654-1661 / Complete line of hunting gear, ammo, and licenses

Bob Michael Gunsmith, Hwy 2 East / 654-1551

MEAT PROCESSORS

L&L Meats, 205 North 1st East / 654-2661

MEDICAL

Phillips County Hospital, 417 South 4th Street East / 654-1100

FOR MORE INFORMATION

Malta Chamber of Commerce
Drawer GG
Malta, MT 59538
406-654-1776

BLM–Malta Field Office
501 South 2nd Street East, Box B
Malta, MT 59538-0047
406-654-1240

Glasgow

Population–3,600 • Elevation–2,612

Glasgow is a ranching community located in a lovely river valley on the Hi-Line of Montana, in the northeast section of the state. It is 12 miles west of the Fort Peck Indian Reservation and 15 miles north of the Fort Peck Recreation Area. The Milk River runs through town. There are a number of block management hunting areas in Valley County. Large blocks of BLM land are situated in the northern and southern part of the county.

The Fort Peck Recreation Area is located in the C.M. Russell National Wildlife Refuge. The Fort Peck Reservoir is 245,000 acres, making it the second largest reservoir in the U.S. The C.M. Russell Wildlife Refuge extends 125 miles up the Missouri River. It contains native prairies, forested coulees, river bottoms, and badlands in its million acres.

ACCOMMODATIONS

Cottonwood Motor Inn, located on Rt 2, ½ mile east of town / 228-8213, toll-free 800-321-8213 / Best Western, 71 units, coin laundry, restaurant / Dogs allowed / 28 units with refrigerators / Indoor pool, sauna, cable / Very nice accommodations at reasonable rates

LaCasa Motel, 2381 Avenue North / 228-9311 / 13 units / Two rooms have 4 double beds each / Refrigerators in some rooms / Cable / Hunters welcome and dogs allowed / Rates very reasonable / Your hosts are Doug and Sharon Adophson

Star Lodge, Hwy West Rt 2 / 228-2494 / 30 units, cable, refrigerators in some rooms / Hunters and dogs welcome / Rates very reasonable / Your hosts are Bill and Shirley Fewer

CAMPGROUNDS AND RV PARKS

Shady Rest RV Park, Rt 2 East / 228-2769 / 4 tent sites, 40 RV / Water, laundry, electric, sewer, shower, store

Trails West Campground, 1½ miles west of Glasgow on Rt 2 / 228-2778 / 15 tent sites, 35 RV / Water, electric, sewer, dump, shower, store

OUTFITTERS

Antelope Creek Outfitters, Rt 1 / 367-5582 / Paul Cornwell / Full accommodations

Billingsley Ranch Outfitters, Box 768. 367-5577, mobile service 367-9751 / Jack Billingsley

RESTAURANTS

Cottonwood Inn Dining Room, located on Hwy 2 in the Cottonwood Motel / 228-8213 / Open for breakfast, lunch and dinner / Prime rib served every evening / Cocktails available, rates reasonable

Sam's Supper Club, 307 1st Avenue North / 228-4614 / Sam's is a popular spot for the local ranchers and town people / They specialize in Montana beef / Cocktails / Very good food at reasonable rates

Johnnie's Cafe, 433 1st Avenue South / 228-4222 / Open 24 hours / This diner is a favorite for Glasgowites

VETERINARIANS

Glasgow Veterinary Clinic, 2 miles east of Glasgow on Hwy 24 / 228-9313 / Dr. Russell Smith, home phone 228-9313

SPORTING GOODS, GUNS, & GUNSMITHS

D&G Sports and Western, 215 4th Avenue South / 228-9363 / Hunting, fishing, guns, and ammo

Leroy's Big Valley Gun Works, 200 1st Avenue North / 228-4867

TAXIDERMISTS

Hagen Taxidermy, HCR 271-1063 / 228-4051

MEAT PROCESSOR

Treasure Trail, 1064 US 2 West / 228-9011

AUTO REPAIR

Dan's Auto Clinic, 802 Second Avenue South / 228-2604

AIR SERVICE

Glasgow International Airport, east of town / 228-4023

MEDICAL

Community Memorial Hospital, 216 14th Avenue South / 482-2120

FOR MORE INFORMATION

Glasgow Chamber of Commerce
and Agriculture
110 5th Street South
Glasgow, MT 59230
406-228-2222

BLM–Glasgow Field Station
Route 1-4775
Glasgow, MT 59230-9796
406-228-4316

Fish, Wildlife & Parks–Region 6 Office
Rural Route 1-4210
Glasgow, MT 59230
406-228-3700

Wolf Point

Population–2,880 • Elevation–2,004

Wolf Point, located on US 2, is home of the "Wild Horse Stampede," the oldest rodeo in Montana. The town is on the mainline of the Burlington Northern Railroad, which services the large grain elevators and farms in the region. Wolf Point is a trading town for farmers and ranchers. It is on the Fort Peck Indian Reservation and home to many Sioux and Assiniboines. The Wolf Point Historical Society exhibits artifacts of Native Americans and the early settlers. The town has grown into a modern shopping center with many services and facilities.

Wolf Point is the county seat of Roosevelt County. East of the Fort Peck Dam, the Missouri River flows down a wide valley lined with cottonwood trees. US 2 also follows the river, which is the southern boundary of Roosevelt County. Wolf Creek, Poplar River, and the Big Muddy flow into the Missouri from the north. In the early 1900s, homesteaders poured into the surrounding area for the "last of the free land," making agriculture the major economy.

ACCOMMODATIONS
Sherman Motor Inn, 200 East Main / 653-1100 or 800-952-1100 / 46 rooms, restaurant, lounge / Dogs allowed / Reasonable rates

Homestead Inn, 101 US 2 East / 653-1300 / 22 rooms / Dogs allowed / Reasonable rates

Big Sky Motel, US 2 East / 653-2300 / 22 rooms / Dogs allowed / Reasonable rates

RBW Campground, 7 miles east on US 2. 525-3740 / Open from May 1– October 1 / 10 tent and 14 RV spaces / Full services

RESTAURANTS
Sherman Motor Inn, 200 East Main Street / 653-1100 / Full menu, 6AM–10PM

Stockman's Bar and Cafe, 217 Main Street / 653-2287

Wolf Point Cafe, 217 Main Street / 653-9610

Elk's Club, Main and 3rd / 653-1920 / 5PM–10PM for dinner

VETERINARIANS
H. A. Hopson, DVM, P.O. Box 302 / 653-1821

SPORTING GOODS
Hi-Line Sports, 420 Hwy 2 / 653-2276 / Complete sportswear and equipment / 8:30AM–5:30PM, Mon–Sat

TAXIDERMISTS
Longhorn Taxidermy, RR37, Box 6076 / 392-5366

MEAT PROCESSOR
Hoch Meat Processing, Hwy 250, north of Wolf Point off US 2 / 392-5533

AUTO REPAIR
K&J Repair, Hwy 2 East / 653-3103
Peter's Auto Service, 225 Hwy 2 / 653-1652

AIR SERVICE
Wolf Point Airport / 653-1621
Big Sky Airlines / 653-2250

MEDICAL
Northeast Montana Medical Group, 301 Knapp / 653-2260
Trinity Hospital, 315 Knapp / 653-2100

FOR MORE INFORMATION
Wolf Point Chamber of Commerce
P.O. Box 237
Wolf Point, MT 59201
406-653-2012

Circle

Population–805• Elevation–2,450

Circle is halfway between Fort Peck and Glendive, 47 miles south of Wolf Point on SR 13 and 49 miles northwest of Glendive on SR 200. The town was named for the simple circle brand of the Mabrey Cattle Corp. On the edge of town is the McCone County Museum with over 5,000 items on display. Circle has overnight accommodations, a campground, restaurants, service stations, and all other facilities necessary for a relaxing stay.

Circle is the county seat of McCone County, with the Missouri River as its northern border and a leg of Fort Peck Lake on the western boundary. The county is mostly plains grassland mixed with over a million acres of grain farmland. The northern area is broken up by the Missouri Breaks along the river.

ACCOMMODATIONS
Traveler Inn Montana, P.O. Box 78 / 485-3323 / 14 rooms / Dogs allowed / Reasonable rates

RESTAURANTS
Tastee Freez, east end of town / 485-3674
Wooden Nickel, Main Street / 485-2575

VETERINARIANS
Circle Veterinary Clinic / 485-2610 or home, 485-2828; no answer, call 485-2208

SPORTING GOODS
Larson True Value Hardware, 112 West Main Street / 485-2690

TAXIDERMIST
Sportsmen's Taxidermy, SR 200 / 485-2355

AUTO REPAIR
Community Auto Repair / 485-2630
Exxon Service Center / 485-3663

AIR SERVICE
County Airstrip, Jeff Skyberg / 485-2481

MEDICAL
McCone County Hospital / 485-3381

FOR MORE INFORMATION
Circle Chamber of Commerce
Box 321
Circle, MT 59215
Orville Quick, 485-2414

Sidney

Population–5,217 • Elevation–1,928

Sidney is nestled in the fertile valley of the lower Yellowstone River at the junction of SR 16 and SR 200 in northeastern Montana, fifteen miles from the North Dakota border. Five motels and hotels provide over 250 rooms. There are many restaurants and a wide variety of stores.

Sidney is the county seat of Richland County and offers a wide scope of recreational opportunities and varied landscapes. There are rugged badlands to the east, while the Yellowstone flows northward towards a majestic confluence with the Missouri River. The Missouri also forms the northern border of Richland County. The western reaches of the county have open grasslands and rolling hills. The county, with a growing season of 140 days, is rich in agricultural lands.

ACCOMMODATIONS

Richland Motor Inn, 1200 South Central Avenue / 482-6400 / 62 rooms / Dogs allowed / Reasonable rates

Angus Ranchouse Motel, 2300 South Central Avenue / 482-3826 / 32 rooms, kitchenettes / Dogs allowed with deposit / Very reasonable rates

Lalonde Hotel, 217 South Central Avenue / 482-1043 / 24-hour desk, 32 rooms / No dogs allowed / Very reasonable / Yellowstone Lounge, dining room

Lone Tree Motor Inn, 990 South Central Avenue / 482-4520 / 40 rooms, continental breakfast / Dogs allowed / Reasonable rates

OUTFITTERS

Montana Experience, Rt 1, Box 1495, Fairview, MT 59221 / 798-3474 / Scott Sundheim, licensed guide for upland birds and big game

RESTAURANTS

Eagle Cafe, 102 East Main / 482-1839 / Breakfast, lunch, and dinner / 5AM–10PM, Mon–Thurs / Fri and Sat 24 hours

Triangle Nite Club, southeast of Sidney / 482-4709 / Dinner, spirits, casino, and live music / 5PM–10PM, Mon–Thurs / Fri and Sat, 5PM–2AM

VETERINARIANS

Douglas Veterinary Clinic, P.O. Box 1766 / 482-1413

SPORTING GOODS, GUNS, & GUNSMITHS

Redwater Trader, 813 South Central Avenue / 482-6737 / Guns, ammunition, and gun parts

AUTO REPAIR

Bloesser Auto, 1440 South Central Avenue / Business 482-5508, home 482-3676

AIR SERVICE
Sidney-Richland Airport / 482-2415, Res. 1-800-882-4475 / Terminal—Big Sky
Airlines

MEDICAL
Sidney Health Center, 216 14th Avenue Southwest / 482-2120

FOR MORE INFORMATION
Sidney Chamber of Commerce
909 South Central Avenue
Sidney, MT 59270
406-482-1916

Plentywood

Population–2,136 • Elevation–2,024

Plentywood, in the extreme northeastern corner of the state on SR 16, is the trading center for the people living in this area. It is 16 miles south of the 24-hour Port of Entry of Regway and only 2 hours from Regina, Saskatchewan. Plentywood is the hub of northeast Montana and the "gateway" to Canada.

Plentywood is the county seat of Sheridan County. The residents of Sheridan County call this area the "Land of the Lazy Mountains." These peaceful "mountains" are really beautiful rolling hills. The main industry is agriculture, with wheat farming and cattle ranching comprising most of the activity. In the early 1900s, Sheridan County had many homesteaders. As a result, there are a great number of county roads along the section lines. Medicine Lake (and Medicine Lake National Wildlife Refuge) lies in the old channel of the Missouri River. This wide valley, dominated by numerous shallow lakes, is a prairie lake ecosystem. Medicine Lake National Wildlife Refuge contains 31,000 acres of water, prairie, and wetlands.

ACCOMMODATIONS

Sheridan Inn, 515 1st Avenue / 765-2810 / 65 rooms, dogs welcome / 24-hour desk service / Coffee, laundry, bird cleaning table, Fryer Tuck's fine dining, and the Robin Hood Lounge / Reasonable rates

Plains Motel, 626 1st Avenue West / 765-1240 / 50 rooms / Reasonable rates

Grandview Hotel, 120 South Main Street / 765-2730 / 13 rooms, lounge, bar / Reasonable rates / Dogs allowed

RESTAURANTS

Cassidy's Bar and Lounge and The Loft Supper Club, 105 South Main Street / 765-2350 / Lunch, 11AM–2PM; dinner, Thurs–Sat, 5PM–10PM

Blue Moon Supper Club, east of Plentywood on Hwy 5 / 765-2491 / Steaks and seafood

Laura Belle's, 121 North Main Street / 765-1080 / Coffee shop, daily specials, soup / Open 8AM–4PM

Alta Vista Cafe, 564 West 1st Avenue / 765-1690 / Fine food / Smorgasbord on Sundays

VETERINARIANS

Plentywood Veterinary Clinic, 622 Sunnyside Avenue / 765-1760 / Robert Kane, DVM

SPORTING GOODS

Hi-Line Sports, 558 West 1st Avenue / 765-1522

TAXIDERMIST

Big Muddy Taxidermy, 161 Lavalley / 765-2413

MEAT PROCESSOR
Ator's Processing, 49 Sentore #A / 765-5645

AUTO REPAIR
Ray's Exxon, 321 West 1st Avenue / 765-1180

AIR SERVICE
Sherwood Airport, Harold DeSilva / 765-2936

MEDICAL
Sheridan Memorial Hospital, 440 West Laurel Avenue / 765-1420 / Emergency
response: 765-1234

FOR MORE INFORMATION
Chamber of Commerce
501 West 1st Street
Plentywood, MT 59254
406-765-1607

Region 6 Guides and Outfitters

Outfitter Services by Species and Specialty

A   Elk, deer, bear, antelope   F   Mountain lion   I   Moose
B   Deer & antelope   G   Sheep   L   Drop Camps
WT Whitetail deer   H   Mountain goat   M   Tent Camps

B	**Chad Beebe** Hi-Line Outfitting P.O. Box 842 Malta, MT 59538 406-654-2437	**BWT** **Wagner Harmon** Montana River Ranch HC 58, Box 9 Bainville, MT 59212 406-769-2404
BWT	**Jack Billingsley** Billingsley Ranch Outfitters P.O. Box 768 Glasgow, MT 59230 406-367-5577	**AB** **Terry Kayser** Terry Kayser Outfitting P.O. Box 152 Dodson, MT 59524 406-658-2189
AF	**Don Burke** Burke Ranch P.O. Box 488 Glasgow, MT 59230 406-367-5247	**AWT** **Rocky Niles** Rocky Outfitters Rt. 2, Box 2930 Fairview, MT 59221 406-747-5051
AB	**Pat Cornwell** Antelope Creek Outfitters Rt. 1, Box 4047 Glasgow, MT 59230 406-367-5582	**AB** **WT** **Eric Olson** Bear Paw Mountains Outfitters Box 23 Havre, MT 59501 406-395-4515
AB **G**	**Roy Ereaux** Triple Creek Outfitters, Inc. P.O. Box 1173 Malta, MT 59538 406-654-2089	**AG** **David Rummel** Little Rockies Outfitting P.O. Box 405 Zortman, MT 59546 406-673-3559
AB	**Thomas Fisher** Lost Coulee Outfitters Box 278 Hinsdale, MT 59241 406-648-5538	**AG** **Ray Shores** Blue Ridge Outfitters Box 1135 Malta, MT 59538 406-654-1780

A	Elk, deer, bear, antelope	**F**	Mountain lion	**I**	Moose
B	Deer & antelope	**G**	Sheep	**L**	Drop Camps
WT	Whitetail deer	**H**	Mountain goat	**M**	Tent Camps

ABG **Matt Simonson**
WT Hiline Outfitters
HC 82, Box 9210
Loring, MT 59537
406-674-5271

ABG **Craig Stiles**
WT Montana Prairie Adventures
Box 1626
Malta, MT 59538
406-654-1649

ABF **Larry Surber**
GWT L.S. Adventures
Box 1603
Chinook, MT 59523
406-357-3459

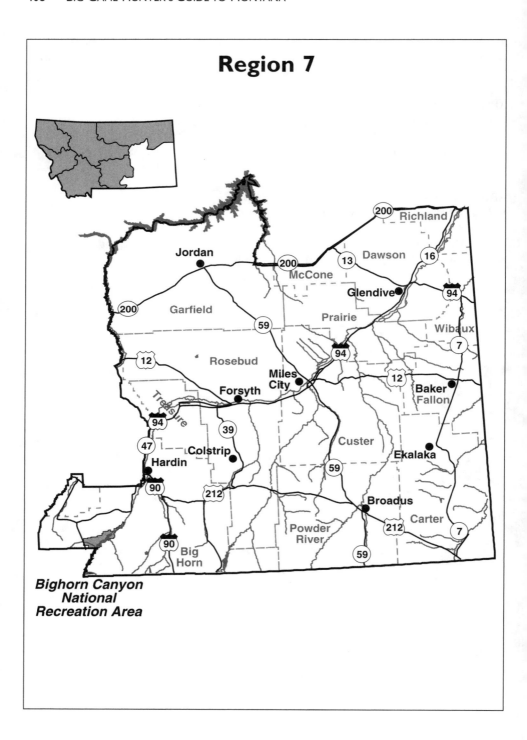

Region 7

Jordan

Richland

200

13 Dawson 16

200
McCone

Garfield

Glendive

200

Prairie

59

94

Wibaux

12

Rosebud

7

Miles
City

Treasure

Forsyth

12

Baker
Fallon

94

39

Custer

Colstrip

Ekalaka

47

Hardin

59

90

212

Broadus

Carter

Powder
River

212

7

90 Big
Horn

59

*Bighorn Canyon
National
Recreation Area*

Region 7

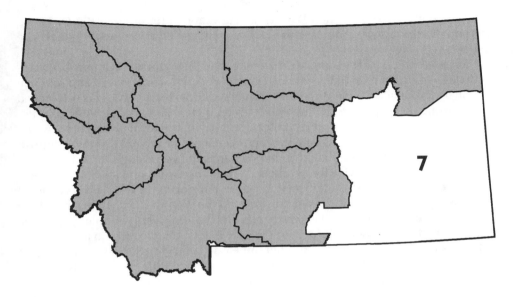

Region 7 is one of those vast spreads of the Great Plains that seems to stretch forever, but just when you think the rolling grass hills will never end, you top a rise and a beautiful, wooded river valley opens before you or a chunk of badlands opens its mysteries. There are quite a few buttes, high ridges, and timbered hills dotting the skyline, enough so that portions of the southeast corner fall under the auspices of the Custer National Forest. Wonderfully empty of man and his developments, yet a high producer of livestock and grain, the region is a mule deer and antelope hunting paradise with excellent, if limited, whitetail hunting in riparian areas. Vehicle access is easy throughout, yet one can choose to hike for miles. Region 7 offers lots of BLM land, Forest Service land, a few sizable chunks of state school lands, the most Block Management land of any region in the state, and public hunting on the south shores of Ft. Peck Reservoir within C.M. Russell National Wildlife Refuge. While ranchers across most of the region will often grant hunting permission to those who request it, down in Carter and Custer Counties almost 70 percent of private land has been leased to outfitters. In addition, the Northern Cheyenne and Crow Indian Reservations in the southwest corner of the region are closed to hunting by nontribal members.

Game Species & Numbers

Year in and year out, this is the "deer factory" of Montana. It produces more mule deer and arguably better mule deer hunting than any other part of the state. The ratio of bucks per 100 does is 40:100 in a bad year, 80:100 in a good year. In contrast, in western Montana, you're lucky to see 25 bucks per 100 does. And Region 7 mule deer bucks are old deer; in 1997, 50% of hunter-harvested mule deer bucks were 4 years old or older. That's the age at which most become 4-pointers and some truly trophy-sized.

Pronghorns also do well here. The buck to doe ratio in 1997 was 60:100. Observed fawn production was outstanding in 1998, averaging 130 fawns per 100 does. The herd is on its way up.

The reason both species are healthier here than in mountain regions is primarily habitat. There is an abundance of cereal grains, superior winter cover, and minimal human disturbance in Region 7. In the mountains, critical winter range is being filled with housing developments, commercial developments, and resorts, while summer range has become overgrown with conifer trees after 100 years of fire suppression.

Despite the dry, shortgrass habitat covering most of the region, whitetails flourish in the irrigated river bottoms and tributaries, venturing surprisingly far into uplands as long as farm crops provide forage and a few trees or shrubs provide hiding cover.

There is no moose, mountain goat, or sheep hunting in the region, but elk herds are growing in the Custer National Forest west of the Powder River, in the Short Pine Hills near the Wyoming border (which offer no hunting yet), and along Ft. Peck Reservoir and the Musselshell River in the north. The bull to cow ratio at Ft. Peck is as high as 70:100, a phenomenal number unheard of outside of Yellowstone National Park. Hunters routinely see 20 bulls with a herd of cows. Rifle hunting is by limited entry permit only, but archers can hunt in unlimited numbers during the archery only season and take either cows or bulls. The Custer National Forest herd supports a small number of permit hunters each year.

Harvest Trend (1992–1996)

Species	Success Rate	Harvest	Hunters
Deer	88%	Mule bucks 9,631–12,315 Mule does 5,580–11,510 Whitetail bucks 2,145–3,781 Whitetail does 2,600–5,111	24,307–28,898
Elk	24%	Bulls 20–74 Cows 40–115	320–685
Pronghorn	65%–82%	Bucks & does 8,802–15,590	11,237–15,391

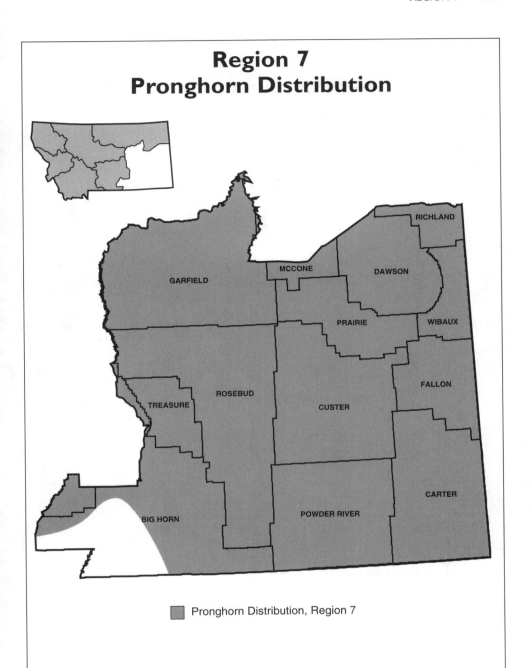

Region 7
Pronghorn Distribution

RICHLAND

MCCONE

DAWSON

GARFIELD

PRAIRIE

WIBAUX

FALLON

ROSEBUD

TREASURE

CUSTER

CARTER

BIG HORN

POWDER RIVER

Pronghorn Distribution, Region 7

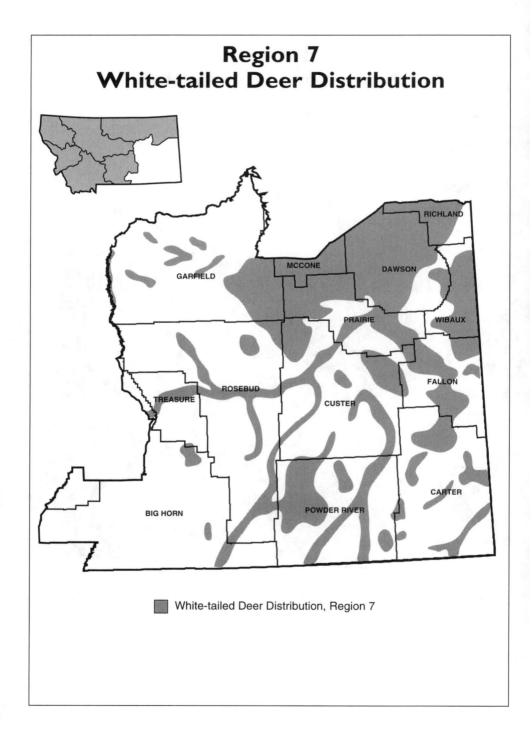

Region 7
White-tailed Deer Distribution

White-tailed Deer Distribution, Region 7

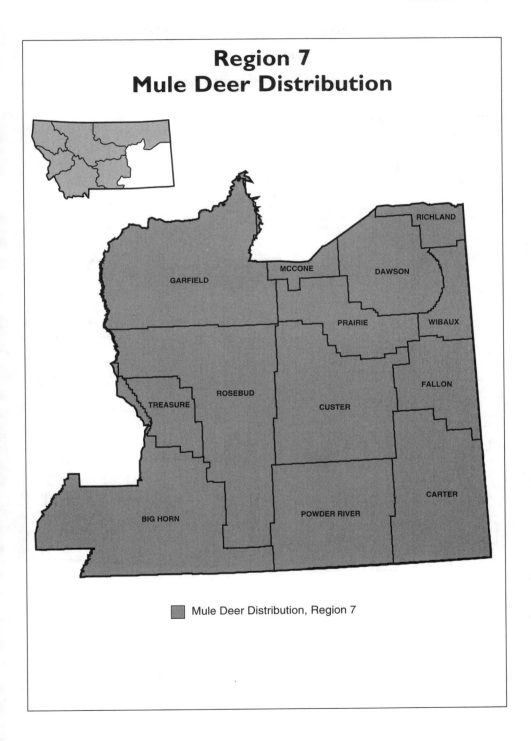

Region 7
Mule Deer Distribution

Mule Deer Distribution, Region 7

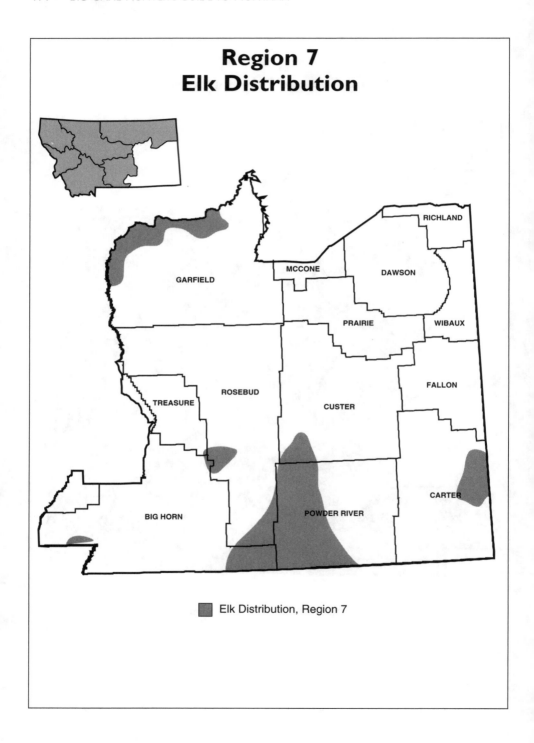

Region 7
Elk Distribution

RICHLAND

MCCONE

DAWSON

GARFIELD

PRAIRIE

WIBAUX

FALLON

ROSEBUD

TREASURE

CUSTER

CARTER

BIG HORN

POWDER RIVER

Elk Distribution, Region 7

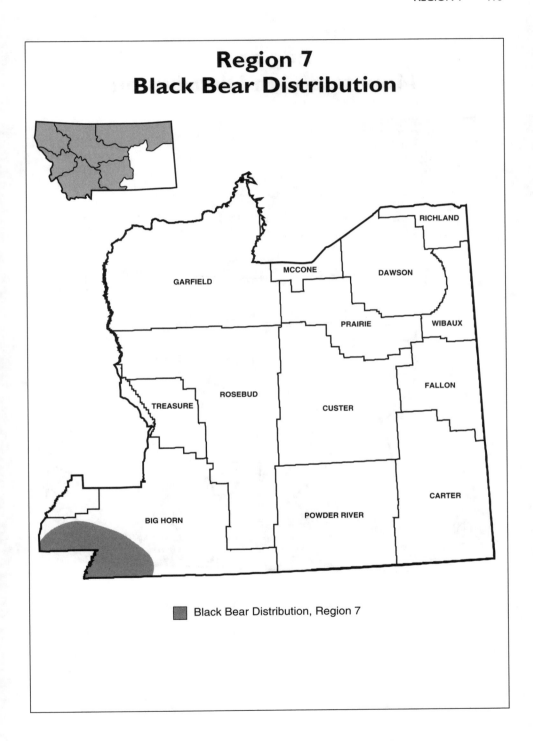

Region 7
Black Bear Distribution

Black Bear Distribution, Region 7

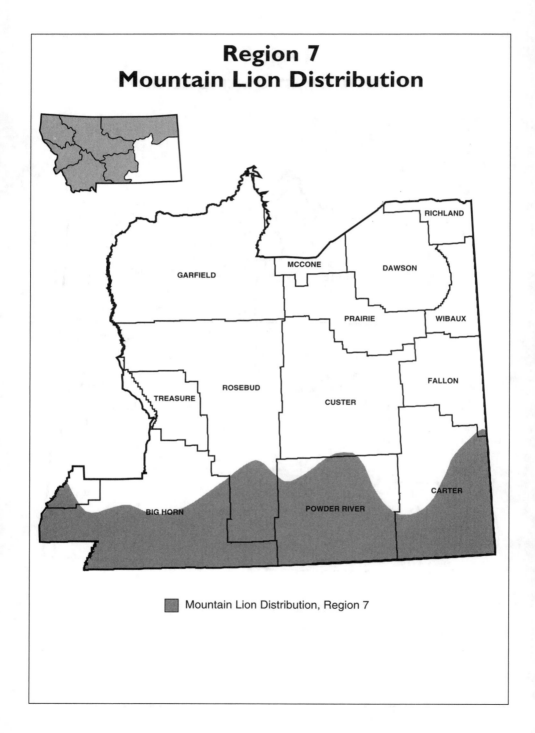

Region 7
Mountain Lion Distribution

Mountain Lion Distribution, Region 7

Physical Characteristics

Most of the region consists of high plains grasslands from 2,200 feet to 5,000 feet elevation broken by buttes and scattered timbered ridges. The entire area is heavily divided by draws, coulees, badlands, and creeks that wriggle their way to the Bighorn, Tongue, and Powder Rivers flowing out of Wyoming north to the Yellowstone; the Musselshell flowing north to the Missouri; and the Missouri itself. River valleys are lined with a mix of cottonwoods, boxelders, ash, willows, and various shrubs. Highlands and attendant canyons support ponderosa pines, junipers, sagebrush, rabbitbrush, and greasewood mixed with various grasses. The major river valleys are irrigated and farmed for corn, sugar beets, soybeans, and alfalfa, all of which attract whitetails and fuel many bucks to impressive antler growth.

Gumbo soils across much of the region make travel hazardous to impossible when wet. Many a hunter has been stuck far from where he wanted to be for a day or two while waiting for gumbo soils to dry enough to drive on.

South of Ekalaka are three units of the Custer National Forest known as the Chalk Buttes, Ekalaka Hills, and Long Pines. Each consists of ridges and buttes covered in a mix of grass and ponderosa pines. Many 4-wheel-drive trails provide access. Farther south on either side of Boxelder Creek are extensive BLM holdings in large enough blocks to accommodate hunting. There are also a couple of large swaths of state school lands in the area.

East of Ashland off US 212 lie 436,210 acres within Custer National Forest. This is a high sandstone plateau between the Tongue River on the west and the Powder River on the east, with Otter Creek running north–south between the two. Most of the area is a jumble of deeply eroded draws and badlands clothed in grass, shrubs, and ponderosa pines, wonderful places for elk and mule deer to hide. Considerable private inholdings along Otter Creek make trespass a concern; watch boundaries carefully.

The huge Charles M. Russell National Wildlife Refuge surrounding Fort Peck Reservoir on the Missouri might look like a big waterfowl refuge on a map, but in reality it is a 1-million-acre reservoir of mule deer, elk, and pronghorns. Though nothing like mountain wilderness, the area is nonetheless rugged, often isolated, and a hunting challenge despite its 700 miles of roads and 4-wheel-drive trails. The uplands rise as much as 1,000 feet above the water, so you can imagine the jumble and tangle of coulees and runoff channels leading to the shores. Badlands are common. While grasses, sagebrush, rabbitbrush, and greasewood cover most of the gumbo shale soil, there are pockets of junipers and deciduous brush throughout the area, as well as extensive stands of juniper and ponderosa pine at the west end, though most of this falls within Regions 4 and 6. Cottonwood and willow thickets are growing up as the upper channels silt in.

There are plenty of 4-wheel-drive access trails into the area, as well as undisturbed hiking for miles. Boat hunting from the reservoir is popular, too; you glass from the water, then land and stalk or camp near shore and hike the hills beyond.

Much of the C.M. Russell NWR borders BLM ground, increasing public hunting acres significantly. Some of the better pronghorn habitat is on this land.

Land Use

The entire region revolves around cattle and sheep. Land is given over to feeding them, towns to collecting and selling them.

You'll also find dryland wheat fields on the flatter land throughout the region, especially north of the Yellowstone. In the Yellowstone valley itself, there's extensive irrigated corn, beans, sugar beets, and alfalfa, in addition to large feedlots for fattening steers.

There's a big coal strip mine at Colstrip, south of Forsyth, scattered oil and gas wells, and that's about it. Region 7 is mostly hard-working cattlemen and sheepmen, honest folks, whose only companions are the many deer and antelope on the big, open Montana plains.

Weather

Most of the region is semiarid, catching 10 to 14 inches of rain each year, mostly as thundershowers between April and September. Following a traditional late summer drought, autumn cold fronts in late September and October often bring a spurt of rain and snow. Be prepared to battle mud and hunt in less than ideal conditions. As is the case anywhere on the plains, winds of 20 to 35 mph are not uncommon. Expect temperatures as high as the 80s in September and as low as –20°F by mid-November. October averages are usually in the mid 40s.

Public Lands and Acreages

National Forests in Region 7	Forest Size (not all acres necessarily within Region 7)
Custer National Forest	2,446,130 acres
C.M. Russell National Wildlife Refuge	**1,100,000 acres** (not all acres necessarily in Region 7)
Block Management Acres	**3,300,000 acres**

Region 7
Mountain Ranges

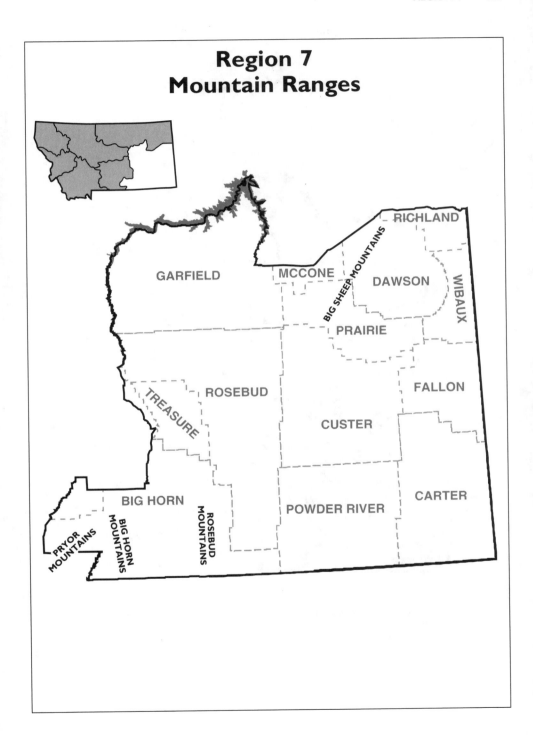

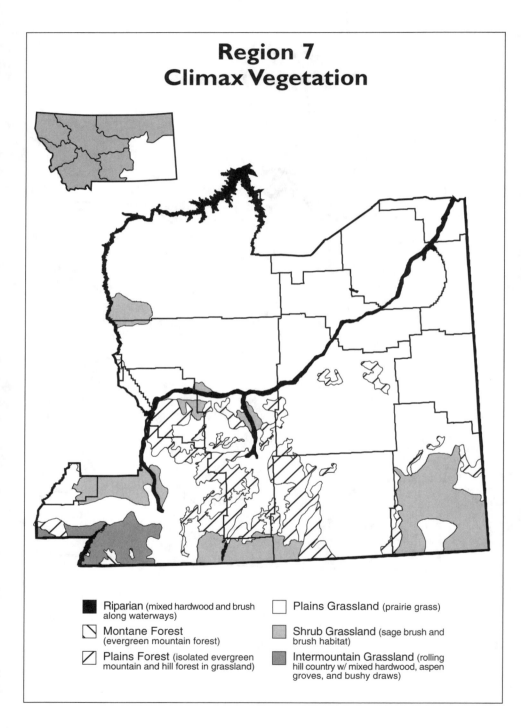

Region 7
Climax Vegetation

Riparian (mixed hardwood and brush along waterways)

Montane Forest (evergreen mountain forest)

Plains Forest (isolated evergreen mountain and hill forest in grassland)

Plains Grassland (prairie grass)

Shrub Grassland (sage brush and brush habitat)

Intermountain Grassland (rolling hill country w/ mixed hardwood, aspen groves, and bushy draws)

Region 7
Land Use

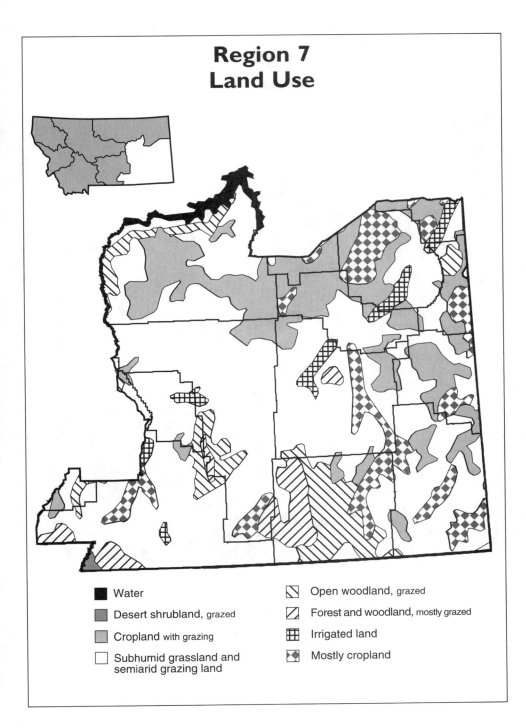

Water

Desert shrubland, grazed

Cropland with grazing

Subhumid grassland and
semiarid grazing land

Open woodland, grazed

Forest and woodland, mostly grazed

Irrigated land

Mostly cropland

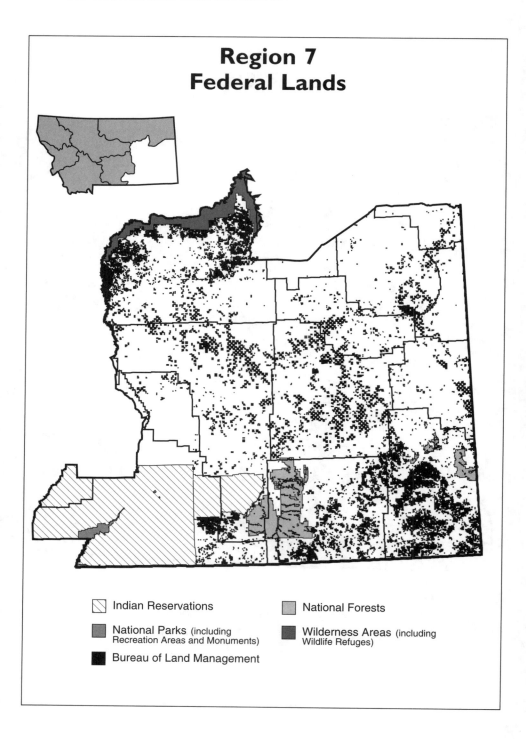

Region 7
Federal Lands

Indian Reservations

National Parks (including Recreation Areas and Monuments)

Bureau of Land Management

National Forests

Wilderness Areas (including Wildlife Refuges)

Region 7 Highlights

C.M. Russell National Wildlife Refuge–Missouri Breaks Elk

Region 7 may be the most productive mule deer and antelope region in Montana, but it also has surprisingly good, if limited, elk hunting. Perhaps the most popular area, at least with bowhunters, is the C.M. Russell National Wildlife Refuge on the south and west ends of Fort Peck Reservoir, especially where the Musselshell River flows in from the south. Bowhunters can hunt here with their general elk license and take bulls or cows during a season that stretches from early September through mid-October. The land is a confusing maze of coulees, breaks, and deep draws covered partially in stands of ponderosa pine and scrub cedar, except in the Musselshell River valley where cottonwoods and willow thickets provide cover. Extensive jungles of willows in the mud flats where the Musselshell dumps its silty waters into the Missouri provide unusual elk cover. Apparently, the animals feel so secure here that they almost refuse to leave, instead shifting and moving to stay out of the way of hunters who have taken to setting up step ladders and hunting from atop them in order to see down into the brush.

In the uplands, the elk are holing up in brushy, isolated draws, then moving out onto private crop fields to feed. Archers attempt to intercept them en route. Sadly, the bulk of the area is surrounded by private lands which are being closed in order to operate leased/outfitted hunts. There are only about three roads into the area: Devil Creek, Snow Creek, and Hell Creek Roads north of Jordan. Boat hunters can access the barren shoreline and hike up. Put-in at ramps at the end of road 321 on the north side of the lake, at Hell Creek State Park at the end of Hell Creek Road, and at the Pines Recreation Area on the north side at the end of refuge road 102.

This is a huge lake, and there are vast distances to cross. Western winds can turn the lake deadly in a matter of minutes. As it is essentially wilderness country, you'll have to depend on your own gear and resources. Use a big, deep boat and lots of caution. Be prepared for hours of riding. Carry a complete camp. A second motor is a great idea. Do not take such a trip lightly.

Yellowstone Valley

The populated, irrigated Yellowstone River valley within Region 7 still provides good whitetail hunting for folks willing to knock on a few doors and make connections. Do this well before the season begins. Some private valley lands are leased near Billings, but farther downstream leasing is rare; let's hope that continues. The entire valley can vary from good to excellent for whitetails, with genuine trophy racks very possible. EHD kills quite a few deer locally in hot, dry summers, but they always seem to bounce back quickly. Bottomland fields in which these deer forage include corn, beets, corn silage (which is cut early), alfalfa, and some beans. The deer hide in the cottonwoods and willows, then come out to feed early and late. They'll hide on

A successful elk hunter cooks breakfast by his backpack tent.

brushy river islands too, sticking tight until you nearly step on them. Pheasant hunters probably find more of them than do deer hunters.

Around Glendive, whitetails have taken to moving out of the river valleys along brushy coulees and creeks, spending their time in deciduous hardwood thickets, tall grass, and bordering dryland wheat fields. Alfalfa and winter wheat really pull them in late in the season after other forage has died back. So do corn fields that have some waste grain. If beans become a more popular crop, expect the deer to learn to love them, too. All of this nearly year-round forage contributes to superb body condition and large antlers.

Some mule deer, mostly doe-fawn groups, stick to valley fields much like whitetails, but muley bucks don't generally join them until the rut. Even then, the old boys move in at night, then trot back into the side hills at dawn to avoid hunters. The rugged hills and brushy draws above the Yellowstone from Forsyth to Sidney are usually good for hiding mule deer. Expect the older bucks to hike several miles back from the river before bedding. They tend to seek the roughest, most isolated or undisturbed terrain for seclusion. They also like to bed high where they can see trouble coming.

Powder River

From the Wyoming line to the Yellowstone River, the Powder River valley is a ribbon of superb whitetail and mule deer habitat. South of Broadus, the flat, often irri-

A hunter approaches a mule deer buck that was shot on high plains grassland.

gated bottomlands are surrounded by rugged hills and breaks that rise to ponderosa pine woodlands on many ridges. Farther north, the river is broader and the valley wider. Alfalfa is the major crop. The river is bordered by old cottonwoods and thickets of willow. About 80 percent of the deer here are muleys until very near the Yellowstone, where whitetails dominate. The downside to the Powder is that virtually all of this prime private land is leased by outfitters or owned and posted by wealthy out-of-state landowners. The only public hunting is on a few Block Management areas on the north river and disjointed chunks of BLM land in the breaks above the river south of Broadus. Many of these are off-limits behind strips of private land bordering the access road. It is possible to find good hunting here if you procure a detailed BLM land ownership map, take careful measurements (a GPS unit would be most useful), and are willing to hike several miles of rough country. Access is off the Powder River East Road and Moorhead (west) Road south of Broadus.

If you'd rather not hassle with maps and compass readings, contact Doug Gardiner, Powder River Outfitters, P.O. Box 1, Boyes, MT 59336, 406-436-2538. Doug

In prime mule deer and pronghorn habitat, a deer hunter shoots from a sitting position beside a yucca plant.

is an honest, hard-working rancher/outfitter who manages the hunting on a major portion of the Powder River valley. He offers reasonably priced guided hunts with impressive results.

Tongue River

The Tongue River is much like the Powder in that it runs north out of Wyoming and cuts through otherwise dry sagebrush and grassy uplands. It is a linear oasis of cottonwoods, willows, and irrigated alfalfa in a land of shortgrass, so it attracts and holds lots of mule deer and whitetails. Also like the Powder, the Tongue is mostly under lease to outfitters and individual hunters. In fact, there is more leased land and fee hunting in Powder and Carter counties in the southeast than in any other part of the state; fully 70 percent of the land is leased. So if you want to enjoy the excellent hunting here, you must scout hard or pay for an outfitted hunt. Thankfully, the 3 million acres of Block Management areas within Region 7 take some of the sting out of this leasing business. You might not get to hunt exactly where you want to, but you should be able to find some place.

The Long Pines and Uplands

In 1988, a big fire burned through the Long Pines, a high ponderosa pine-covered ridge south of Ekalaka near the North Dakota line. Folks were very distressed

Keith Atcheson drags out a pronghorn buck with 15-inch horns taken in eastern Montana.

about the "devastation" while wildlife biologists were gleeful. Now, ten years later, the biologists have been proven right. By wiping out some 50 percent of the decadent pines, the ground was opened up and fertilized for the regeneration of aspens, chokecherry, plum, serviceberry, and similar trees and shrubs that deer can actually eat. All that food and brush are supporting some good whitetails these days, and hunting pressure isn't too bad in this little chunk of Custer National Forest. The Long Pines stretch about 25 miles, mostly north to south. Road access is good.

A real surprise for mule deer hunters is the bleak shortgrass flats beginning about 20 miles west of the Long Pines. This is top-drawer pronghorn country, most of it under BLM control, and every year numerous large mule deer bucks move onto these barrens to escape hunting pressure. The tallest tree in the area is probably an eight-inch sage, so the deer use small dips and coulees to lay up while watching across miles of bleak terrain for danger. It would take an exceptional stalker to out-smart one, but they are there.

The rest of the uplands from the Yellowstone to Wyoming offer similar honey holes for hunters dedicated enough to search them out. The vast landscape simply has too many places to hide for all the big bucks to be taken each year. That's why most of Montana's largest mule deer come out of this region year after year, including a few B&C heads. The poorest regions are those heavily farmed for dryland wheat around Baker, Wibaux, northwest of Glendive, and north of Miles City. The cover is much reduced in these areas, and too many roads make the deer easy targets. The best mule deer habitat in these areas are the intermittent sections with rugged breaks, coulees, and badlands. Such terrain is scattered here and there and worth seeking out.

REGION 7 HUB CITIES*
Colstrip

Population–3,000 • Elevation–2,540

Colstrip is as good as its name. It originated in 1924 as a place where coal was dug to supply the Northern Pacific railroad. During the 1970s energy crunch, the tiny town was built up considerably to house and supply workers at the nearby coal strip mines where giant shovels unearth coal to fuel four huge electricity generating plants. The 692-foot chimneys are the highest man-made structures in the state.

Colstrip lies 29 miles south of I-94 on State Route 39 amid typical eastern Montana shortgrass plains interspersed with pine-covered, rocky sandstone buttes and ridges and cut with broad, shallow valleys where mule deer and antelope play. Most surrounding land is privately owned. In 1998, about 85,000 acres nearby were open under the Block Management Program.

ACCOMMODATIONS
Fort Union Inn, 5 Dogwood / 748-2553
Super 8, 6227 Main Street / 748-3400
Debby Vetsch Bed & Breakfast / 748-3653 or 888-525-3262

RESTAURANTS
Bob's Place, 17 Cherry / 748-2566. Colstrip Super Stop / 748-4514
Jimmy's Subs & Such, 310 Water Avenue / 748-4485
Subway, 6230 Main / 748-2101

VETERINARIANS
Clark Veterinary Clinic, Light Industrial Park / 748-4282

SPORTING GOODS
Ace Hardware, Main Street / 748-3450

AIR SERVICE
Colstrip Airport, Bill Mayo / 748-2406 / Strip is 5,100' by 75' at elevation 3,425'

AUTO REPAIR
Childer's Auto Repair / 748-3585
CAR Auto Repair, Terry Olsen / 748-3338

MEDICAL
Colstrip Medical Center, 6230 Main / 748-3600
Emergency Services— Sheriff, 303 Willow Avenue / 748-2211

* See also Hardin in Region 5 and Circle and Sidney in Region 6.

Forsyth

Population– 2,178 • Elevation– 2,515

Forsyth is located in southeastern Montana on the banks of the Yellowstone River at the junction of Interstate 94 and US 12, 100 miles east of Billings and 46 miles west of Miles City. Forsyth, a friendly small town, provides full services and has many recreational opportunities.

Forsyth is the county seat of Rosebud County, which is the third largest county in Montana, four times larger than the state of Rhode Island. The Yellowstone River runs east to west across the center of the county and provides rich agricultural land and whitetail habitat along the waterway. Rosebud Creek and the Tongue River are the other main water systems. Part of the southern portion of the county is the Northern Cheyenne Reservation.

ACCOMMODATIONS

Best Western Sundowner Inn, Interstate 90, Exit 93, 1018 Front Street / 356-2115 / Reservations: 800-332-0921 / 40 rooms, in-room coffee bars, refrigerators / Dogs allowed (vacant lot adjacent for exercise) / Reasonable rates

Rails Inn Motel and Cafe, Intestate 94, Exit 93, 3rd and Front / 354-2242 / 50 rooms, Side Track Lounge / Dogs allowed / Reasonable rates

Rest Well Motel, 810 Front Street, Interstate 94, Exit 93 / 356-2771 / Reservations: 800-548-3442 / 18 rooms / Continental breakfast, refrigerators, 5 kitchenettes / Dogs allowed with restrictions / Reasonable rates

RESTAURANTS

Speedway Diner, 811 Main Street / 356-7987 / Home cooking / Open 24 hours

Rails Inn Cafe and Side Track Lounge, 3rd and Front / Family dining, home-made soups, daily specials / 6AM–8PM

VETERINARIANS

Animal House Veterinarian Service, 100 Prospect Avenue / 356-7731 / After hours phone, 356-2315

SPORTING GOODS

Clark Hardware, 1195 Main / 356-2529

Forsyth Hardware / 356-2405

TAXIDERMISTS

Diamond Willow Taxidermy, 165 West Cedar / 356-2606

MEAT PROCESSOR

Fjelstad Processing, 1145 Main / 356-9881

AUTO REPAIR

Art's Tire Service, 1487 Main Street / 356-7718

D&K Auto, Rosebud Drive / 356-2071

AIR SERVICE
Tillet Field Airport, Rosebud County / 356-9950

MEDICAL
Rosebud Health Care Center, 383 North 17th / 356-2161

FOR MORE INFORMATION
Forsyth Chamber of Commerce
P.O. Box 448
Forsyth, MT 59327
Contact Cal MacConnel at 406-356-2529

Broadus

Population– 571 • Elevation– 3,027

Broadus is located on US 212, 79 miles south of Miles City in the southeastern corner of the state, near the junction of the Powder and the Little Powder Rivers. The Powder River starts in Wyoming and travels north across the county. It has been described as "a mile wide and an inch deep, too wet to plow and too thick to drink." Broadus is the gateway to the Black Hills in South Dakota and is often called the "biggest little town in the west."

Broadus is the county seat of Powder River County. Custer National Forest is in the western portion of the county. Powder River County offers a smorgasbord of rugged landscape—picturesque cottonwood, creeks, river bottoms, agricultural lands, and the abundance of game.

ACCOMMODATIONS

C-J Motel, US 212, west side / 436-2671 / 30 rooms / Dogs allowed for a $5 fee / Reasonable rates

Quarterhorse Motor Inn, US 212, center of town / 436-2626 / 10 rooms / Dogs allowed for a $5 fee / Reasonable rates

Buckskin Inn /436-2929 / 11 rooms / Dogs allowed for a $5 fee / Reasonable rates

OUTFITTERS

Oakwood Lodge, South Pumpkin Creek, 25 miles west of Broadus, 3 miles south of Hwy 212 / 427-5474 / Three spacious rooms with individual baths, home-made breakfast, peaceful and quiet / Professional guide for big game, spring and fall turkey, and upland gamebirds

RESTAURANTS

Montana Bar and Cafe / 436-2454 / Breakfast, lunch, and dinner / Red Velvet dining room, homemade rolls and pies

Homestead Inn / 436-2615 / Full menu, restaurant and lounge / 7 days, 6:30AM–10PM

Chuck's Tastee Freez, west side of Broadus / 436-2818 / Complete menu

VETERINARIANS

Broadus Veterinary Clinic, 436-2772

SPORTING GOODS, GUNS, & GUNSMITHS

Cobbs True Value Hardware / 436-2811 / Guns and ammunition

TAXIDERMISTS

Mountain Prairie Taxidermy, East Powderville Road / 436-2993

Powder River Taxidermy, 708 South Park Street / 436-2538

AUTO REPAIR
Powder River Rebuild / 436-2889
Alderman Oil Conoco, south end / 436-2898 / Open 7 days, 5:30AM–10PM

AIR SERVICE
Fly West Air Inc. / 436-2966

MEDICAL
Powder River Medical Clinic / 436-2651

FOR MORE INFORMATION
Broadus Chamber of Commerce
P.O. Box 484
Broadus, MT 59317
406-436-2611

Baker

Population– 1,818 • Elevation– 2,929

Baker is 81 miles east of Miles City on US 12, just inside the Montana-North Dakota border. This friendly city serves as a market town for the surrounding grazing and farming area. Baker, the county seat of Fallon, has a museum and a new trap-shooting and target range. The Medicine Rocks State Park is west of town. The county has no major rivers, but does have Fallon Creek to the south. Fallon County terrain is primarily plains grasslands with agricultural land interspersed.

ACCOMMODATIONS
Montana Motel, 716 East Montana Avenue / 778-3315 / 12 rooms / Reasonable rates
Sagebrush Inn, 518 US 12, Box 1157 / 778-3341 / 40 rooms / Dogs allowed / Reasonable rates
Roy's Motel and Campground, 327 Montana Avenue / 778-3321 / 40 rooms / Dogs allowed / Reasonable rates

RESTAURANTS
Sakelaris Kitchen, Lake City Shopping Center / 778-2202 / Full family dining, 5:30AM–8PM / Sun 7AM–3PM
Corner Bar, 11 South Main / 778-3278 / 1PM–Midnight / Lunch and dinner
The Loft, 19 South Main / 778-3557 / Supper club and bar / 5PM–Midnight

VETERINARIANS
Fallon County Vet, North of Baker / 778-3532 / After hours, 365-2898

SPORTING GOODS, GUNS, & GUNSMITHS
Gunrunner Gun Shop, 29½ South 2nd West / 778-3443 / Guns and ammunition

AUTO REPAIR
Baker Body Shop, 26 Southwest 3rd / 778-2024

AIR SERVICE
Baker Municipal Airport / 778-3508

MEDICAL
Fallon Medical Complex, 202 South 4th Street West / 778-3331
Community Clinic, 320 Hospital Drive / 778-2833

FOR MORE INFORMATION
Baker Chamber of Commerce
P.O. Box 849
Baker, MT 59313
406-778-2266

Ekalaka

Population– 439 • Elevation– 4,806

Ekalaka is 116 miles south of Glendive. Known as "the town at the end of the road," Ekalaka has only one paved road. Though small, it meets all the needs for a pleasant stay. The primary industries are sheep and cattle production.

Ekalaka is the county seat of Carter County, located in the southeastern corner of Montana. The county is comprised of wide open spaces where arid prairie and shrub grassland rise to meet the Chalk Buttes, Ekalaka Hills, and the Long Pines which are part of Custer National Forest. Carter County is a mixture of sagebrush prairie, grassland prairie, and agriculture. Ponderosa pine, juniper breaks, and hardwood bottoms are found along Box Elder Creek and the Little Missouri.

ACCOMMODATIONS

Guest House, 4 Main Street, P.O. Box 296 / 775-6337 / 5 rooms / Dogs allowed with restrictions / Reasonable rates

Midway Motel, Main Street, P.O. Box 484 / 775-6619 / 6 rooms, some dogs allowed / Reasonable rates

CAMPGROUNDS AND RV PARKS

Cline Camper Court, west of town near fairgrounds / 775-6619 / Open May 1– December 1 / 15 RV and 6 tent spaces / Water, electric, sewer, showers

RESTAURANTS

B&B Grill and Bar, Main Street / 775-6484 / Breakfast, lunch, and dinner / Full menu, 7AM–10PM

Wagon Wheel Cafe, Main Street / 775-6639 / Full menu, 6AM–8PM

VETERINARIANS

James G. Tooke, DVM, north of town on Hwy 7 / 775-6494 office, 775-6493 home

SPORTING GOODS, GUNS, & GUNSMITHS

W&S Propane, 775-6221 / Guns and ammunition

AUTO REPAIR

Fruit Repair, Main Street / 775-6542 / Full service and repair

AIR SERVICE

Ekalaka Airport, Ernest Tooke / 775-6542

MEDICAL

Dahl Memorial Hospital, Park Avenue / 775-8730

FOR MORE INFORMATION

Chamber of Commerce
P.O. Box 297
Ekalaka, MT 59324
775-6658

Miles City

Population– 8,461 • Elevation– 2,627

Miles City, "Cowboy Capital of Montana," is just off Interstate 94. The city's many services have made it the hub of southeastern Montana. This is a modern community that still retains its western culture.

Miles City is the county seat of Custer County. The Tongue River from the south meanders by the western edge of Miles City where it joins the Yellowstone River. The wide Powder River, with its cottonwood bottoms, flows the length of the county. Good access roads follow the major creeks and rivers in Custer County. Custer County's terrain provides a diversity of land patterns, with its vast, wide-open plains grasslands carved with an array of topographical extremes. Here is some of the best whitetail, mule deer, and pronghorn hunting in Montana.

ACCOMMODATIONS

Motel 6, 1314 South Haynes Avenue / 232-7040. Reservations, 800-891-6161 / Interstate 90, Exit 138 / 113 rooms / Dogs allowed / Reasonable rates
The Olive Hotel, 501 Main Street / 232-2450, 800-228-2000 / 34 rooms, lounge / Dogs allowed / Expensive rates
Days Inn, 1006 South Haynes Avenue, Interstate 90, Exit 138 / 232-3550 / 58 rooms, continental breakfast / Dogs allowed / Reasonable rates
Best Western War Bonnet Inn, Interstate 90, Exit 138, Hwy 312 / 232-4560, 800-528-1234 / 54 units, indoor pool, continental breakfast / Dogs allowed / Reasonable rates

CAMPGROUNDS

KOA Miles City, Palmer Street / 232-3991 / Open April through October / Full facilities

RESTAURANTS

Louie's Olive Dining Room, 501 Main Street / 232-0743 / Steaks and seafood, nightly specials / Cocktails
Club 519, 519 Main Street / 232-5133
Cellar Casino and Bar, 719 Main Street / 232-5611 / Daily lunch and dinner specials, full menu
600 Lounge and Cafe, 19 South 7th Street / 232-3860
Hole in the Wall, 602 Main Street / 232-9887 / Dinner specials, 5PM–10PM / Sunday buffet, 11AM–3PM

VETERINARIANS

East Main Animal Clinic, 2719 Main Street / 232-6900; after hours 412-5588
Miles City Veterinary, west of Miles City / 232-2559

SPORTING GOODS, GUNS, & GUNSMITHS
Red Rock Sporting Goods, 2900 Valley Drive East / 232-2716 or 800-367-5560 /
  Complete sporting needs / 9AM–5:30PM
Coast to Coast Hardware, 818 Main Street / 232-4168 / Sporting goods /
  Mon–Sat 8AM–6PM; Sun 1PM–5PM
Blue Sky Guns, 602 Palmer Street / 232-2263

TAXIDERMISTS
Faber Taxidermy, 713 Knight Street / 232-3200
Western Wildlife Studios, Hwy 59 North / 232-3820

MEAT PROCESSORS
Butcher Block Specialtes, 713 Knight Street / 232-3556

AUTO RENTAL AND REPAIR
Mac's Frontierland Ford, Mercury, and Lincoln, 3016 Valley Drive East /
  232-2456 / Rentals and service
Jack's Body Shop, 700 7th Street / 232-1661 / Complete car care, 24-hour
  towing

AIR SERVICE
Miles City Airport, East Hwy 59 / 232-1354 / Big Sky Commuter Service

MEDICAL
Holy Rosary Health Center, 2101 Clark Street / 232-2540 or 800-843-3820
Miles City Health Care Clinic, 2600 Wilson / 233-2572

FOR MORE INFORMATION
Miles City Chamber of Commerce
901 Main Street
Miles City, MT 59301
406-232-2890

BLM–Miles City Field Office
111 Garryowen Road
Miles City, MT 59301
406-233-2800

Fish, Wildlife & Parks–Region 7 Office
P.O. Box 1630
Miles City, MT 59301
406-232-4365
Block Management: 232-0930

Glendive

Population– 4,802 • Elevation– 2,069

Glendive is in eastern Montana along the Yellowstone River off Interstate 94. Located on the outskirts of town is the 8,000-acre Makoshika State Park of Primitive Terrain, where dinosaurs once roamed.

The Big Sheep Mountains in western Dawson County have hardwood draws, plains grasslands, rolling hills, and agricultural land extending to the Yellowstone River. Irrigated land is found along the river, and some dryland farming occurs elsewhere in the county.

ACCOMMODATIONS

Super 8, 1904 North Merrill / 365-5671 / 53 rooms / Dogs allowed / Reasonable rates

Day's Inn, 2000 North Merrill / 365-6011 / 60 rooms / Dogs allowed / Reasonable rates

Budget Hosts Riverside Inn, Interstate 94 and Hwy 16 / 365-2349 / 36 rooms / Dogs allowed / Reasonable rates

Parkwood Motel, 1002 West Bell / 365-8221 / 16 rooms / Dogs allowed for a $5 charge / Very reasonable

Glendive Campground, I-94, Exit 215 / 365-6721 / Open all year / 7 tent and 60 RV spaces / Full services

CAMPGROUND

Glendive Campground, Merrill Avenue / 365-6721 / Open April–October / 88 sites / Full facilities

RESTAURANTS

Twilite Dining, Lounge and Casino, 209 North Merrill / 365-8705 / Prime rib, steak, and seafood

Jordan Motor Hotel and Coffee Shop, 223 North Merrill / 365-5655 / Fine dining in the Blue Room

Trail Star Truck Stop and Trail Star II, Hwy 16, Exit 213 / 365-3901 / Open 24 hours / Good, home-cooked meals

Bacios Italian Dining, 302 West Towne / 365-9664 / Take out and delivery available

VETERINARIANS

Glendive Veterinary Clinic and Supply, 821 North Sargent / 365-3475, home 365-2898 / Ivan Dyekman, DVM

SPORTING GOODS, GUNS, & GUNSMITHS

Friendly True Value, P.O. Box 1089 / 365-8233 / Guns and ammunition

First National Pawn, 101 South Merrill Avenue / 365-3933

AUTO REPAIR
Cenex, Hwy 16 and Interstate 94 / 365-8403 / Open 24 hours

AIR SERVICE
Big Sky Airlines, P.O. Box 1086 / 687-3360

MEDICAL
Glendive Medical Center, 202 Prospect Drive / 365-3306
Clinic / 365-8901

FOR MORE INFORMATION
Chamber of Commerce and Agriculture
200 North Merrill, P.O. Box 930
Glendive, MT 59330
406-365-5601 / Fax 365-3302

Jordan

Population– 485 • Elevation– 2,800

Jordan is 130 miles east of Lewistown on SR 200 and 84 miles northwest of Miles City on SR 59. It is the county seat of Garfield County, nicknamed the "Big Lonesome." The county has the lowest population density in Montana, one person to every three square miles. The C.M. Russell Wildlife Refuge and Fort Peck Lake cover a large portion of Garfield County. The rest of the county is large ranches, plains grassland, gumbo buttes, mixed sagebrush prairie, and Missouri Breaks badlands—a pronghorn and mule deer paradise.

ACCOMMODATIONS
Fellman's Motel, Hwy 200, Box 89 / 557-2209 or 1-800-552-2689 / 16 rooms / Dogs allowed / Reasonable rates

Garfield Hotel and Motel, Hwy 200 and Main, Box 374 / 557-6215 / 12 rooms / No dogs allowed / Reasonable rates

OUTFITTERS
Hell Creek Guest Ranch, P.O. Box 325 / 557-2224 / John and Sylvia Trumbo / Turkey and big game hunting

RESTAURANTS
QD's, west of Jordan on Hwy 200 / 557-2301 / Full service, 6AM–10PM

VETERINARIANS
The closest veterinarian is in Circle, Region 6:
Circle Veterinary Clinic / 485-2610 or home, 485-2828

SPORTING GOODS
Fellman's Ace Hardware / 557-2206

TAXIDERMY
Daryl's Taxidermy, Hellcreek Road / 557-2709

MEAT PROCESSOR
Ryan's Processing Plant, Main Street / 557-6219

AUTO REPAIR
Pioneer Garage / 557-2263

AIR SERVICE
Garfield County Airport, Vivienne Schrank / 557-2565

MEDICAL
Garfield County Health Center, Inc. / 557-2500

FOR MORE INFORMATION

Chamber of Commerce
P.O. Box 370
Jordan, MT 59337
406-557-2248 or 557-2232

Region 7 Guides and Outfitters

Outfitter Services by Species and Specialty

A	Elk, deer, bear, antelope	F	Mountain lion	I	Moose
B	Deer & antelope	G	Sheep	L	Drop Camps
WT	Whitetail deer	H	Mountain goat	M	Tent Camps

AB   **Keith Bales**
Bales Hunts
HC 39, Box 33
Otter, MT 590623
406-784-2487

BWT   **Jamie Byrne**
J&J Outfitter
HC Box 962
Mill Iron, MT 59342
406-775-8891

AB
WT   **Ross Childers**
7-Ranch
Brussett, MT 59318
406-557-2845

BWT   **Alvin Cordell**
Mon-Dak Outfitters
P.O. Box 135, Mont. Rt.
Camp Crook, SD 57724
605-797-4539

BWT   **Scott Cornell**
Yellowstone River Hunting
Box 183, 431 S. 3rd St.
Forsyth, MT 59327
406-356-2511 or 406-342-5830

BWT   **Robert Dolatta**
Robert Dolotta Outfitters
HC77 Box 6557
Terry, MT 59349
406-846-5736

B   **Sy Gilliland**
SNS Outfitter & Guide Service
P.O. Box 4187
Casper, WY 82160
307-266-4229

AB
WT   **Ken Greslin & Doug Gardiner**
Powder River Outfitters
P.O. Box 1
Boyes, MT 59336
406-436-2538

AB
WT   **Russ Greenwood**
Doonan Gulch Outfitters
P.O. Box 501
Broadus, MT 59317
406-427-5474

B   **Thomas Haack**
Ridge Runner Outfitters
P.O. Box 426
Sheboygan, WI 53082
414-565-4155

AB
WT   **James Haynie**
Lost Creek Outfitting
Box 468
Circle, MT 59215
406-485-2234

B   **Rick Kasper**
Rawhide Creek Ranch & Blue
Rock Outfitters
899 Spruce Hill
Thousand Oaks, CA 91320
805-498-1518

A	Elk, deer, bear, antelope	**F**	Mountain lion	**I**	Moose
B	Deer & antelope	**G**	Sheep	**L**	Drop Camps
WT	Whitetail deer	**H**	Mountain goat	**M**	Tent Camps

BWT **Robert May, Jr.**
Silver Bullet, Inc.
2335 Habersham Dr., SW
Marietta, GA 30064
770-424-6696

B **Paul Mobley**
Twin Buttes Outfitters
P.O. Box 110
Olive, MT 59343
406-554-3456

B **Dan Murphy**
Lakeview Outfitters, Inc.
P.O. Box 1000
Lake City, CO 81235
303-944-2401

B **J. Perkins**
Ray Perkins Outfitter
1906 Main Street
Miles City, MT 59301
406-232-4283

BWT **David Potts**
Sage & Sun Outfitters
P.O. Box 5022
Forsyth, MT 59327
406-354-7461

BWT **Richard N. Rumph**
Rumph Ranch
Box 343
Biddle, MT 59327
406-427-5452

BWT **Claude Saylor**
Barr Y 7 Ranch
HC 60, Box 10
Brusell, MT 59318
406-557-6150

B **Ed Schaffer**
Indian Creek Adventures
HC 39, Box 22
Otter, MT 59062
406-784-2889

AB **Patrick Sinclair**
Snowline Outfitters
P.O. Box 471
Jordan, MT 59337
406-557-2646

ABG **Craig Stiles**
WT Montana Prairie Adventures
Box 1626, 213 S. 2nd St. E.
Malta, MT 59538
406-654-1649

BWT **John Stuver**
Cedar Breaks Outfitters, Inc.
Box 121
Broadus, MT 59317
406-427-5796

B **Cal Thornberg**
Cat Track Outfitters
Box 1311
Forsyth, MT 59327
406-356-2692

A	Elk, deer, bear, antelope	F	Mountain lion	I	Moose
B	Deer & antelope	G	Sheep	L	Drop Camps
WT	Whitetail deer	H	Mountain goat	M	Tent Camps

ABF **Herb Weiss**
WT River Road Outfitters
259 River Rd.
Glendive, MT 59330
406-365-5796

BWT **James Wilkins**
Otter Creek Outfitters
Box 31
Otter, MT 59062
406-784-6185

BWT **John Wilkinson**
Cottonwood Outfitters
P.O. Box 6241
Miles City, MT 59301
406-232-4910

B **Dale Williams**
Seven Bar Cross Ranch
Sonnette, MT 59348
406-427-5210

Outfitters and Guides

The difference between outfitters and guides is that outfitters supply you with room and board as well as guiding service; guides just guide. The relation between the two is that generally guides work for outfitters.

In many cases, the guides that outfitters hire are kids fresh out of guide school with little or no intimate knowledge of an area's animals or their habits. Some outfitter/guides dump clients in RVs or trailers at the end of logging roads where they take the client out wandering the public forest close to roads where, of course, the client could do just as well himself. Some book you, take your money, and don't even show up at the airport.

On the other hand, some outfitters treat you like royalty, wake you with a cup of coffee, feed you steak and lobster, put you up in lavish cabins or tent camps 20 miles from the nearest road, saddle your horse, pack your lunches, and point you toward trophy bucks and bulls. About all you have to do is show up and enjoy yourself.

So how do you get a good guide? First determine what you expect of one. Do you want to hunt on foot, horse, or from roads? Do you want to stay in tents, cabins, or a motel in town? Do you want to hunt wilderness areas, national forests, or private land? Do you want a Boone & Crockett head, a representative head, or just good meat? Do you want to hunt hard from dawn to dusk or take it easy and nap at midday? Assess your wants and needs honestly and accurately. Then start shopping for an outfitter to fill them.

The best place to start is with a recommendation from a friend who has been there. Short of such advice, check ads and editorials in hunting magazines. Hunting clubs and conservation organizations like Safari Club International, The Rocky Mountain Elk Foundation, and the Foundation for North American Wild Sheep often maintain lists of recommended outfitters. You can get a complete list of Montana guides, where they operate, and what species they guide for from the Montana Outfitters & Guides Association, 33 South Last Chance Gulch, Suite 2B, Helena, MT 59601-4132, 406-449-3578.

Armed with this list, narrow your choices and write or call a few. Ask them to send you their literature. Give extra credence to operators who've been in business in the same location for ten years or more; they wouldn't last that long if they were no good, and if they've been in business that long they should know their territory and game intimately. Ask where and how they hunt, what accommodations they use, etc. If it doesn't sound like your style, try another outfitter. When you find a likely candidate, discuss your list of wants and needs and your philosophy of hunting and ask if he thinks his operation is compatible. Then get a long list of his recent clients, those who didn't shoot game as well as those who did, and call these folks, asking their honest assessment not only of the lodging, food, country, and game, but also the attitudes and atmosphere at camp. Were the guides genuine, honest, conscientious, patient, and helpful? How much game did they see? How large were the antlers or

Guide John Law brings firewood into a canvas wall tent.

horns? How many hunters went home satisfied? If you like what you've heard, call the
outfitter again and ask to see a contract. Usually you're expected to pay half the cost
of the trip when you book it, the other half when you arrive to hunt.

Before you book, contact Montana Fish, Wildlife & Parks and inquire as to the
status of your target species where you're planning to book a hunt. Sometimes winter weather, clearcutting, fires, etc. can change populations and opportunities dras-
tically in a single year.

Some of today's best outfitted hunting is done on large private ranches where
harvests are tightly controlled. You don't have to put up with hordes of locals and can
enjoy hunting without fear of a buck being shot out from under you. Ask how long
the ranch has been under trophy management and the average age and size of animals taken in the past five years. As explained above in booking an outfitter, get a list
of references and confirm the reports for yourself.

Hunting guide Lance Williams enjoys a cup of coffee.

Stay away from guides who hunt from a vehicle on public roads and public land. To my way of thinking, any experienced outdoorsman who knows wildlife and knows his way about the woods and mountains can hunt from roadsides on his own.

One way to shorten your research is to book through a reputable hunting con-sultant—reputable, meaning someone who's been in the business for at least five years. Two recommendations are Jack Atcheson & Sons, Inc. (3210 Ottawa, Butte, MT 59701, 406-782-3498) and Cabela's Outdoor Adventures (812 13th Ave., Sidney, NE 69160, 800-346-8747; on the net at www.cabelas.com). At no cost to you, consultants match you with the appropriate outfitter. Just tell them how you like to hunt, what you'd like to accomplish, and the sort of folks you like to hunt with. They'll make the match, subject to your approval. They can usually make all travel arrangements, too, and they'll be full of helpful information about weather, gear, travel, side trips, local scenic wonders, etc.

A hot meal at the end of a long day's hunt is truly a pleasure.

Remember to be honest in your self-appraisal. Don't tell your outfitter you're ready to climb 4,000 feet and hike 12 miles a day when you're 50 pounds overweight and can't climb into bed without panting. Even old geezers who hobble have had successful elk hunts when they've warned their guides up front so they could plan and prepare. And go to camp with a "have fun, can do" attitude. That can make all the difference in your enjoyment of the hunt.

Warranties and Guarantees

No one can *guarantee* a trophy, and you should shy away from any outfitter who does. No one can predict the vagaries of wildlife and weather, let alone your shooting skills. You don't want to get mixed up with outfitters who turn loose pen-raised critters just to meet a guarantee; what you want is an honest try for free-ranging wild game in good country.

However, some outfitters will *warranty* such things as weather. They may, for instance, offer to guide you again next year for half-price if your hunt is completely snowed out or if you see absolutely no game. Ask about such warranties up front.

Drop Camps

You can hire some outfitters to pack you into the backcountry and drop you off with their tents, stoves, kitchen tools, and sometimes food and horses. You do the cooking, woodcutting, hunting, and meat care on your own. The advantage of such drop camps are many: you don't need to buy a camping outfit or maintain it; you get far enough from roads to avoid most casual hunters; you don't have to put up with strangers telling you when to get up, where to hunt, and how to shoot; you can hunt at your own pace; you eat meals you plan and cook; and it generally costs less than a fully guided hunt. The downside is that you spend more time doing chores and less time hunting. Also, an outfitter is unlikely to drop you in his best hunting area; he'll save that for his better paying, fully guided clients.

If you feel comfortable in the mountain wilderness, can handle horses and survival situations, and can care for meat and trophies, a drop camp might be just what you need.

Hunting Public and Private Lands

These days it isn't enough to know where game is; you also have to know on whose property it roams. More than 25 million acres in Montana are controlled by the state, the U.S. Forest Service, the Bureau of Land Management, and the U.S. Fish & Wildlife Service, and most of this land is open to hunting without permission unless posted otherwise (safety zones, special resource management areas, etc.). The upside to public land is easy access: no fuss, no begging permission; just go hunting. The downside is that everyone and his dog hunts it, so game is often spooky, sometimes scarce, and rarely of trophy quality unless isolation, rugged terrain, or a limited permit system limits buck or bull harvest.

Private land, on the other hand, can be exceedingly difficult to access. Montana state law requires that big game hunters receive permission from the landowner, lessee, or their agent to hunt any private property, whether owned by individuals, companies, or corporations, regardless of whether or not the property is posted. It is the hunter's responsibility to know property boundaries! Know before you go. To be safe, get permission to hunt private lands in writing. Many hunters have been prosecuted for trespass after they received verbal permission from brothers, cousins, neighbors, and casual acquaintances of the real landowner. Some ranches are closed to all hunting, many are leased for hunting, some charge a fee for hunting, and a few are still open to those who merely ask. Ranches with tightly controlled hunting often produce old-age bucks and bulls. Limited competition makes for isolated, relaxing hunting.

STATEWIDE OVERVIEW MAPS

Your first investment in any hunting trip to Montana should be a good map. An excellent general-purpose map for all of Montana is the DeLorme Mapping Company *Montana Atlas & Gazetteer*. In addition to counties, roads, lakes, and rivers, this magazine-format collection of maps shows private, BLM, state, and Forest Service land ownership. It also depicts Indian reservation boundaries, most jeep and many foot trails, springs, swamps, woodlands, public campgrounds, and boat launch sites. The gazetteer section lists and describes all federal lands by location, size, and permitted uses. The DeLorme *Atlas* cannot, of course, show individual road closures or emergency land closures instituted by various management agencies. You must consult these agencies or their latest maps for such information.

Topographic Maps

The most detailed maps for showing land forms, elevation, springs, ponds, swamps, woods, trails, etc. are United States Geological Survey (USGS) topographic

Montana Federal Lands

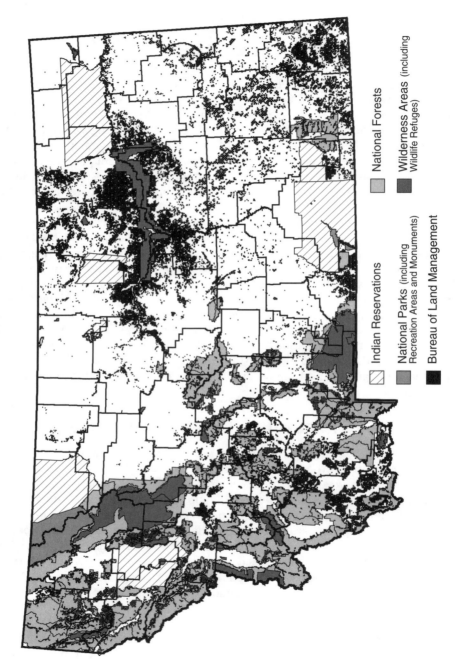

Indian Reservations

National Parks (including Recreation Areas and Monuments)

Bureau of Land Management

National Forests

Wilderness Areas (including Wildlife Refuges)

maps. These are what mountaineers and backpack hunters use to find their way in the wilderness. Experienced hunters also use them to decipher likely deer and elk travel routes and suitable hiding places based on isolation, forest cover, impassable cliffs and rivers, saddles between high mountains, etc. Combined with surface ownership maps, topos are the ultimate in detailed mapping. Depending on the year in which they were charted, USGS topographic maps may be from a 15-minute series or 7.5-minute series. The 15-minute series details land surface areas about 13 miles east-to-west and 17 miles north-to-south, with contour intervals (lines depicting elevation) of 80 or 100 feet. The 7.5-minute series covers about 6.5 miles by 8.5 miles, with contour intervals of 40 feet. They are your best option for detailed hunt planning. Each map is called a quadrangle (quad) and is identified by a name and by its latitude and longitude position. For example, the Bozeman Pass Quadrangle is latitude 45°37'30" and longitude 110°45'00". To determine which quad covers your chosen hunting area, you'll need to study an index grid map which overlays quad names over the entire state. Locate your chosen hunting grounds on the index map, note which quads cover it, and order those.

You can obtain a Montana topo map index from the USGS, Box 25286, Federal Center, Denver, CO 80225. You can also call 1-800-USA-MAPS and follow automated instructions to order your maps, or reach a real person for advice and assistance. USGS topo maps cost $4 as of July 1998.

Many sporting goods and backpacking supply stores throughout Montana sell USGS topo maps popular in their areas.

STATE SCHOOL LANDS

State school trust lands, scattered across the state in square-mile blocks, are open to hunting if you possess a current $10 State Lands Recreational Use License available from Fish, Wildlife & Parks offices and license agents statewide. Carry this license with you at all times because under the law, ranchers who lease state school lands for grazing have the right to ask recreationists for proof they are licensed to use said school lands. They cannot force you off the land if you are not licensed, but they can call law enforcement. The best way to identify state school lands is by referring to land status maps available from the BLM (addresses and phone numbers are listed below under BLM). While many school lands are isolated and provide minimum habitat for big game, some are accessible and support pronghorn, mule deer, white-tails, and even elk.

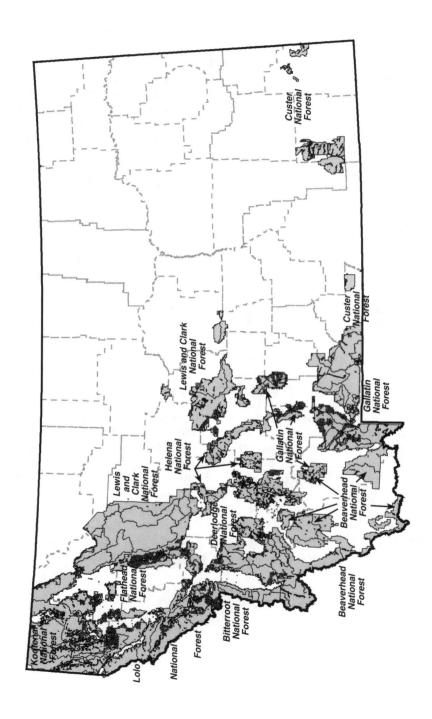

Montana National Forests

United States Forest Service

The U.S. Forest Service sells detailed maps of all National Forests within Montana. These show land ownership, roads and trails, road closures and other travel restrictions and can be purchased at many sporting goods stores, at most local Forest Service offices and ranger stations, or directly from the regional USFS office. Call first for pricing and payment options. The quickest way to get any Forest Service map is via phone and credit card payment from the Northern Region Office in Missoula. This office handles all Montana National Forest maps:

U.S.D.A. Forest Service
Northern Region Office
200 E. Broadway, Box 7669
Missoula, MT 59807
406-329-3511

Regional Forest Service offices require cash or check payment and may not have maps of every National Forest in the state. They should have the most up-to-date information on closed roads, fires, floods, and other calamities that could interfere with your travel plans. Addresses are:

Beaverhead-Deerlodge National Forest
420 Barrett St.
Dillon, MT 59725-3572
406-683-3900

Bitterroot National Forest
1801 N. 1st St.
Hamilton, MT 59840
406-363-7167

Custer National Forest
1310 Main St., P.O. Box 50760
Billings, MT 59105
406-248-9885

Flathead National Forest
1935 3rd Ave. East
Kalispell, MT 59901
406-758-5200

Gallatin National Forest
10 E. Babcock Ave., Federal Building
P.O. Box 130
Bozeman, MT 59771
406-587-6701

Helena National Forest
2880 Skyway Drive
Helena, MT 59601
406-449-5201

Kootenai National Forest
506 U.S. Highway 2 West
Libby, MT 59923
406-293-6211

Lewis & Clark National Forest
1101 15th St. North
P.O. Box 869
Great Falls, MT 59403
406-791-7700

Lolo National Forest
Building 24, Ft. Missoula
Missoula, MT 59804
406-329-3750

Montana Bureau of Land Management Lands

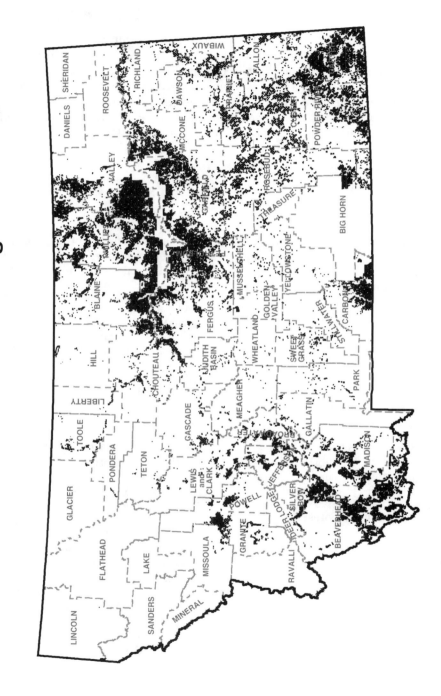

BUREAU OF LAND MANAGEMENT

Some 8 million acres of public land, much of it scattered and in checkerboard parcels mixed with private and state land, are managed by the BLM in Montana. Most of it is open for hunting, but it must be reached via public roads or waterways; you cannot cross private land to reach BLM land without permission from the private landowner. By the same token, holders of grazing leases on specific BLM lands cannot keep hunters out or maintain locked gates, post "No Hunting" signs, or employ similar tactics designed to turn back hunters. If you believe BLM land has been improperly blocked or posted, contact the nearest BLM office.

The BLM maintains Recreation and Surface Management maps that depict land ownership, as well as roads, trails, and waterways. The state BLM headquarters office sells more than 90 maps covering all of the state, and they accept credit card orders over the phone. That address is:

Montana State BLM Office
222 N. 32nd St.
P.O. Box 36800
Billings, MT 59107-6800
406-255-2888

Regional BLM offices may not have every map of BLM lands in Montana, but they will have the most up-to-date information on local conditions, flooded roads, snow depth, and similar factors affecting travel. Much of eastern Montana soil is a gumbo clay so slippery that even a light rain can render 4-wheel-drive vehicles nearly useless. After rains, it is useful to know which roads and trails are graveled, and thus suitable for driving, and which are gumbo and impassable. The regional Montana BLM offices are:

Butte Field Office
106 N. Parkmont, Box 3388
Butte, MT 59701-3388
406-494-5059

Havre Field Station
1704 Second St. West, Drawer 911
Havre, MT 59501-0911
406-265-5891

Dillon Field Office
1005 Selway Drive
Dillon, MT 59725-9431
406-683-2337

Great Falls Field Office
812 14th St. North
Great Falls, MT 59401
406-727-0503

Missoula Field Office
3255 Fort Missoula Road
Missoula, MT 59804-7293
406-329-3914

Malta Field Office
501 S. Second St. East, Box B
Malta, MT 59538-0047
406-654-1240

Lewistown Field Office
Airport Road, Box 1160
Lewistown, MT 59457
406-538-7461

Glasgow Field Station
Rt. #1-4775
Glasgow, MT 59230-9796
406-228-4316

Montana Indian Reservations

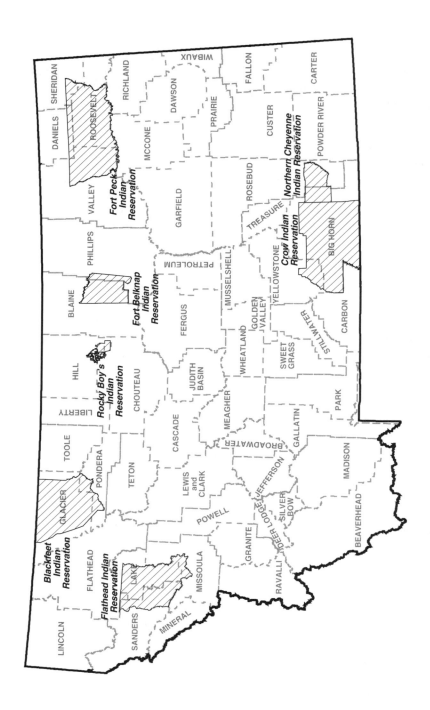

Miles City Field Office
111 Garryowen Road
Miles City, MT 59301
406-233-2800

Billings Field Office
810 East Main Street
Billings, MT 59105-3395
406-238-1540

Hunting on Indian Reservations

Montana is home to seven reservations representing 11 tribes. Each features a wealth of cultural institutions and historic sites. Together, the reservations cover over 7 million acres.

When traveling on reservations, be particularly respectful of the people you encounter. Many tribes work to attract visitors, but others feel that tourists invade their privacy and compromise the integrity of their traditional culture. In order to make your visit pleasant for everyone, be sensitive to your surroundings and obey all tribal laws and regulations.

Each reservation is a sovereign governing body with sole management and control of its wildlife resources. Non-tribal members may only hunt big game on Indian tribal lands with permission of and under the regulations of each tribal government. Some tribes permit non-member hunting for select species, some do not, and this changes from year to year. For up-to-date information, contact tribes at the addresses listed.

Blackfeet Reservation

- 1.5 million acres
- Blackfeet Nation
  Box 850
  Browning, MT 59417
  406-338-7207
- Closed to big game hunting by non-tribal members.

The Blackfeet Reservation is located in northwestern Montana along the Rocky Mountain Front. Canada borders it to the north, and Glacier National Park to the west.

Crow Indian Reservation

- 2.4 million acres
- Crow Indian Reservation
  Crow Agency, MT 59022
  406-638-2601
- Closed to all hunting by non-tribal members.

Located in southeastern Montana, the Crow Reservation's northern boundary lies just south of Billings, and its southern boundary is Wyoming. The famous Little Bighorn River, noted for its fabulous trout fishing and the Little Bighorn Battlefield, flows through the center of the reservation.

Flathead Reservation

- 1.2 million acres
- Confederated Salish & Kootenai Tribe
  Tribal Fish and Game Conservation Program
  Box 278
  Pablo, MT 59855
  406-675-4700 or 1-800-634-0690
- Closed to big game hunting by non-tribal members.

The Flathead Reservation is located north of I-90 between Missoula and Kalispell in the beautiful Mission Valley. It is open to waterfowl and upland game bird hunting through a cooperative agreement with FWP, and has excellent pheasant, Hungarian partridge, duck, and goose hunting. Inquire with the Tribal Fish and Game Conservation Program for details.

Fort Belknap Reservation

- 705,000 acres
- Fort Belknap Tourism Office
  RR1, Box 66
  Fort Belknap Agency
  Harlem, MT 59526
  406-353-2205
- Open to limited big game hunting for antelope, bison, and deer by permit only.

Fort Belknap offers some of Montana's best antelope hunting, along with deer, prairie dog, upland bird, waterfowl, and even a limited number of permits for buffalo. The reservation occupies nearly 700,000 acres of grasslands, interspersed with riparian areas, reservoirs, and ponds. The Milk River forms the northern boundary and the Little Rocky Mountains mark the southern. Big game licenses and regulations may be acquired by contacting the Fort Belknap Fish & Wildlife Program at RR 1 Box 66, Fort Belknap Agency, Harlem, MT 59526, 406-353-2205 ext. 428.
As of 1998:

- Antelope Season: September 1—October 31
  Permits: Buck $600 per tag; Doe $75 per tag; maximum of 2 tags for each gender available per person.
- Bison Season: October 1—February 28 (4 permits available)
  Permits: 1 each: trophy class bison, $6,000; 3 each: 4- to 6-year-old bulls, $3,000 each.
- Deer Season: October 1—December 16 (10 permits available)
  Permits: Bucks only, $1,000

Fort Peck Reservation

- 2 million acres
- Fort Peck Assiniboine & Sioux Tribes
  Box 1027
  Poplar, MT 59255
  406-678-5155
- Closed to big game hunting by non-tribal members.

The Fort Peck Reservation is home to the Assiniboine and Sioux tribes. It is located on the Hi-Line in northeastern Montana, 50 miles from the Canadian border. The Missouri River forms its southern boundary.

Northern Cheyenne Reservation

- 445,000 acres
- Northern Cheyenne Reservation
  Box 991
  Lame Deer, MT 59043
  406-477-6284
- Closed to all hunting by non-tribal members.

The reservation is located in southeastern Montana, bounded on the east by the Tongue River and on the west by the Crow Reservation.

Rocky Boy's Reservation

- 108,000 acres
- The Chippewa-Cree Business Committee
  Box 544, Rocky Boy Route
  Box Elder, MT 59521
  406-395-4282
- Open to hunting for by permit only.

The Rocky Boy's Reservation is located on the Hi-Line in Hill County, about 20 miles south of Havre. The terrain consists of plains grasslands and montane forest. The Bears Paw Mountains grace the southern part of the reservation. Hunting licenses are available at the police station located on Lower Box Elder Road.

Montana Wilderness Areas and National Wildlife Refuges

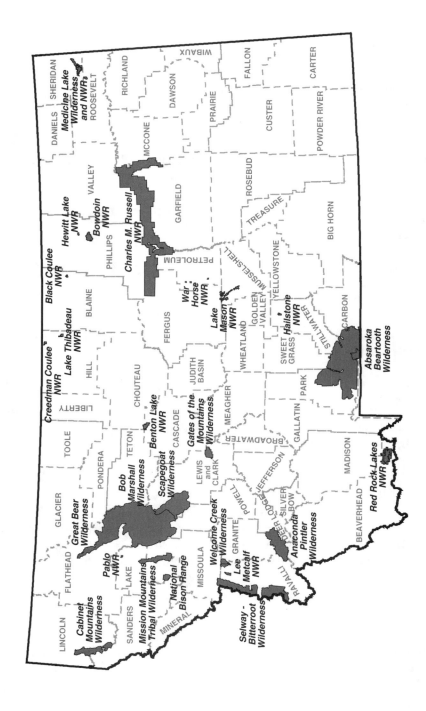

NATIONAL WILDLIFE REFUGES

Montana has nine National Wildlife Refuges that allow hunting. A Montana state hunting license is required to hunt refuge lands. However, each refuge also has its own set of regulations and seasons; call or write to request maps and regulations. The following is a listing of those refuges in Montana that allow hunting, their acreage, addresses, and phone numbers.

Charles M. Russell NWR
1,100,000 acres
P.O. Box 110
Lewiston, MT 59457
406-538-8706

Benton Lake NWR
12,383 acres
P.O. Box 450
Black Eagle, MT 59414
406-727-7400

Bowdoin NWR
15,500 acres
HC 56, Box 5700
Malta, MT 59538
406-654-2863

Hailstone NWR
1,828 acres
P.O. Box 110
Lewiston, MT 59457
406-538-8706

Lake Mason NWR
18,600 acres
P.O. Box 110
Lewiston, MT 59457
406-538-8706

Lee Metcalf NWR
2,800 acres
P.O. Box 257
Stevenville, MT 59870
406-777-5552

Medicine Lake NWR
31,457 acres
223 N. Shore Road
Medicine Lake, MT 59247
406-789-2305

Red Rock Lakes NWR
43,500 acres
Monida Star Route, Box 15
Lima, MT 59739
406-276-3536

War Horse NWR
3,192 acres
P.O. Box 110
Lewiston, MT 59457
406-538-8706

BLOCK MANAGEMENT PROGRAM

One of the newest programs for hunter access on private land is the Block Management Program, which has made more than 7.5 million acres of private land available to licensed hunters. Here's how it works: funds from nonresident, variable-priced, outfitter-sponsored big game licenses are used to compensate landowners for opening their property to hunters. Each landowner negotiates a deal with FWP as to how access is granted, whether or not vehicles are allowed, what species can be hunted, how long the lands will remain open, etc.

Because regulations are variable, hunters must obtain the current Block Management booklet from FWP that lists lands open under the program and outlines procedures hunters must follow to gain access. Sometimes this is as simple as crossing onto the property and starting to hunt, sometimes it requires signing in at the ranchhouse, sometimes it means making an advanced reservation with the landowner for hunting days. For complete and current information on Block Management, contact the FWP office in the region you plan to hunt.

Region 1
490 North Meridian Road
Kalispell, MT 59901
406-752-5501
fwprg1@mt.gov

Region 2
3201 Spurgin Road
Missoula, MT 59804
406-542-5500
fwprg2@mt.gov

Region 3
1400 South 19th
Bozeman, MT 59718
406-994-4042
fwpgen@mt.gov

Helena Area Resource Office
930 Custer Ave. W.
Helena, MT 59620-0701
406-444-4720

Butte Area Resource Office
1820 Meadowlark Lane
Butte, MT 59701
406-494-1953

Region 4
4600 Giant Springs Road, P.O. Box 6610
Great Falls, MT 59406-6610
406-454-5840
fwprg4@mt.gov

Region 5
2300 Lake Elmo Drive
Billings, MT 59105
406-247-2974
fwprg5@mt.gov

Region 6
Rural Route 1-4210
Glasgow, MT 59230
406-228-3700
fwprg6@mt.gov

Havre Area Resource Office
2165 Hwy 2 East
Havre, MT 59501
406-265-6177
fwphao@mt.gov

Region 7
P.O. Box 1630
Miles City, MT 59301
406-232-0930
fwprg7@mt.gov

Captain May I

As soon as the sixth mule deer buck bounced from the buffaloberry thicket beside the creek, my brother knew we'd found the place for our deer hunt. "Did you see the size of that last one?" he asked as I stood slack jawed, still staring at the knoll behind which the deer had fled. "I thought the fifth one was big, but that last one! Wow! I get him."

We jabbered happily as we hiked back to the truck, no longer interested in the shotguns we carried or the sharptails we were supposed to be hunting. "Do you think they'll still be here when deer season opens? Do you think anyone else knows about them? Do you think anyone else will be hunting here?" Our musings were exciting, but premature.

"Maybe we should ask the rancher if we can hunt deer," Bob suggested.

"Why couldn't we? He likes us. He said we can hunt."

"Yeah, birds. Maybe not deer." We stopped at the house on our way out. Bob was right.

"Gee, fellas, I'd like to let you but I've got the place leased for deer."

"Leased?"

"Yup. Several guys from Billings with money wanted it all to themselves and they made me an offer I couldn't refuse. Doctors and lawyers and such is what they are. I hate to turn down folks like you, but, well, times being what they are…"

We got the picture. After that we started asking for deer hunting permission after every bird hunt we made on private land. The answer was always the same. Sorry. Full up. Promised to family and friends. Leased out. No room. Nada. That was back in the days before the Block Management Program. Today several of these same ranches are now open to hunting by regular Joes like me and my friends. The satisfying part is that those same wealthy hunters who formerly leased us out of the market are now paying for the Block Management leases on which we can hunt. The high fees non-residents pay for outfitter-sponsored elk and deer licenses fund Block Management. Oh, some prime ranches are still leased to individuals, clubs, and outfitters, but some 7 million private acres that weren't open ten years ago are now open to some form of hunting under Block Management.

That's not the Montana of 1805, but it's progress.

Equipment Checklists

Camping Gear

Vast distances, wilderness, and an aesthetic desire to live close to the land makes camping popular with Montana hunters. For many sportsmen, it wouldn't be hunting without a snug camp. In addition to private campgrounds and RV parks, Montana is dotted with Forest Service, state, county, and municipal campgrounds, but many of these are closed during big game seasons. Fortunately, hunters may legally camp on Forest Service and Bureau of Land Management lands except where posted otherwise. Come October, old logging roads, logging decks, cottonwood draws, and creek bottoms are sprinkled with tents, campers, and campfires. Here's what you'll need for a comfortable vehicle camp:

_____ Tent. External or internal aluminum-frame cottage or umbrella tents often collapse under Montana snow. In addition, small nylon backpack tents may be great for sleeping in, but are poor for drying gear and cooking in because of their lack of room. A better option is the canvas wall tent supported by sturdy poles, 2×4s, or steel pipe frames. Outfit it with a sheet-metal stove, and you'll be cozy even when it's well below freezing outside. The minimal size for two hunters and gear is 8×10 feet, and you'll find that 4-foot sidewalls add considerable space over 3-foot walls. Some hunters like a wall tent for their kitchen, dining, and drying room, and separate small tents for sleeping. In this way, a relatively small wall tent can serve quite a few hunters.

_____ Poles, stakes, guy ropes.

_____ Pickup camper or RV. Pickup campers are self-contained, versatile, and handy. Anywhere the truck goes, they go. RVs and trailers are even more lavish and comfortable, but many are too large to go where you might wish to camp.

_____ Tarps. One or more canvas, plastic, or nylon tarps erected overhead as roofs provide shelter for cutting and storing wood, dressing, cooking, sitting around the fire, etc. Just don't place them directly over the fire.

_____ Extra nylon-sheathed rope in various diameters for hanging game, erecting tarps, shoring up tents, etc.

_____ Sleeping bag.

_____ Sleeping pad. Therm-a-rest, closed-cell foam, or open-cell foam.

_____ Cot.

_____ Pillow.

_____ Lanterns. Pump-up gas models are fine, but propane versions are cleaner and easier to maintain. Battery-powered units aren't as bright, and you also run the risk that the battery may go dead.

A wall tent camp kitchen contains frying pans, kettles, and a gas stove.

Cooking on a Coleman gas stove inside a canvas wall tent.

_____ Cook stove. As with lanterns, pump-up gas versions require more work and mess than propane.

_____ Heater. These can be campfires banked in front of open-sided tents, sheet-metal wood-burning stoves inside closed tents, or propane/gas/kerosene heaters.

_____ Table and chairs. Log chunks are okay, but a backrest is heavenly after a few days of hard hunting. Folding tables make kitchen work and dining much more pleasant.

_____ Plates, cups, bowls, flatwear.

_____ Kettles, fry pan, mixing bowls, spatula, ladle, measuring cup, etc.

_____ Aluminum foil, paper towels, plastic wrap.

_____ Coolers for groceries and game meat.

_____ Water jugs with dispenser spouts, 3 to 5 gallons, plastic or galvanized metal.

_____ Salt for capes & hides.

_____ Hatchet or mallet for pounding tent stakes.

_____ Hatchet or ax for chopping limbs.

_____ Splitting maul for firewood.

_____ Bow saw.

_____ Chain saw, if you expect to cut lots of firewood. They're also good for removing fallen trees from roads and trails.

_____ Chain saw oil, gas, and maintenance tools, if you do decide to bring that chainsaw.

_____ Frame pack for hauling out meat.

_____ Wire and duct tape.

_____ Tools: Saw, hammer, pliers, wrenches, screwdrivers, etc. for maintenance and repair of vehicles and equipment.

_____ Buckets for water.

_____ Shower bag.

_____ Rugs, straw, or wooden flooring.

_____ Food! Plan your meals ahead of time and prepackage them if possible. Pre-cooked soups, stews, and casseroles can be frozen and heated for serving in camp with minimum fuss. Instant oatmeal simplifies cooking and clean up. Unless you love to spend time in camp, sacrifice food quality for field time.

Vehicle Emergency Kit

In the wilds, even a 4×4 truck can get stuck or break down. Every hunting vehicle should have a good set of emergency tools: ax; saw; hammer; wrenches; wire; duct and electricians' tape; assorted nails, bolts, nuts, and screws; spare hose clamps; spare radiator hose; extra fan belts; extra spare tire; battery-powered air compressor; jumper cables; flares; sand shovel; snow shovel; hand winch, tow rope, or chain; matches; sleeping bag; candy; and emergency food and water. Be prepared to repair anything and to weather bad storms.

Driving isn't always necessary. With his rifle and pack, a hunter makes use of a mountain bike and logging roads to get into good habitat in a western forest.

Backpack Camp

Backpack hunting is serious work. You must carry not only all your hunting gear but also your shelter and food. And on the way out, you may be packing 100 to 500 pounds of meat. This takes stamina and time. If you hunt 10 miles from your vehicle, figure on packing out 100 pounds of meat per day. One man will need at least four days to pack an elk out, generally by ferrying 100 pounds each day from camp. Then he still has to retrieve the camp. That doesn't leave much time for hunting on a one-week trip.

Think things through carefully before backpack hunting, and always go with at least one able companion. Test yourself and all your gear on several summer backpack trips before the hunt. You're on your own out there; if any part of you or your equipment fails, help is a long way off. Maximize hunting time by carrying lightweight meals that need only be soaked in boiling water to prepare.

Here's a suggested equipment list in addition to clothing:

_____ Backpack. External frames support more weight, but internal frames flex more and are more comfortable off-trail and in brush and forests. You'll need between 4,000 and 5,000 cubic inches of internal space. One or two big pockets leave more space for big loads, but a variety of smaller pockets, especially around the perimeter of the pack, help organize small items and keep them accessible. There should be plenty of lash tabs and load tightening straps on the pack; this way, you can generally tie your sleeping bag, tent, and pad to the outside of the bag, leaving the larger pockets/compartments for clothing, food, and the animal you'll hopefully pack out. Most important is a well-padded, well-designed hip belt and shoulder straps to distribute the load. You should be able to carry the weight on your hips; if your arms start going numb or blue, you should readjust your load or pack lighter.

_____ Sleeping bag and pad.

_____ Tent & fly. Don't skimp here. This is your protection against storms. You may be rained or snowed on for up to five days. Self-supporting tents can be erected on hard ground, and a few guy lines and staked corners will keep it anchored. Rather than a big, heavy tent, I carry a small tent & fly, plus a lightweight, 10x14-foot nylon fly to erect over the tent and surrounding ground to give me someplace to store and dry gear if it rains.

_____ Collapsible, 3-gallon water bucket.

_____ Lightweight stove and fuel. I like the 1.6-pound Peak 1 Feather 400.

_____ Extra fuel in an aluminum tank.

_____ 2-quart cooking pot.

_____ Small fry pan (optional).

_____ Metal spoon & fork.

_____ Sierra cup.

_____ Water filter such as those made by First Need or PUR.

Sporting a full backpack, a big game hunter looks down into steep valleys from a ridgetop.

_____ 2 wide-mouth, 1-quart plastic water bottles.

_____ Multi-tool pliers or Hunter model Swiss Army Knife.

_____ Hunting knife.

_____ Knife sharpener.

_____ Compact binocular.

_____ Compass.

_____ Topo maps.

_____ Small flashlight, extra batteries.

_____ Butane cigarette lighter.

_____ Waterproof matchcase with compass in lid.

_____ Emergency fire starters (waxed sawdust, etc.).

A backpacking big game hunter prepares a meal.

_____ Large, heavy-duty plastic bag to cover your pack during rain or for hauling meat.

_____ Large garbage bags for lining your pack while hauling meat; otherwise, the residual scent of blood will bring the bears running from miles around when you take your next backpacking trip in the summer. Besides, it's a mess to clean up.

_____ Cloth meat bags for hanging and cooling meat.

_____ Cooler (to be left at car for storing packed-out meat).

_____ Small bar soap.

_____ 100-feet of nylon-sheathed cord for lashing meat, securing your fly or tent, etc.

_____ Light sandals or shoes for wearing around camp while your boots dry.

_____ Wire saw.

_____ First Aid kit.

_____ Rifle & 10-15 rounds of ammo, or bow and arrows.

_____ Licenses and tags.

Leaving his tent for the day, a backpacking hunter takes a pack filled with survival gear along.

First Aid Kit

If you can't hunt with a doctor or emergency medical technician, at least have a good first aid kit on hand and rudimentary knowledge in its use. A basic emergency/first aid how-to book should be in every vehicle or camp. Common hunting injuries can include sprains and broken bones, cuts and abrasions, foreign objects in eyes, blisters, burns, frostbite, choking, and heart attacks.

First Aid Kit

_____ Scissors

_____ Tweezers

_____ Needle and thread

_____ Needle-nosed pliers

_____ Razor blade

_____ Ace bandages, 2-inch and 4-inch

_____ Triangular bandage (dish towel will work)

_____ Sterile gauze pads, 2x2-inch

_____ Band-Aids, assorted sizes

_____ Betadine antiseptic wash

_____ Saline solution eye wash

_____ White adhesive tape, 1/2-inch

_____ Sterile eye pads

_____ Antibiotic ointment

_____ Antacids

_____ Aspirin, Tylenol, Motrin

_____ Milk of Magnesia

_____ Cough drops

_____ Antihistamines

_____ Lomotil (stops diarrhea)

_____ Snake bite kit

_____ CELLULAR PHONE—To call for real help. See emergency numbers in the hub cities sections of this book.

An early snowfall catches a hunter in the mountains with minimal gear, although the wool vest, hat, and pants are good precautions.

Clothing

Montana is one of those states where, if you don't like the weather, all you have to do is wait five minutes; it'll change. In autumn, especially, temperatures may vary from +80° to -15°F. You might choke on dust, drown in rain, or drift over with snow. Hunting success hinges on how well you dress.

Most outdoorsmen recognize the value of layering with modern, hydrophobic fabrics and insulation. Instead of a single down or heavy wool parka, pack a waterproof shell, an insulated vest, and a jacket filled with Holofil, Qualofil, Thinsulate, or similar insulation that maintains loft even when wet. Add or remove layers as temperatures dictate. The manmade materials are lighter than natural fibers, too. Their biggest drawback is that they melt from campfire sparks, so stand clear and never use a fleece or polypro glove to lift a hot pan or kettle from the stove.

Here's a recommended clothing list to cover a week of all the weather Montana can throw at you:

_____ 2-3 sets hydrophobic long underwear, tops and bottoms, in polypropylene, Thermastat, Capilene©, MTP, or similar, spun-plastic fabrics.

_____ 4-6 pairs thin hydrophobic socks and 4-6 pairs of thick wool, fleece, or polypro socks.

_____ 1 pair light or medium wool, Cabela's MTO50, Stealth Cloth, or fleece pants, 1 pair jeans or canvas pants, and 1 pair heavy wool or fleece pants. For truly Arctic conditions, 1 pair insulated bibs or coveralls.

_____ Waterproof, zip-leg overpants for rain and wind protection.

_____ 2 cotton, long-sleeved undershirts or t-shirts for early season, hot weather.

_____ 2 flannel, wool, Worsterlon, fleece, or micro-fiber button-down, long-sleeved shirts.

_____ Insulated vest.

_____ Insulated or medium-weight fleece jacket.

_____ Heavy parka for late season.

_____ Waterproof/windproof parka shell, ¾ length.

_____ Stocking cap, balaclava.

_____ Fleece neck gaiter or face mask.

_____ Brim hat or cap for sun/rain.

_____ 2 pairs of gloves, heavy and light.

_____ Waterproof boots, 8- to 10-inch tops, 400- to 800-grams Thinsulate insulation, bobbed soles for secure grip on wet rocks, logs, and grass. For mountain hunting, soles should be stiff and sharp edged for cutting edge-wise into steep slopes.

Boot Options

An army marches on its stomach. A hunter marches in his boots. You won't hunt far with sore and blistered feet, so get good boots and break them in well before your hunt. Montana terrain calls for three basic boot types: mountain, plains, and wetlands or river bottoms.

Mountain Boots

Today's best mountain hunting boots feature leather or Cordura uppers (all those parts above the sole). Cordura is lighter; leather is more dust and water-resistant and perhaps more durable. The less stitching, the better, because stitches fray or pop long before soles or uppers wear out, especially when scree, boulders, and sharp sticks are abrading them. Shop for uppers with a minimum of overlapping pieces sewn together. One smooth piece of leather from the sole up over the toe to the ankle is best. Stitch-down soles (Goodyear welt construction) are easy to replace when soles wear out, but the stitches might give way first. Modern cemented soles are durable and rarely de-laminate.

To prevent pebbles and twigs from dropping inside boots, wear 8-inch to 10-inch uppers. A soft-leather achilles "hinge" and soft-leather, cushioned "rock guard" collar around the top two or three inches improve comfort considerably and reduce weight.

The farther eyelets continue down the boot toward the toes (lace-to-toe construction), the more effectively they can be adjusted for comfortable fit over a wider variety of foot widths and sock layers. Hook eyelets are fastest to lace up, but they often catch the looped laces of the opposite boot and trip the wearer; this can be dangerous on cliffs and steep, rocky slopes. D-rings are nearly as fast and much safer. Backset eyelets at the instep snug the boot more securely around the ankle for increased lateral support, also important on steep terrain.

The sole of a mountain boot should be thick to cushion against sharp rocks, hard to resist abrasion and to support the foot at sharp angles, sharp-edged to cut into sidehills and snowfields, and deeply lugged for traction and to grab protrusions of rock. For years, hard-rubber Vibram lug soles were the ultimate, but now a number of softer rubber compositions and tread patterns are better. Bobbed soles seem to be the most versatile for woods, meadows, and rocks. The softer rubber bobs grip wet rocks and logs better than do slick, hard-rubber soles; a rim of sharp-edged cleats around the edge of the sole cuts into hillsides. As a bonus, bobbed soles don't pick up much mud.

In my experience, no amount of mink oil, snow seal, or silicone will keep boots waterproof after a morning or two of walking in wet grass. However, modern GoreTex boots remain leak-free over two or three seasons of hard use. Make sure any GoreTex boots you buy have the "Guaranteed to Keep You Dry" tag; this means they were built properly and are guaranteed to work. GoreTex is a thin layer of a teflon-like, white "plastic" porous enough to pass vapor but not water. It is sandwiched between a boot's outer material and inner liner, so you never see it. GoreTex will reduce, but not stop, your feet from sweating. If you sweat in regular, non-waterproof boots, why wouldn't you sweat in GoreTex boots? Like leather, GoreTex will eventually wear out, but two or three years of dry feet are worth an extra $20 to $40.

Don't worry about whether or not 200 Grams of Thinsulate insulation in a boot will be too hot. I have sweaty feet, and I can hike 12 miles a day at 70°F in 200-gram Thinsulate boots without discomfort. The Thinsulate also functions as padding to dull the rough edges of leather and stitching, prevent blisters, and cushion against sharp stones. At 400 grams, Thinsulate begins to warm things up. I find 400 grams perfect for temperatures between 20° and 40°F if I'm active. For stand hunting, 800 to 1,000 grams is better.

If you plan to hunt after mid-November, you may face a cold weather challenge. At 0° to –20°F, you can keep your feet tolerably warm by hiking steadily, but stop for an hour or more and you'll be in trouble no matter how much insulation is in your boot, especially if you've filled your socks with perspiration. Wet socks will suck heat from your feet at a painful rate. So will the thickest layer of wet felt inside pac boots. Carry spare socks and/or felts, and change frequently to keep that essential insulating layer dry. Some hunters treat their feet with anti-perspirant to reduce sweating. Others cover their feet in plastic wrap or plastic bags before donning socks. Their feet stay damp, but their socks stay dry, and dry socks are the key to warmth.

Pac boots are de rigeur for deep snow hunting, but many folks find them poorly designed for walking. Their feet slip inside. You might try 1,000- to 1,600-gram Thinsulate insulated leather boots for a tighter, more secure "boot-like" fit and feel. Air-filled Mickey Mouse boots may also work for you.

Plains Boots

Mountain boots perform adequately on the plains, but are really more than you need. You can get by with lighter materials, less support, and a less aggressive tread design. Softer rubber, crepe-type soles suffice on rolling ground. Soft-rubber soles reduce noise, so they're better for stalking. GoreTex is still a good idea. It rains and snows on the plains, too. Stick with the 8-inch uppers and minimum exposed stitching. Many hunters like Bean-style rubber boots with leather uppers, but prickly pear cactus may puncture them. Forget cowboy boots with smooth soles; they slip and slide on the slightest grassy incline and provide little ankle support.

Wetland Boots

Whitetail hunters working river bottoms will likely need extra water protection for crossing creeks and sloughs. Since they mostly sit on stand or still-hunt short distances, support and traction are of minor concern. Ankle-fit rubber boots 12-inches to 16-inches high, hip boots, and, rarely, waders are called for. Insulated versions may be necessary for cold days.

Rifles, Ammunition, and Sights

Advising a hunter as to which rifle, sight, and ammunition to use is akin to telling a commuter which car to drive. Beyond some broad guidelines, it's personal choice. Given that plenty of deer and elk are killed every year with arrows and muzzleloaders, even the mildest centerfire rifle would seem adequate for the job as long as it is used within its effective range. Nevertheless, there are widely accepted standards and popular cartridges for all of Montana's big game hunting; consider these before choosing your favorite. And regardless of which rifle/cartridge you ultimately select for any hunting chore, never push it beyond its limits. As a general rule, when downrange energy levels drop below 1,500 foot-pounds, a bullet has become marginally effective for elk, moose, and bear; figure 1,000 ft-lbs. for deer-sized game. You can find these figures in Federal, Remington, and Winchester ammunition catalogs, as well as reloading handbooks.

RIFLE ACTIONS AND STYLES

Modern centerfire rifles are built around five basic actions: single shot, including falling block, rolling block, and break-action; turnbolt or bolt-action; lever-action; pump or slide action; and autoloading action. Autoloaders offer the fastest follow-up shots for average shooters. Experts can cycle pumps and levers just as fast, and even a few bolt-action shooters can nearly match that speed. The worth of this talent remains moot; ideally you shouldn't need a second shot, and a perfectly placed first shot should be your goal. Once the game is alert and running, each follow-up shot becomes tougher. For this reason, more hunters are choosing bolt-action and single-shot rifles for their superior, first-shot accuracy potential.

Modern bolt-action and single-shot rifles can be fine-tuned to consistently put five shots inside a half-inch circle or less. Both are also chambered for the latest, flattest shooting, hardest hitting cartridges using the best pointed, aerodynamically efficient, premium bullets. All this adds up to maximum long-range trajectory, accuracy, and power. The best turnbolt rifle in a large magnum caliber is powerful elk medicine up to 400 yards or more, though such long shots should be taken in emergency situations only, such as anchoring wounded game. Modern bolt-action rifles include the Winchester M70, Remington M700, Browning A-Bolt, Ruger M77, Kimber K770, Marlin MR7, and Savage M110. Modern single-shot rifles include the Dakota M10, Ruger #1, Browning M1885 High Wall, and H&R Ultra.

That said, it is only fair to note that some autoloaders and pumps feature free-floating barrels and shoot almost as accurately as bolt-actions, so don't rule them out as long range tools. The BOSS system on Browning pump and autoloader rifles often helps them group into an inch or less at 100 yards. Some suggested autoloaders and pumps with these features are the Browning BAR and BPR, and the Remington M7400 and M7600.

Rifle hunter shoots down into a frosty pine forest from a limestone ridge.

Realistically, any rifle that groups three shots inside a 2-inch circle at 100 yards is accurate enough for shooting to 300 yards. Most of the rifles mentioned above should match or better that. If you limit shots to 200 yards or less, any rifle that throws five bullets inside 3 inches will do the job. Much western Montana moose, elk, bear, and mule deer habitat is so dense that 100-yard shots are considered long.

Lever action repeaters are on average the least accurate and least powerful rifles. Models with tube magazines (Winchester M94 and Marlin 336) must shoot flat-nosed bullets to prevent spontaneous ignition upon recoil. Sharp bullet tips that touch primers of cartridges ahead of them in the magazine act as firing pins when the rifle recoils, initiating a disastrous chain reaction. Flat bullets don't detonate primers, but they do push a lot of wind, which slows them down quickly. The resultant trajectory and energy loss limits their effective range. Even large capacity cases such as the 45-70 Govt. and .444 Marlin are effective to only 200 yards or so. Lever actions like the

Browning BLR feature clip magazines and can handle sharp-pointed bullets in modern cartridges like .270 Win. and 7mm Rem. Mag. and are legitimate 300-yard guns.

Single-shots in any action are tools for experienced, careful hunters willing to wait for perfect shooting opportunities. Their biggest drawback is the lack of a quick second shot, should one be needed to anchor an escaping crippled animal. A well-tuned single-shot can be as accurate as the best turnbolt rifle.

Centerfire .22s for Big Game

Montana permits the use of centerfire .22 cartridges for hunting big game, and a few experts use them with good effect. Hundreds of teenagers and women have used .222 Rem., .223 Rem., .22-250 Rem., and .220 Swift rifles to cleanly kill hundreds of pronghorns, deer, and even elk. Still, .22 centerfires are not recommended for average hunters. Why? Primarily because bullet weights and construction are not ideal for adequate penetration. Slip a 55-grain .22 slug traveling at 3,000 fps between the ribs of a whitetail, and the tiny bullet will transfer 1,114 ft.-lbs. of kinetic energy and massive shock to the nervous system. But stick that same projectile on a hip or shoulder and it could explode on the muscle and bone, creating only a severe flesh wound.

Equally important, tiny .22 bullets do not retain energy well downrange. Even a super-fast .220 Swift .55-grain bullet leaving the muzzle at 3,900 fps and carrying 1,857 ft.-lbs. of energy will retain only about 900 ft.-lbs. of that energy at 300 yards, 700 ft.-lbs. at 400 yards. That's minimal for big deer.

Most factory .22 centerfire ammunition is loaded with thin jacketed, highly frangible varmint bullets. Only Federal offers a true Premium big game bullet, the 55-grain Trophy Bonded Bear Claw in the .22-250 Rem. and .220 Swift. Folks who load their own ammunition should use this bullet or the 50- and 53-grain Barnes X bullets. In tests, these slugs have reportedly penetrated farther than a partition-type bullet fired from a .338 Win. Mag.

If you insist on shooting big game with a centerfire .22, use a premium bullet, load it hot, and stalk as closely as you can, preferably inside 250 yards.

Shooting from a sitting position with a single-shot Dakota M10 rifle supported by shooting sticks.

AMMUNITION

Cartridges for Specific Species

Despite arguments for the "all-round gun," different cartridges perform better for some species and styles of hunting than others. The bullet is actually more critical than the case that launches it. Still, the .30-06 Springfield remains an ideal choice for all Montana big game species, including moose and bear. Shoot 150- to 165-grain boat tail bullets for adequate knockdown power and flat trajectory for open country muleys, whitetails, pronghorns, sheep, and goats. Step up to 180-grain, possibly 200-grain, slugs for elk, bear, and moose.

Truth be known, you can do much the same thing with a .270 Winchester or .280 Remington. They are simply the .30-06 case necked to smaller diameters. Go with 130- and 140-grain .270 bullets for deer-sized game, 150- to 160-grain for bigger stuff. Try 130- to 150-grain .284 slugs for deer in the .280 Remington, 150- to 175-grain for larger critters.

Ballistic experts can nitpick until doomsday about arcane "advantages" of the .284 Winchester over the 7mm-08 Remington or the 7mm STW over the 7mm Remington Magnum, but game rarely knows if it was shot through both lungs with a .25-06 Remington or a .338 Winchester Magnum. Did you realize, for example, that the difference in trajectory between the old .30-06 and the powerful .300 Weatherby Magnum at 300 yards is 2 inches? That's all! The Weatherby does pack 500 ft.-lbs. more kinetic energy, but the .30-06 is still carrying over 2,000 ft.-lbs., more than enough to shoot through an elk with the right premium bullet.

Study trajectory tables and you'll see that most of today's centerfire cartridges are quite similar in power and trajectory and more than adequate for Montana game. Pick one, and then get down to the serious business of learning to judge range and shoot.

Bullets

More critical than cartridge selection is bullet selection. A thin-skinned, frangible bullet may fly true and hit hard, but upon striking flesh and bone it could disintegrate into dozens of lightweight, ineffective particles unable to penetrate to the vitals. As a rule, larger animals require longer, heavier slugs in any caliber so that sufficient bullet mass remains behind the mushroomed tip to drive it deep. If all or most of the slug mushrooms, the broad pancake of metal drags and stops before penetrating adequately. Equally important is bullet integrity or toughness. A big game bullet must stay in one piece so that it can carry its energy through the target.

To ensure deep penetration, use a "premium" bullet for anything larger than big buck whitetails. Examples include Barnes X, Winchester Fail Safe, Nosler Partition, Combined Technologies Partition Gold, Trophy Bonded Bear Claw, Swift A-Frame, and Speer Grand Slam. These slugs also perform well on smaller game, but aren't necessary.

Lighter game can be taken with traditional jacketed bullets such as Winchester SilverTip and Power Point, Remington Core-Lokt, Federal Hi-Shok, Sierra GameKing and ProHunter, Speer Soft Point and Mag Tip, Hornady Interlock, Nosler Ballistic Tip,

Barnes Original, etc. Do not use thinly jacketed, frangible "varmint" bullets for any big game hunting; they are designed to break up upon impact with small, thin-skinned animals smaller than a coyote.

Shoot Through

For years, hunters have argued whether it was better for a bullet to punch through an animal, leaving two holes and a good blood trail, or penetrate just to the off-side skin, thus expending all kinetic energy inside the beast. Both approaches have worked well for decades, but recent research suggests that "shot through" game dies sooner and travels less distance after being hit.

Recommended Cartridges

Game	Habitat	Cartridges
Pronghorn, sheep, mule deer, whitetail, mountain goat, cougar.	Open plains, long range	.243 Win., 6mm Rem., .240 Weath. Mag., 250 Savage, .257 Roberts, .25-06 Rem., .257 Weath. Mag., 6.5X55 Swedish Mauser, .260 Rem., .264 Win. Mag., .270 Win., .270 Weath. Mag., 7x57mm Mauser 7mm-08 Rem., 7x64mm Brenneke, .280 Rem., .284 Win., 7mm Rem. Mag., 7mm Weath. Mag., 7mm STW, .308 Win., .30-06 Spring., .300 H&H Mag., .300 Win. Mag., .300 Weath. Mag., 8mm Rem. Mag. .338 Win. Mag., .35 Whelen, .350 Rem. Mag.
Pronghorn, sheep, mule deer, whitetail, mountain goat, cougar.	Forests, close range	Any of the above cartridges plus 7-30 Waters, .30 Rem., .30-30 Win., 300 Savage, .30-40 Krag, 307 Win., .303 Savage, .303 British, .32 Win. Special, 8mm Mauser, .348 Win., .35 Rem., .356 Win., .358 Win.
Elk, black bear, moose	Open country, long range	All cartridges listed for long range deer except those smaller than .25-06 Rem. using a 120-grain premium bullet. Many consider the .270 Win. with 150-grain premium bullet minimum for elk and moose. Although many elk have been taken with .243 Win. and even .22-250 Rem., these calibers are considered too small for such large animals. Add the .375 H&H Mag. and the potent new .30-378 Weath. Mag.
Elk, black bear, moose	Forests, close range	Any of the long range cartridges discussed above plus 7-30 Waters, .30 Rem., .30-30 Win., .300 Savage, .30-40 Krag, .307 Win. .303 Savage, .303 British, .32 Win. Special, 8mm Mauser, .340 Weatherby Mag., .348 Win., .35 Rem., .356 Win., .358 Win., .350 Rem. Mag., .375 Win., .375 H&H Mag., .378 Weath. Mag., .416 Rem. Mag., .416 Rigby, .416 Weath. Mag. .444 Marlin, .45-70 Govt., .458 Win. Mag.

Using a Browning A-Bolt SS with a Leupold scope and Harris bipod, a hunter aims from a brushy draw in grassland.

SIGHTS

Telescopic sights are almost universal on today's big game rifles. Modern scopes are so rugged and reliable that few shooters are willing to do without them. The advantage they offer over open sights is precise aiming at long range, allowing one to take advantage of the long-range potential of most modern cartridges. Why use a rifle that will shoot accurately to 350 yards if you can't see to aim it beyond 200 yards?

If you do prefer the challenge of hunting with iron sights, try a peep. Experienced shooters insist the peep is more effective than buckhorn, V, and similar open sights.

A basic 4× scope can handle 98 percent of all big game sighting chores. If you want to save money, get a tough, bright 4× and go hunting. If, however, you're enthralled by technology and the lure of greater magnification, there are plenty of variable power scopes to scratch your itch. The most practical and versatile fall in the 2–8× and 3–9× range, give or take a number at either end. Unless you plan to shoot small varmints at 300 yards, you don't need more power, so why carry it?

Avoid large objective lens scopes, the ones with front lenses the diameter of Pepsi cans. Yes, these 44mm to 50mm objectives do transmit more light than smaller lenses, but most of it you never need because the pupil in your eye cannot open wide enough to take it all in. Only at the edge of night and at 6× magnification or more does that extra, heavy glass become useful. Do you really want to pack it around all day for five or ten minutes of possible use? When it gets that dark you shouldn't be shooting anyway. Stick with a 3–9× with a 36mm objective for general-purpose hunting.

Something you do want in any scope is a fully multi-coated lens, usually found on top-line models in any brand. Anti-reflective coatings of magnesium flouride and other elements on all lens surfaces do more to increase light transmission than anything else. Make sure the scope is advertised as fully multi-coated, meaning all, not just some, air-to-glass surfaces have been multi-coated. Proven scopes include top-line models from Leupold, Bushnell, Burris, Pentax, Simmons, Zeiss, Swarovski, and Nikon.

Understanding Optics

A good binocular or spotting scope can save a hunter miles of walking and help locate wary game he or she would otherwise miss. Sit high at dawn and dusk and you will spot more undisturbed game than you ever would by walking and watching with your naked eye. You can even watch and pattern shy bottomland whitetails from a distant bluff.

A good, general-use binocular is a 7× or 8×, magnifications most folks can hand hold and get a clear, steady view; some people can hold a 10× binocular. Higher magnifications are generally difficult to view because the image appears to shake; in reality, it's due to the fact that our bodies naturally have a certain amount of continual movement, and we simply can't hold the binocular perfectly still. Spotting scopes that zoom from 15× to 45× are the most versatile, but at those powers they must be steadied on a tripod or sandbag. It's best to scan for game at 15×, then zoom up for a closer look. Often atmospheric haze or heat waves make 30× and higher magnifications unusable.

The last number in a designation like 7×35 or 8×42 represents the objective lens diameter in millimeters. Objective lens size determines how much light will enter the telescope, so the bigger the objective, the brighter the image, all else being equal. Magnification and objective lens diameter together determine the size of its exit pupil.

The exit pupil is the circle of light through which a magnified image is passed. You can see it by holding a binocular or scope about 18-inches from your eye, pointing it at the sky or a bright ceiling, and looking at the eyepiece lens; in it you'll see the circle of light. The diameter of this exit pupil corresponds to the size of your own eye's pupil. If the exit pupil is smaller than your pupil, the image will look darker than it is. If the exit pupil is larger than your pupil, the extra brightness will be wasted. The human pupil dilates to about 7mm in darkness, so you'll want a binocular with a 7mm exit pupil for low-light viewing—i.e., a 7×50mm. In bright daylight, the human pupil will shrink to 2mm or 3mm. Under these conditions, an 8×28mm binocular with its 3mm exit pupil will transmit an image that appears just as bright as that seen through an 8×42mm binocular.

So, if you plan to do all of your glassing in good light, you may enjoy the minimum weight of a compact binocular weighing less than a pound. Look to 7×26, 8×22, 10×26, and similar combinations. If you wish to peer into the shadows after sunset, you'll have to lug around those 7×50s. The 5mm exit pupil of a 7×35 or 8×42 binocular is sufficient until about a half-hour after sunset.

Remember that rifle scopes and spotting scopes are subject to this same magnification/objective lens diameter relationship. At 20×, a spotting scope would need a 60mm objective lens to achieve at 3mm exit pupil. Zoom that scope to 30×, and the exit pupil would shrink to 2mm. This is why 77mm spotting scopes are so bright.

Because glass reflects about four percent of the light striking it, any telescope's apparent brightness can be improved by coating each surface with an air-to-glass, anti-reflectant compound such as magnesium flouride; such coatings reduce light reflection to less than 1 percent. The best scopes and binoculars transmit 90 to 95 percent of light that enters them. Only optics advertised as fully multi-coated will have all air-to-glass lens surfaces multi-coated.

Other things to look for in a good binocular or spotting scope include armor coating for durability, solid construction, long eye relief and/or roll-down rubber cups if you wear glasses, a waterproof guarantee, comfortable and convenient focus controls, and adjustable eyepiece controls that stay put. With optics, you pretty much get what you pay for. Buy the best you can afford. Some of the better binocular bargains I've seen in recent years are the Pentax phase-coated 8×42 DCF WP, the Bushnell Discoverer 7×42, and the Simmons Presidential 8×42. All offer superb clarity at a good price, and they're waterproof to boot. For more money and a slightly better view, try Bushnell Elites, top-of-the-line Zeiss, Leitz, and Swarovskis.

Chris Yeoman glasses with a Bausch & Lomb Elite 15–45× spotting scope.

TRAVELING WITH GUNS

A tangle of state gun laws makes traveling with firearms problematic. To avoid complications when crossing various state lines, pack all firearms unloaded in a hard case, preferably locked, with ammunition packed separately. If possible, break the gun down or remove the bolt. Transport it in the trunk, a camper, or the backseat; the less accessible the gun, the better. Generally, transporting long firearms is perfectly legal in all states, so long as they are cased and unloaded. Handguns, however, are a different story. Some states are real sticklers about them; reportedly you can't even drive through Massachusetts with one. Consult local authorities for specifics.

Flying with firearms is relatively simple. Again, pack the unloaded firearm—rifle, shotgun, or handgun—in a locked, hard case without ammunition. Ammunition may not be carried on your person, so store it in a checked bag other than the one containing the firearm. When you arrive at the ticket counter to check baggage, announce to the agent that you are checking a firearm. She or he may or may not ask to see the firearm but will give you a firearms card that you must sign, date, and place inside the case. You are no longer required to place this card on the outside of the case (where it announces "steal me" to all observers); that was an old FAA regulation that has since been rescinded. Place the card inside your gun case, lock the case, and send it on its way.

Many of the cheap plastic cases don't stand up to baggage handlers. Heavy-duty aluminum cases by Impact Case Co. of Spokane, WA, lock solidly and are virtually indestructible. You can ship raw eggs in them and they'll arrive intact. A top loading, hard plastic case with wheels called ToughPak was designed to ship golf clubs, but it holds up to six long guns. It has a built-in lock and, best of all, it doesn't look like a gun case. You put your rifle in a soft case first and pack clothes, sleeping bag, boots, etc. around it.

Half-length cases designed for take-down shotguns are handy and don't look like rifle cases, but you can still carry a standard bolt-action rifle in them. Just unscrew the barreled action from the stock and place both inside. Put all screws, magazine springs, suitable screwdrivers, and other loose parts inside a zip-lock bag. You might want to wrap a towel around the stock in case it rubs against the action.

Some tricks for camouflaging gun cases include wrapping them in cardboard and duct tape; labeling them as musical instruments, electrical equipment, nursery stock, etc.; and plastering them with golf or tennis stickers. I've been flying with guns since 1988 and haven't had one stolen yet. Knock on wood.

Backups for Broken Rifles

What if your rifle breaks during a hunt? The simplest recourse is to bring an extra rifle along. Folks with less room often take a second scope along, as this is the hardware most likely to break. Mount the backup scope in quick-release rings that match the bases on your rifle, sight in before leaving home, and it will be ready in minutes.

If you have basic gunsmithing skills, take along replacement scope mount screws, firing pins, or extractors. Use a spare sling as a carry strap on your luggage.

Blackpowder hunters take leave of their mud-covered Suburban.

Using Skyline snow camouflage, this bowhunter stalks his quarry with a recurve bow.

In full camouflage, a bowhunter shooting a compound bow kneels on a sagebrush-covered ridge.

Archery Information and Equipment

Bowhunters are an independent lot. They use a confusing variety of equipment— everything from homemade longbows with cedar arrows and stone broadheads to overdraw carbon compound bows with carbon arrows, pin sights, launcher rests, peep sights, and mechanical release aids. And it all works!

By Montana law, however, all equipment must meet minimum standards. Arrows must be tipped with broadheads with at least two cutting edges. Bows must be long, recurve, or compound. No crossbows are permitted during archery only seasons, though they can be used during the general seasons. Sights may not be enhanced via electricity, luminous chemicals, or artificial light of any kind; fiber optic sights are strictly illegal. Poison, chemical, or explosive tips are also illegal. Anyone hunting with a bow during rifle seasons must comply with rifle season regulations, including wearing a minimum of 400 square inches of hunter orange material above the waist.

Beyond these basic regulations, archers are free to work with the wide variety of bow and arrow materials on the market. Because mule deer and antelope are relatively small-bodied, thin-skinned animals and often shot at long range (for bowhunting), arrow trajectory is important. You might want to try high-speed bows, light arrows, and over-draw setups to increase speed and flatten trajectory. For heavier-bodied black bear, elk, and moose, you'll need the superior penetration a heavy arrow and broadhead provide; short, light arrows and overdraw set-ups are not recommended for these species.

A small, lightweight range finder can help eliminate incorrect yardage guesses and prevent shooting at animals too far away. Also keep in mind that it is difficult to judge distances over steep up- and downhill angles in the mountains. Steep angles affect arrow flight, causing higher than normal hits. Practice shooting at steep angles before any mountain hunt.

After a stalk through montane forests, this hunter aims at a mule deer buck quartering away from him.

Shot Placement

Projectiles, whether bullets or arrows, kill by destroying vital body organs.

A shot to the brain or spine ends or interrupts neural function and results in instant death or paralysis. An animal that falls in its tracks has either been hit in the brain/spine or so close to it that the massive shock of the bullet either kills outright or temporarily stuns. Always hurry to any animal that falls instantly, prepared to shoot it again; many a "dead" deer has jumped up and fled after recovering from a superficial neck or spine wound that merely stunned it. Because of this short-term stunning effect, most big game hunters avoid head and neck shots. Both are small targets that can move quickly, resulting in complete misses or non-lethal injuries.

The heart/lung area in the front half of the body cavity of all big game animals is a much larger target. This is why experienced hunters prefer to place their shots just behind their quarry's shoulder so as to penetrate broadside through the chest cavity. Animals struck here usually don't fall instantly. In fact, they often run a hundred yards of more as if uninjured. But soon they either run out of oxygen or their blood pressure drops too low to sustain life, and they expire. Shoot low in an animal's chest and you should hit the heart or lower lungs. If your shot goes high, you punch through the upper lungs and they bleed into the lower lungs, putting both out of commission. If a shot goes even higher, it usually strikes the spine for an instant kill. A shot that lands slightly forward often breaks the shoulder before penetrating the heart or lungs, destroying some edible meat, but ensuring that the animal will not be able to run far. This latter is a wise shot on black bears, cougars, and mountain goats. The first two are soft-footed and difficult to track, and goats often will walk to a ledge and fall. Choose your shots and terrain carefully.

A shot aimed behind the shoulder that strikes too far back may catch the liver or kidneys; while eventually fatal, such shots are slow acting and to be avoided. A paunch or gut shot is even worse. If you believe you've struck an animal behind the heart/lungs, keep shooting to put it down.

Placing a bullet for a quick, clean kill on any big game animal is a matter of anatomy and angles. The objective is to angle the projectile through both lungs. Thus, if the animal is standing broadside, you aim just behind the bend of the shoulder and below the centerline (the heart sits low in the chest). The line of flight pushes the bullet or arrow through both lungs. If the animal is standing slightly away (quartering away), you aim as far back as necessary so that the bullet catches the back of the near-side lung before driving forward to catch the middle or front half of the off-side lung. You can visualize these bullet/arrow paths by drawing imaginary lines from your position through the animal. An old hunter's saying is to "aim for the offside shoulder." That's good advice. Use it on an elk quartering toward you, and you'd place your sights ahead of his near-side shoulder.

Two exceptions to this rule involve animals facing directly at or away from you. The head-on shot is trickier than it looks because most ungulates (hoofed animals) have rather narrow chests that taper to a thin brisket. Bullets strike this sharp junction of ribs and glance off, sliding around them instead of punching inside to the "boiler room." The result is a nasty flesh wound behind the shoulder and the animal's side. A better shot would be the middle of the neck, if you can't wait for your quarry to turn and present a broadside shot.

If you're forced to take a "straight-away" shot, aim for the base of the tail and use a top-grade, premium bullet that will stay together to penetrate. Ideally, you will hit the spine and anchor the game. Move in quickly for a finishing shot. If you are above an animal facing away, you may be able to aim between its shoulders. This way a shot that is either high or low should hit the spine somewhere between the head and tail. If it's off to the side, it should catch a lung.

Common Shot Angles

Broadside

This is the best possible shot with the greatest margin for shooter error on any big game animal. Aim for the center of the chest just behind the bend of the front leg or shoulder. If your shot goes low, you should hit the heart or lower lungs; high, and you punch through the upper lungs; higher still, and you hit the spine. If it hits forward, you break the shoulder and still hit both lungs. Too far back, however, leads to a paunch or gut shot, and this should be avoided at all costs.

Quartering to Shooter

Aim for the off-side shoulder. Based on your knowledge of game animal anatomy and the position of the far-side front leg as seen underneath the animal, draw an imaginary line from your rifle or bow to that far-side shoulder, or slightly behind it if you don't want to damage any meat. Aim accordingly, which in this case would be in front of the near-side shoulder.

Quartering away from Shooter

Again, aim so that your bullet or arrow would catch the far-side shoulder. In this case, you hold your sights nearly on the last rib of the near-side. This is just about the horizontal center of the animal and would be too far back for a broadside shot, but in this case the bullet catches the rear of the near-side lung, angles forward, and catches the front half of the off-side lung.

Tail/Rump to Shooter

Many hunters eschew the "Texas heart shot," as this is called, but a steady shooter using a powerful cartridge and heavy, premium bullet can take it with confidence. It will destroy a lot of meat, however. Aim for the base of the tail. If the shot is true, you will break several vertebrae and paralyze the beast; rush in for a finishing shot. If you shoot slightly left or right, you should break the pelvis or one of the back legs; again, the animal should go down immediately. If you are low and your bullet is tough enough, it should penetrate forward sufficiently to reach the lungs/heart. Many times, it will even exit through or near a front shoulder. There is also a good chance you could strike and sever one of the femoral arteries in a back leg; this kills surprisingly fast.

Front-on Shot

This is a poorer shot choice than the "Texas heart shot" because the ribs of most big game join like the prow of a ship at a sharp angle. The angled brisket/ribs will turn even a stout bullet, which then follows along the ribs, sliding between them and the front shoulder to create a bad flesh wound without breaking bones or damaging internal organs. If you must take this shot, aim slightly high and try for the base of the spine/neck. Better yet, wait until the animal turns and offers a better shot.

Black bears are an exception to this rule. They are broad across the chest and offer a good target for the heart/lung area. Be careful, though, that a high shot doesn't hit the skull if you want it for a trophy.

Caring for Meat

Hunters need to understand three things about meat: it must be kept clean, cool, and dry.

Care for the meat starts with your choice of shots. For tender, tasty meat, shoot animals that are calm; heat and lactic acid build up in the muscles of running game, making them tough. And once you've dressed the carcass, the sooner you cool it, the better.

There are numerous ways to field dress game. First off, any critter shot in the chest will have bled out internally; there is no need to cut its throat. As for the rest, the most common method for dressing big game is to roll the animal on its back and open the body cavity from anus to sternum or on up through the chest cavity and then to pull the innards out. Reach as far up the trachea and esophagus as possible and cut them off, then pull back to remove the lungs and heart. Next, slice the large diaphragm muscle from the sidewalls of the body cavity and continue pulling the offal toward the anus, cutting tissue as necessary near the spine to facilitate removal. Done right, all internal organs roll out in one connected unit.

You have two options at the pelvis: you may split the pelvis bone to expose and free the last few inches of large intestine, or leave the bone and cut around the anus from the outside like reaming the core from an apple. Anus and large intestine are then pulled back through the pelvis into the body cavity and out through the main opening in the belly. On a buck or bull, the penis and testicles must first be sliced free of the belly skin and back over the pelvis. They will then slip through with the anus.

If temperatures are above 30°F, skin the carcass as soon as possible. Hides and pelts are great insulators; left on they'll hold body heat for hours, especially on large animals like elk. Muscle mass on elk and moose are so great that even skinned carcasses can remain warm next to the bone 12 hours after the killing. It's best to quarter them.

A second field butchering technique skips opening the body cavity. Instead, the game is skinned as it lies, and muscles are cut from the skeleton. This is especially handy on elk and moose. Start anywhere by poking a knife tip under the hide and slicing it open. Skin down to expose the shoulder, ribs, and rear haunch. Because the front leg is attached only with muscle, not bone, you can slice between it and the ribs to free it in one piece; hang it from a limb to cool while you finish dressing the animal. Alternatively, leave the shoulder attached to the carcass and fillet the meat from it, keeping the knife close to the bones. The meat does not need to come off in one piece; small pieces can be cut into stew meat or ground for hamburger. Toss the pieces into a cloth bag or place atop a plastic garbage bag to cool.

You may cut down from the spine toward the ball-and-socket joint of the rear leg to remove it. Hang it from a limb to cool while you continue. If you'd rather fillet it in place, find a bone close to the surface and begin cutting. You'll notice compact groups of muscle separated by thin, translucent layers of tissue. By following these tissue "joints" and pulling them apart, you can remove entire muscle groups with minimum cutting. Set them aside to cool.

The loins or backstrap can be cut free from the spine and tops of ribs in one long piece. Just cut down along the spine, then forward to the neck. Your second cut follows the horizontal projection of vertebrae and the tops of ribs. You'll see this easily as you progress.

Fillet meat from the neck bones. When the first side of the carcass is filleted clean, roll it over and repeat the cutting on the other side, stretching out the skinned hide to serve as a clean operating base. When that side is finished, you will have a skeleton with belly intact. At this point you may slice remaining meat from the ribs and brisket or saw the ribs free. Open the belly if desired to remove the liver and tenderloins that lie tight against the spine.

Here are a few tips to consider when working with meat:

- To prevent tainting elk meat with urine-soaked belly hair, use one knife to cut through the belly and a fresh knife to cut next to the meat. A thin film of oily urine on your knife can taint pounds of meat. Alternatively, carefully skin away the dirty, dark belly hide, cut it free from the rest of the hide, and wash your knife and hands thoroughly before resuming butchering. Carry soap, water, and paper towels for this. Plastic "operating room" gloves for handling the belly hair are another option.

- Avoid touching the oily, urine-soaked tarsal glands of mule deer and whitetails with knife or hand. Have one person hold the legs out of the way while another does the butchering, or slice away the tarsal glands by skinning the section of leg hide to which they are attached. Wash knife and hands afterward.

- The "stink" of a pronghorn comes from its oily black "cheek patch." Avoid touching this. You might want to cape the head and place it out of the way, then wash up before proceeding with butchering.

- If you plan to mount a head, cape it before butchering. (See caping illustrations.) It's important to leave enough brisket and shoulder hide intact. Do not cut its throat and do not slice up through the chest. Remove the head from the neck at the last vertebrae or continue skinning out the head, being careful to cut deep through the ears and around the eyes, lips, and nose. Novice skinners should stop skinning at the last vertebrae and have an experienced taxidermist finish the job. The head and cape need to be heavily salted and transported quickly to a local taxidermist, and it is a good idea to know in advance which ones will accept the job on short notice. If you are sending the cape and antlers to a non-local taxidermist, the head will, of course, have to be completely caped before boxing and shipping. Follow the instructions detailed in the sidebar "Caping Heads."

- Pronghorns have a reputation for "gamey" meat. Generally, this is because they are improperly butchered in hot weather. When properly cared for, pronghorn flesh is tender, mild, and delicious. Do not shoot them after they've been run hard. Remove the hide as quickly as possible and put the meat on ice. Do not simply gut and stuff the carcass in a pickup bed or car trunk.

- If meat gets dirty, do not try to wash it clean; let it dry to a crust. This will preserve the inside perfectly as long as it remains cool. At home, fillet off the dirty, dry external layer and discard. The remaining meat will be perfectly clean and moist.
- If game meat is cooled quickly, hung in the shade, and allowed to develop a dry crust, it should keep for at least a week, even if daytime temperatures climb to 70°F.
- If flies are present, hang carcasses, quarters, or boned meat in cheesecloth or muslin bags in the shade, or place it inside plastic bags atop ice in coolers. Do not let the meat get soaked by melted ice.
- The fat and bone marrow of whitetails and mule deer have a strong, gamey taste that many people don't like. Keep venison tasting mild by removing all fat and by not sawing through any bones.
- Pillowcases make good meat bags.
- While butchering, touch up your knife blade often with a ceramic stick or steel.

Shipping Meat

If you're from out of state and plan to take your meat with you, there are several things you should know.

First, it is illegal to transport dry ice via air domestically; if you plan to bring your meat with you on the plane, you'll need to find another alternative for keeping it cool. Two methods that work well include:

- Freezing the meat solid, packing it in a styrofoam container, and then placing this in a leak-proof or cardboard box. In this fashion, the meat should keep for at least 48 hours.
- Place the meat—either frozen or not, but preferably frozen or cool—in a small box, and place this box inside a larger cooler containing blocks—not cubes—of ice. Blocks take longer to melt, and will keep the meat cooler longer.

As a last note, airlines vary widely in policy regarding shipping animal racks. Many will accept the racks if you simply pad and tape the skull and tips. Others ask that you box them prior to check-in. As always, contact your airline before your trip.

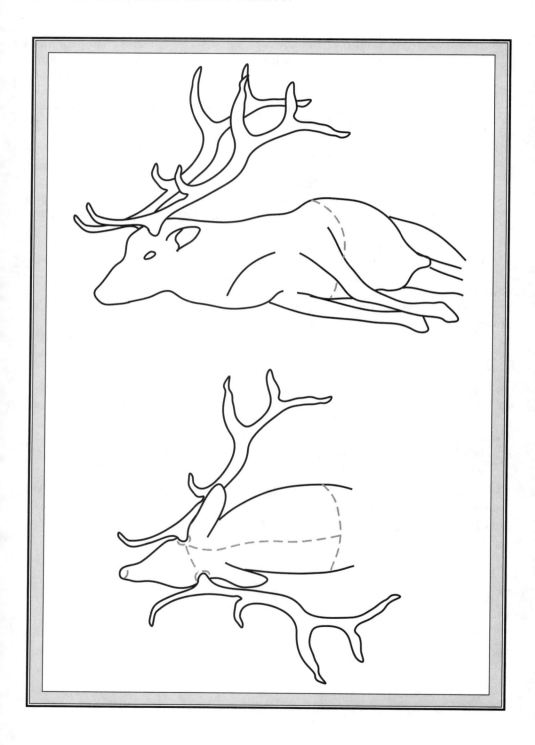

Caping Heads

To preserve a game head for a taxidermy shoulder mount, slice the hide around the animal behind the shoulders, then up the center of the neck to a point between the horns. Skin the lower neck hide forward to the jaw or until the head can be cut and twisted from the last neck vertebrae. If temperatures are below 40°F, a skin will keep in this condition for several days.

For complete caping, continue skinning by working the hide from around the antlers or horns with a screwdriver tip or knife tip. Then skin down to the ears and cut through them close to the head. Peel and skin down to the eyes, being careful to cut deeply under the lids and especially at the glands below each eye. Be careful around the nose, and cut it off well back from the nostrils. Leave plenty of the fleshy inner lip. Pour salt liberally on the flesh side of the cape and roll it up. After a day or two, shake out the salt, pour off the moisture, re-salt, and roll it again. A cape will keep for weeks this way, but you should deliver it to a taxidermist as soon as possible.

Choosing a Taxidermist

The quality of taxidermy varies widely from outstanding to horrible. The best work might come out of a small shop in an artist's basement while the sorriest looking, overstuffed critters might be pieced together in a professional-looking building on Main Street. So don't judge a taxidermist by the location or appearance of his shop; judge instead by the looks of his finished product. Try to see work he's done for others in addition to the displays in his shop. Some taxidermists display work they've put extra time and effort into while cranking out mediocre work for run-of-the-mill clients. Specify that you expect the same quality as you've seen in his trophy room or on a previous client's wall.

Ask what methods the taxidermist employs, or specify the method yourself. Shortcut taxidermy includes "pickled" capes that dry hard and eventually crack. Specify tanned capes and hides for your mounts. Make sure all horns will be boiled off the skull core to remove inner cartilage, then neatly remounted. Slap-dash taxidermists simply let horns dry to their cores, inviting odors and destructive burrowing insects that can eat away the horns from the inside.

Get a work order/receipt from your taxidermist that clearly spells out the species you brought in and the size of the cape and antlers or horns. He should punch an identifying mark or initial in a corner of the hide. Photograph all horns and antlers from several angles before you leave them. If possible, carve a small distinguishing mark in an inconspicuous spot on antlers and horns, especially trophy-sized ones; more than one trophy rack has "disappeared" from a taxidermist's studio over the years. The work order should clearly state what you want; for example, a shoulder-mount mule deer with left head-turn, ears back, lip curled up.

Finally, get a firm date for delivery of the finished mount. Some taxidermists take years to finish mounts. It is easier and cheaper to transport a cape and horn to a taxidermist near your home than to ship a completed mount across the country. However, the extra shipping charge could be worth it for superior quality work, and Montana taxidermists might charge sufficiently less for their work than Eastern taxidermists, nullifying the extra cost of shipping anyway. It never hurts to investigate. The hassle of flying a raw cape and rack home might be worth the extra shipping for a quality, completed mount.

Neither the author nor publisher of this book guarantees the work of any taxidermists listed herein. Some may be outstanding, others less than mediocre. Some may have gone out of business. Some might only mount fish or birds. Call ahead and look before you leap.

List of Sources

Montana Fish, Wildlife & Parks

State Headquarters
Montana Fish, Wildlife & Parks
1420 East Sixth Avenue, P.O. Box 200701
Helena, MT 59620-0701
406-444-2535
fwp.state.mt.us

Region 1 Office
490 North Meridian Road
Kalispell, MT 59901
406-752-5501
fwprg1@mt.gov

Region 2 Office
3201 Spurgin Road
Missoula, MT 59804
406-542-5500
fwprg2@mt.gov

Region 3 Office
1400 South 19th
Bozeman, MT 59718
406-994-4042
fwpgen@mt.gov

Helena Area Resource Office
930 Custer Ave. W.
Helena, MT 59620-0701
406-444-4720

Butte Area Resource Office
1820 Meadowlark Lane
Butte, MT 59701
406-494-1953

Region 4 Office
4600 Giant Springs Road
P.O. Box 6610
Great Falls, MT 59406-6610
406-454-5840
fwprg4@mt.gov

Region 5 Office
2300 Lake Elmo Drive
Billings, MT 59105
406-247-2940
fwprg5@mt.gov

Region 6 Office
Rural Route 1-4210
Glasgow, MT 59230
406-228-3700
fwprg6@mt.gov

Havre Area Resource Office
2165 Hwy 2 East
Havre, MT 59501
406-265-6177
fwphao@mt.gov

Region 7 Office
P.O. Box 1630
Miles City, MT 59301
406-232-0900
fwprg7@mt.gov

State Travel Office
Montana Departement of Commerce
Tourism Office
1424 South 9th Avenue
Helena, MT 59620-0533
1-800-VISIT MT or 406-444-2654

Block Management Office
Montana Fish, Wildlife & Parks
Field Services Division
1420 East Sixth Avenue
Helena, MT 59620
406-444-2602

US Department of Agriculture Forest Service

Northern Region Headquarters
USDA—Forest Service
P.O. Box 7669
Missoula, MT 59807
406-329-3511

Gallatin National Forest
10 E. Babcock Ave., Federal Building
P.O. Box 130
Bozeman, MT 59771
406-587-6701

Beaverhead-Deerlodge National Forest
420 Barrett St.
Dillon, MT 59725-3572
406-683-3900

Helena National Forest
2880 Skyway Drive
Helena, MT 59601
406-449-5201

Bitterroot National Forest
1801 N. 1st St.
Hamilton, MT 59840
406-363-7167

Kootenai National Forest
506 U.S. Highway 2 West
Libby, MT 59923
406-293-6211

Custer National Forest
1310 Main St.
P.O. Box 50760
Billings, MT 59105
406-248-9885

Lewis & Clark National Forest
1101 15th St. North
P.O. Box 869
Great Falls, MT 59403
406-791-7700

Flathead National Forest
1935 3rd Ave. East
Kalispell, MT 59901
406-758-5200

Lolo National Forest
Building 24, Ft. Missoula
Missoula, MT 59804
406-329-3750

Bureau of Land Management

Montana State BLM Office
222 N. 32nd St., P.O. Box 36800
Billings, MT 59107-6800
406-255-2888

Butte Field Office
106 N. Parkmont, Box 3388
Butte, MT 59701-3388
406-494-5059

Dillon Field Office
1005 Selway Drive
Dillon, MT 59725-9431
406-683-2337

Missoula Field Office
3255 Fort Missoula Road
Missoula, MT 59804-7293
406-329-3914

Lewistown Field Office
Airport Road, Box 1160
Lewistown, MT 59457
406-538-7461

Havre Field Station
1704 Second St. West, Drawer 911
Havre, MT 59501-0911
406-265-5891

Great Falls Field Office
812 14th St. North
Great Falls, MT 59401
406-727-0503

Malta Field Office
501 S. Second St. East, Box B
Malta, MT 59538-0047
406-654-1240

Glasgow Field Station
Rt. #1-4775
Glasgow, MT 59230-9796
406-228-4316

Miles City Field Office
111 Garryowen Road
Miles City, MT 59301
406-233-2800

Billings Field Office
810 East Main Street
Billings, MT 59105-3395
406-238-1540

Outfitter and Guide Organizations

Montana Outfitters &
Guides Association
33 South Last Chance Gulch, Suite 2B
Helena, MT 59601-4132
406-449-3578

Montana Board of Outfitters
Department of Commerce
111 North Jackson
Helena, MT 59620
406-444-3788

Road and Weather Conditions

Statewide conditions
800-226-ROAD(7623) or 406-444-6339

For local road reports:
Billings 406-252-2806
Bozeman 406-586-1313
Butte 406-494-3666
Glendive 406-365-2314
Great Falls 406-453-1605
Havre 406-265-1416
Kalispell 406-755-4949
Lewistown 406-538-7445
Miles City 406-232-2099
Missoula 406-728-8553
Wolf Point 406-653-1692

Index

WILDERNESS ADVENTURES GUIDE SERIES

If you would like to order additional copies of this book or our other Wilderness Adventures Press guidebooks, please fill out the order form below or call **800-925-3339** or **fax 800-390-7558.** Visit our website for a listing of over 2500 sporting books—the largest online: **www.wildadv.com**

Mail to: Wilderness Adventures Press, P.O. Box 627, Gallatin Gateway, MT 59730

☐ **Please send me your free catalog on hunting and fishing books.**

Ship to:

Name _____

Address _____

City _____ State _____ Zip _____

Home Phone _____ Work Phone _____

Payment: ☐ Check ☐ Visa ☐ Mastercard ☐ Discover ☐ American Express

Card Number _____ Expiration Date _____

Qty	Title of Book and Author	Price	Total
	Big Game Hunter's Guide to Colorado (*due Fall 1999*)	$26.95	
	Wingshooter's Guide to Montana	$26.00	
	Flyfisher's Guide to Montana	$26.95	
	Wingshooter's Guide to Idaho	$26.95	
	Flyfisher's Guide to Idaho	$26.95	
	Wingshooter's Guide to South Dakota	$26.95	
	Wingshooter's Guide to North Dakota	$26.95	
	Total Order + shipping & handling		

**Shipping and handling: $4.00 for first book,
$2.50 per additional book, up to $11.50 maximum**